YELLOW

BY
MAKOTO TATENO

DMP
DIGITAL MANGA
PUBLISHING

YELLOW 2

Translation & Adaptation	**G. Genki**
Lettering	**Studio Cutie**
Graphic Design	**Eric Rosenberger**
Editing	**Stephanie Donnelly**
Editor in Chief	**Fred Lui**
Publisher	**Hikaru Sasahara**

English Edition Published by
DIGITAL MANGA PUBLISHING
A division of DIGITAL MANGA, Inc.
1487 W 178th Street, Suite 300
Gardena, CA 90248

www.dmpbooks.com

First Edition: September 2005
ISBN: 1-56970-951-3

1 3 5 7 9 10 8 6 4 2

Printed in Canada

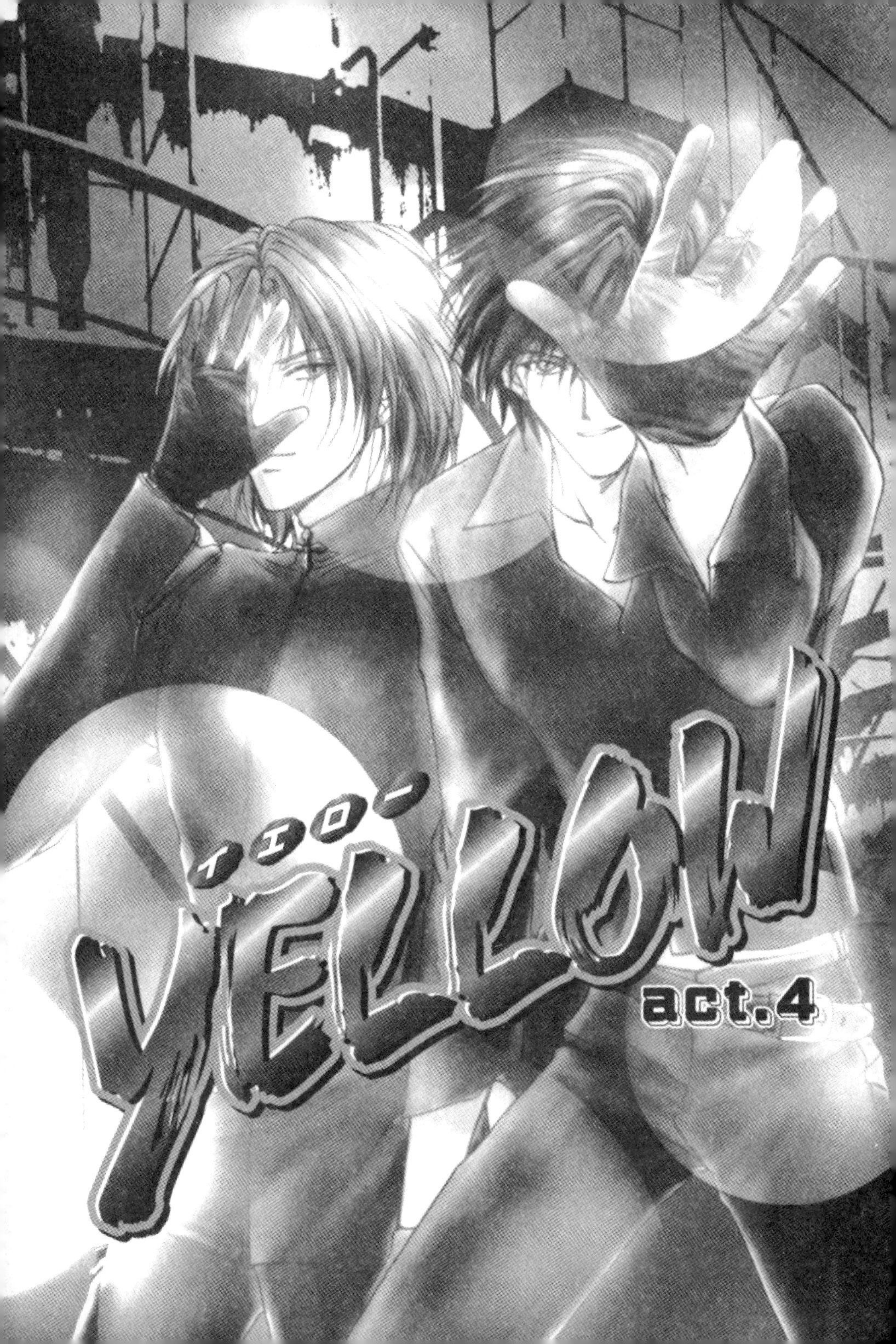
イエロー
YELLOW
act.4

PROFILE

Suspect #1

name

GOH

age

22

height and weight

184 CM / 72 KG

blood type

O

occupation

DRUG SNATCHER

special qualifications

LOCK BREAKER

personality

POSITIVE AND
FORWARD-LOOKING

background

HIS IDENTITY IS A SECRET,
EXCEPT THAT HE'S GAY.

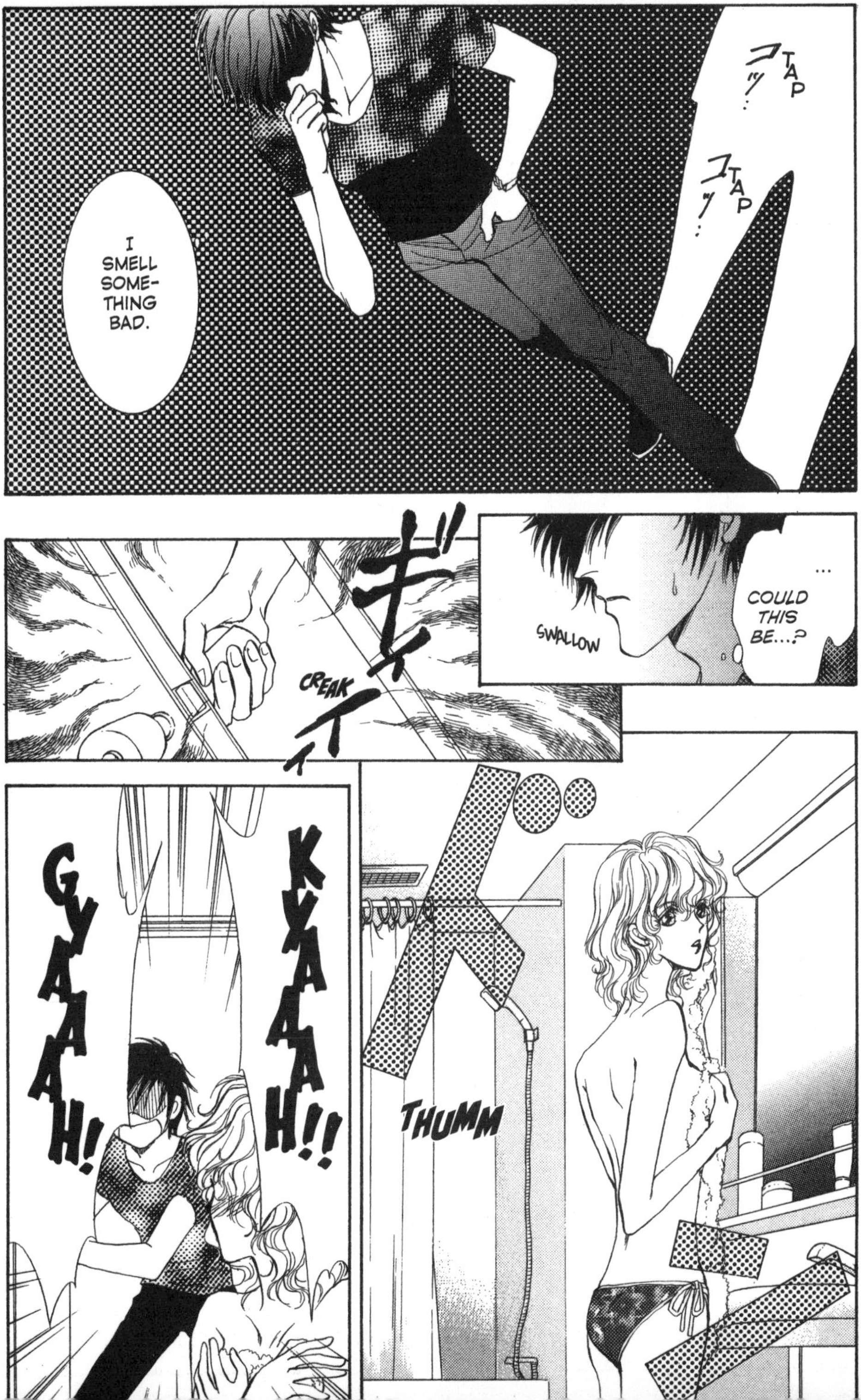

TAP
TAP
I SMELL SOME-THING BAD.
...COULD THIS BE...?
SWALLOW
CREAK
THUMM
KYAAAAH!!
GYAAAAH!

THERE ARE PEOPLE THAT ARE TOTAL OPPOSITES IN THE WORLD.

GOH!

FOR INSTANCE, US.

TAKI!!

YOU SCUM!! DIDN'T I TELL YOU A HUNDRED TIMES NOT TO BRING A WOMAN IN HERE?!

CAFE

OPEN

MEN ARE OKAY! I'M A MAN! YOU'RE A MAN! THIS IS A CASTLE OF MEN!!

THE SMELL OF PERFUME, LIPSTICK-STAINED CUPS AND PANTYHOSE WITH HOLES ARE NOT ALLOWED!

YOU BRING HOME MEN ALL THE TIME, DON'T YOU?

NEVER, EVER!!

TAKI

QUIVER QUIVER

6

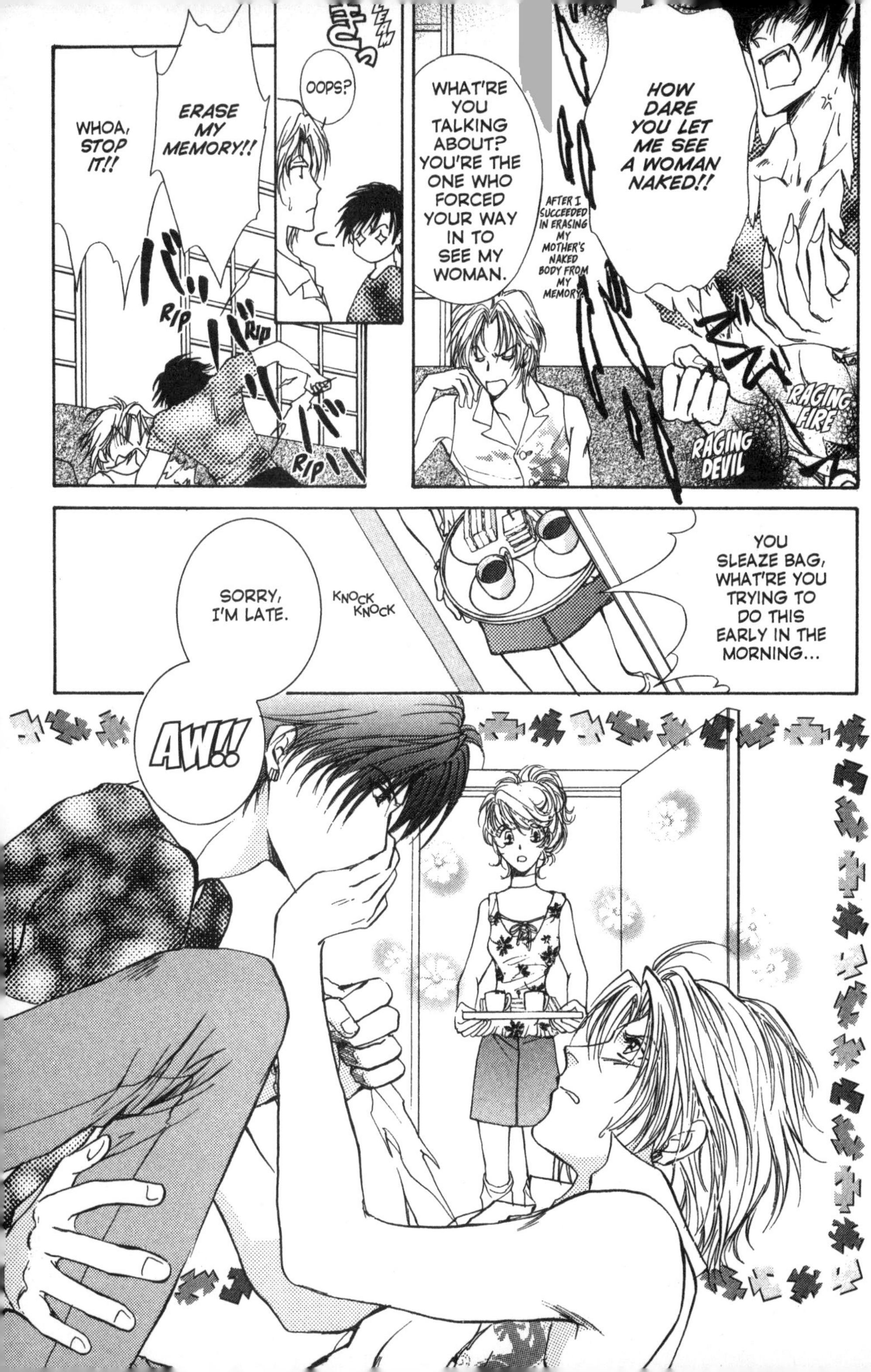
HOW DARE YOU LET ME SEE A WOMAN NAKED!!
RAGING FIRE
RAGING DEVIL
WHAT'RE YOU TALKING ABOUT? YOU'RE THE ONE WHO FORCED YOUR WAY IN TO SEE MY WOMAN.
AFTER I SUCCEEDED IN ERASING MY MOTHER'S NAKED BODY FROM MY MEMORY.
OOPS?
ERASE MY MEMORY!!
WHOA, STOP IT!!
RIP
RIP
RIP
YOU SLEAZE BAG, WHAT'RE YOU TRYING TO DO THIS EARLY IN THE MORNING...
KNOCK KNOCK
SORRY, I'M LATE.
AW!!

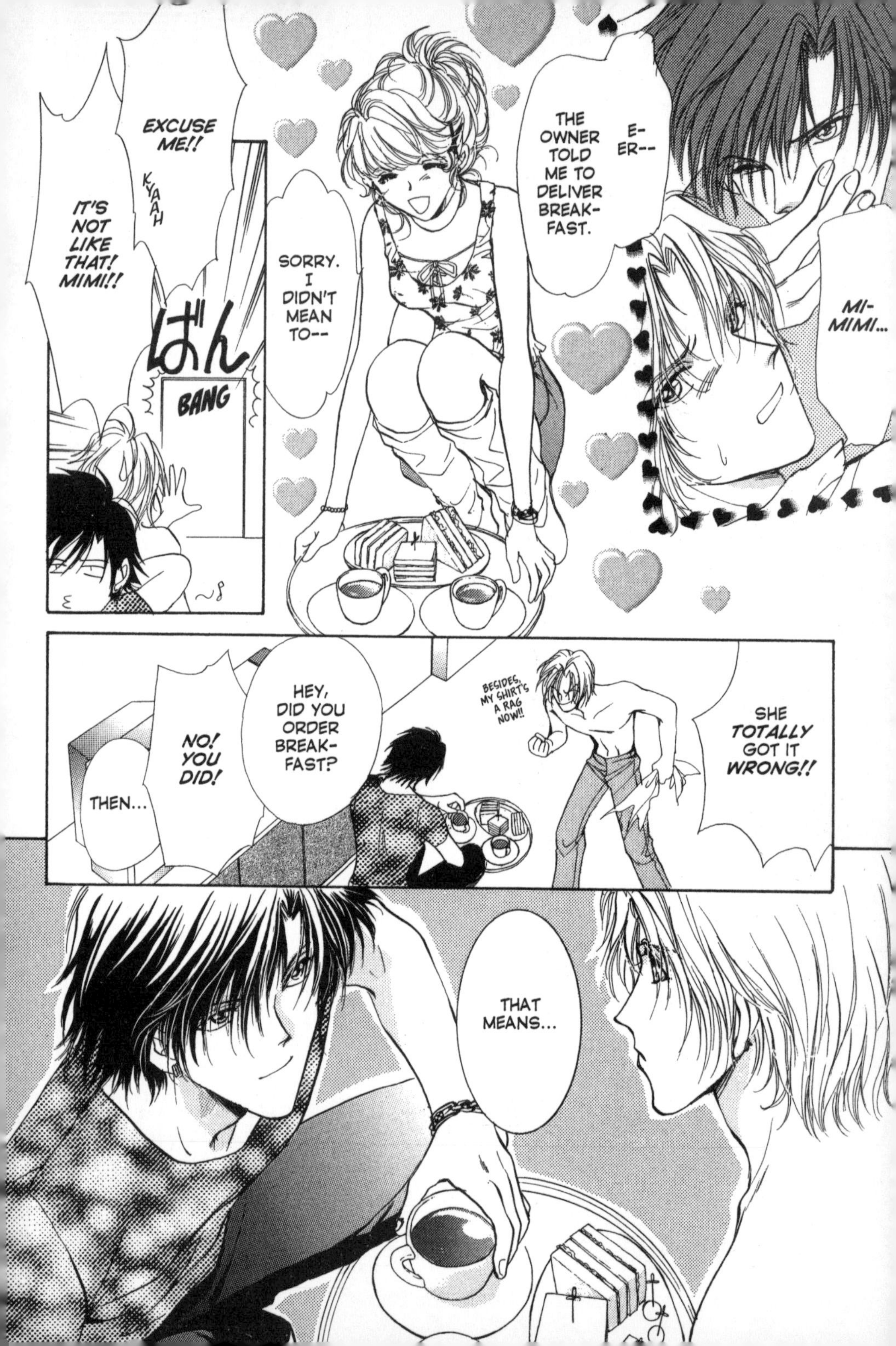
E-
ER--
THE OWNER TOLD ME TO DELIVER BREAKFAST.
MI-MIMI...
SORRY. I DIDN'T MEAN TO--
EXCUSE ME!!
KYAAH
IT'S NOT LIKE THAT! MIMI!!
ばん
BANG
SHE TOTALLY GOT IT WRONG!!
BESIDES, MY SHIRT'S A RAG NOW!!
HEY, DID YOU ORDER BREAKFAST?
NO! YOU DID!
THEN...
THAT MEANS...

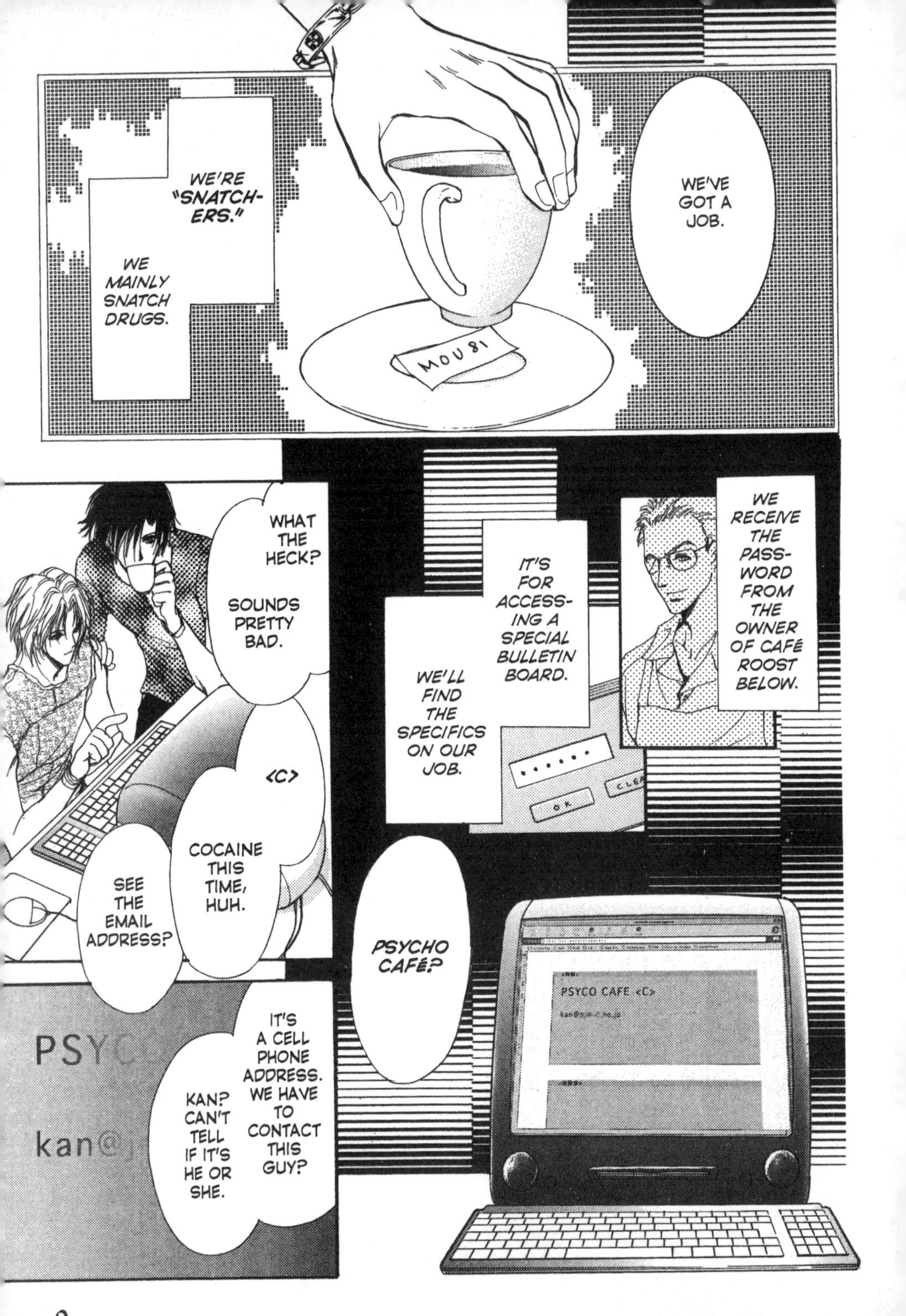

WE'VE GOT A JOB.
WE'RE "SNATCHERS."
WE MAINLY SNATCH DRUGS.
MOU81
WE RECEIVE THE PASSWORD FROM THE OWNER OF CAFÉ ROOST BELOW.
IT'S FOR ACCESSING A SPECIAL BULLETIN BOARD.
WE'LL FIND THE SPECIFICS ON OUR JOB.
OK
CLEA
WHAT THE HECK?
SOUNDS PRETTY BAD.
<C>
COCAINE THIS TIME, HUH.
SEE THE EMAIL ADDRESS?
PSYCO CAFE <C>
PSYCHO CAFÉ?
PSYC
kan@j
IT'S A CELL PHONE ADDRESS. WE HAVE TO CONTACT THIS GUY?
KAN? CAN'T TELL IF IT'S HE OR SHE.

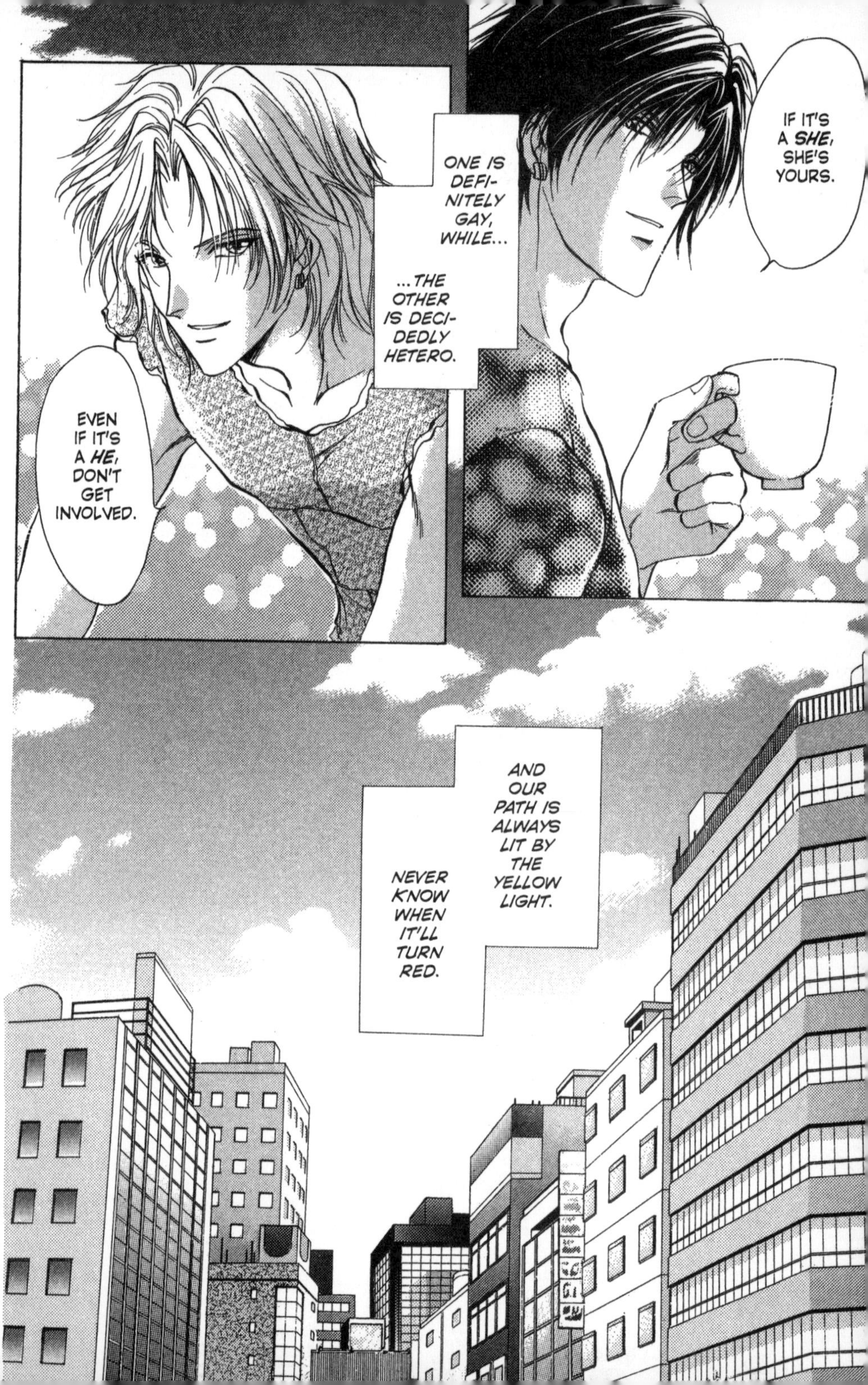
IF IT'S A SHE, SHE'S YOURS.
ONE IS DEFINITELY GAY, WHILE...
...THE OTHER IS DECIDEDLY HETERO.
EVEN IF IT'S A HE, DON'T GET INVOLVED.
AND OUR PATH IS ALWAYS LIT BY THE YELLOW LIGHT.
NEVER KNOW WHEN IT'LL TURN RED.

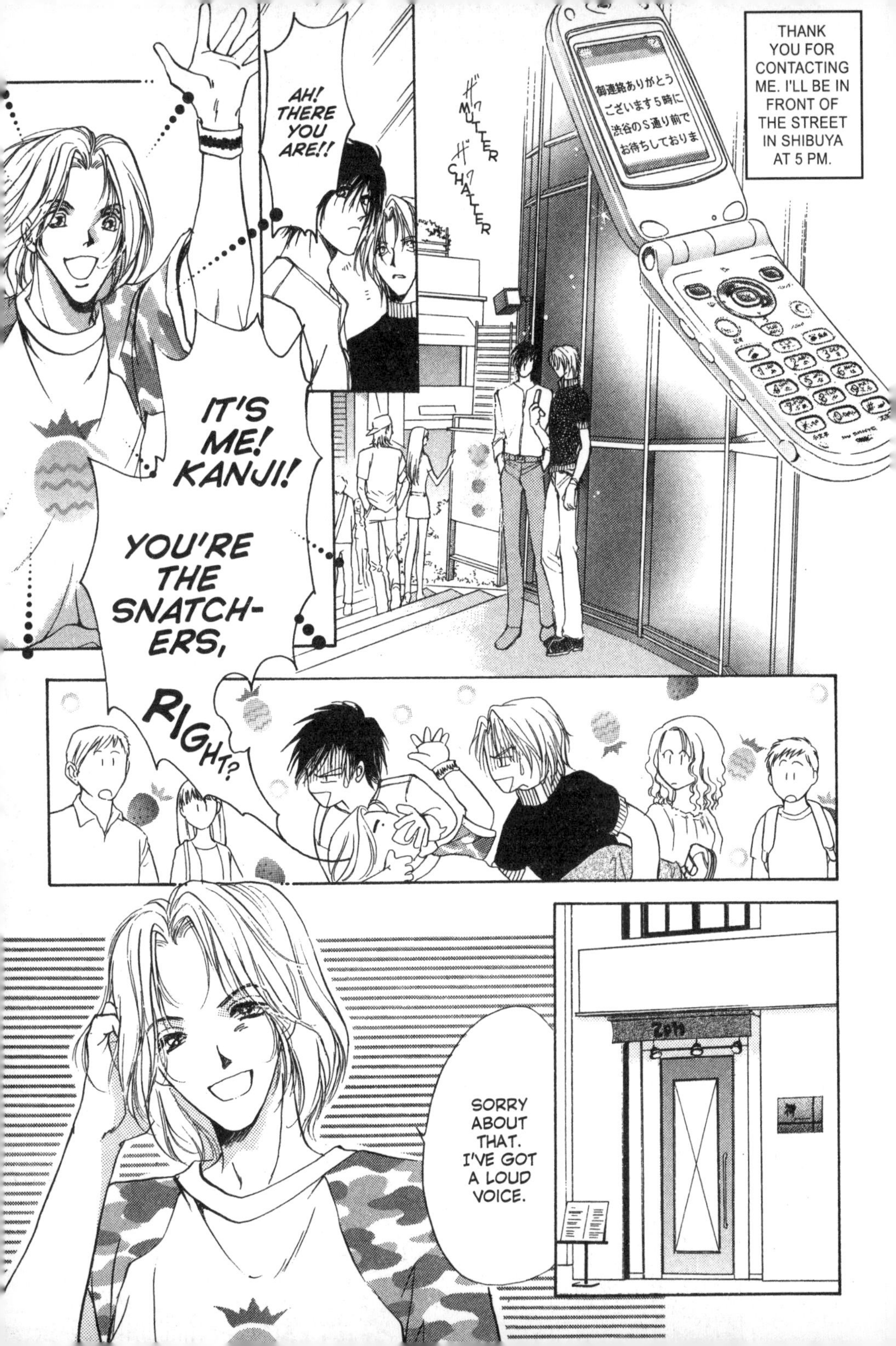

THANK YOU FOR CONTACTING ME. I'LL BE IN FRONT OF THE STREET IN SHIBUYA AT 5 PM.
御連絡ありがとう
ございます5時に
渋谷のS通り前で
お待ちしておりま
MUTTER
CHATTER
AH! THERE YOU ARE!!
IT'S ME! KANJI!
YOU'RE THE SNATCHERS, RIGHT?
SORRY ABOUT THAT. I'VE GOT A LOUD VOICE.

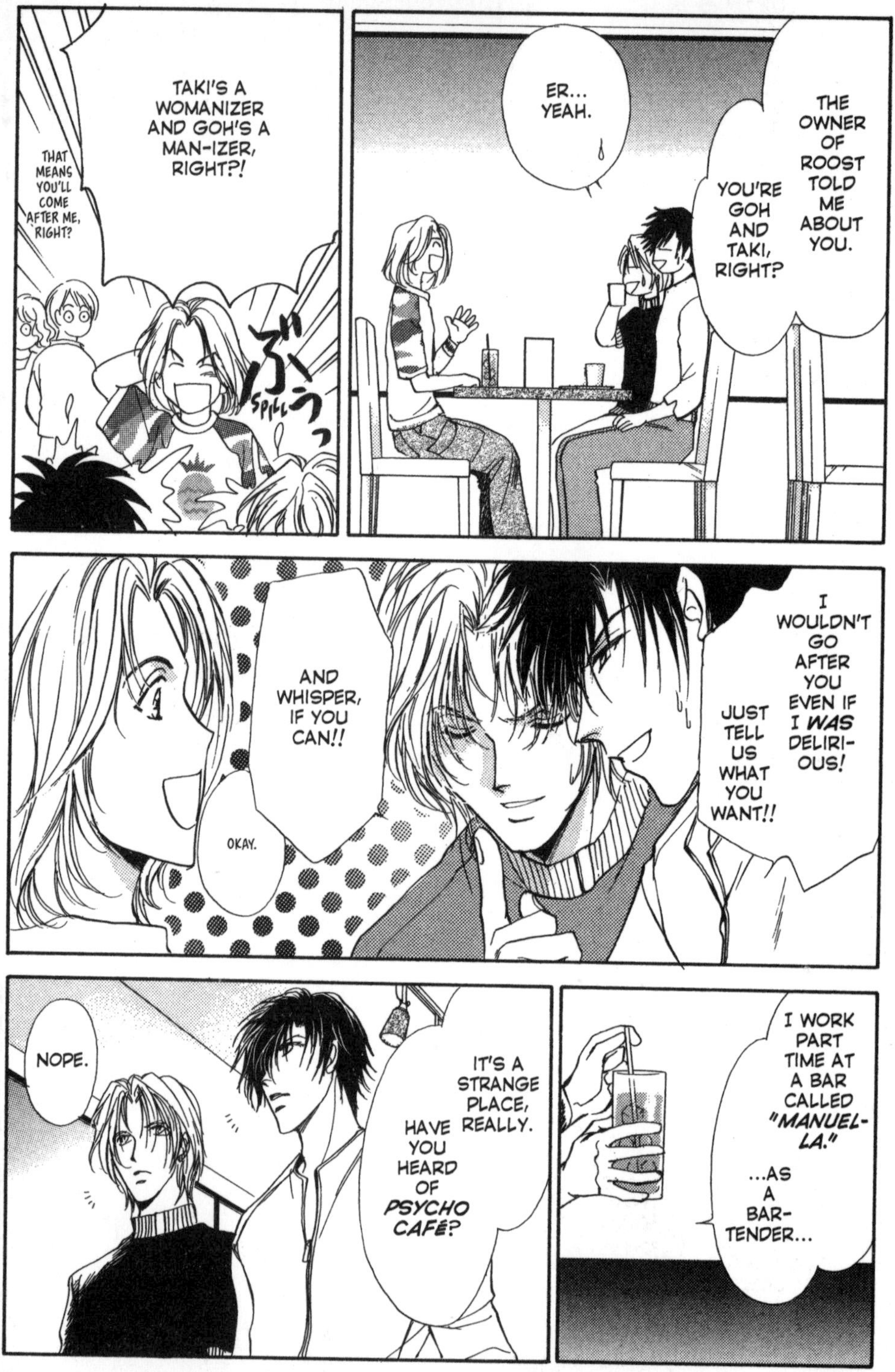
THE OWNER OF ROOST TOLD ME ABOUT YOU.
YOU'RE GOH AND TAKI, RIGHT?
ER... YEAH.
TAKI'S A WOMANIZER AND GOH'S A MAN-IZER, RIGHT?!
THAT MEANS YOU'LL COME AFTER ME, RIGHT?
ぶうっ
SPILL
I WOULDN'T GO AFTER YOU EVEN IF I *WAS* DELIRIOUS!
JUST TELL US WHAT YOU WANT!!
AND WHISPER, IF YOU CAN!!
OKAY.
I WORK PART TIME AT A BAR CALLED *"MANUELLA."*
...AS A BARTENDER...
IT'S A STRANGE PLACE, REALLY.
HAVE YOU HEARD OF *PSYCHO CAFÉ*?
NOPE.

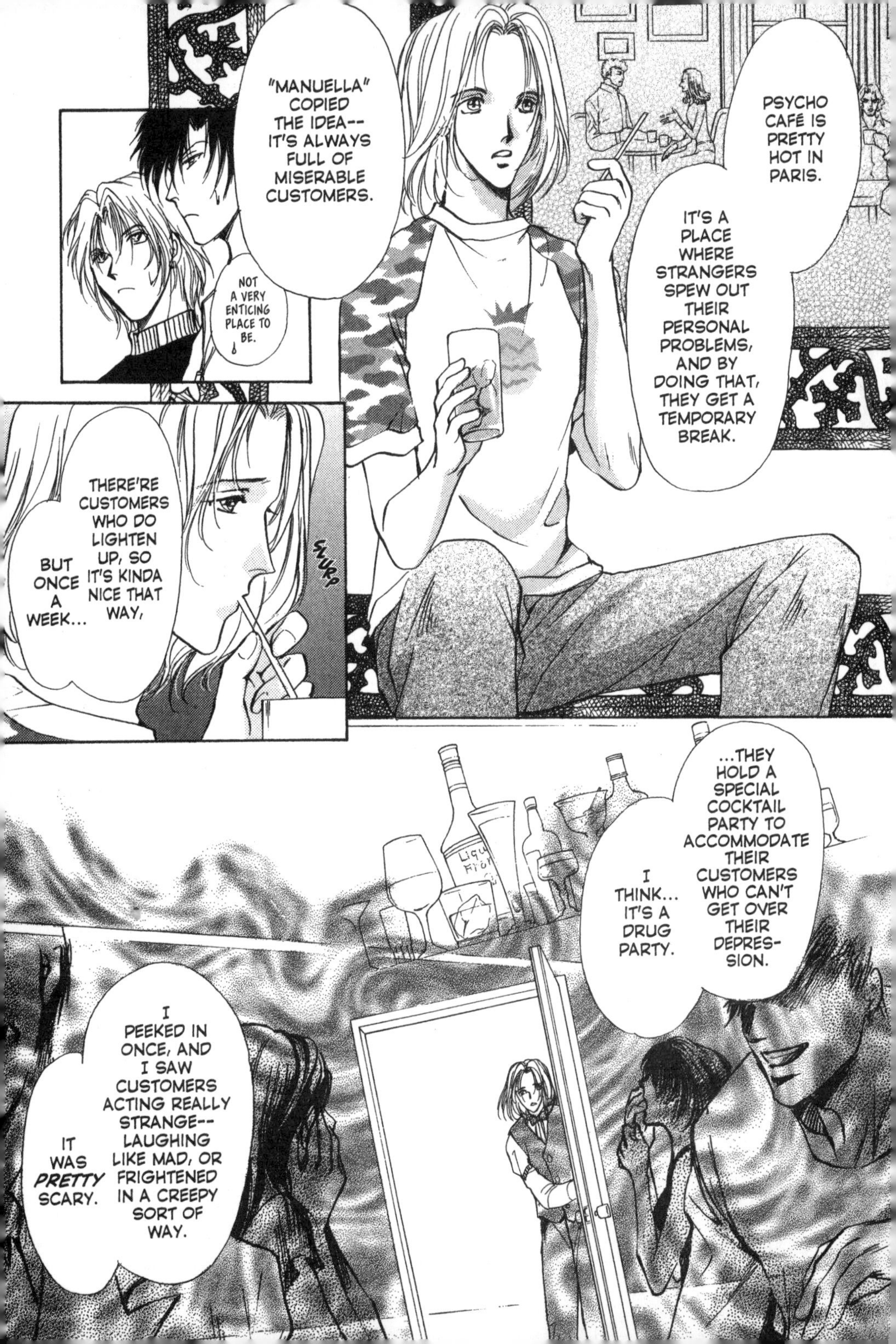
PSYCHO CAFÉ IS PRETTY HOT IN PARIS.
IT'S A PLACE WHERE STRANGERS SPEW OUT THEIR PERSONAL PROBLEMS, AND BY DOING THAT, THEY GET A TEMPORARY BREAK.
"MANUELLA" COPIED THE IDEA-- IT'S ALWAYS FULL OF MISERABLE CUSTOMERS.
NOT A VERY ENTICING PLACE TO BE.
THERE'RE CUSTOMERS WHO DO LIGHTEN UP, SO IT'S KINDA NICE THAT WAY,
SLURP
BUT ONCE A WEEK...
...THEY HOLD A SPECIAL COCKTAIL PARTY TO ACCOMMODATE THEIR CUSTOMERS WHO CAN'T GET OVER THEIR DEPRES-SION.
I THINK... IT'S A DRUG PARTY.
I PEEKED IN ONCE, AND I SAW CUSTOMERS ACTING REALLY STRANGE-- LAUGHING LIKE MAD, OR FRIGHTENED IN A CREEPY SORT OF WAY.
IT WAS *PRETTY* SCARY.

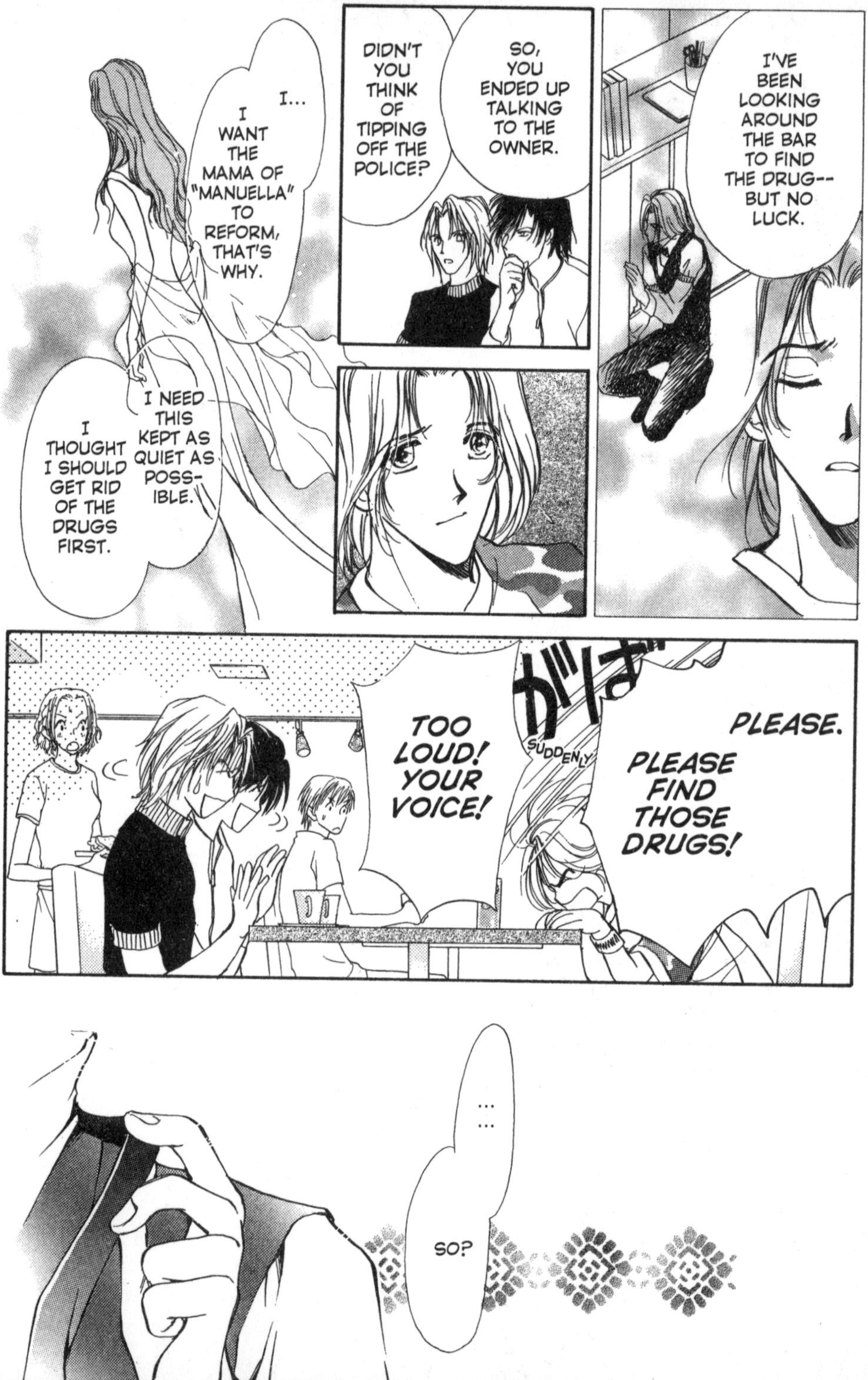
I'VE BEEN LOOKING AROUND THE BAR TO FIND THE DRUG-- BUT NO LUCK.
SO, YOU ENDED UP TALKING TO THE OWNER.
DIDN'T YOU THINK OF TIPPING OFF THE POLICE?
I... I WANT THE MAMA OF "MANUELLA" TO REFORM, THAT'S WHY.
I NEED THIS KEPT AS QUIET AS POSS-IBLE.
I THOUGHT I SHOULD GET RID OF THE DRUGS FIRST.
PLEASE.
PLEASE FIND THOSE DRUGS!
がばっ
SUDDENLY
TOO LOUD! YOUR VOICE!
……
SO?

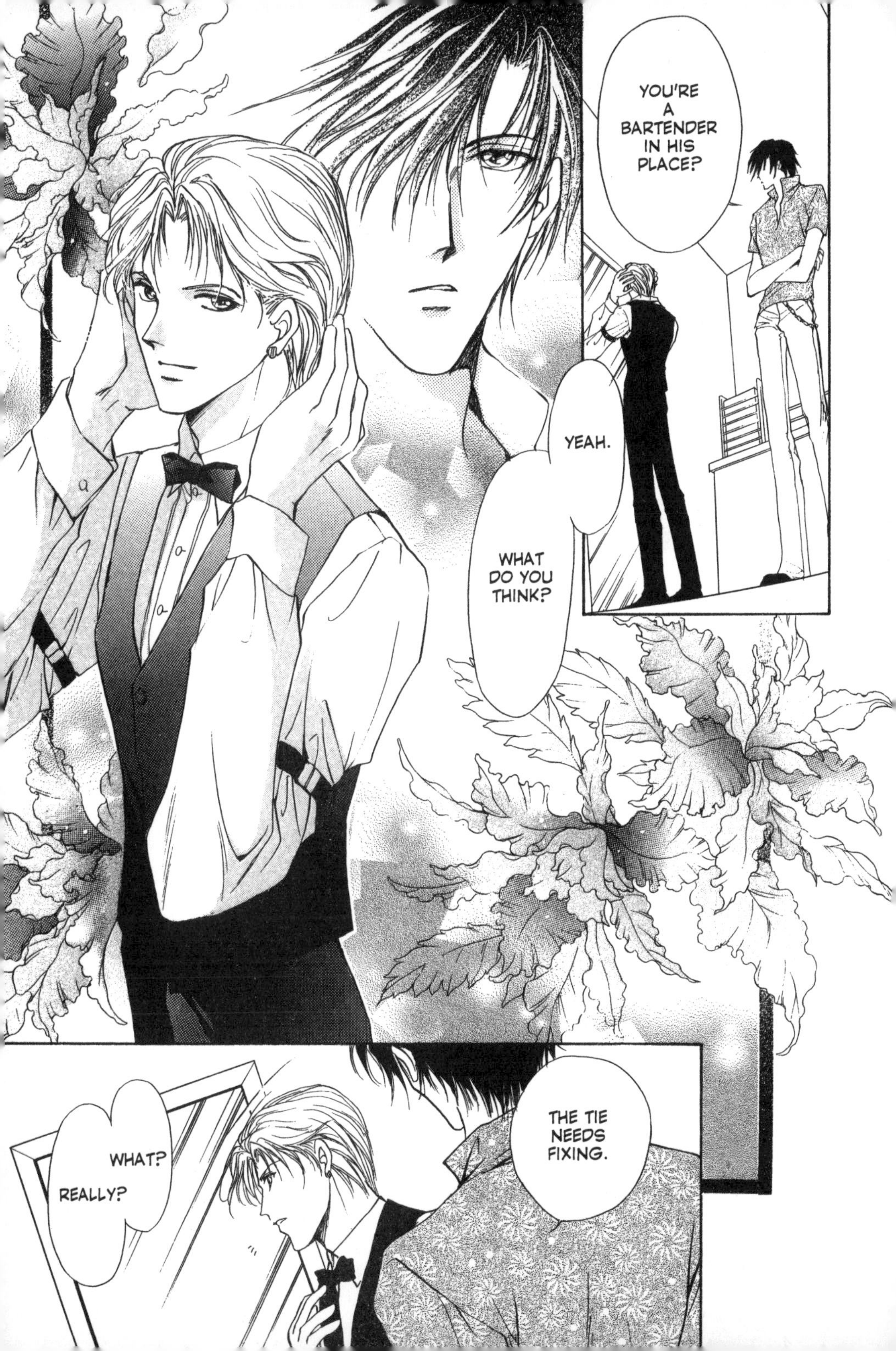
YOU'RE A BARTENDER IN HIS PLACE?
YEAH.
WHAT DO YOU THINK?
THE TIE NEEDS FIXING.
WHAT? REALLY?

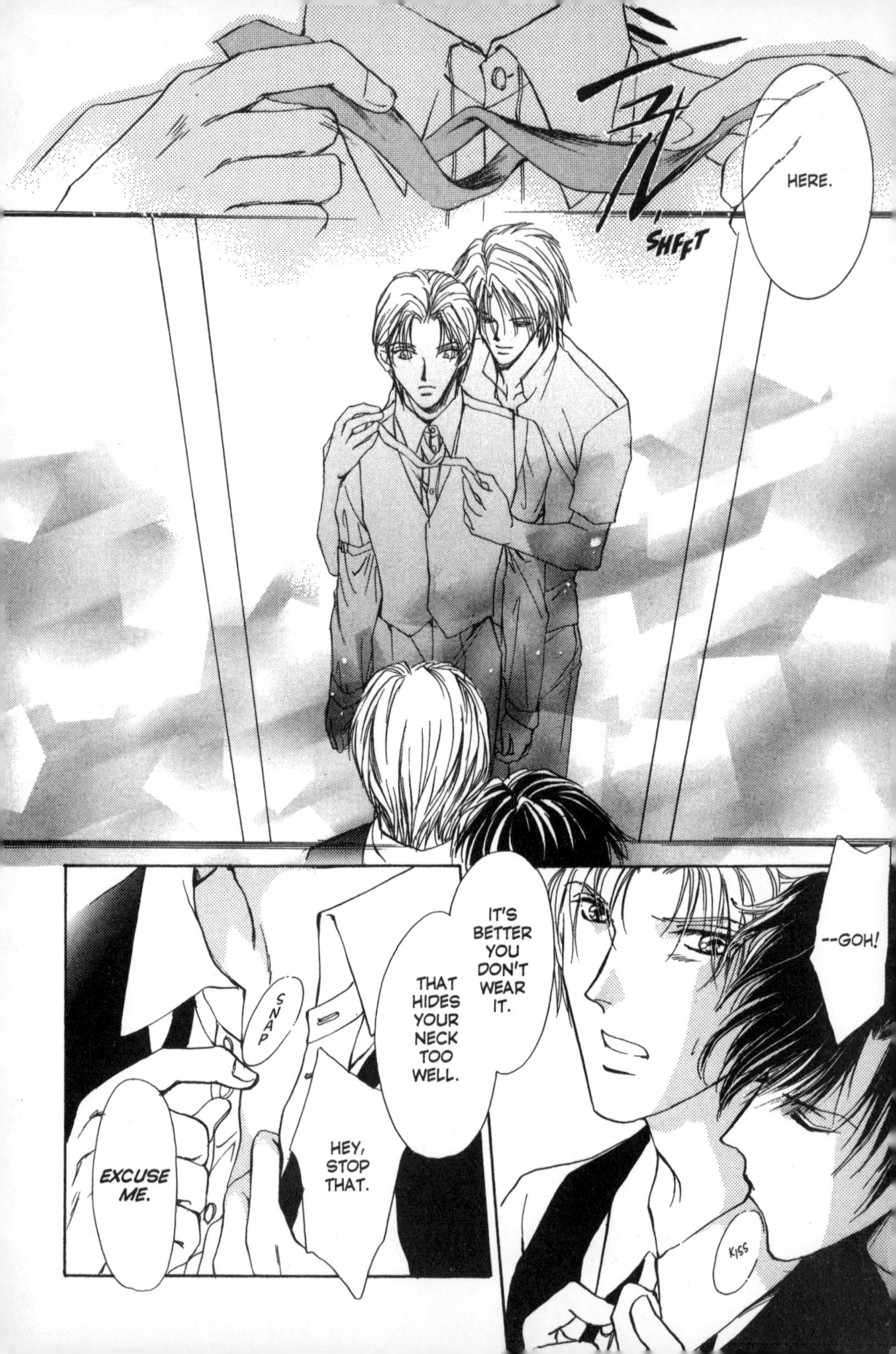
HERE.
SHFFT
--GOH!
KISS
IT'S BETTER YOU DON'T WEAR IT.
THAT HIDES YOUR NECK TOO WELL.
HEY, STOP THAT.
SNAP
EXCUSE ME.

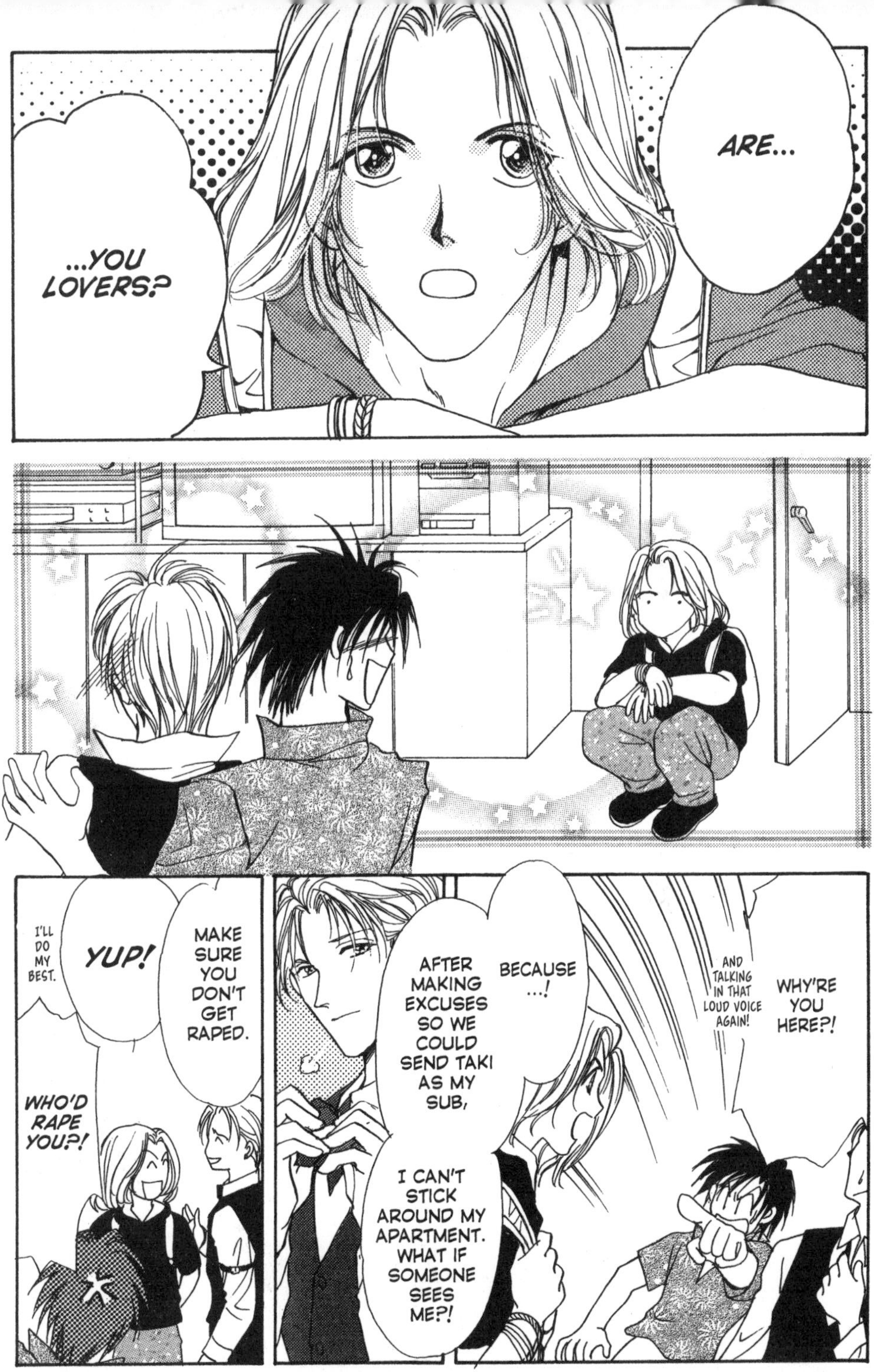
ARE...
...YOU LOVERS?
WHY'RE YOU HERE?!
AND TALKING IN THAT LOUD VOICE AGAIN!
BECAUSE ...!
AFTER MAKING EXCUSES SO WE COULD SEND TAKI AS MY SUB,
I CAN'T STICK AROUND MY APARTMENT. WHAT IF SOMEONE SEES ME?!
MAKE SURE YOU DON'T GET RAPED.
YUP!
I'LL DO MY BEST.
WHO'D RAPE YOU?!

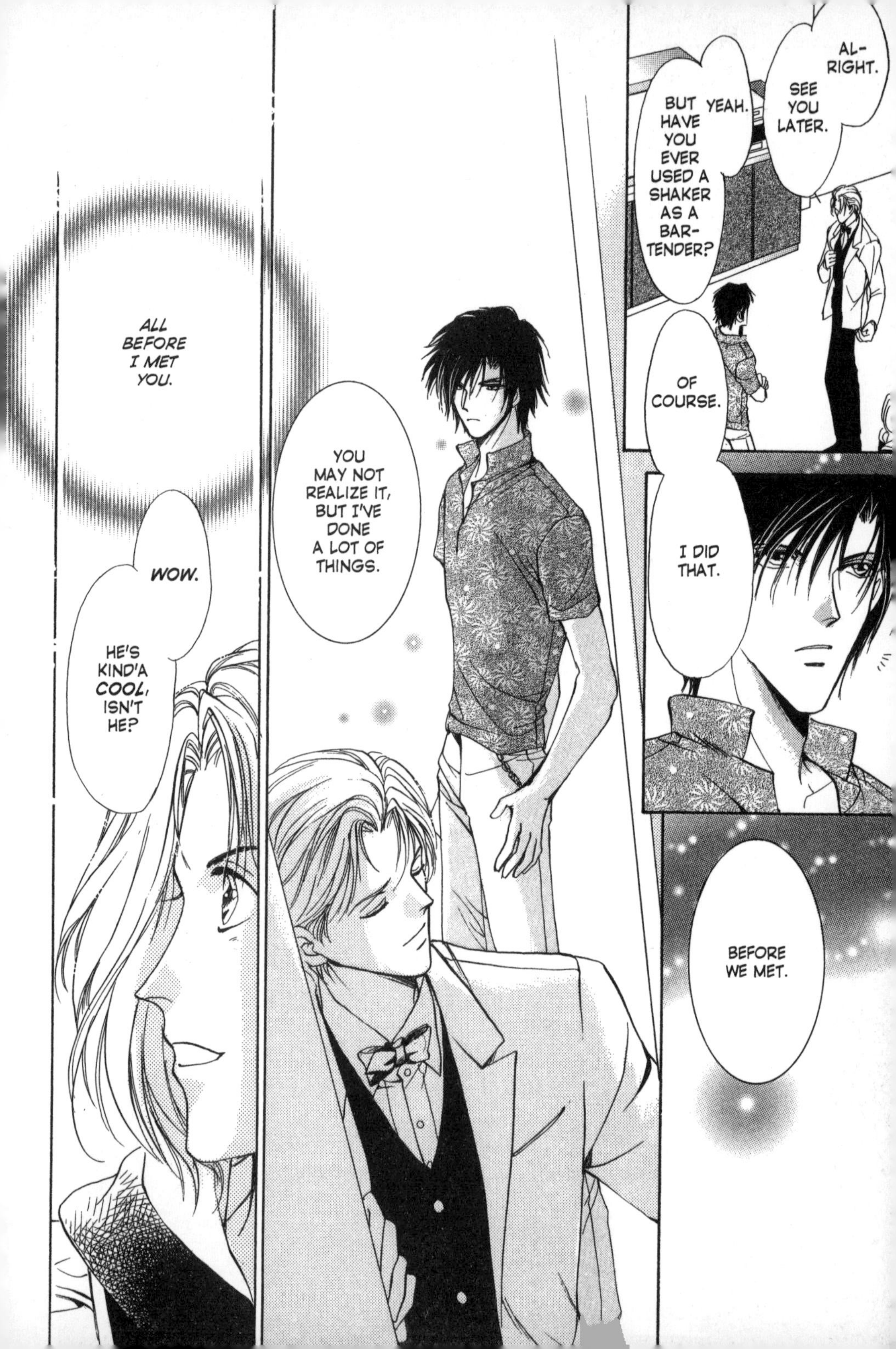
AL-RIGHT. SEE YOU LATER.
YEAH.
BUT HAVE YOU EVER USED A SHAKER AS A BAR-TENDER?
OF COURSE.
I DID THAT.
BEFORE WE MET.
YOU MAY NOT REALIZE IT, BUT I'VE DONE A LOT OF THINGS.
ALL BEFORE I MET YOU.
WOW.
HE'S KIND'A COOL, ISN'T HE?

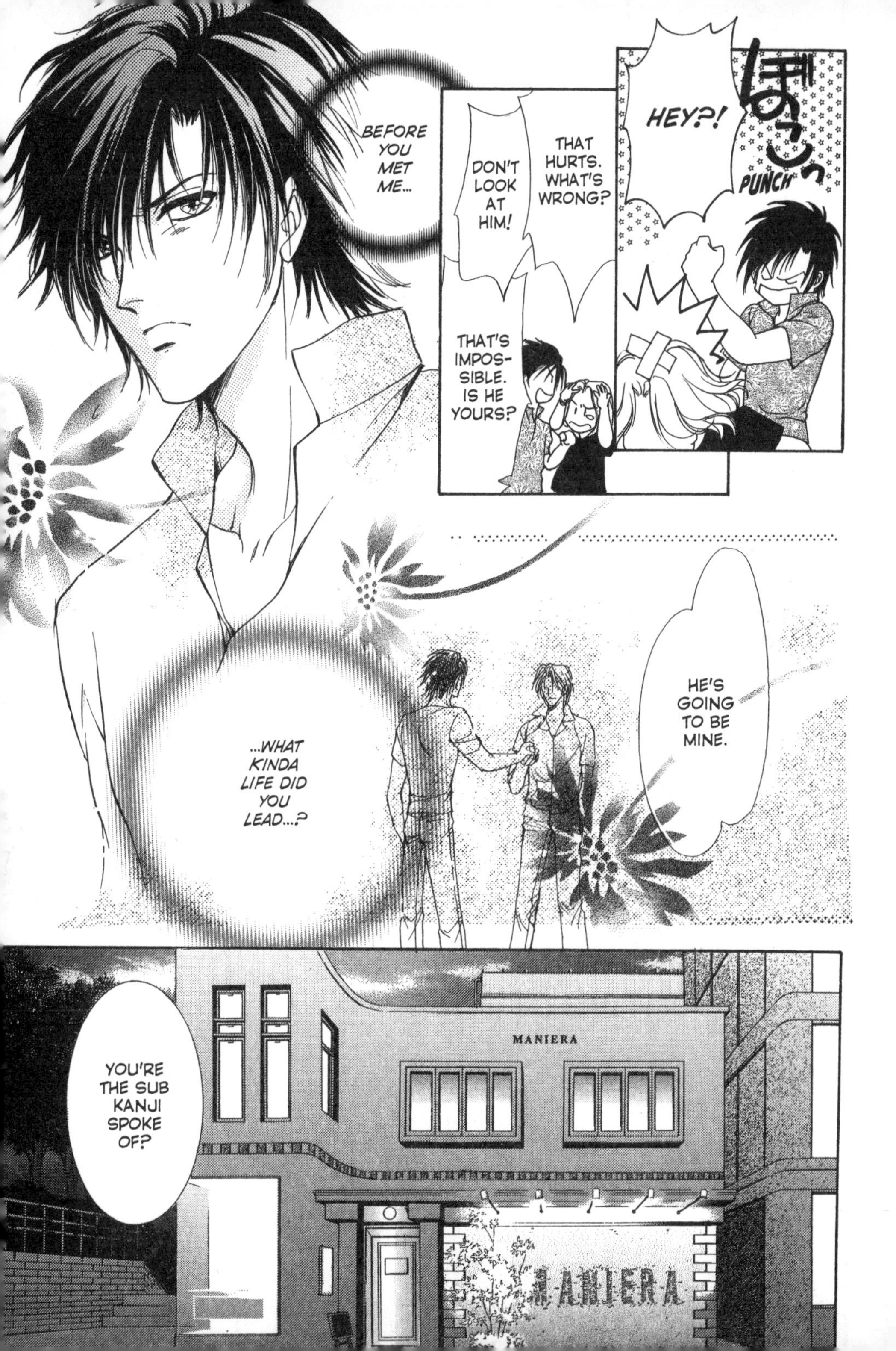
HEY?!
PUNCH
THAT HURTS. WHAT'S WRONG?
DON'T LOOK AT HIM!
THAT'S IMPOS-SIBLE. IS HE YOURS?
BEFORE YOU MET ME...
HE'S GOING TO BE MINE.
...WHAT KINDA LIFE DID YOU LEAD...?
MANIERA
YOU'RE THE SUB KANJI SPOKE OF?
MANIERA

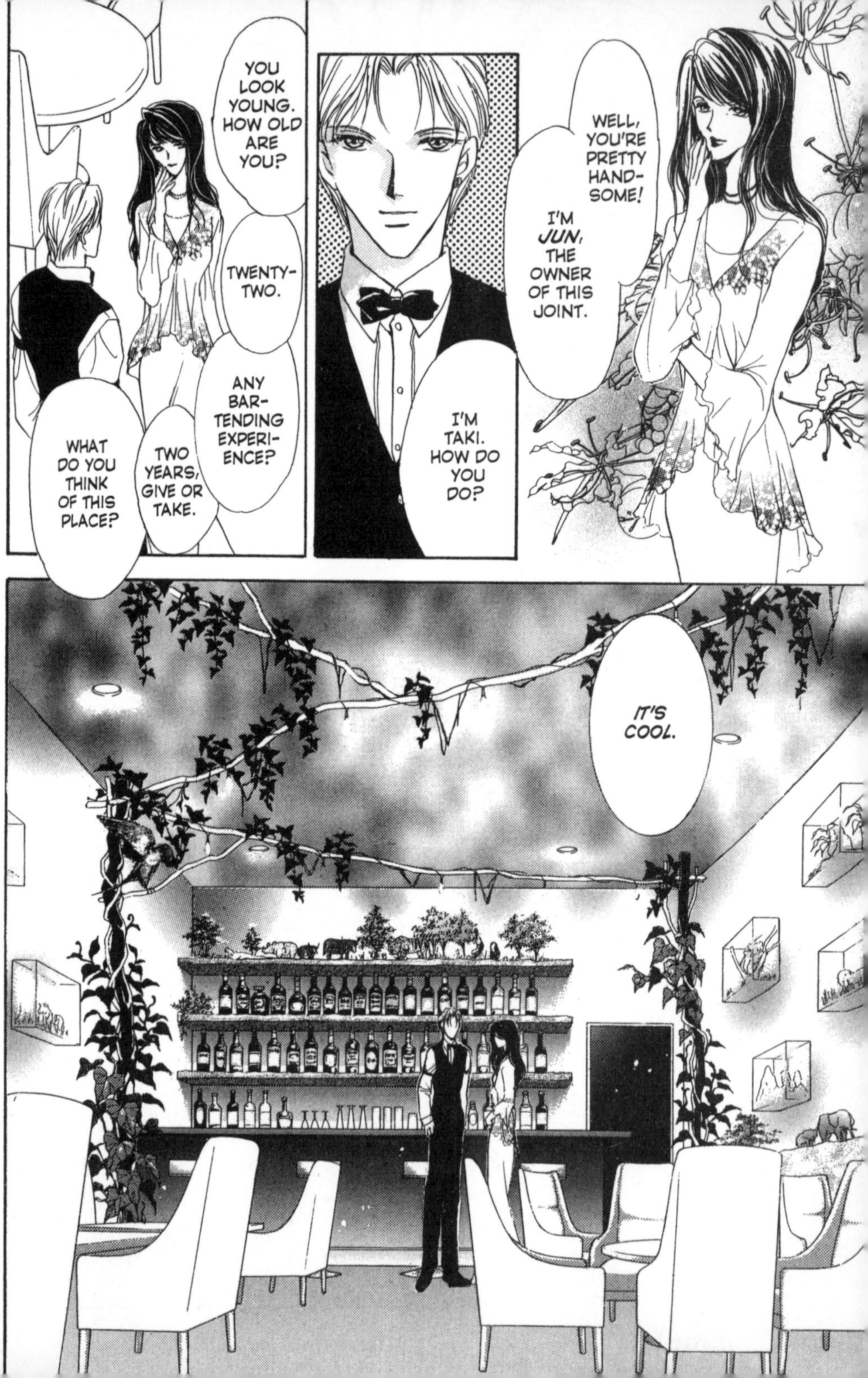
WELL, YOU'RE PRETTY HANDSOME!
I'M *JUN*, THE OWNER OF THIS JOINT.
I'M TAKI. HOW DO YOU DO?
YOU LOOK YOUNG. HOW OLD ARE YOU?
TWENTY-TWO.
ANY BARTENDING EXPERIENCE?
TWO YEARS, GIVE OR TAKE.
WHAT DO YOU THINK OF THIS PLACE?
IT'S COOL.

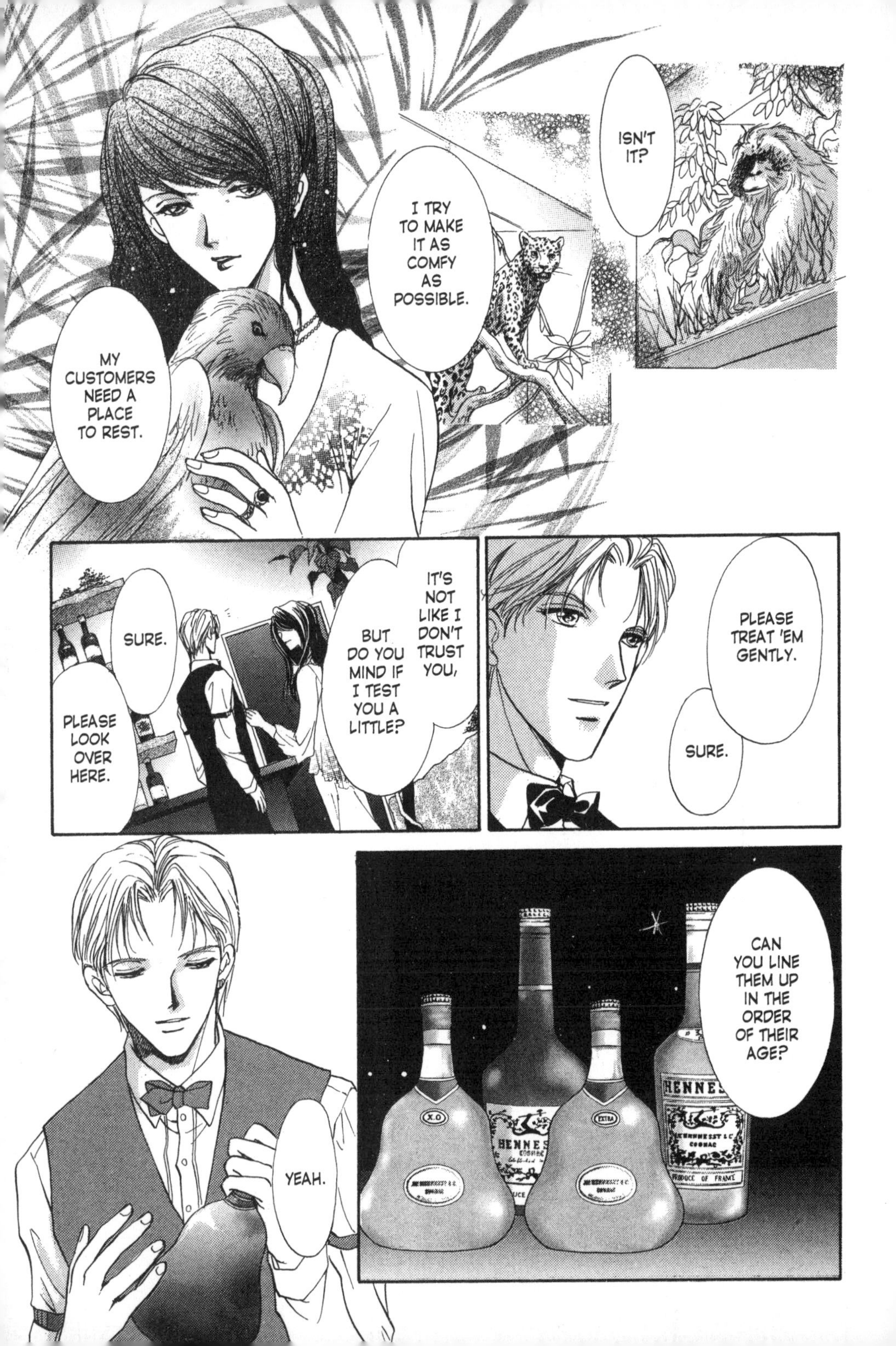
ISN'T IT?
I TRY TO MAKE IT AS COMFY AS POSSIBLE.
MY CUSTOMERS NEED A PLACE TO REST.
PLEASE TREAT 'EM GENTLY.
SURE.
IT'S NOT LIKE I DON'T TRUST YOU,
BUT DO YOU MIND IF I TEST YOU A LITTLE?
SURE.
PLEASE LOOK OVER HERE.
CAN YOU LINE THEM UP IN THE ORDER OF THEIR AGE?
X.O
EXTRA
YEAH.

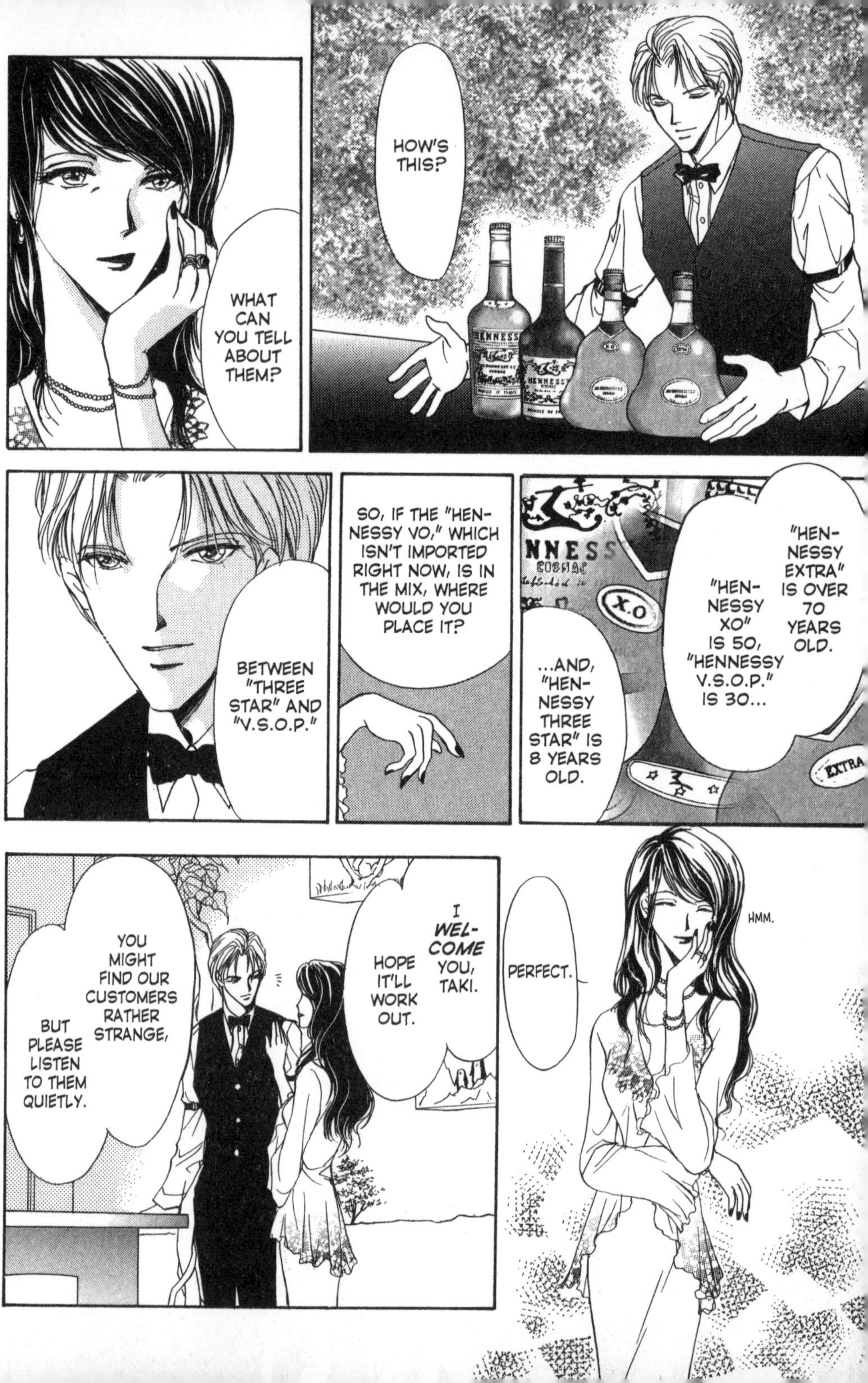
HOW'S THIS?
WHAT CAN YOU TELL ABOUT THEM?
"HENNESSY EXTRA" IS OVER 70 YEARS OLD.
"HENNESSY XO" IS 50, "HENNESSY V.S.O.P." IS 30...
...AND, "HENNESSY THREE STAR" IS 8 YEARS OLD.
SO, IF THE "HENNESSY VO," WHICH ISN'T IMPORTED RIGHT NOW, IS IN THE MIX, WHERE WOULD YOU PLACE IT?
BETWEEN "THREE STAR" AND "V.S.O.P."
HMM.
PERFECT.
I *WELCOME* YOU, TAKI.
HOPE IT'LL WORK OUT.
YOU MIGHT FIND OUR CUSTOMERS RATHER STRANGE,
BUT PLEASE LISTEN TO THEM QUIETLY.

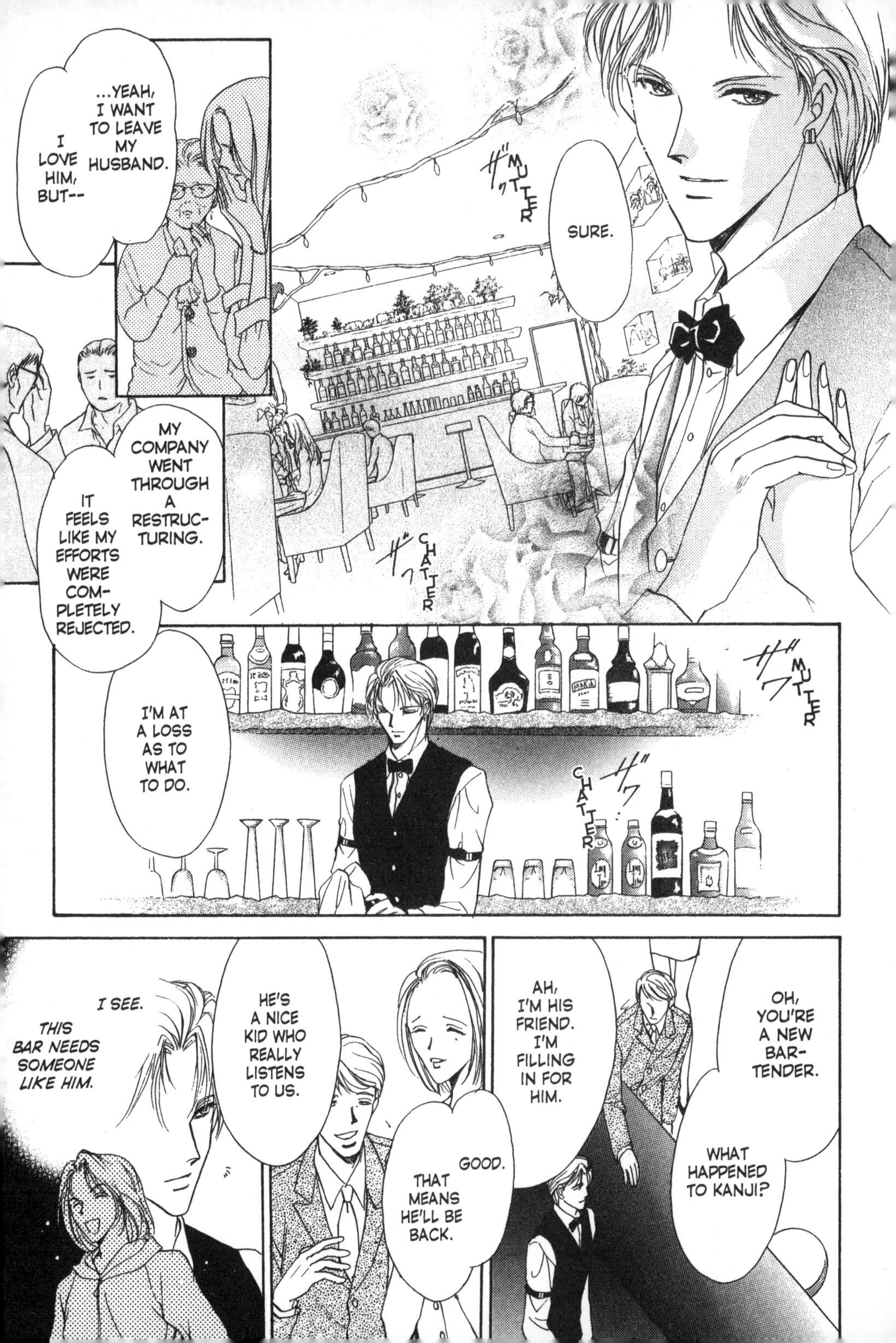
SURE.
MUTTER
CHATTER
...YEAH, I WANT TO LEAVE MY HUSBAND.
I LOVE HIM, BUT--
MY COMPANY WENT THROUGH A RESTRUC-TURING.
IT FEELS LIKE MY EFFORTS WERE COM-PLETELY REJECTED.
MUTTER
CHATTER
I'M AT A LOSS AS TO WHAT TO DO.
OH, YOU'RE A NEW BAR-TENDER.
AH, I'M HIS FRIEND. I'M FILLING IN FOR HIM.
WHAT HAPPENED TO KANJI?
HE'S A NICE KID WHO REALLY LISTENS TO US.
GOOD.
THAT MEANS HE'LL BE BACK.
I SEE.
THIS BAR NEEDS SOMEONE LIKE HIM.

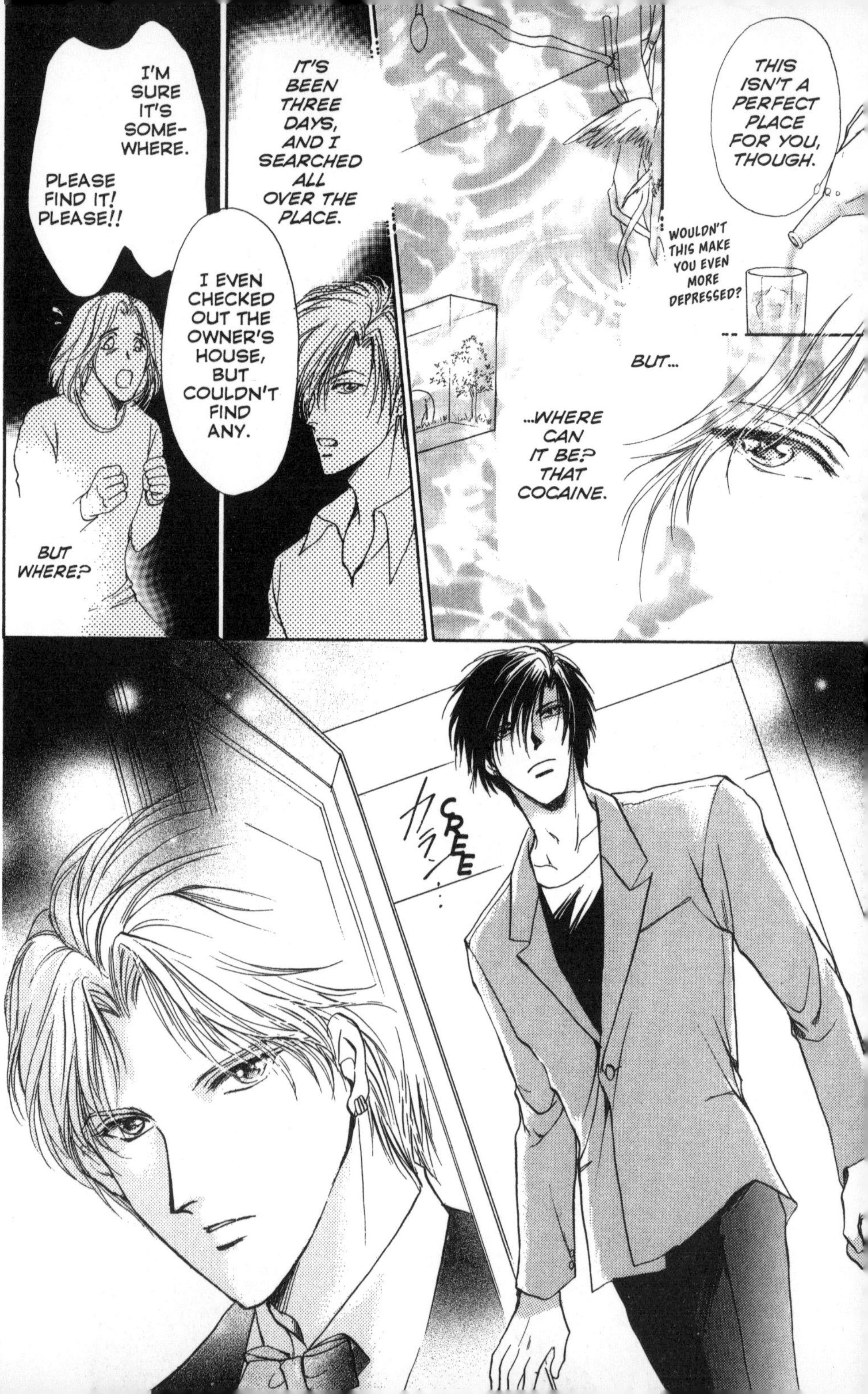
THIS ISN'T A PERFECT PLACE FOR YOU, THOUGH.
WOULDN'T THIS MAKE YOU EVEN MORE DEPRESSED?
BUT...
...WHERE CAN IT BE? THAT COCAINE.
IT'S BEEN THREE DAYS, AND I SEARCHED ALL OVER THE PLACE.
I EVEN CHECKED OUT THE OWNER'S HOUSE, BUT COULDN'T FIND ANY.
I'M SURE IT'S SOME-WHERE.
PLEASE FIND IT! PLEASE!!
BUT WHERE?
CREEE

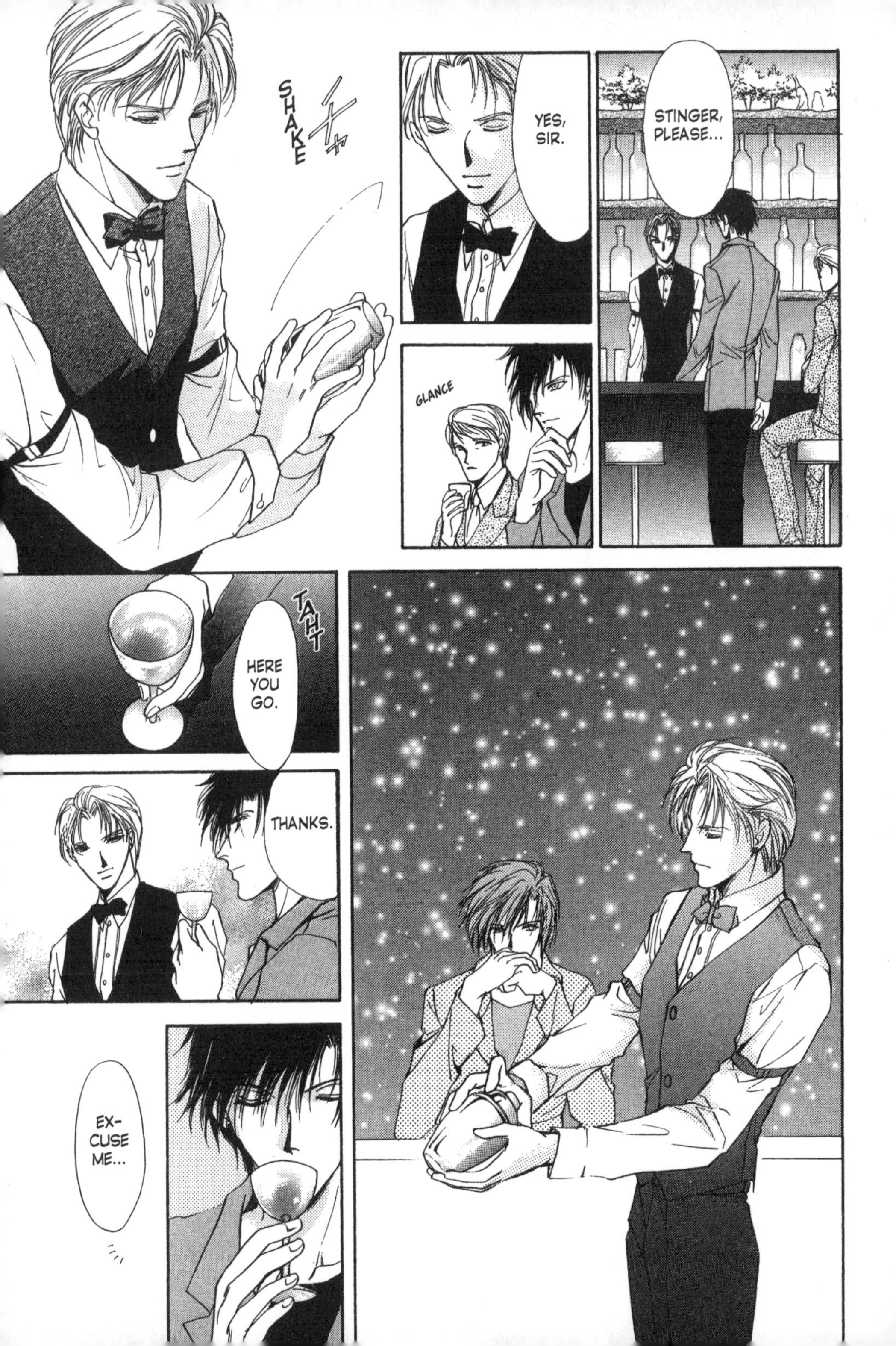
STINGER, PLEASE...
YES, SIR.
GLANCE
SHAKE
TAHT
HERE YOU GO.
THANKS.
EX-CUSE ME...

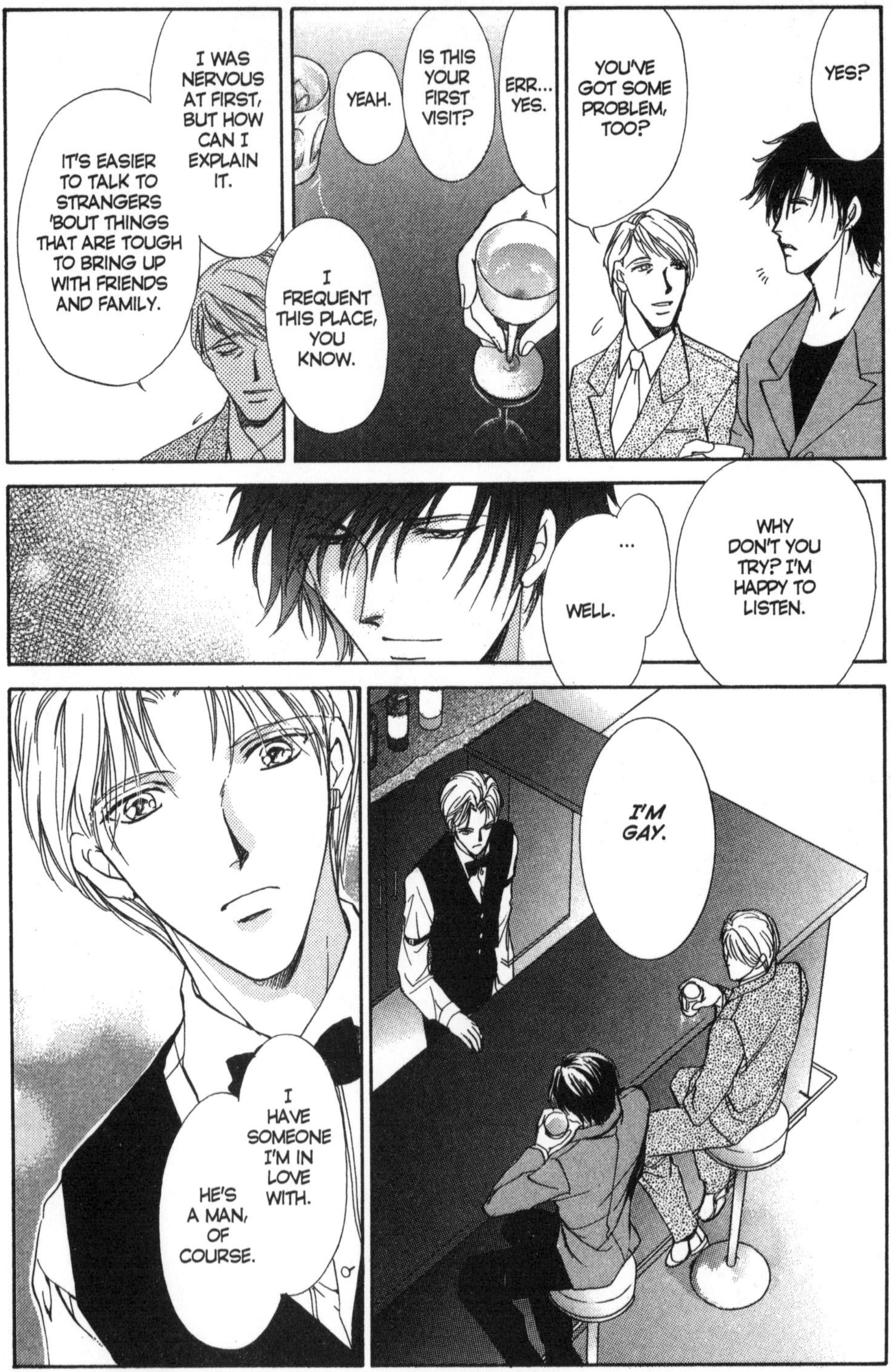
YES?
YOU'VE GOT SOME PROBLEM, TOO?
ERR... YES.
IS THIS YOUR FIRST VISIT?
YEAH.
I FREQUENT THIS PLACE, YOU KNOW.
I WAS NERVOUS AT FIRST, BUT HOW CAN I EXPLAIN IT.
IT'S EASIER TO TALK TO STRANGERS 'BOUT THINGS THAT ARE TOUGH TO BRING UP WITH FRIENDS AND FAMILY.
WHY DON'T YOU TRY? I'M HAPPY TO LISTEN.
... WELL.
I'M GAY.
I HAVE SOMEONE I'M IN LOVE WITH.
HE'S A MAN, OF COURSE.

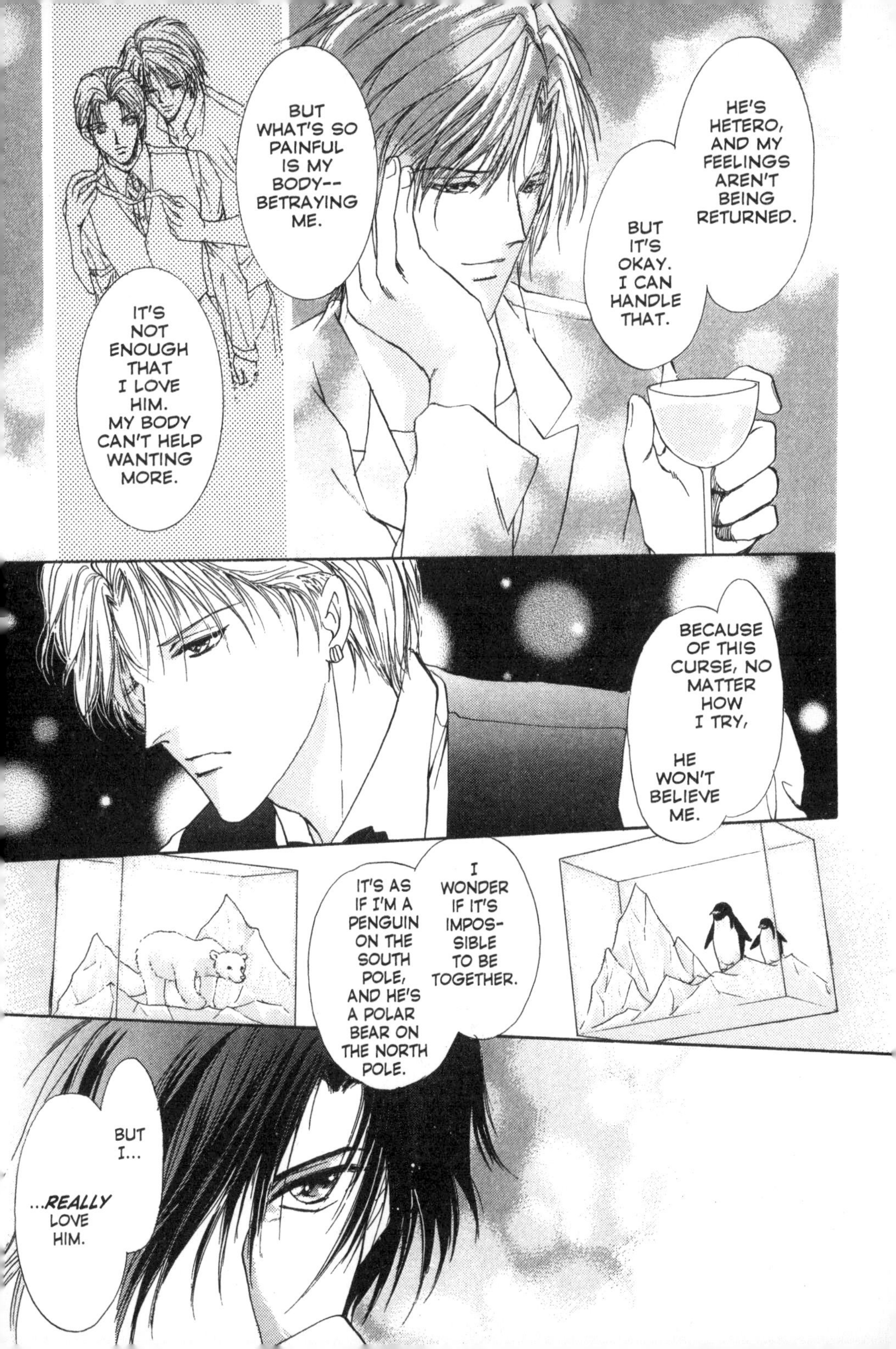
HE'S HETERO, AND MY FEELINGS AREN'T BEING RETURNED.
BUT IT'S OKAY. I CAN HANDLE THAT.
BUT WHAT'S SO PAINFUL IS MY BODY--BETRAYING ME.
IT'S NOT ENOUGH THAT I LOVE HIM. MY BODY CAN'T HELP WANTING MORE.
BECAUSE OF THIS CURSE, NO MATTER HOW I TRY,
HE WON'T BELIEVE ME.
I WONDER IF IT'S IMPOS-SIBLE TO BE TOGETHER.
IT'S AS IF I'M A PENGUIN ON THE SOUTH POLE, AND HE'S A POLAR BEAR ON THE NORTH POLE.
BUT I...
...*REALLY* LOVE HIM.

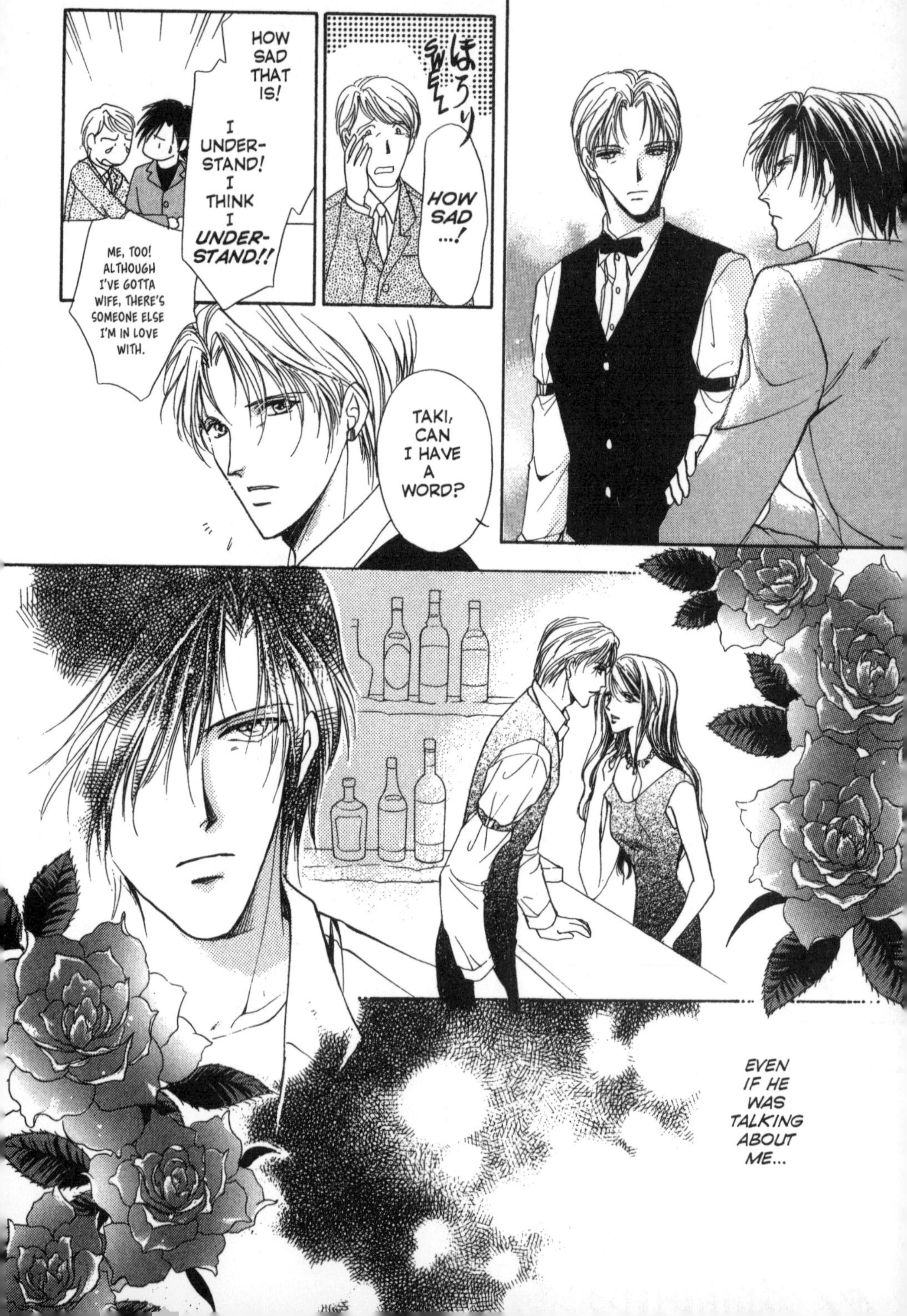
ほろり
SWELL
HOW SAD ...!
HOW SAD THAT IS!
I UNDERSTAND! I THINK I UNDERSTAND!!
ME, TOO! ALTHOUGH I'VE GOTTA WIFE, THERE'S SOMEONE ELSE I'M IN LOVE WITH.
TAKI, CAN I HAVE A WORD?
EVEN IF HE WAS TALKING ABOUT ME...

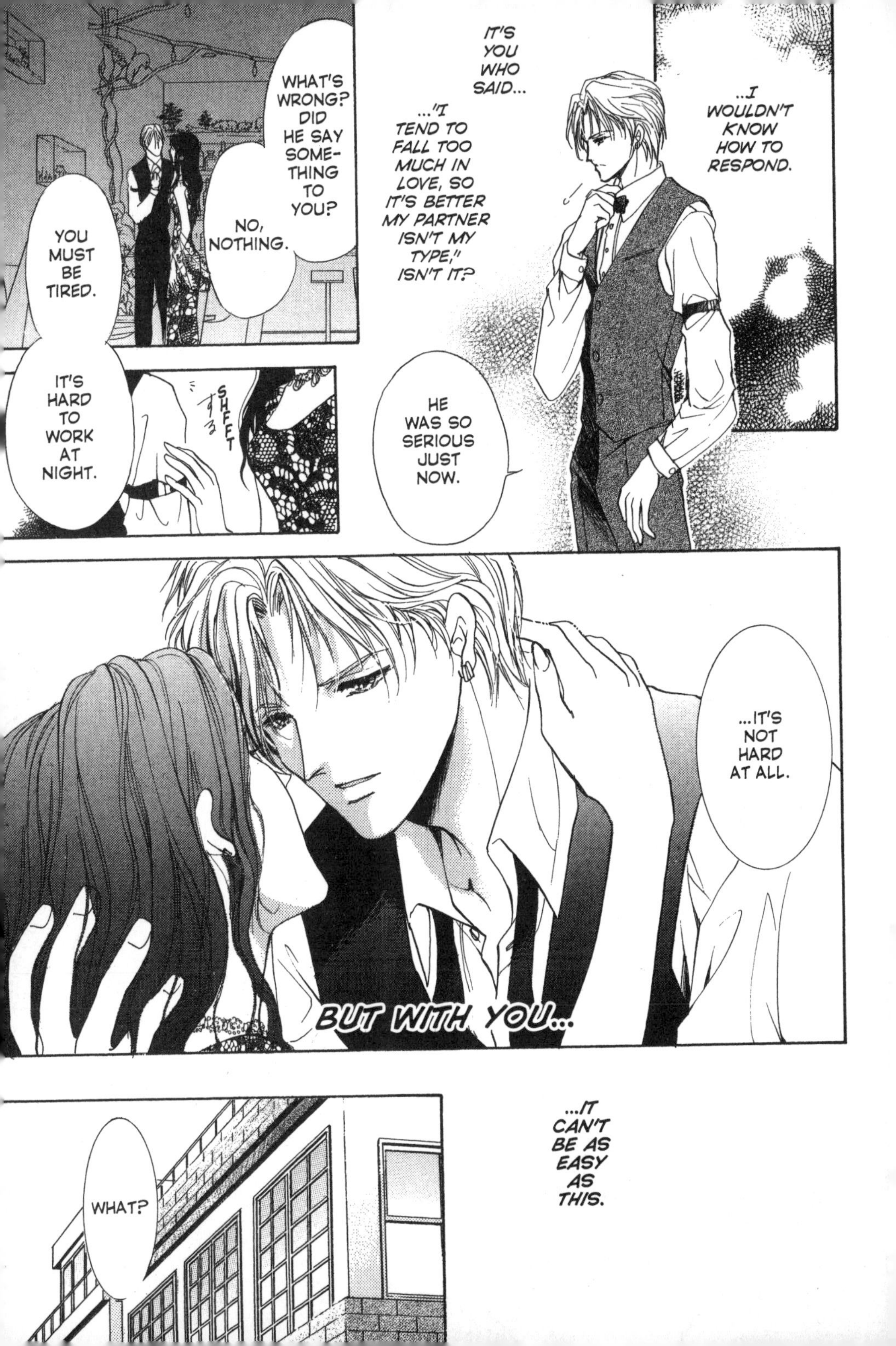
..I WOULDN'T KNOW HOW TO RESPOND.
IT'S YOU WHO SAID...
..."I TEND TO FALL TOO MUCH IN LOVE, SO IT'S BETTER MY PARTNER ISN'T MY TYPE," ISN'T IT?
HE WAS SO SERIOUS JUST NOW.
WHAT'S WRONG? DID HE SAY SOME-THING TO YOU?
NO, NOTHING.
YOU MUST BE TIRED.
SHFFT
IT'S HARD TO WORK AT NIGHT.
...IT'S NOT HARD AT ALL.
BUT WITH YOU...
...IT CAN'T BE AS EASY AS THIS.
WHAT?

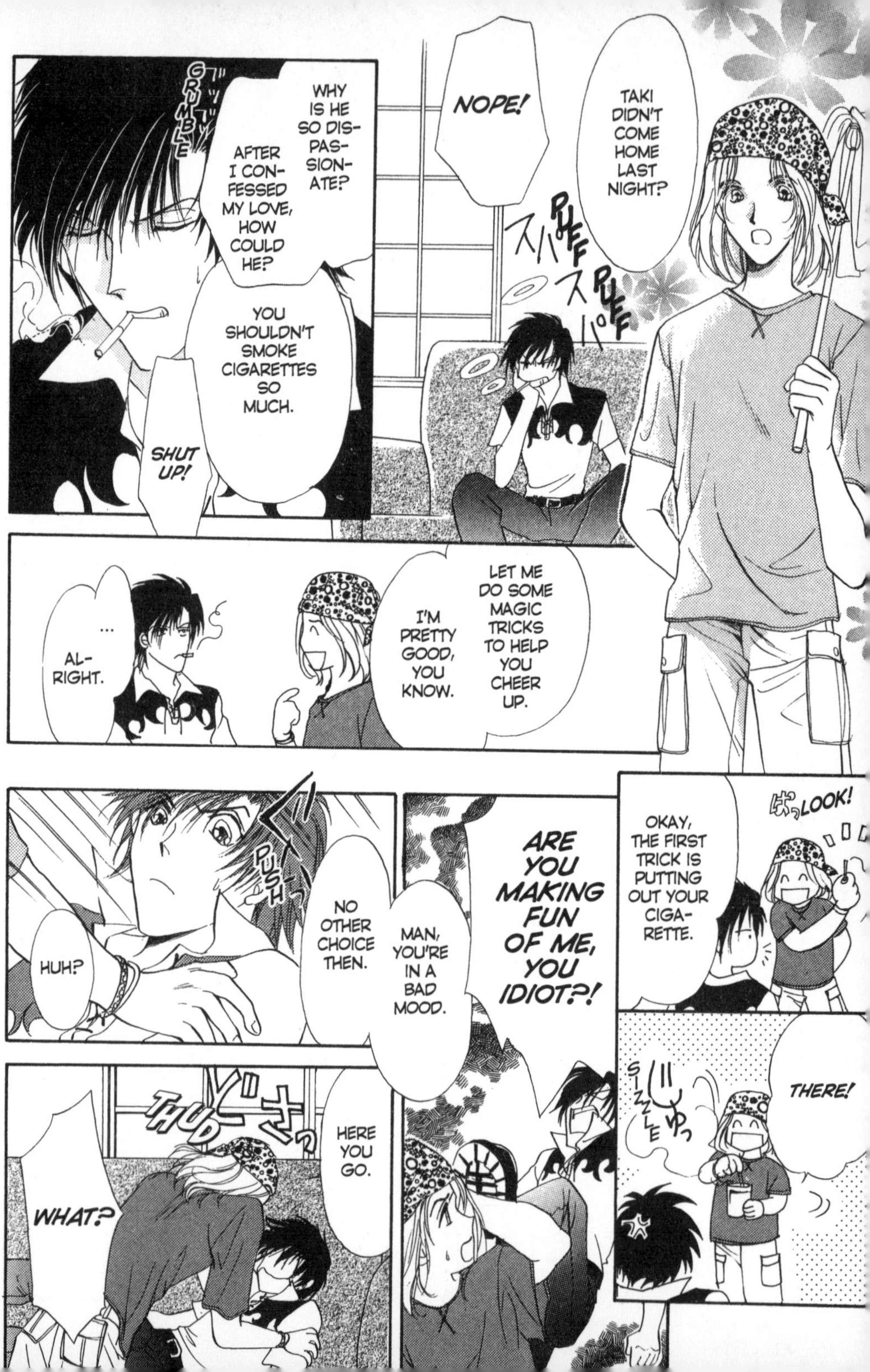
TAKI DIDN'T COME HOME LAST NIGHT?
NOPE!
PUFF PUFF
WHY IS HE SO DISPASSIONATE?
AFTER I CONFESSED MY LOVE, HOW COULD HE?
GRUMBLE
YOU SHOULDN'T SMOKE CIGARETTES SO MUCH.
SHUT UP!
LET ME DO SOME MAGIC TRICKS TO HELP YOU CHEER UP.
I'M PRETTY GOOD, YOU KNOW.
... ALRIGHT.
LOOK!
OKAY, THE FIRST TRICK IS PUTTING OUT YOUR CIGARETTE.
SIZZLE
THERE!
ARE YOU MAKING FUN OF ME, YOU IDIOT?!
MAN, YOU'RE IN A BAD MOOD.
NO OTHER CHOICE THEN.
PUSH
HUH?
THUD
HERE YOU GO.
WHAT?

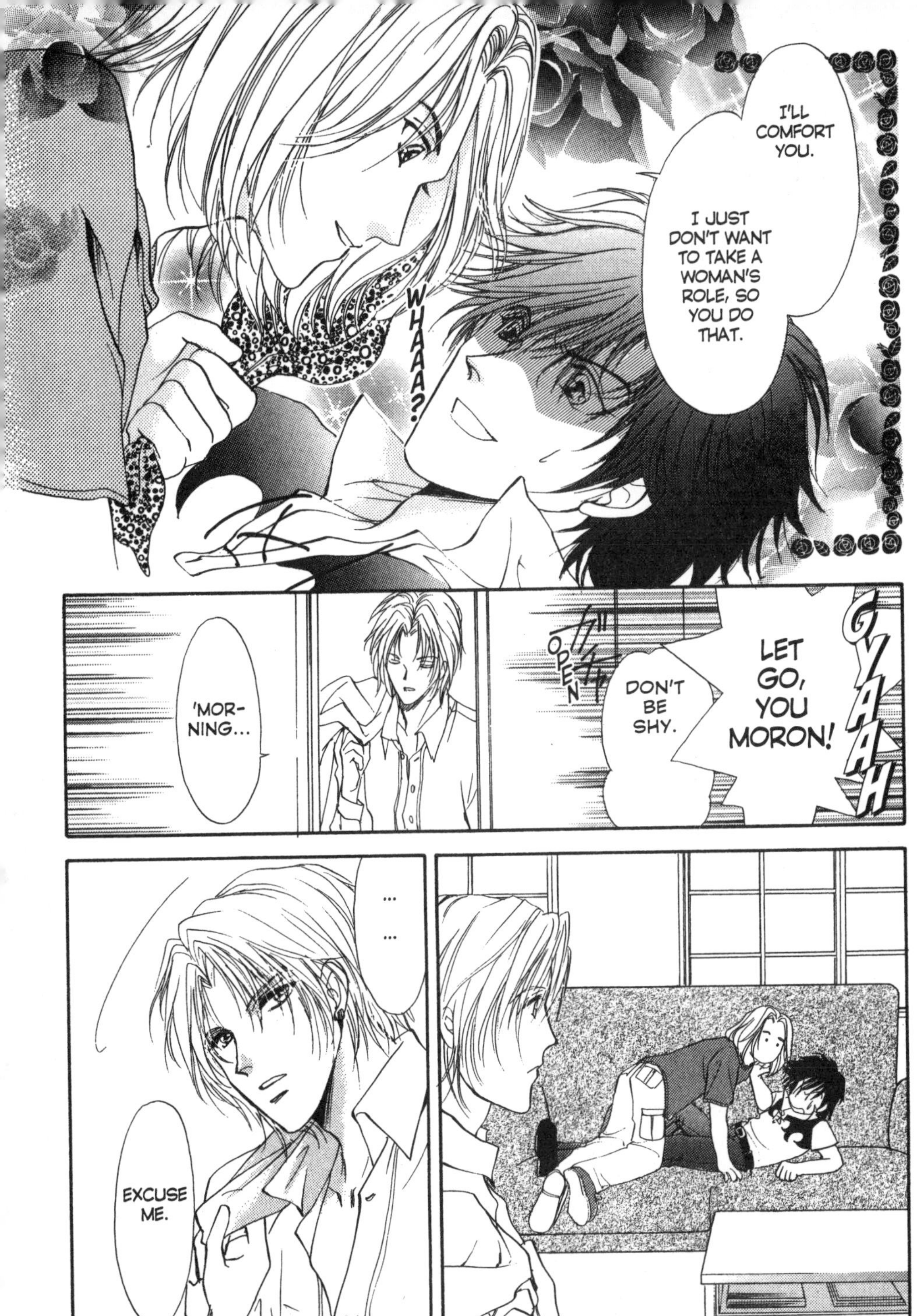
I'LL COMFORT YOU.
I JUST DON'T WANT TO TAKE A WOMAN'S ROLE, SO YOU DO THAT.
WHAAA?
GYAAAH
LET GO, YOU MORON!
DON'T BE SHY.
OPEN
'MOR-NING...
...
...
EXCUSE ME.

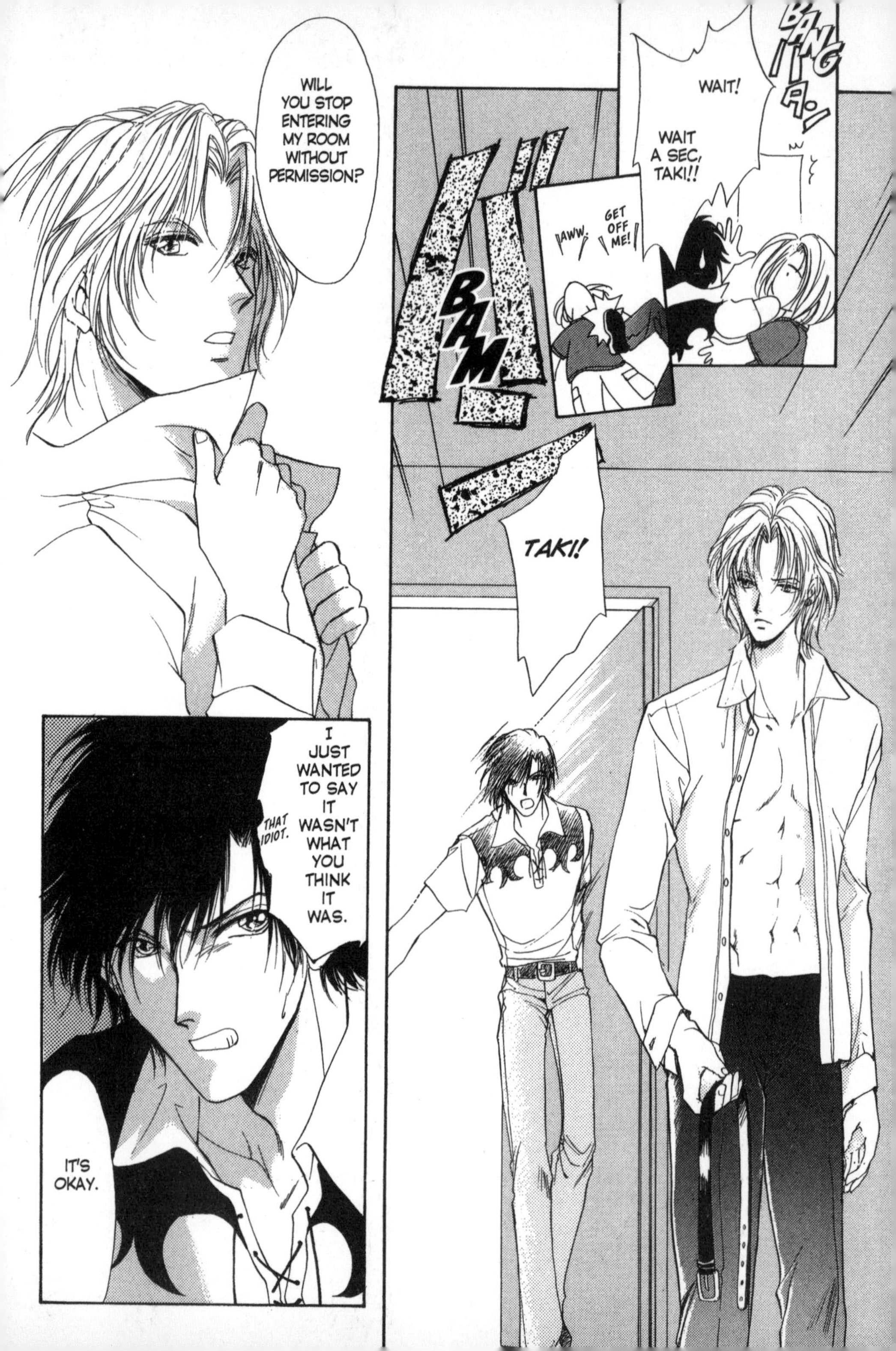
BANG
WAIT!
WAIT A SEC, TAKI!!
AWW.
GET OFF ME!
BAM
TAKI!
WILL YOU STOP ENTERING MY ROOM WITHOUT PERMISSION?
I JUST WANTED TO SAY IT WASN'T WHAT YOU THINK IT WAS.
THAT IDIOT.
IT'S OKAY.

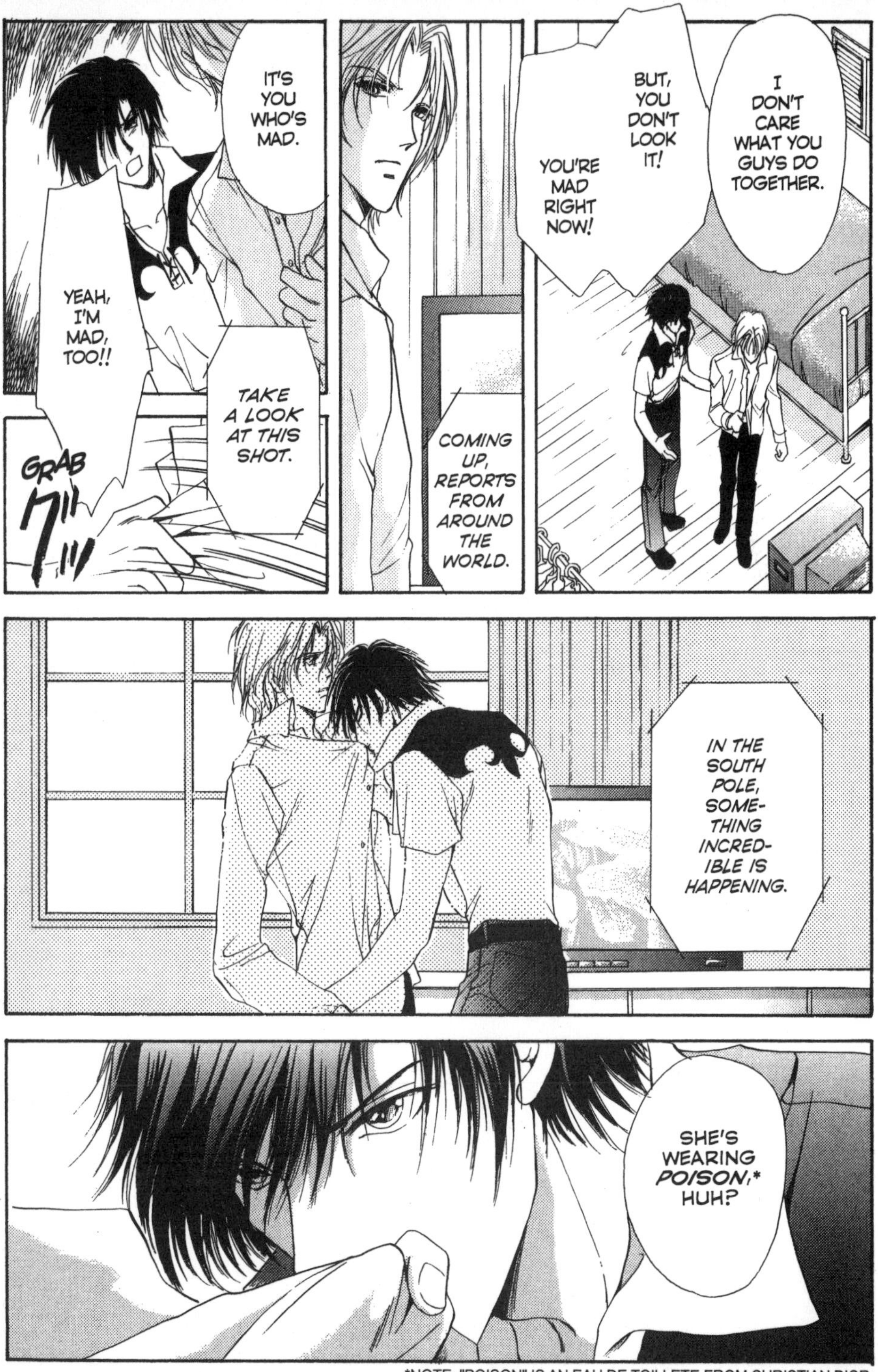
I DON'T CARE WHAT YOU GUYS DO TOGETHER.
BUT, YOU DON'T LOOK IT!
YOU'RE MAD RIGHT NOW!
COMING UP, REPORTS FROM AROUND THE WORLD.
IT'S YOU WHO'S MAD.
YEAH, I'M MAD, TOO!!
TAKE A LOOK AT THIS SHOT.
GRAB
グッ
IN THE SOUTH POLE, SOMETHING INCREDIBLE IS HAPPENING.
SHE'S WEARING POISON,* HUH?

*NOTE: "POISON" IS AN EAU DE TOILLETE FROM CHRISTIAN DIOR.

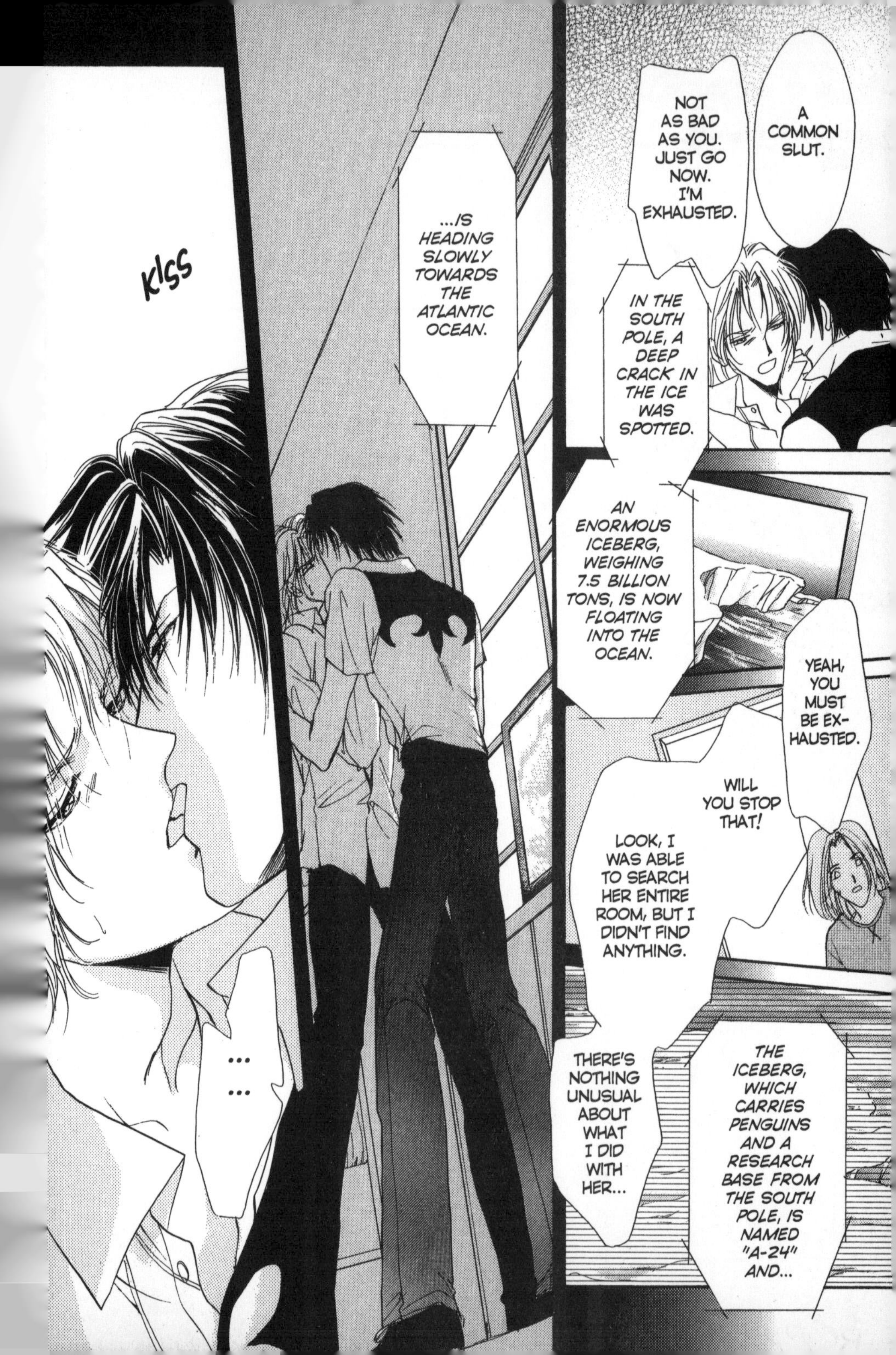
A COMMON SLUT.
NOT AS BAD AS YOU. JUST GO NOW. I'M EXHAUSTED.
IN THE SOUTH POLE, A DEEP CRACK IN THE ICE WAS SPOTTED.
AN ENORMOUS ICEBERG, WEIGHING 7.5 BILLION TONS, IS NOW FLOATING INTO THE OCEAN.
YEAH, YOU MUST BE EX-HAUSTED.
WILL YOU STOP THAT!
LOOK, I WAS ABLE TO SEARCH HER ENTIRE ROOM, BUT I DIDN'T FIND ANYTHING.
THE ICEBERG, WHICH CARRIES PENGUINS AND A RESEARCH BASE FROM THE SOUTH POLE, IS NAMED "A-24" AND...
THERE'S NOTHING UNUSUAL ABOUT WHAT I DID WITH HER...
...IS HEADING SLOWLY TOWARDS THE ATLANTIC OCEAN.
KISS
...
...

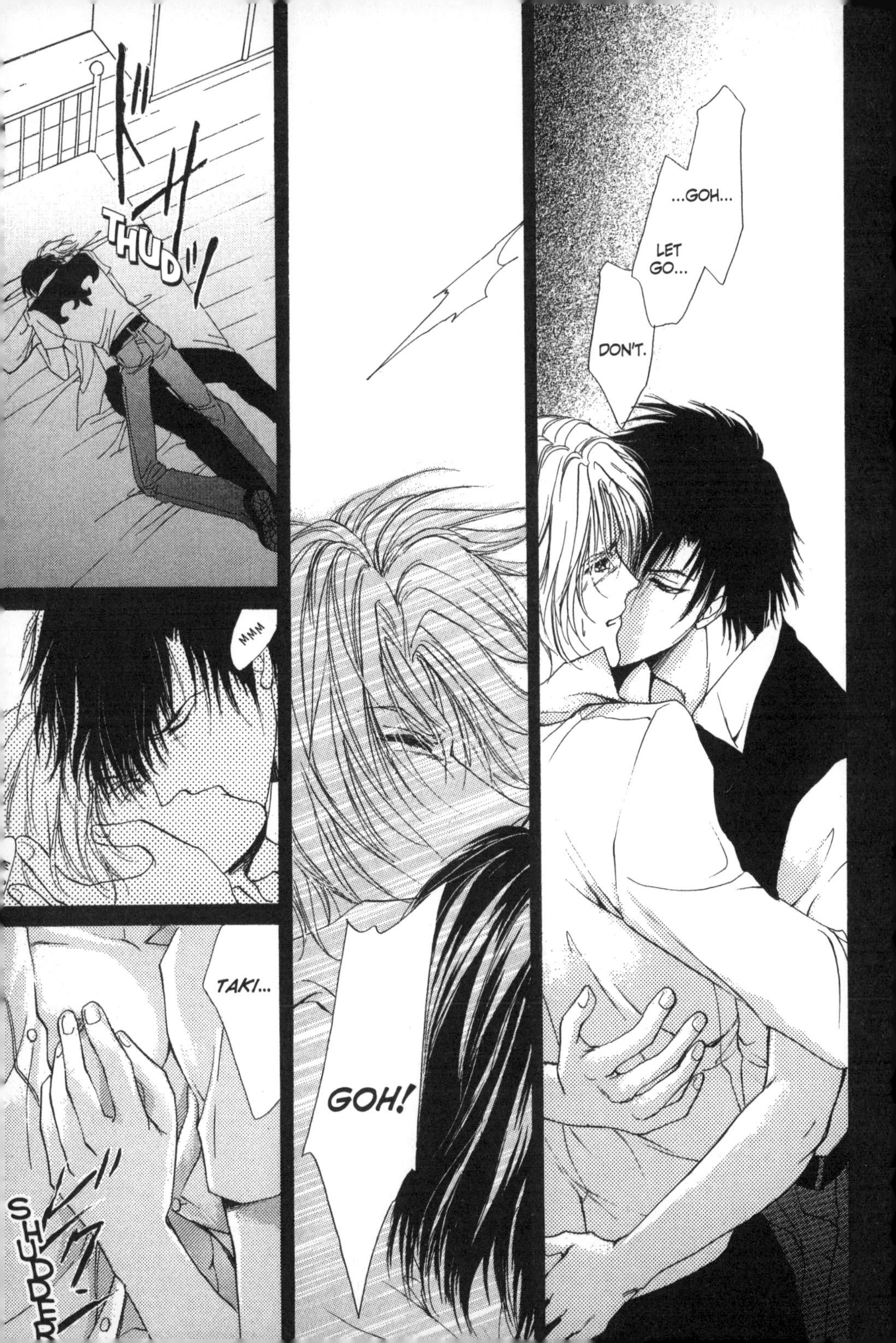
...GOH...
LET GO...
DON'T.
GOH!
THUD
MMM
TAKI...
SHUDDER

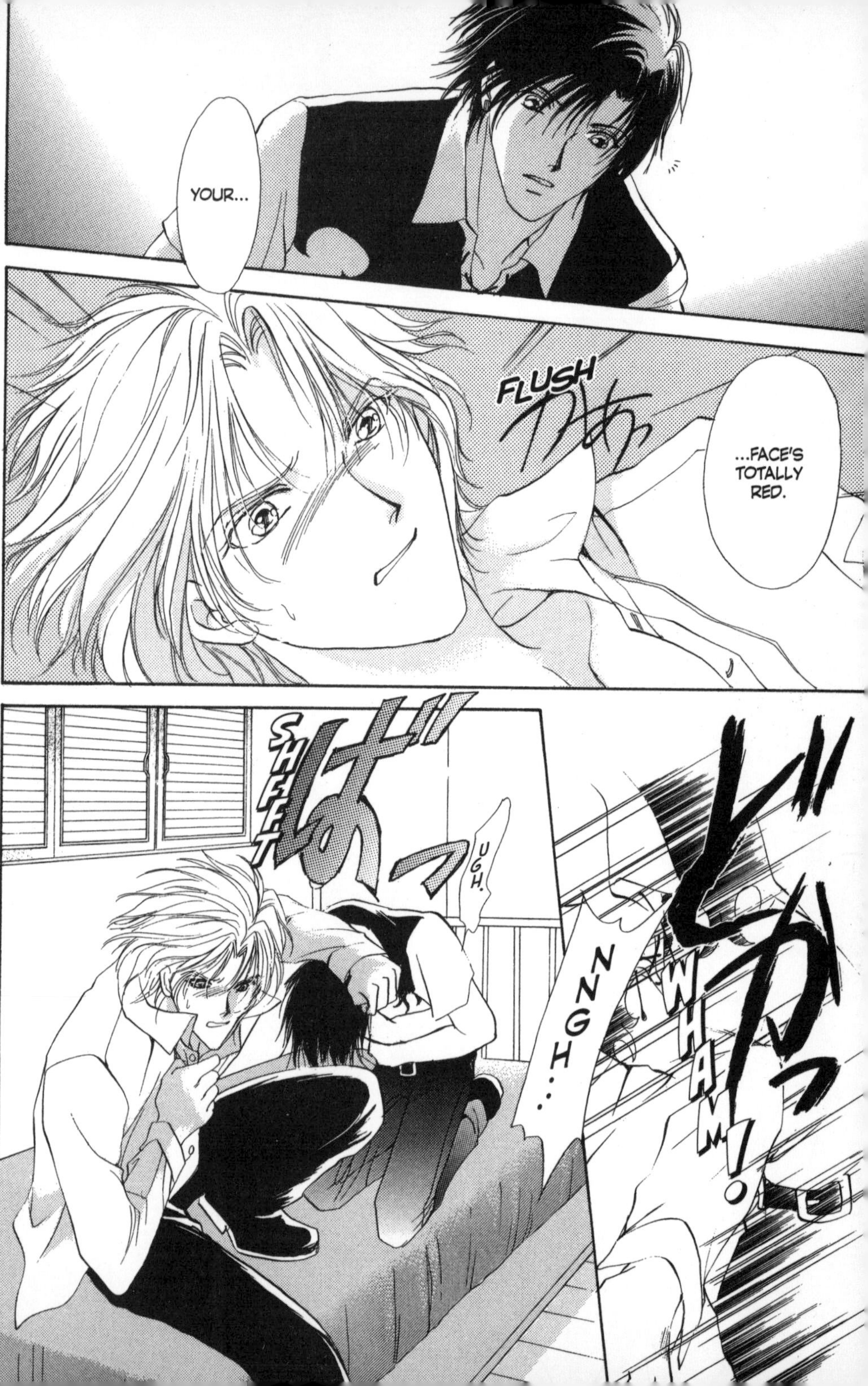
YOUR...
...FACE'S TOTALLY RED.
FLUSH
WHAM!
NNGH...
SHFFT
UGH.

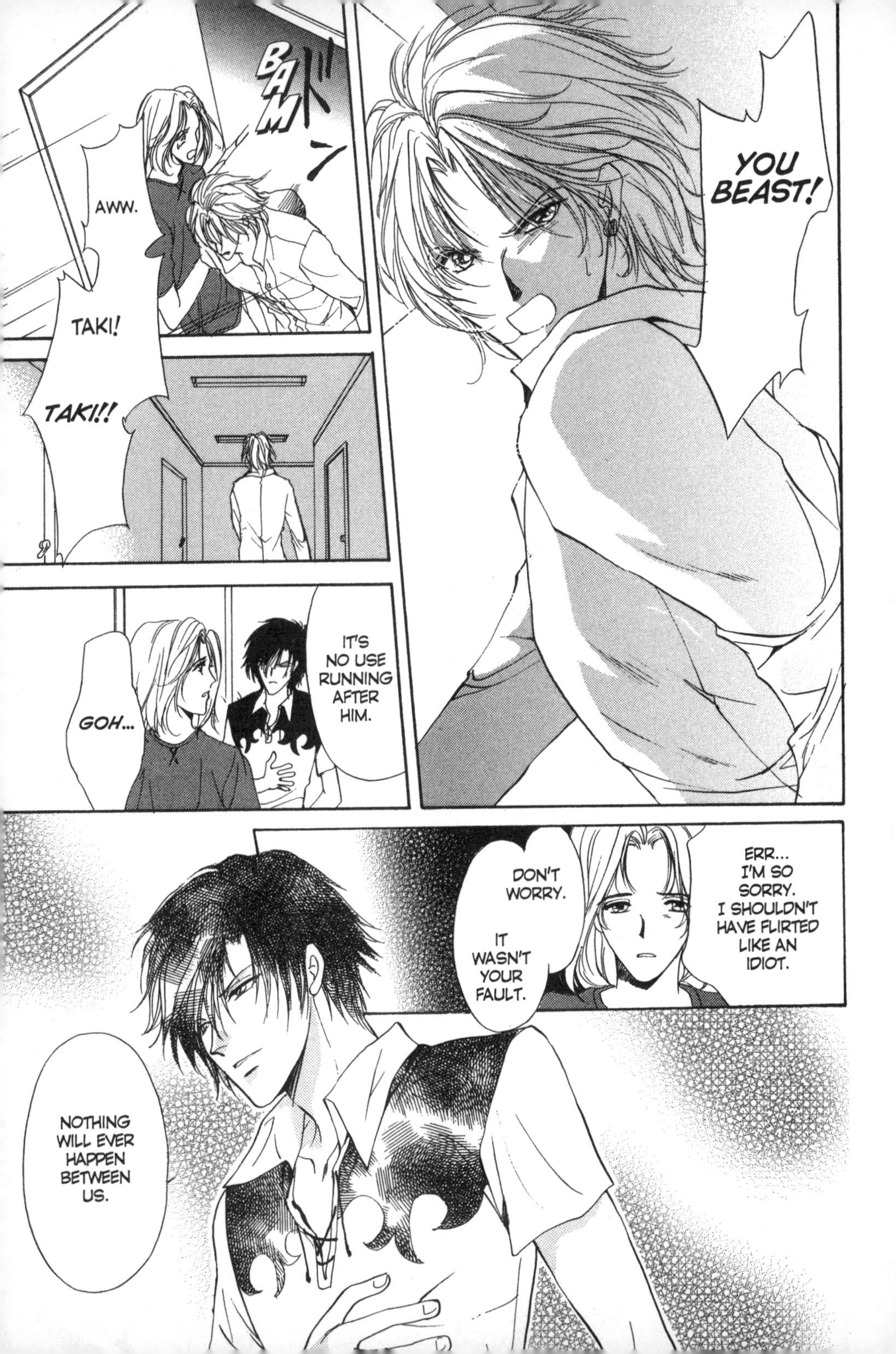
YOU BEAST!
BAM
ドン
AWW.
TAKI!
TAKI!!
IT'S NO USE RUNNING AFTER HIM.
GOH...
ERR... I'M SO SORRY. I SHOULDN'T HAVE FLIRTED LIKE AN IDIOT.
DON'T WORRY.
IT WASN'T YOUR FAULT.
NOTHING WILL EVER HAPPEN BETWEEN US.

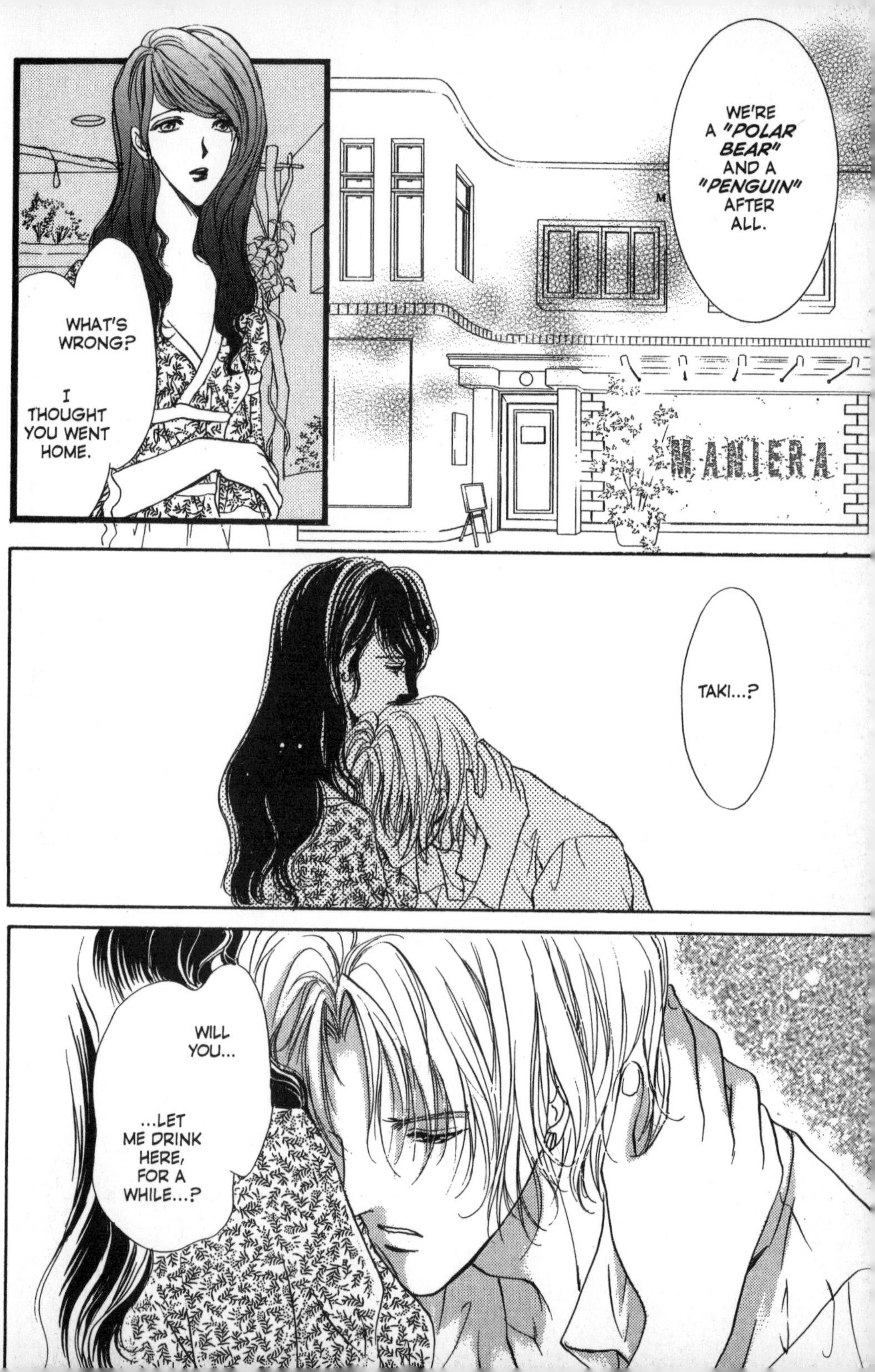
WE'RE A *"POLAR BEAR"* AND A *"PENGUIN"* AFTER ALL.
MANIERA
WHAT'S WRONG?
I THOUGHT YOU WENT HOME.
TAKI...?
WILL YOU...
...LET ME DRINK HERE, FOR A WHILE...?

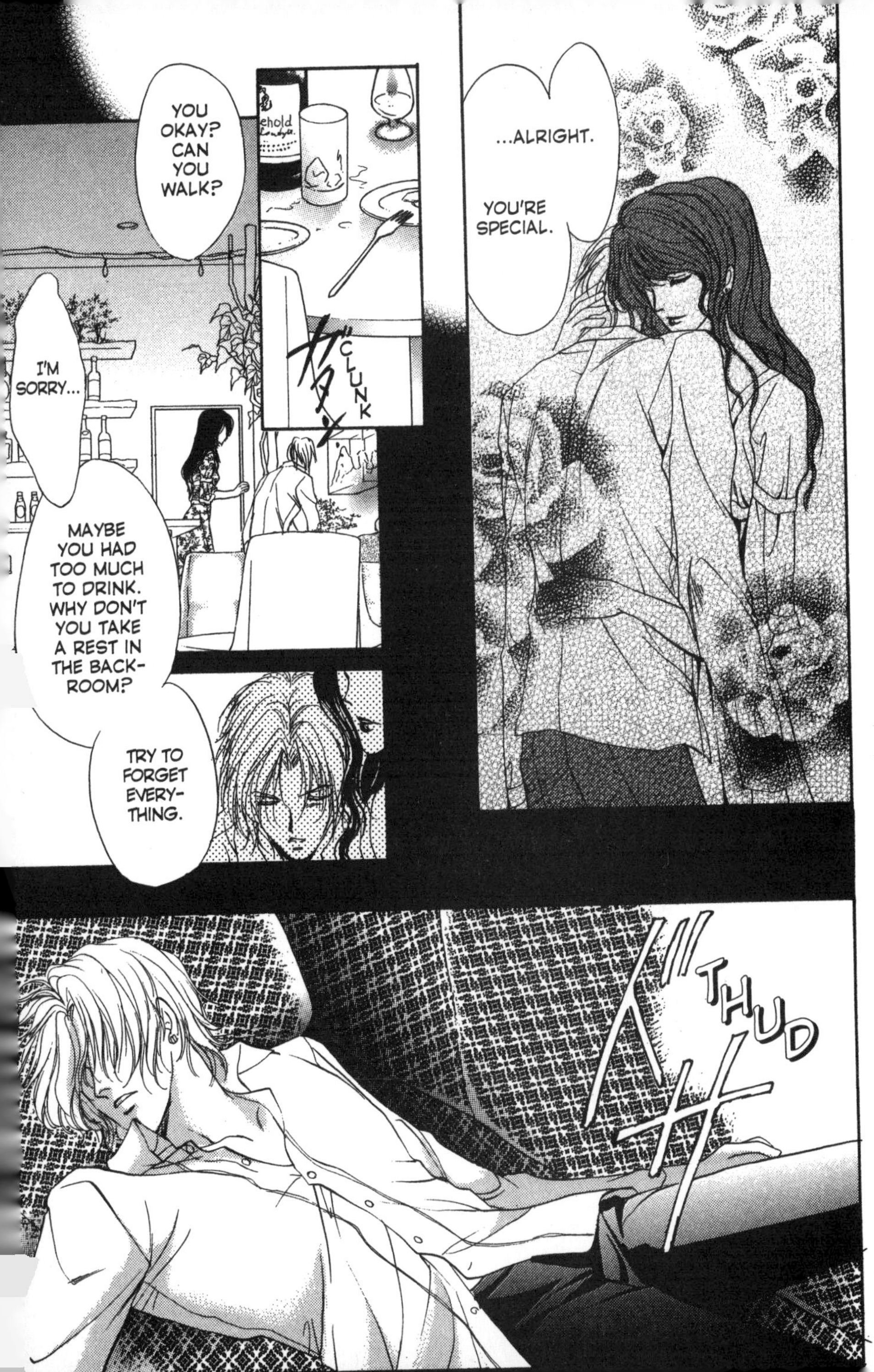
...ALRIGHT.
YOU'RE SPECIAL.
CLUNK
YOU OKAY? CAN YOU WALK?
I'M SORRY...
MAYBE YOU HAD TOO MUCH TO DRINK. WHY DON'T YOU TAKE A REST IN THE BACK-ROOM?
TRY TO FORGET EVERY-THING.
THUD

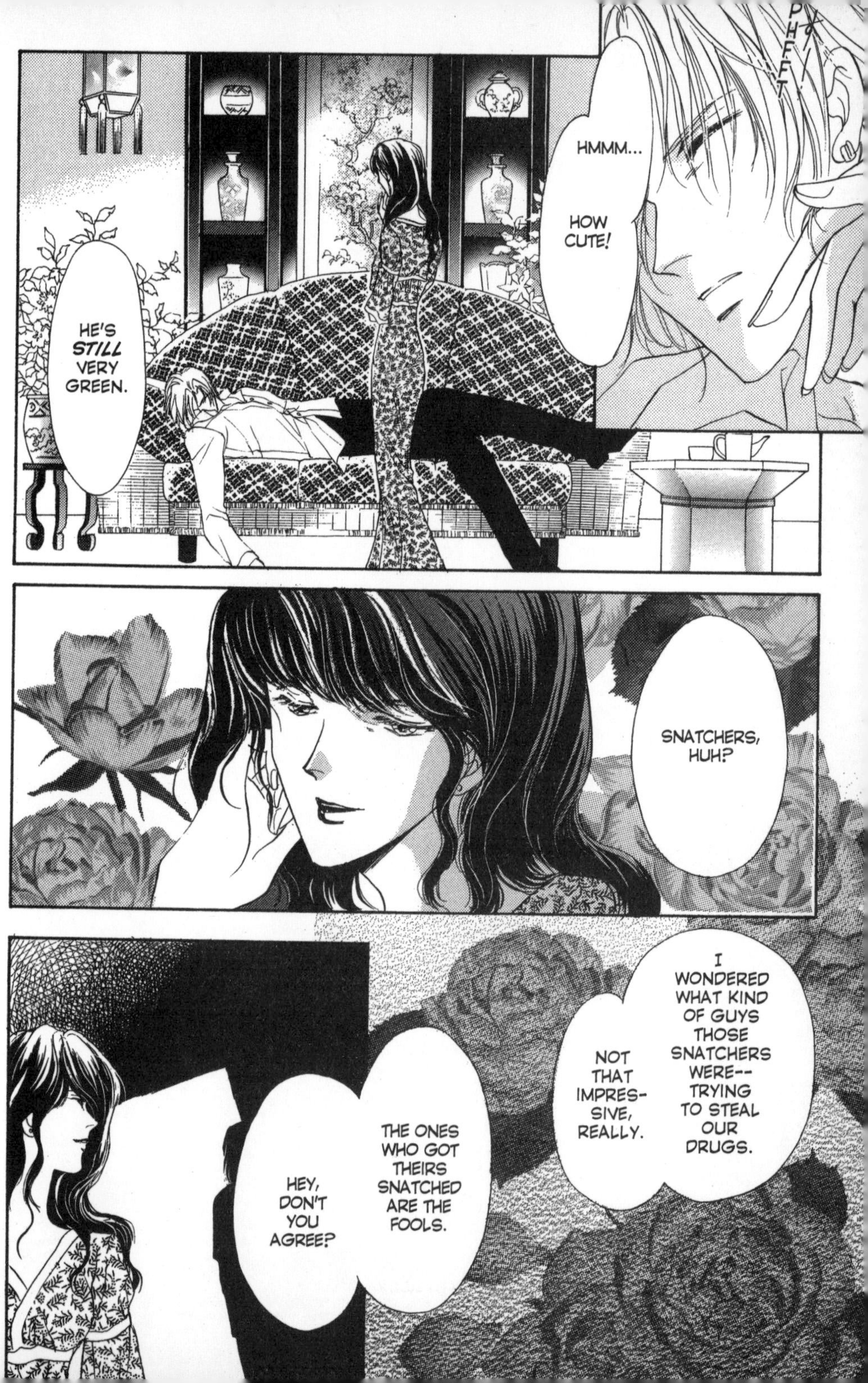
PHFFT
HMMM...
HOW CUTE!
HE'S *STILL* VERY GREEN.
SNATCHERS, HUH?
I WONDERED WHAT KIND OF GUYS THOSE SNATCHERS WERE-- TRYING TO STEAL OUR DRUGS.
NOT THAT IMPRES-SIVE, REALLY.
THE ONES WHO GOT THEIRS SNATCHED ARE THE FOOLS.
HEY, DON'T YOU AGREE?

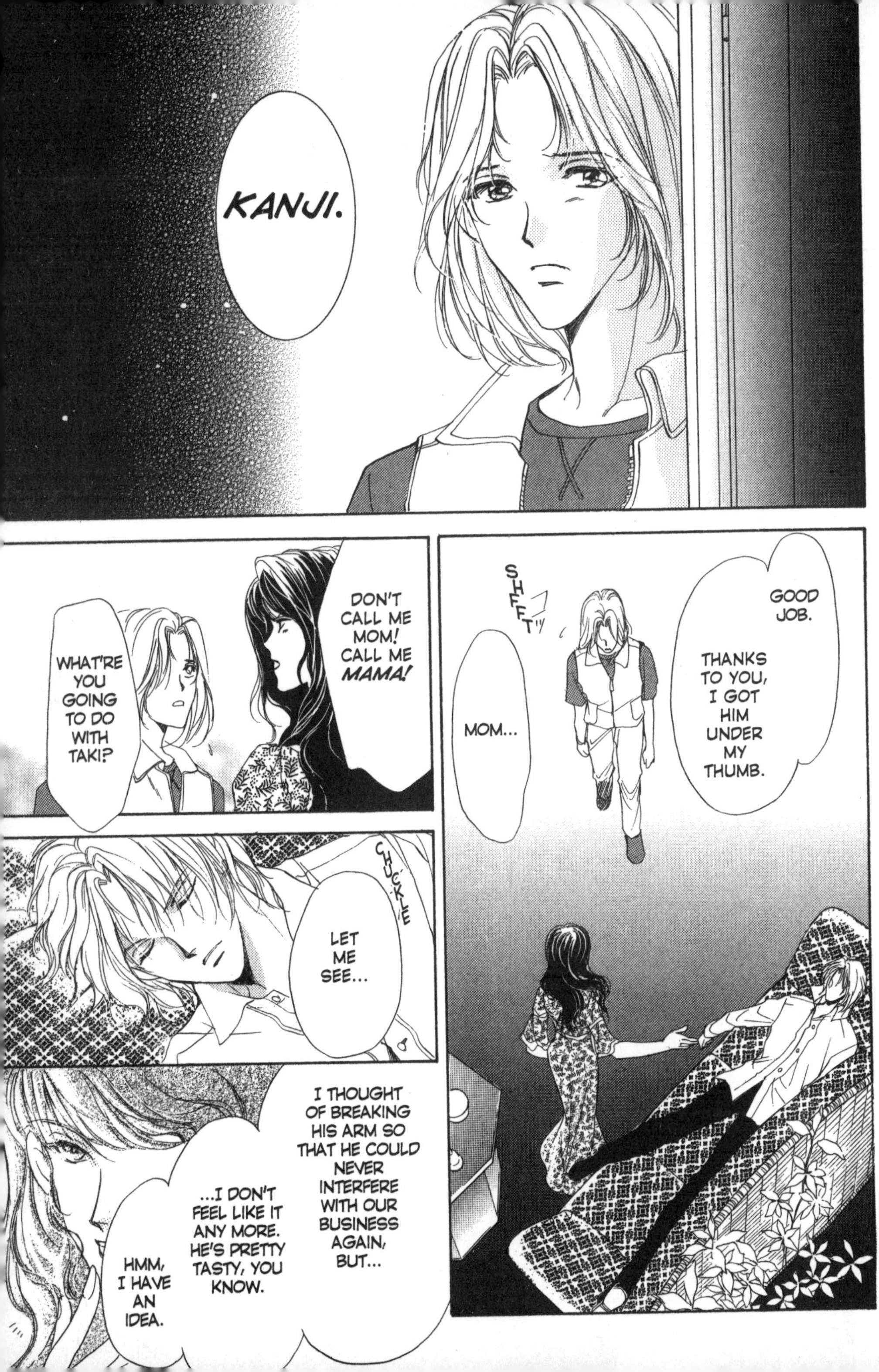
KANJI.
GOOD JOB.
THANKS TO YOU, I GOT HIM UNDER MY THUMB.
SHFFT
MOM...
DON'T CALL ME MOM! CALL ME MAMA!
WHAT'RE YOU GOING TO DO WITH TAKI?
CHUCKLE
LET ME SEE...
I THOUGHT OF BREAKING HIS ARM SO THAT HE COULD NEVER INTERFERE WITH OUR BUSINESS AGAIN, BUT...
...I DON'T FEEL LIKE IT ANY MORE. HE'S PRETTY TASTY, YOU KNOW.
HMM, I HAVE AN IDEA.

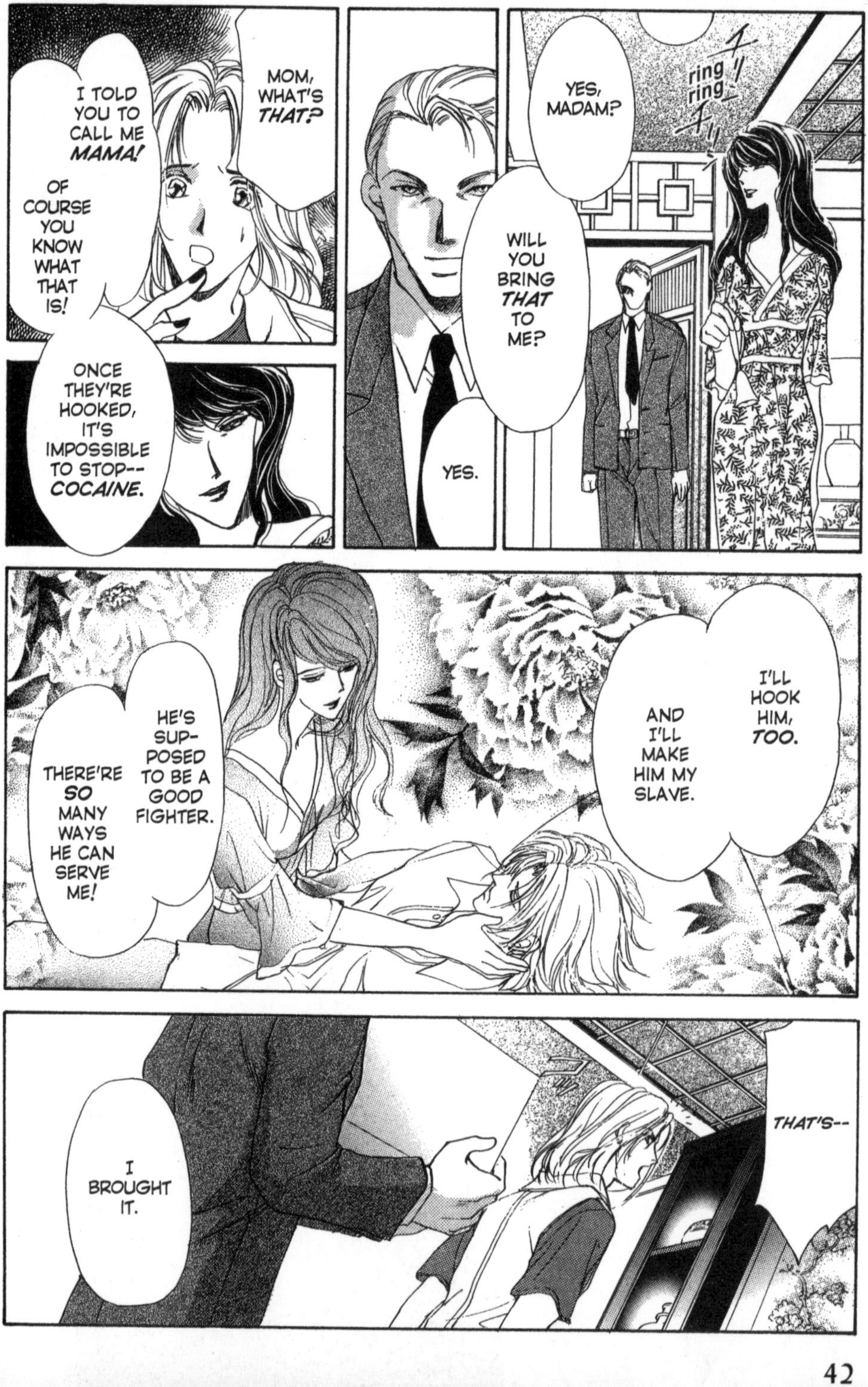
ring ring
YES, MADAM?
WILL YOU BRING *THAT* TO ME?
YES.
MOM, WHAT'S *THAT?*
I TOLD YOU TO CALL ME *MAMA!*
OF COURSE YOU KNOW WHAT THAT IS!
ONCE THEY'RE HOOKED, IT'S IMPOSSIBLE TO STOP-- *COCAINE.*
I'LL HOOK HIM, *TOO.*
AND I'LL MAKE HIM MY SLAVE.
HE'S SUP-POSED TO BE A GOOD FIGHTER.
THERE'RE *SO* MANY WAYS HE CAN SERVE ME!
THAT'S--
I BROUGHT IT.

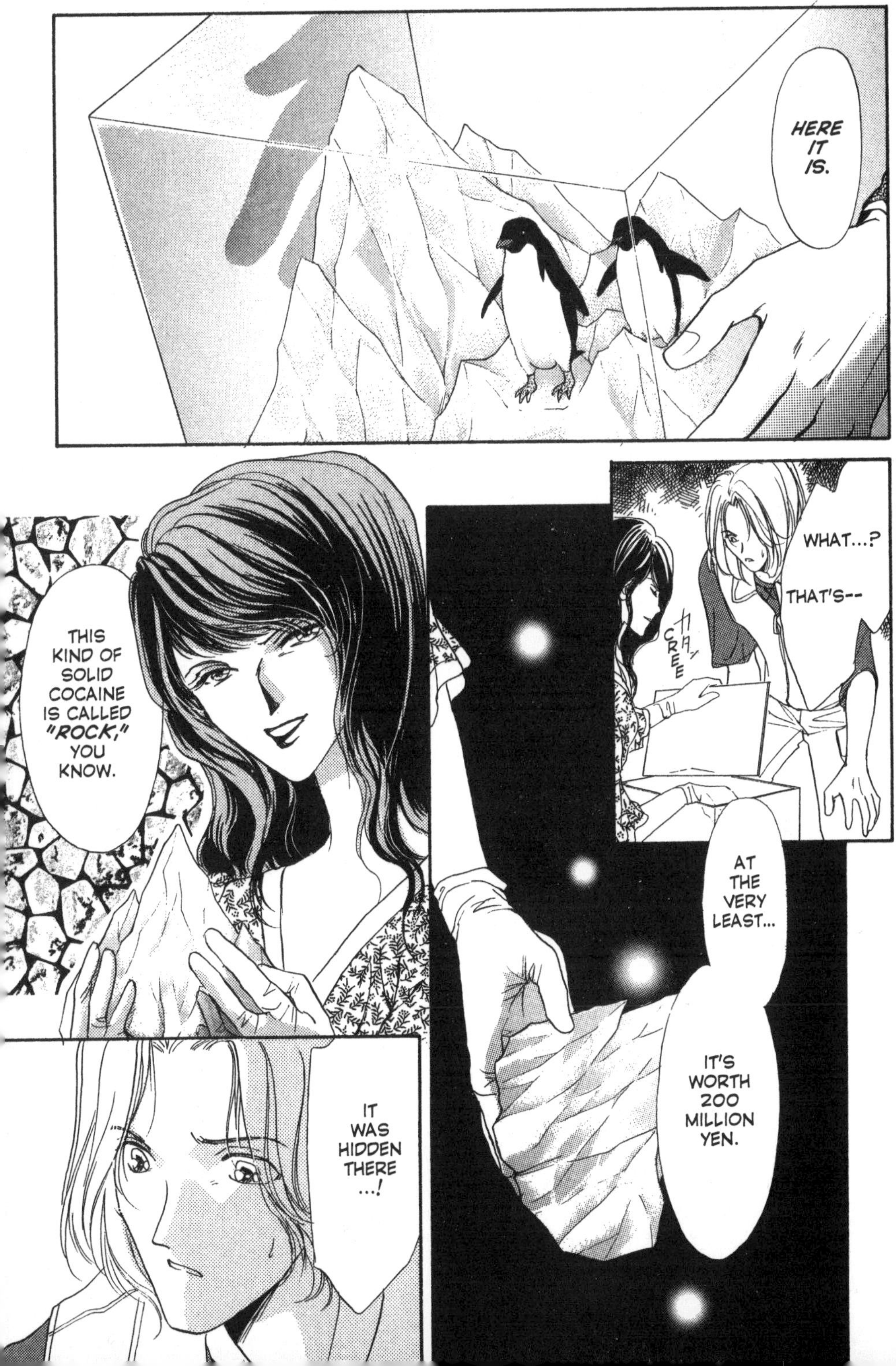
HERE IT IS.
WHAT...?
THAT'S--
CREE
AT THE VERY LEAST...
IT'S WORTH 200 MILLION YEN.
THIS KIND OF SOLID COCAINE IS CALLED "ROCK," YOU KNOW.
IT WAS HIDDEN THERE...!

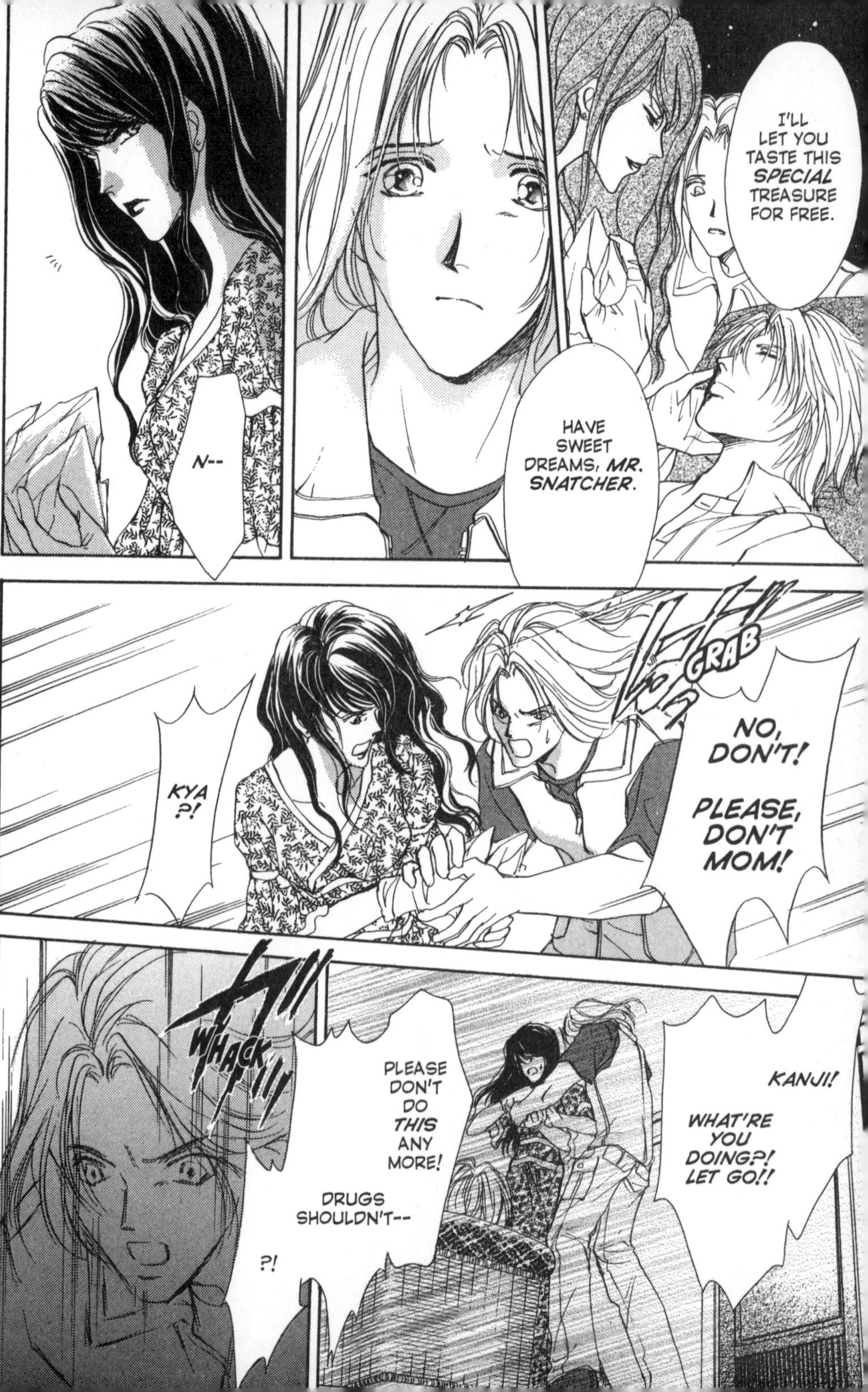
I'LL LET YOU TASTE THIS *SPECIAL* TREASURE FOR FREE.
HAVE SWEET DREAMS, ***MR. SNATCHER***.
N--
GRAB
NO, DON'T!
PLEASE, DON'T MOM!
KYA ?!
KANJI!
WHAT'RE YOU DOING?! LET GO!!
PLEASE DON'T DO ***THIS*** ANY MORE!
DRUGS SHOULDN'T--
WHACK
?!

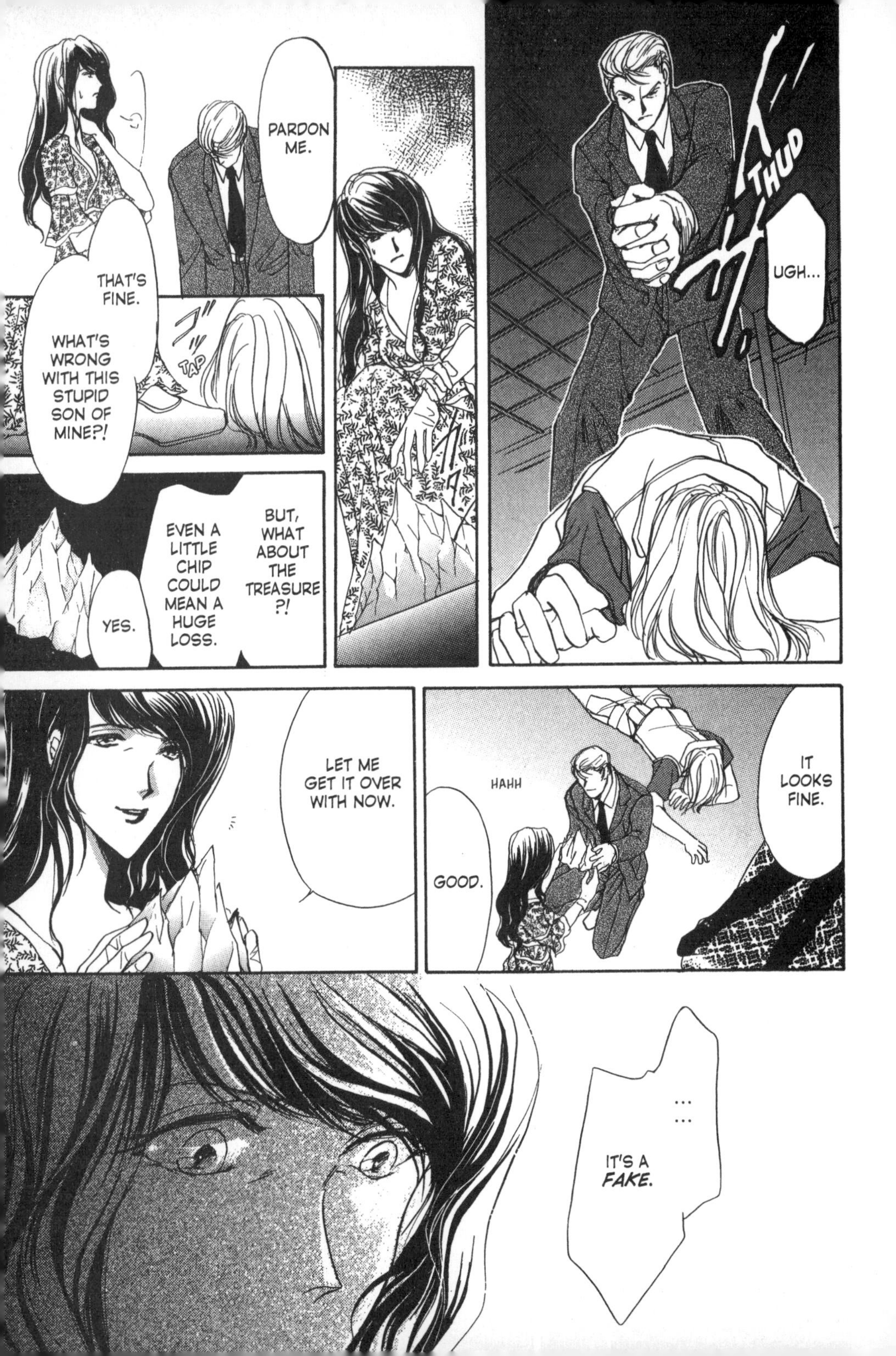
THUD
UGH...
PARDON ME.
THAT'S FINE.
WHAT'S WRONG WITH THIS STUPID SON OF MINE?!
TAP
BUT, WHAT ABOUT THE TREASURE?!
EVEN A LITTLE CHIP COULD MEAN A HUGE LOSS.
YES.
IT LOOKS FINE.
HAHH
GOOD.
LET ME GET IT OVER WITH NOW.
......
IT'S A FAKE.

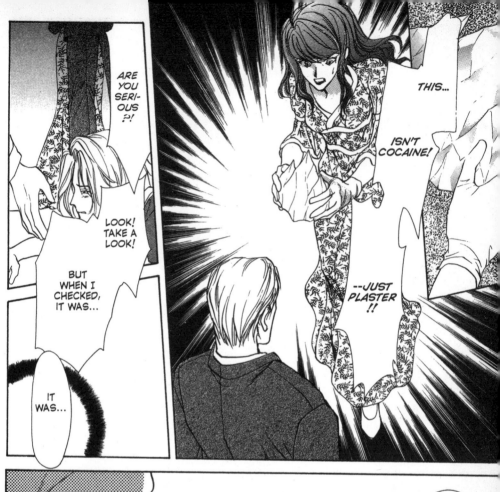

ARE YOU SERIOUS?!

LOOK! TAKE A LOOK!

BUT WHEN I CHECKED, IT WAS...

IT WAS...

THIS...

ISN'T COCAINE!

--JUST PLASTER!!

...REAL UNTIL A MOMENT AGO.

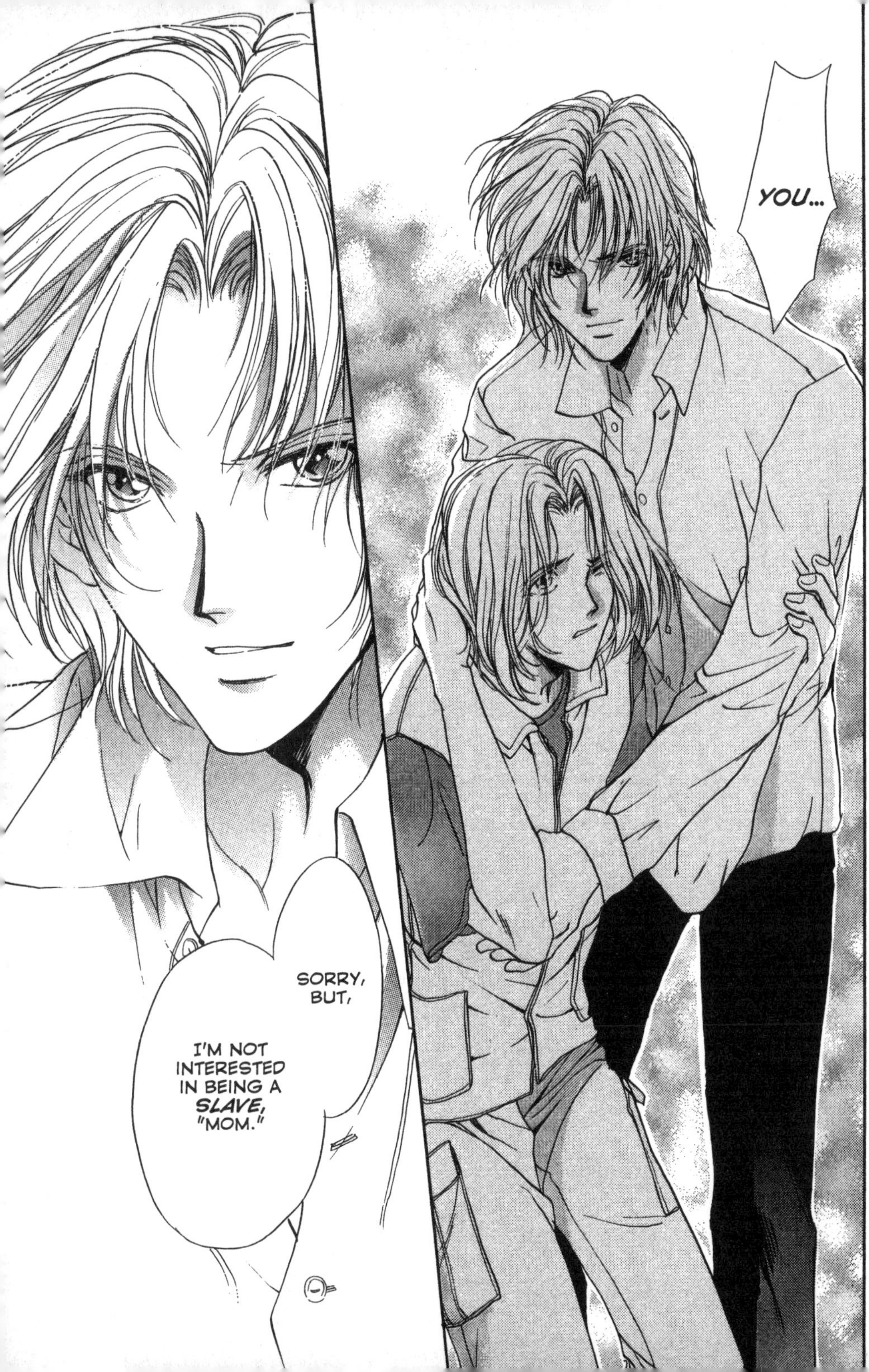
YOU...
SORRY, BUT,
I'M NOT INTERESTED IN BEING A *SLAVE,* "MOM."

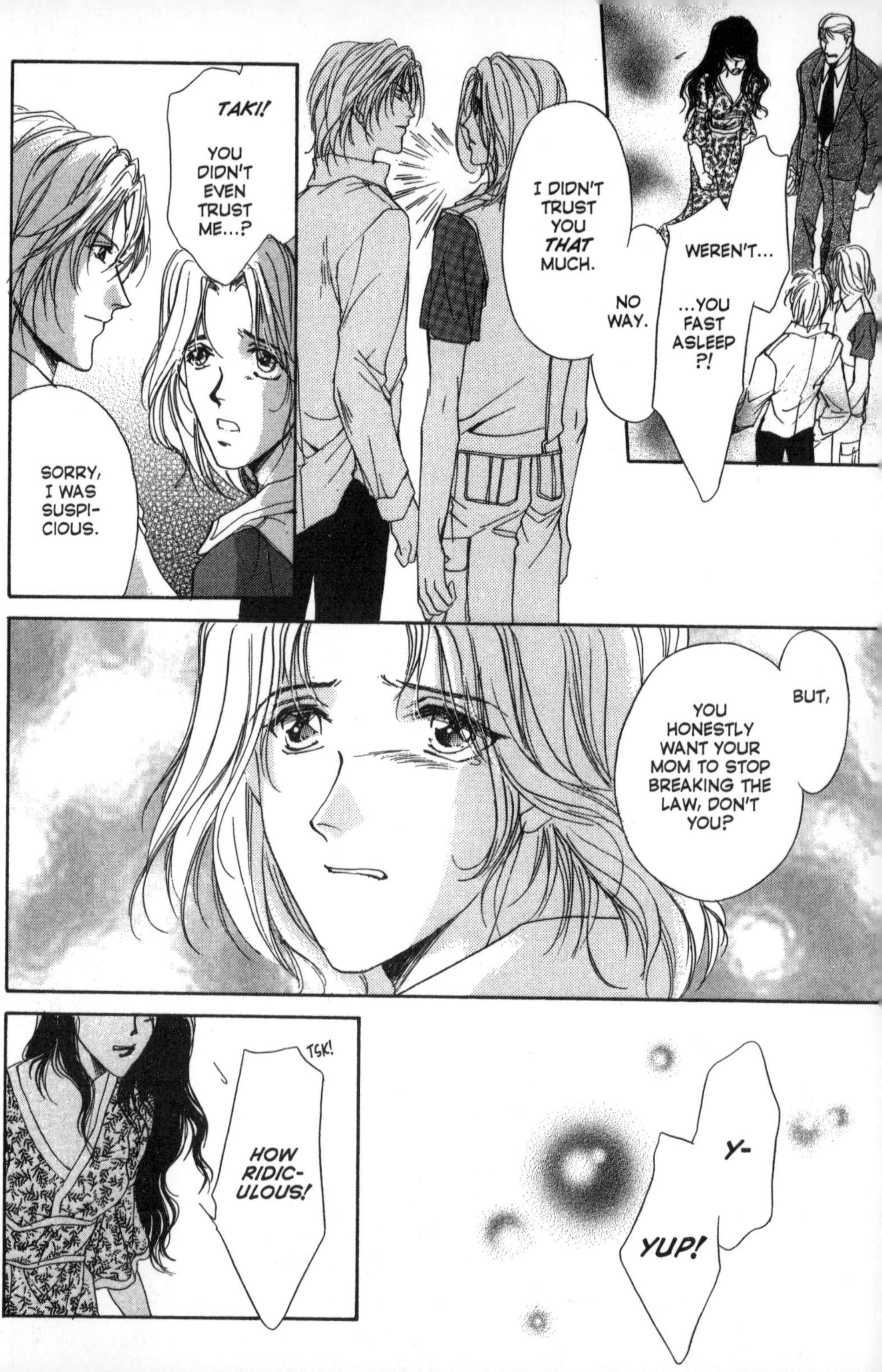
WEREN'T...
...YOU FAST ASLEEP?!
NO WAY.
I DIDN'T TRUST YOU *THAT* MUCH.
TAKI!
YOU DIDN'T EVEN TRUST ME...?
SORRY, I WAS SUSPICIOUS.
BUT,
YOU HONESTLY WANT YOUR MOM TO STOP BREAKING THE LAW, DON'T YOU?
Y-
YUP!
TSK!
HOW RIDICULOUS!

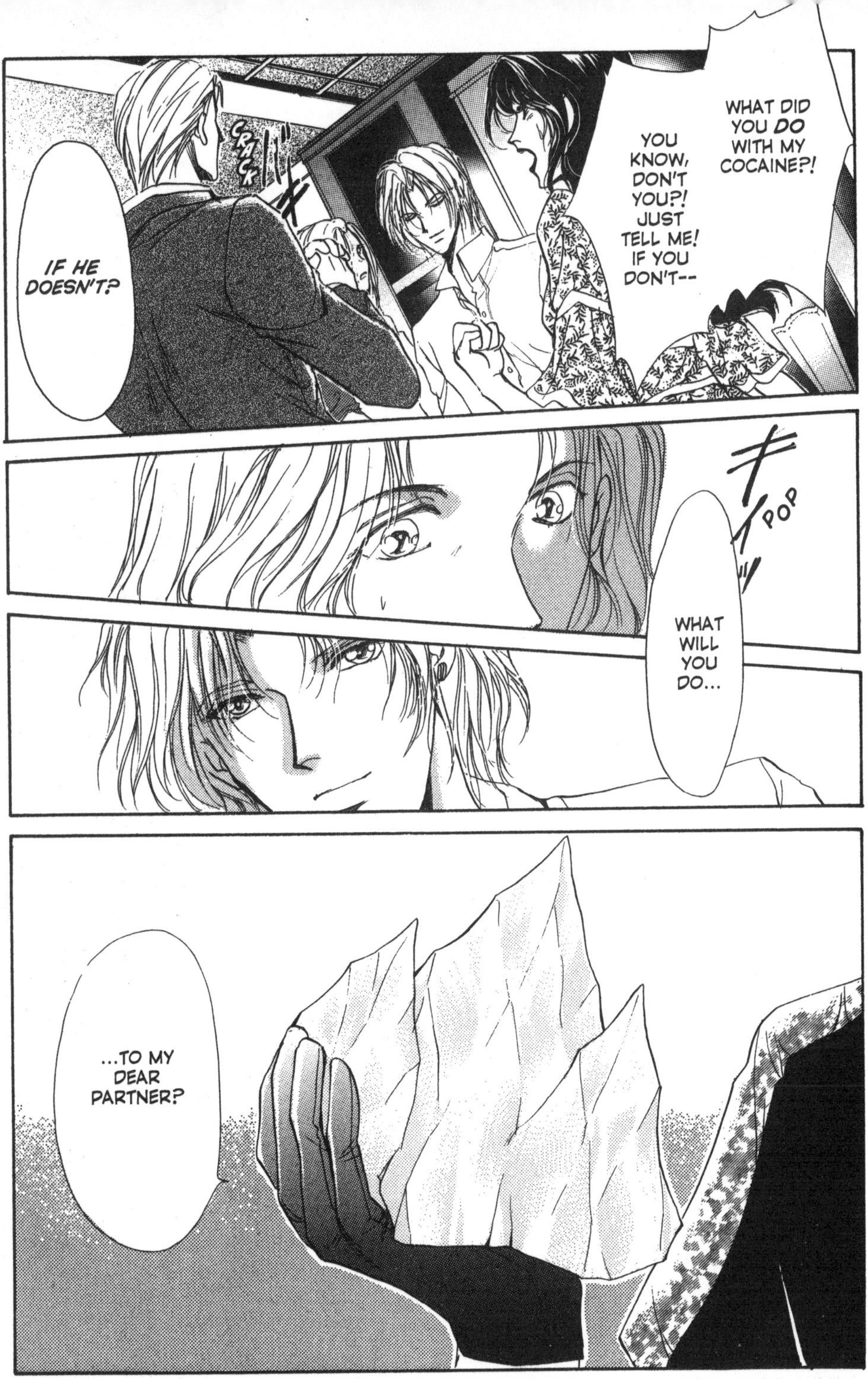
WHAT DID YOU *DO* WITH MY COCAINE?!
YOU KNOW, DON'T YOU?! JUST TELL ME! IF YOU DON'T--
CRACK
IF HE DOESN'T?
POP
WHAT WILL YOU DO...
...TO MY DEAR PARTNER?

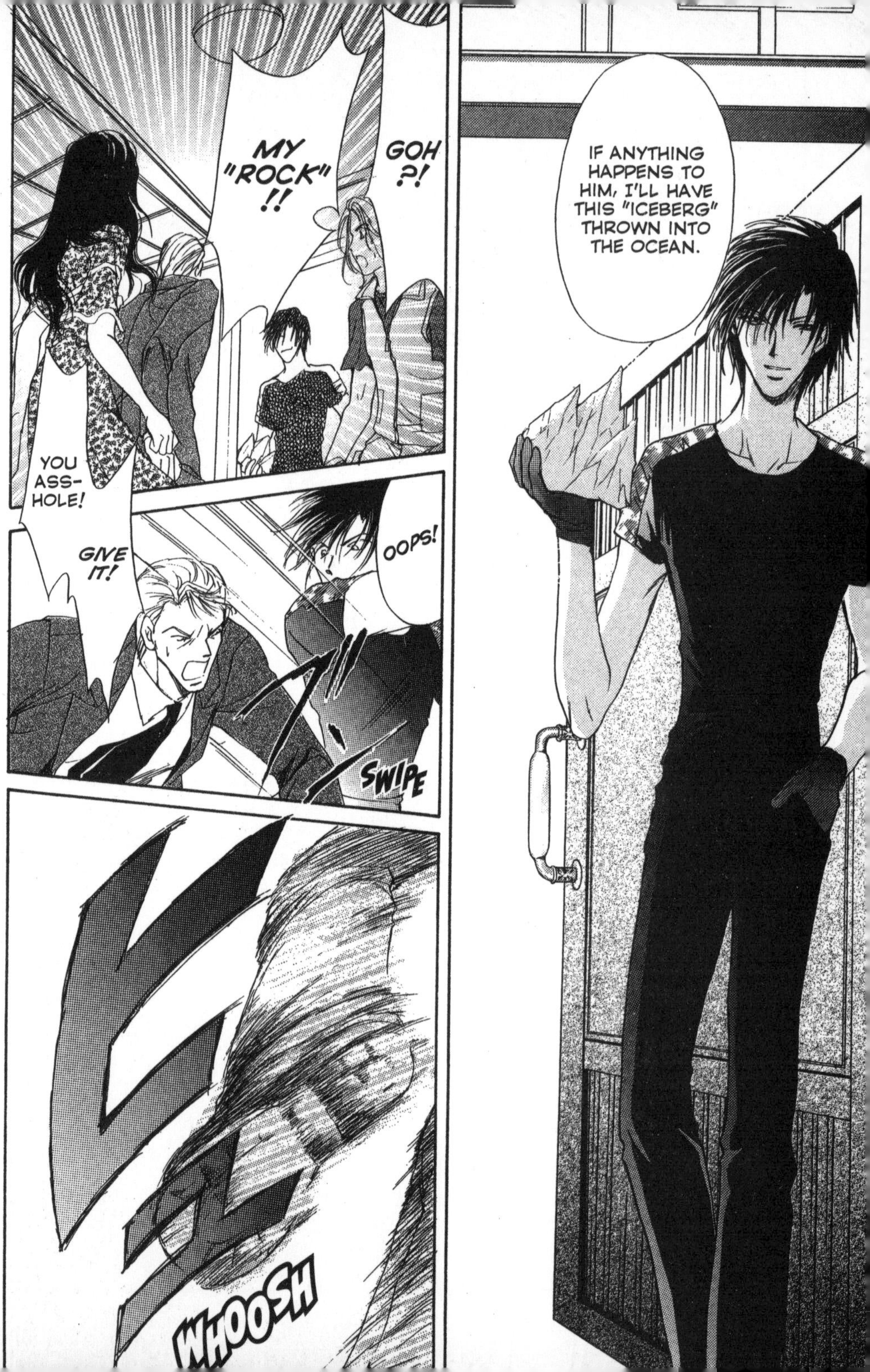
IF ANYTHING HAPPENS TO HIM, I'LL HAVE THIS "ICEBERG" THROWN INTO THE OCEAN.
GOH ?!
MY "ROCK" !!
YOU ASS-HOLE!
OOPS!
GIVE IT!
SWIPE
WHOOSH

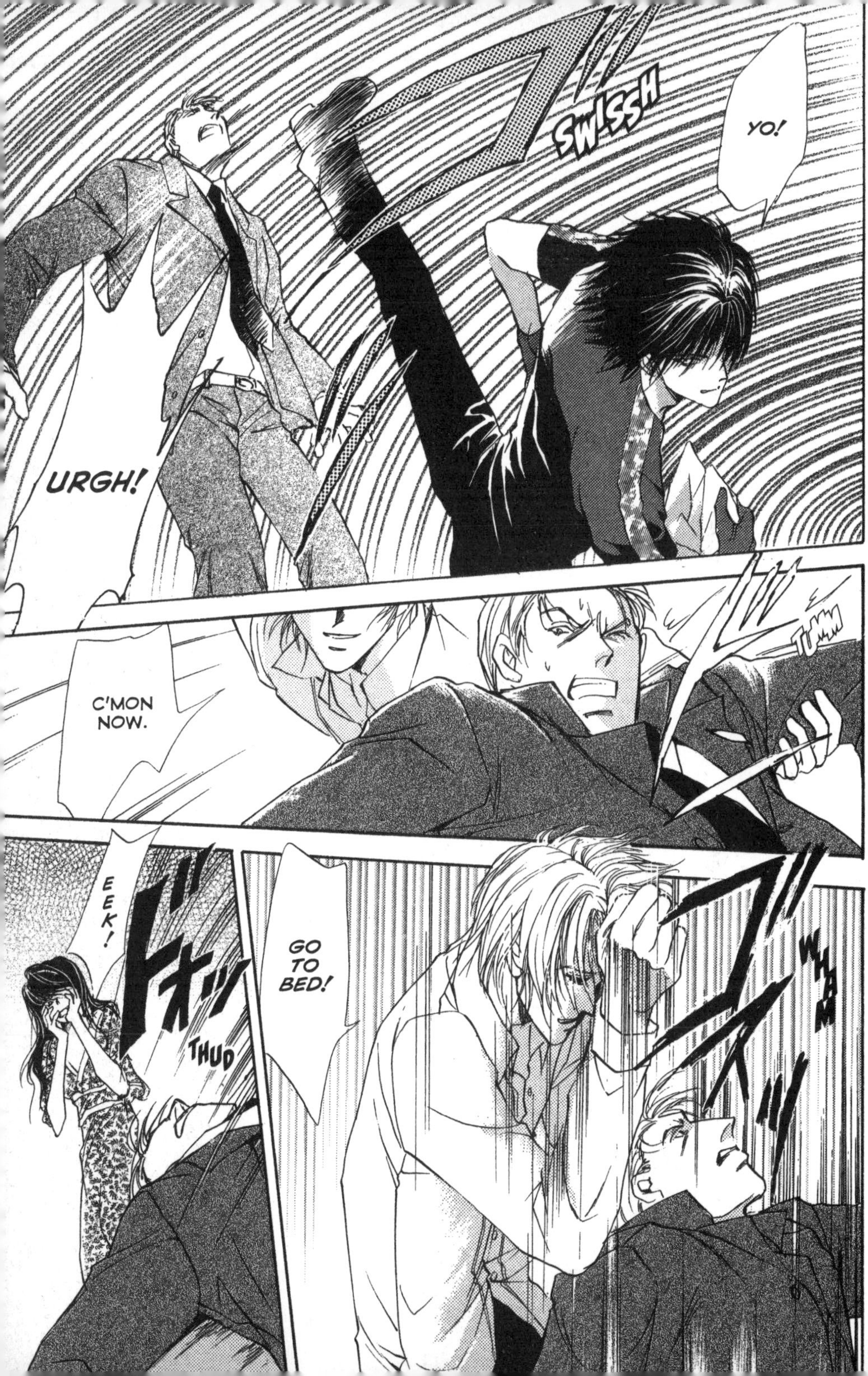
YO!
SWISSH
URGH!
TUMM
C'MON NOW.
GO TO BED!
WHAM
EEK!
THUD

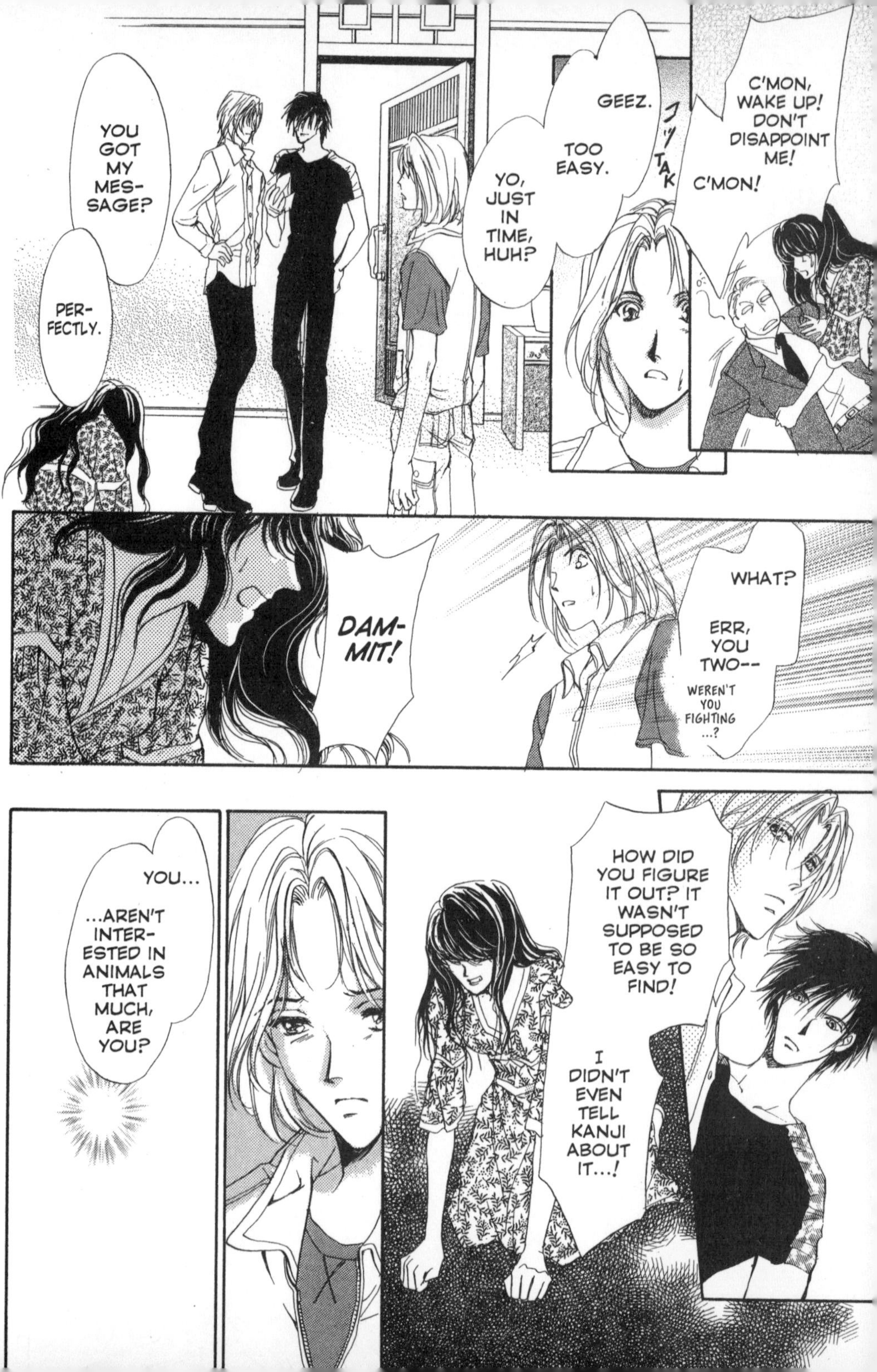

C'MON, WAKE UP! DON'T DISAPPOINT ME!
C'MON!
コツ
TAK
GEEZ.
TOO EASY.
YO, JUST IN TIME, HUH?
YOU GOT MY MES-SAGE?
PER-FECTLY.
WHAT?
ERR, YOU TWO--
WEREN'T YOU FIGHTING ...?
DAM-MIT!
HOW DID YOU FIGURE IT OUT? IT WASN'T SUPPOSED TO BE SO EASY TO FIND!
I DIDN'T EVEN TELL KANJI ABOUT IT...!
YOU...
...AREN'T INTER-ESTED IN ANIMALS THAT MUCH, ARE YOU?

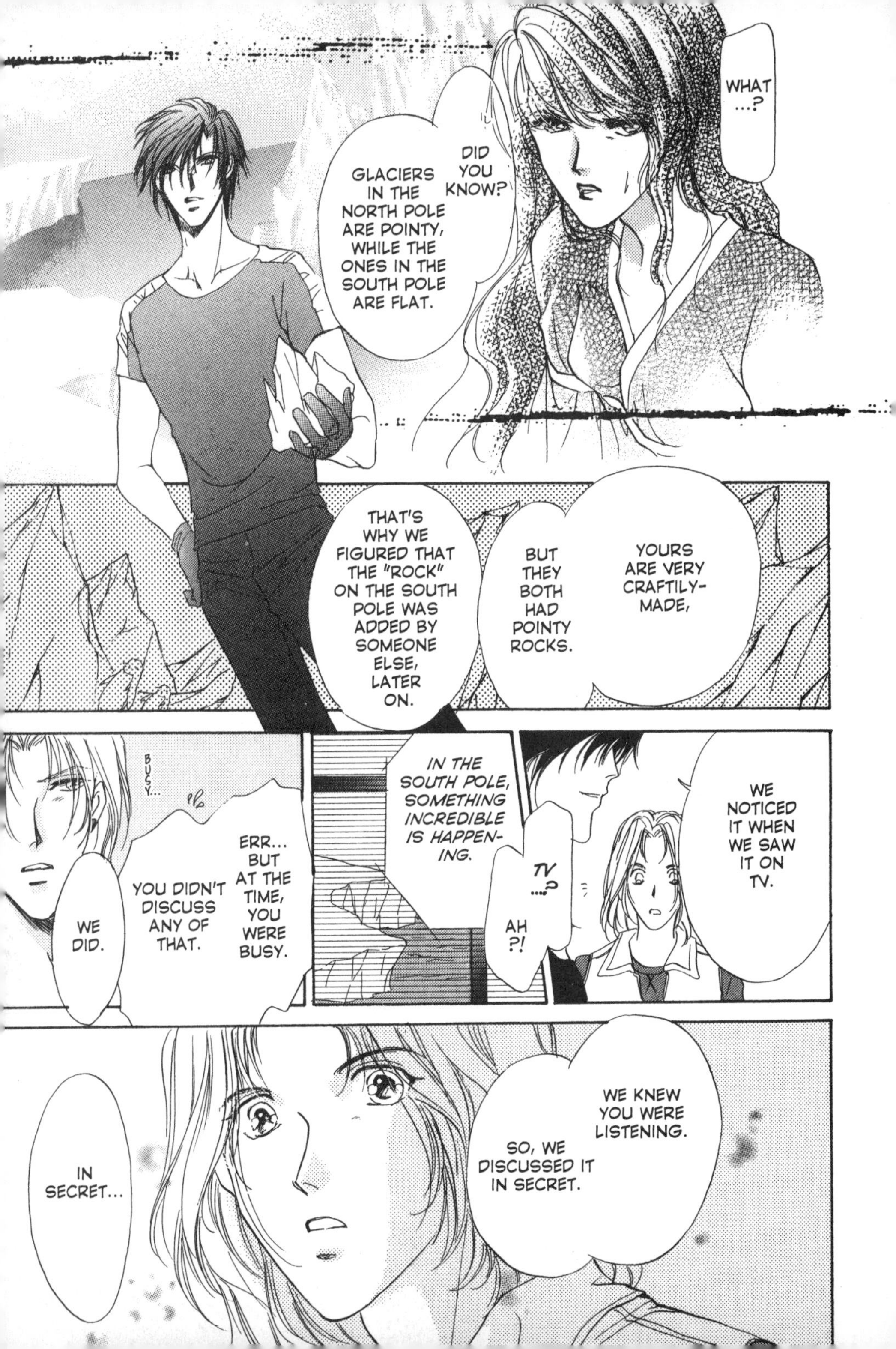
WHAT...?
DID YOU KNOW?
GLACIERS IN THE NORTH POLE ARE POINTY, WHILE THE ONES IN THE SOUTH POLE ARE FLAT.
YOURS ARE VERY CRAFTILY-MADE,
BUT THEY BOTH HAD POINTY ROCKS.
THAT'S WHY WE FIGURED THAT THE "ROCK" ON THE SOUTH POLE WAS ADDED BY SOMEONE ELSE, LATER ON.
WE NOTICED IT WHEN WE SAW IT ON TV.
TV...?
AH?!
IN THE SOUTH POLE, SOMETHING INCREDIBLE IS HAPPEN-ING.
ERR... BUT AT THE TIME, YOU WERE BUSY.
BUSY...
YOU DIDN'T DISCUSS ANY OF THAT.
WE DID.
WE KNEW YOU WERE LISTENING.
SO, WE DISCUSSED IT IN SECRET.
IN SECRET...

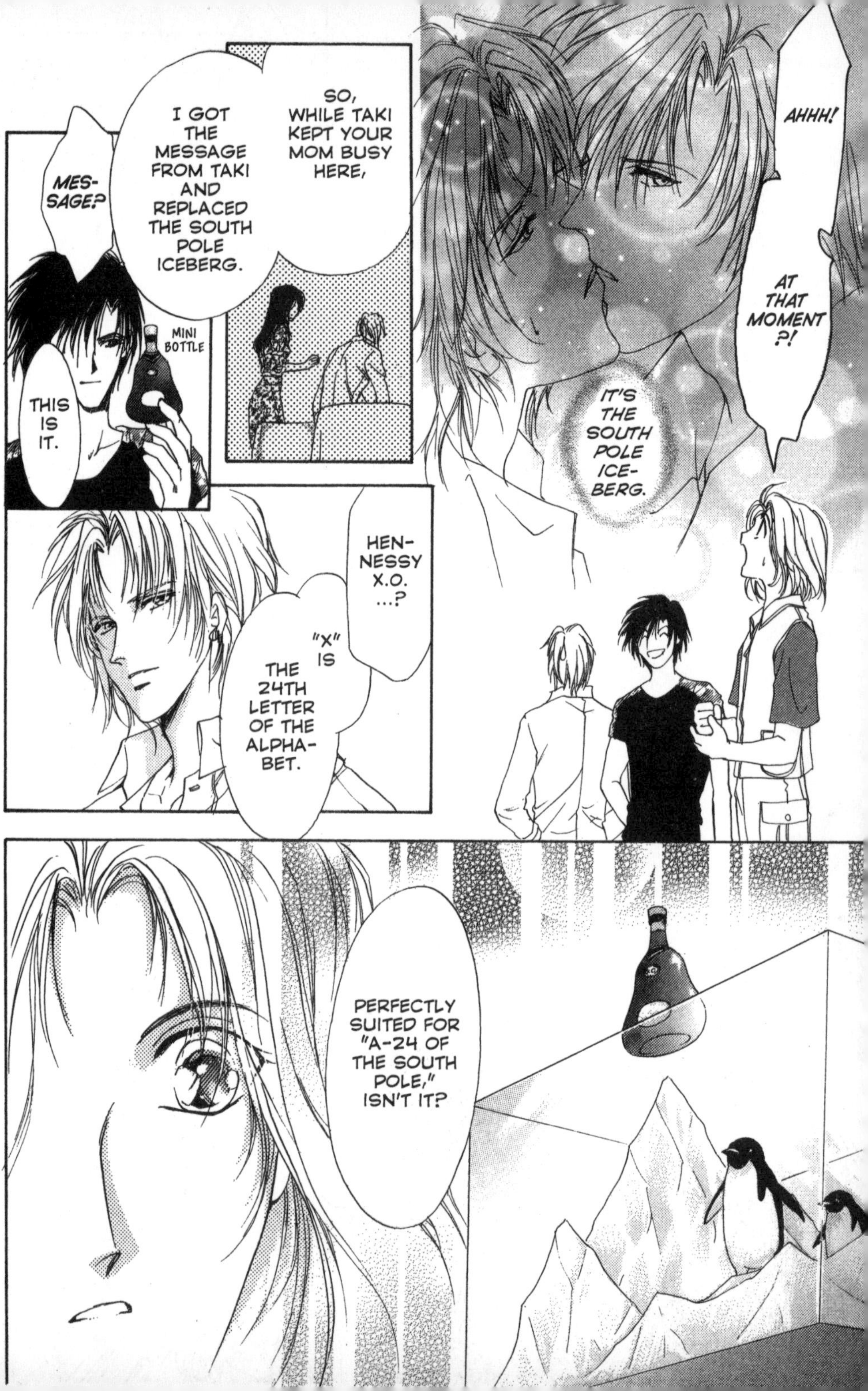
AHHH!
AT THAT MOMENT ?!
IT'S THE SOUTH POLE ICE-BERG.
SO, WHILE TAKI KEPT YOUR MOM BUSY HERE,
I GOT THE MESSAGE FROM TAKI AND REPLACED THE SOUTH POLE ICEBERG.
MES-SAGE?
MINI BOTTLE
THIS IS IT.
HEN-NESSY X.O. ...?
"X" IS THE 24TH LETTER OF THE ALPHA-BET.
PERFECTLY SUITED FOR "A-24 OF THE SOUTH POLE," ISN'T IT?

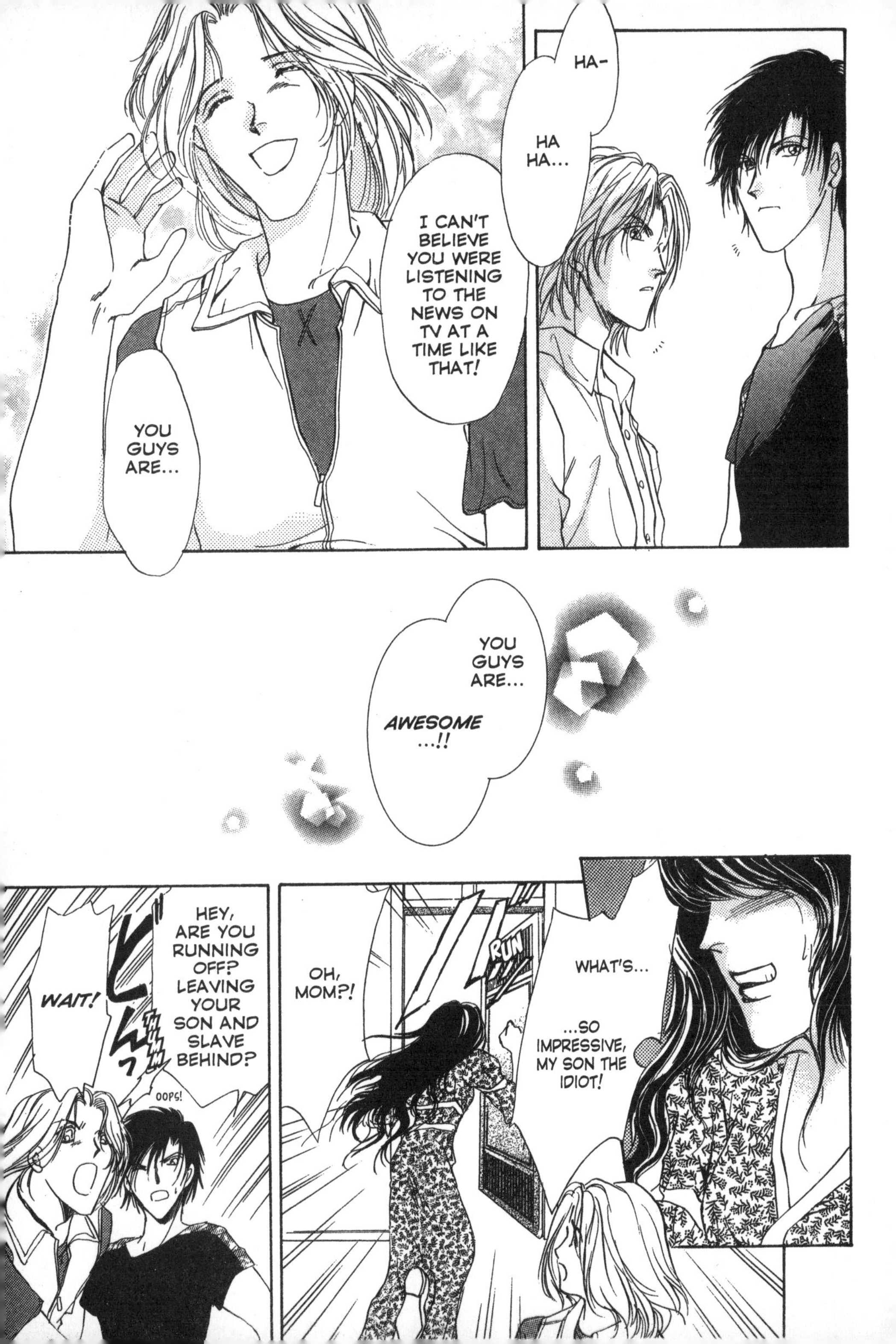
HA- HA HA...
I CAN'T BELIEVE YOU WERE LISTENING TO THE NEWS ON TV AT A TIME LIKE THAT!
YOU GUYS ARE...
YOU GUYS ARE...
AWESOME ...!!
WHAT'S...
...SO IMPRESSIVE, MY SON THE IDIOT!
RUN
OH, MOM?!
HEY, ARE YOU RUNNING OFF? LEAVING YOUR SON AND SLAVE BEHIND?
WAIT!
OOPS!

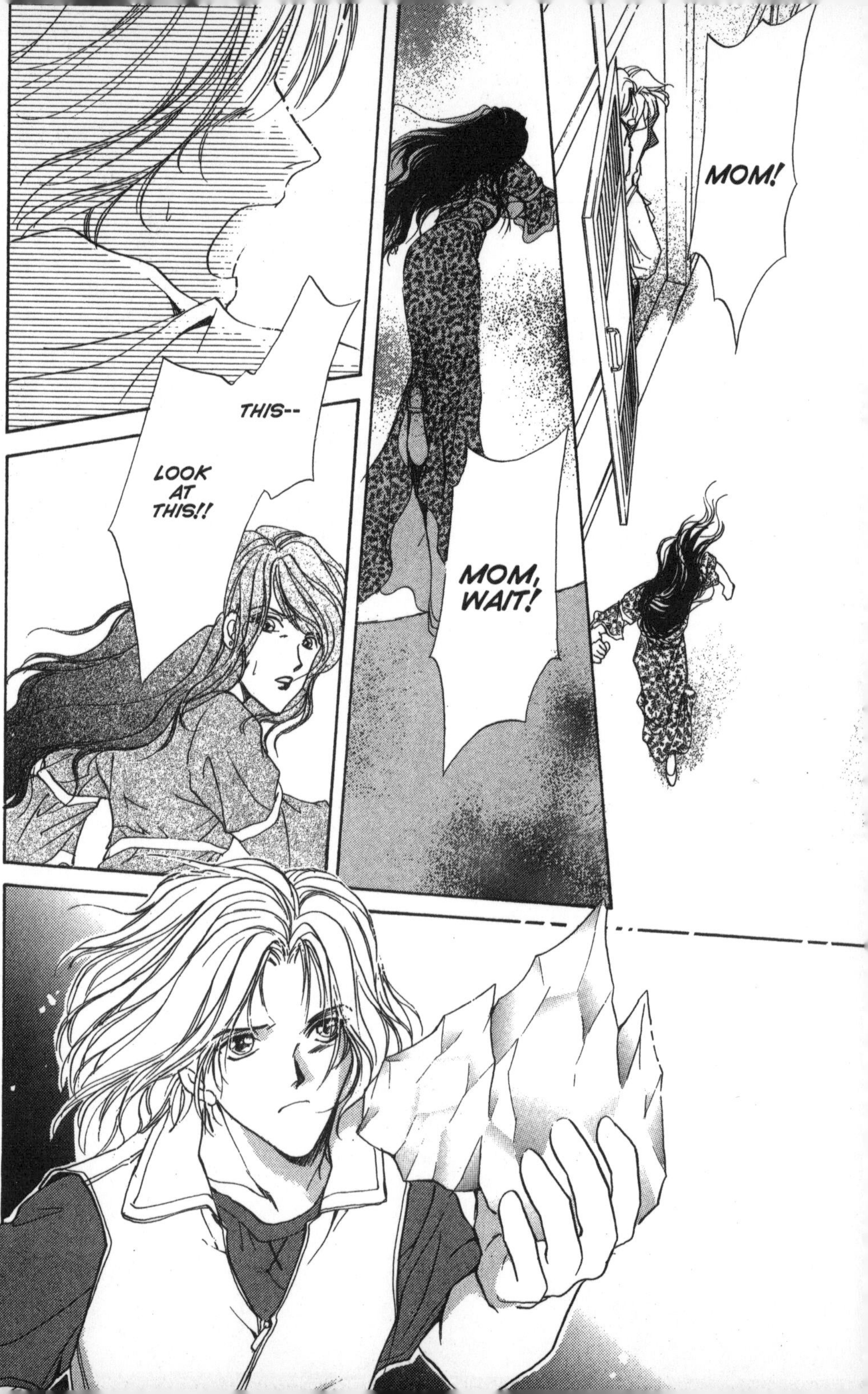
MOM!
MOM, WAIT!
THIS--
LOOK AT THIS!!

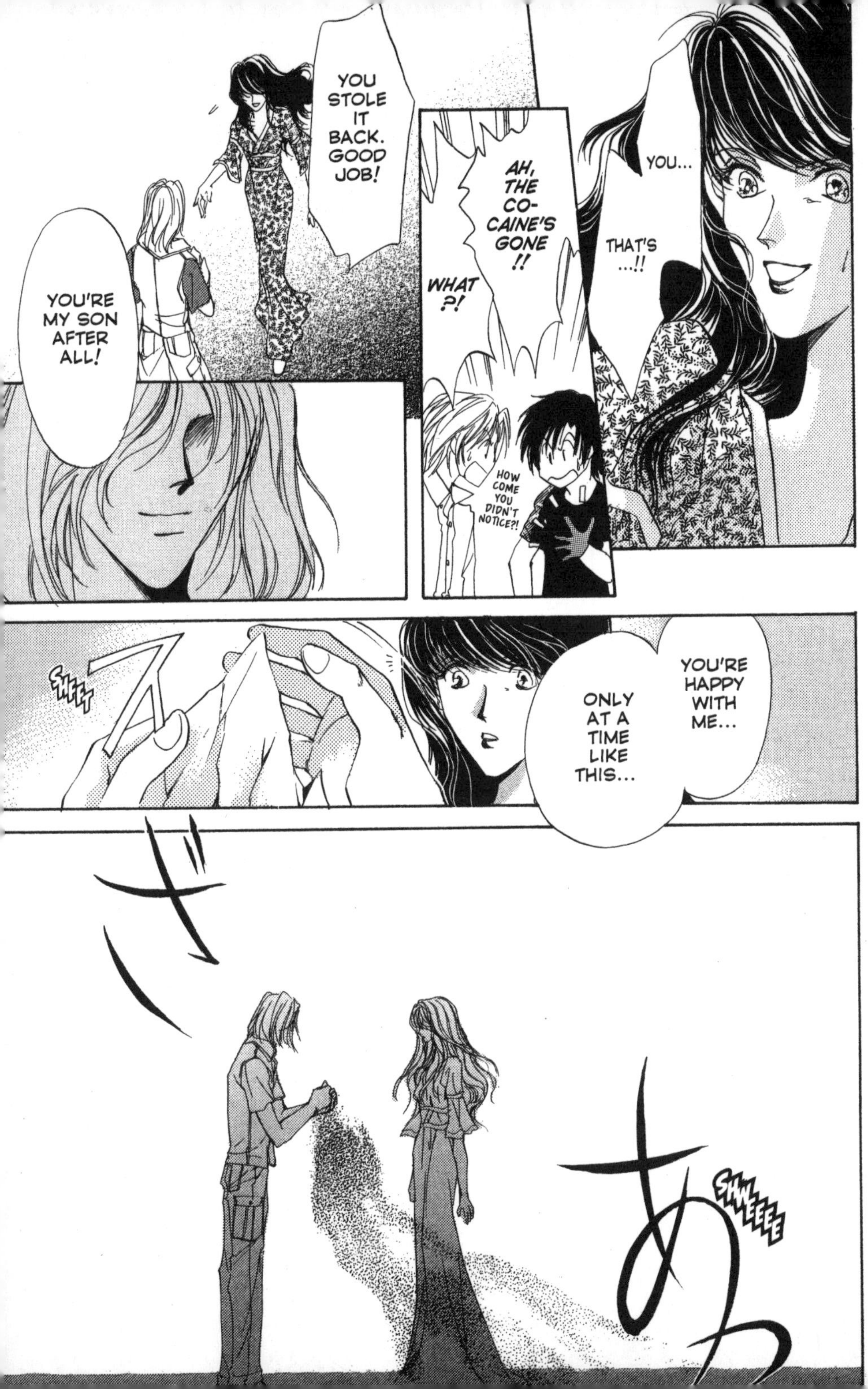
YOU...
THAT'S ...!!
AH, THE CO-CAINE'S GONE!!
WHAT?!
HOW COME YOU DIDN'T NOTICE?!
YOU STOLE IT BACK. GOOD JOB!
YOU'RE MY SON AFTER ALL!
YOU'RE HAPPY WITH ME...
ONLY AT A TIME LIKE THIS...
SHFFT
あ
SHWEEEE
ザ

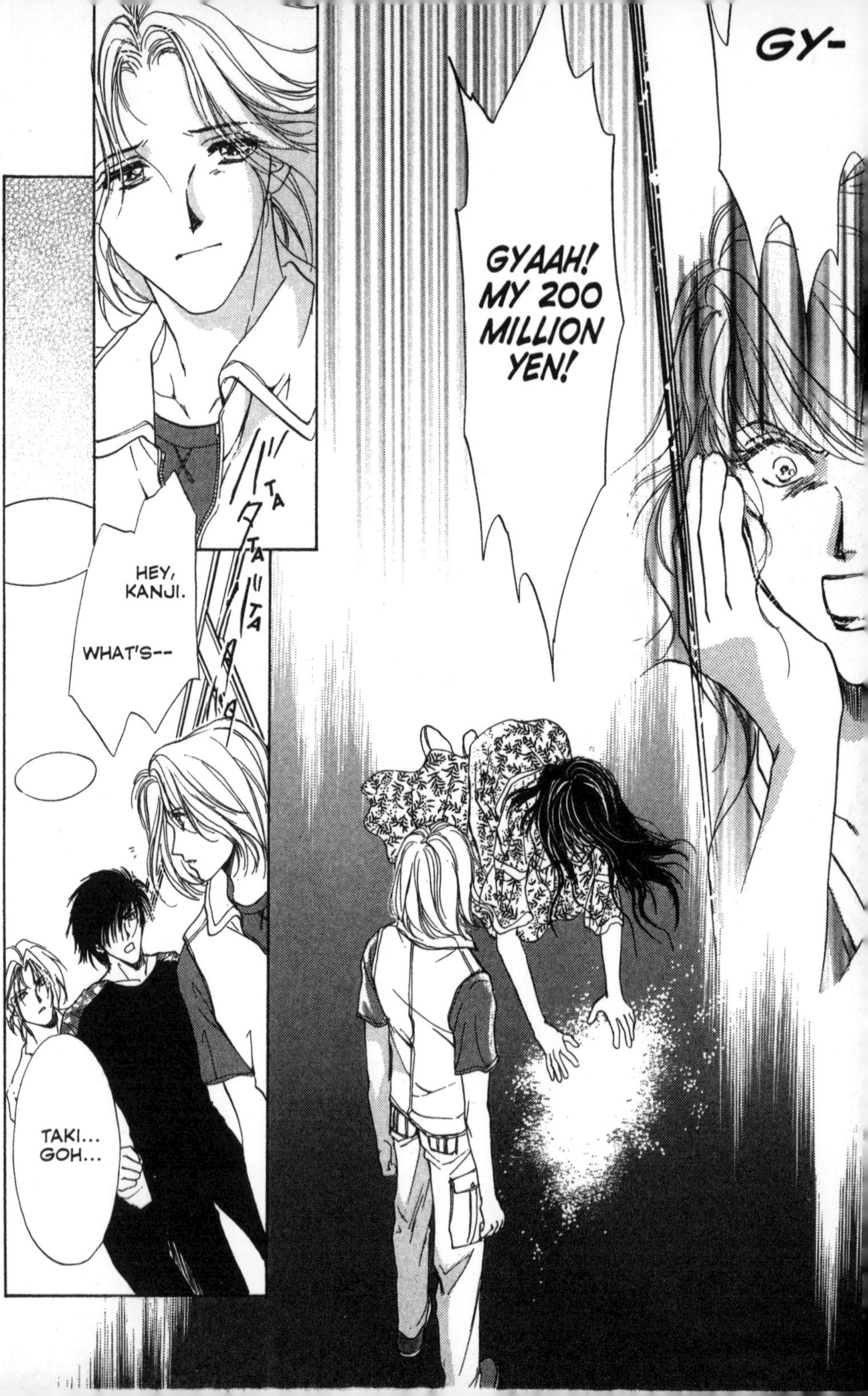
GY-
GYAAH! MY 200 MILLION YEN!
TA TA TA TA
HEY, KANJI.
WHAT'S--
TAKI... GOH...

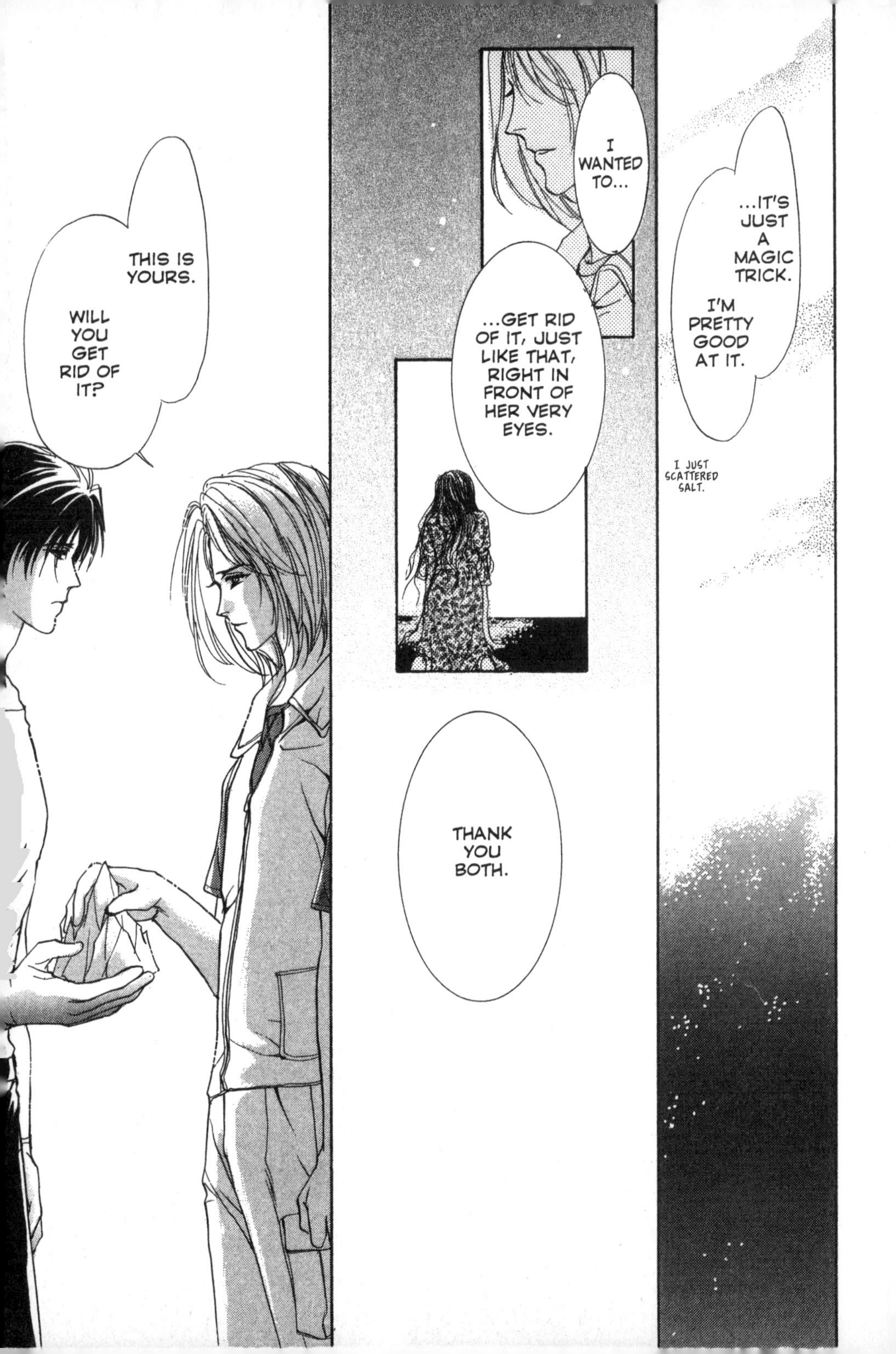

...IT'S JUST A MAGIC TRICK.
I'M PRETTY GOOD AT IT.
I JUST SCATTERED SALT.
I WANTED TO...
...GET RID OF IT, JUST LIKE THAT, RIGHT IN FRONT OF HER VERY EYES.
THANK YOU BOTH.
THIS IS YOURS.
WILL YOU GET RID OF IT?

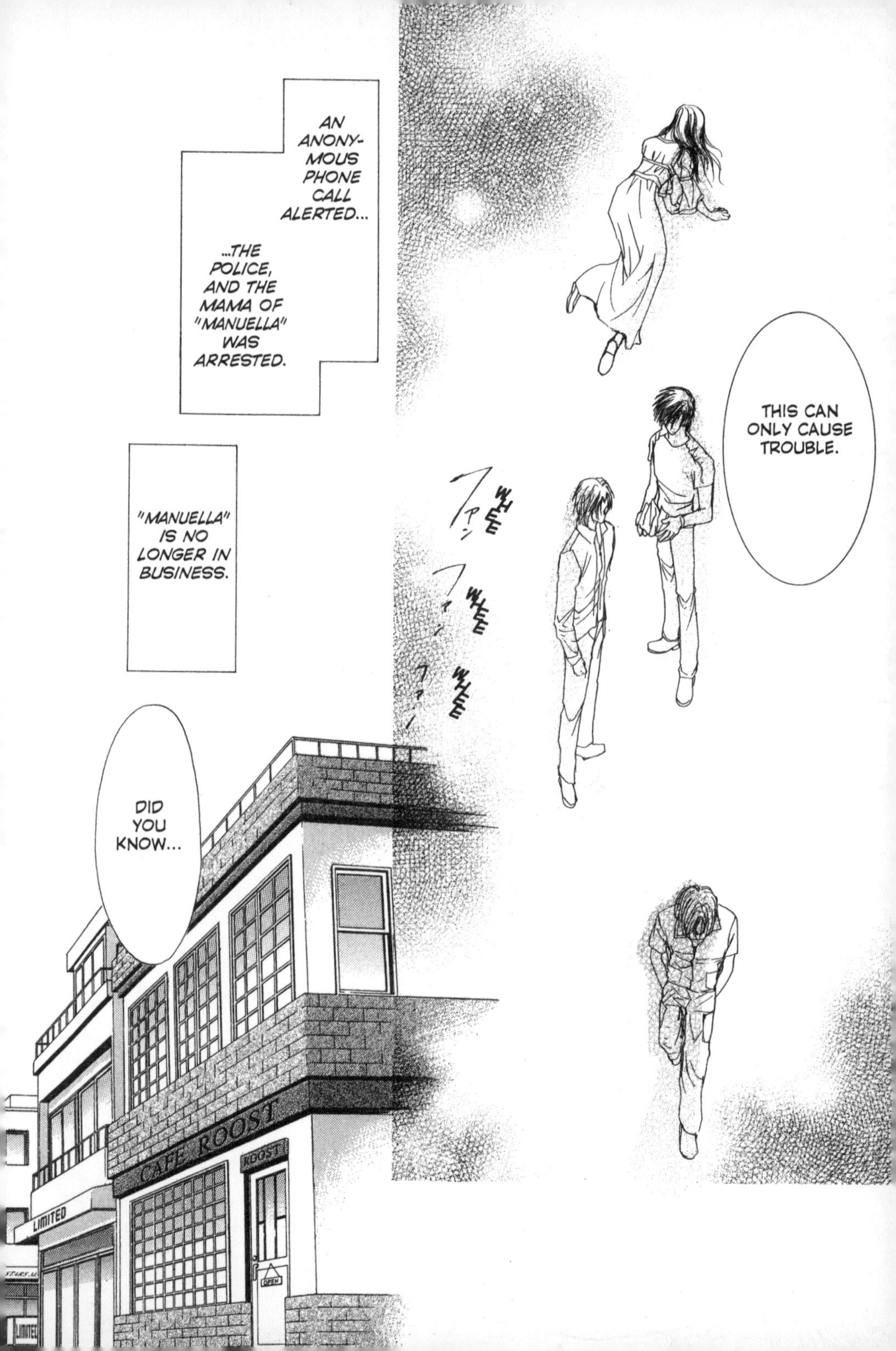
THIS CAN ONLY CAUSE TROUBLE.
WHEE
WHEE
WHEE
AN ANONYMOUS PHONE CALL ALERTED...
...THE POLICE, AND THE MAMA OF "MANUELLA" WAS ARRESTED.
"MANUELLA" IS NO LONGER IN BUSINESS.
DID YOU KNOW...
CAFE ROOST
ROOST
LIMITED
OPEN

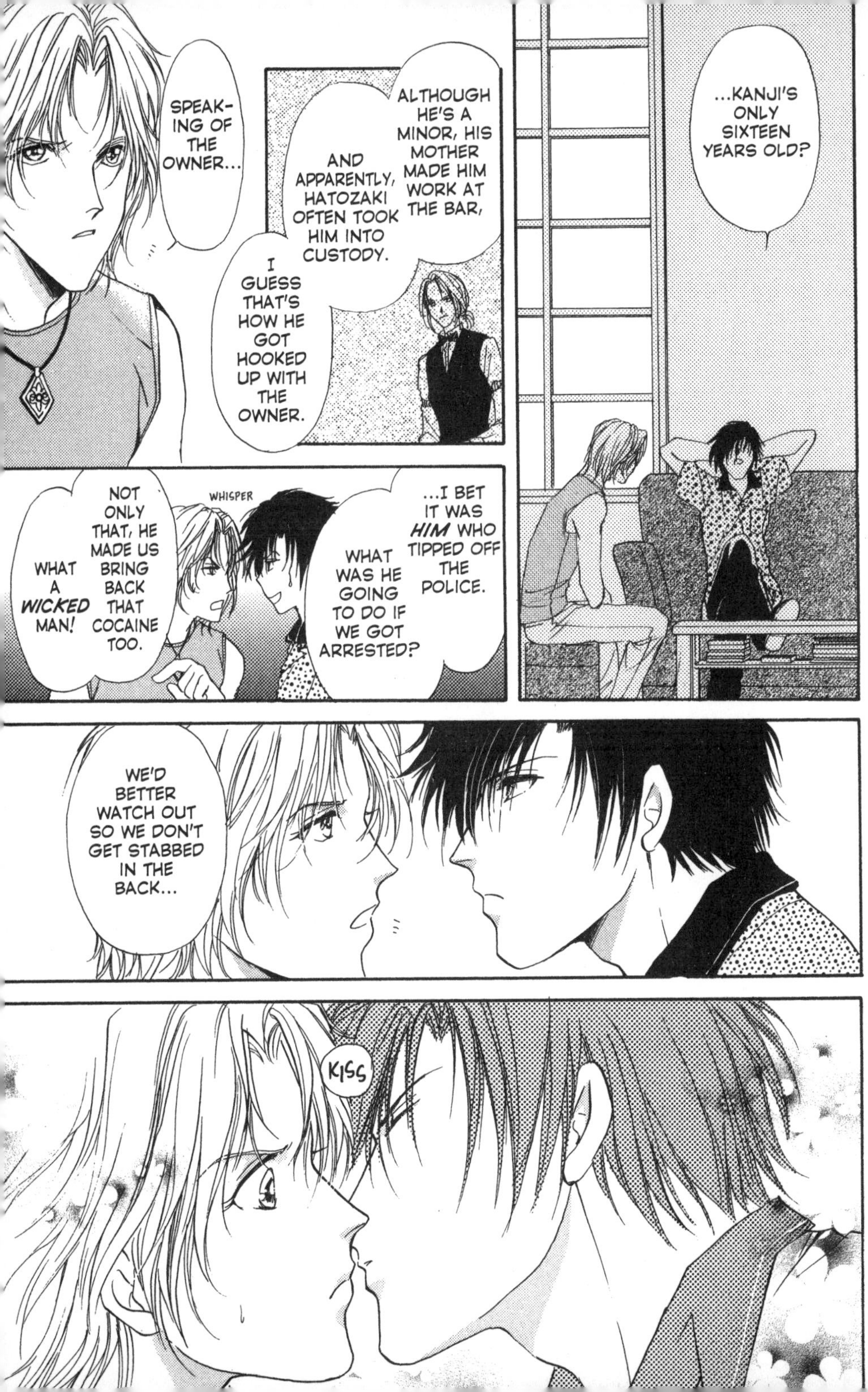
...KANJI'S ONLY SIXTEEN YEARS OLD?
ALTHOUGH HE'S A MINOR, HIS MOTHER MADE HIM WORK AT THE BAR,
AND APPARENTLY, HATOZAKI OFTEN TOOK HIM INTO CUSTODY.
I GUESS THAT'S HOW HE GOT HOOKED UP WITH THE OWNER.
SPEAK-ING OF THE OWNER...
...I BET IT WAS *HIM* WHO TIPPED OFF THE POLICE.
WHAT WAS HE GOING TO DO IF WE GOT ARRESTED?
WHISPER
NOT ONLY THAT, HE MADE US BRING BACK THAT COCAINE TOO.
WHAT A *WICKED* MAN!
WE'D BETTER WATCH OUT SO WE DON'T GET STABBED IN THE BACK...
KISS

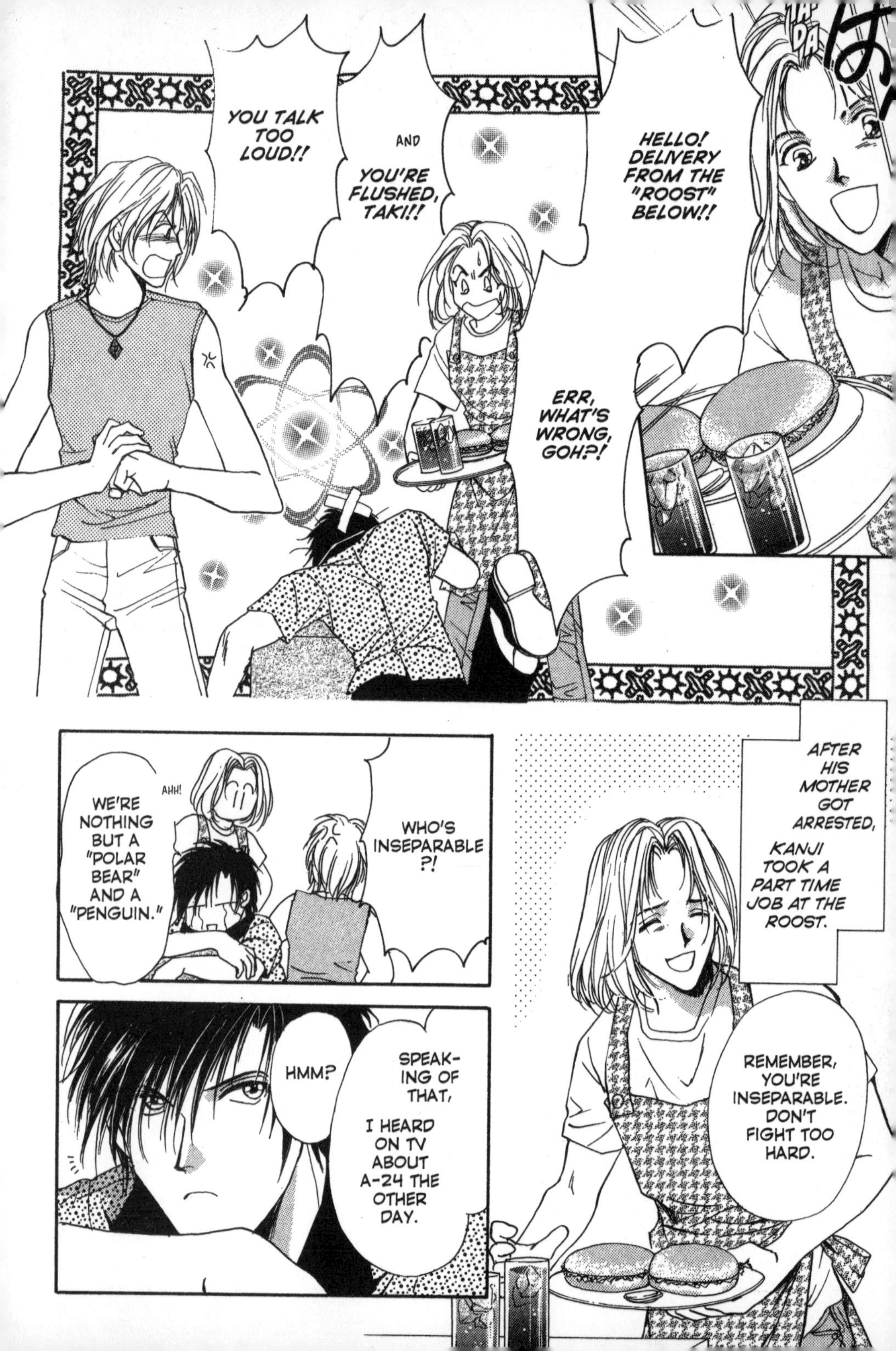
HA DA
HELLO! DELIVERY FROM THE "ROOST" BELOW!!
ERR, WHAT'S WRONG, GOH?!
YOU TALK TOO LOUD!!
AND
YOU'RE FLUSHED, TAKI!!
AFTER HIS MOTHER GOT ARRESTED,
KANJI TOOK A PART TIME JOB AT THE ROOST.
REMEMBER, YOU'RE INSEPARABLE. DON'T FIGHT TOO HARD.
WHO'S INSEPARABLE ?!
AHH!
WE'RE NOTHING BUT A "POLAR BEAR" AND A "PENGUIN."
SPEAK-ING OF THAT,
I HEARD ON TV ABOUT A-24 THE OTHER DAY.
HMM?

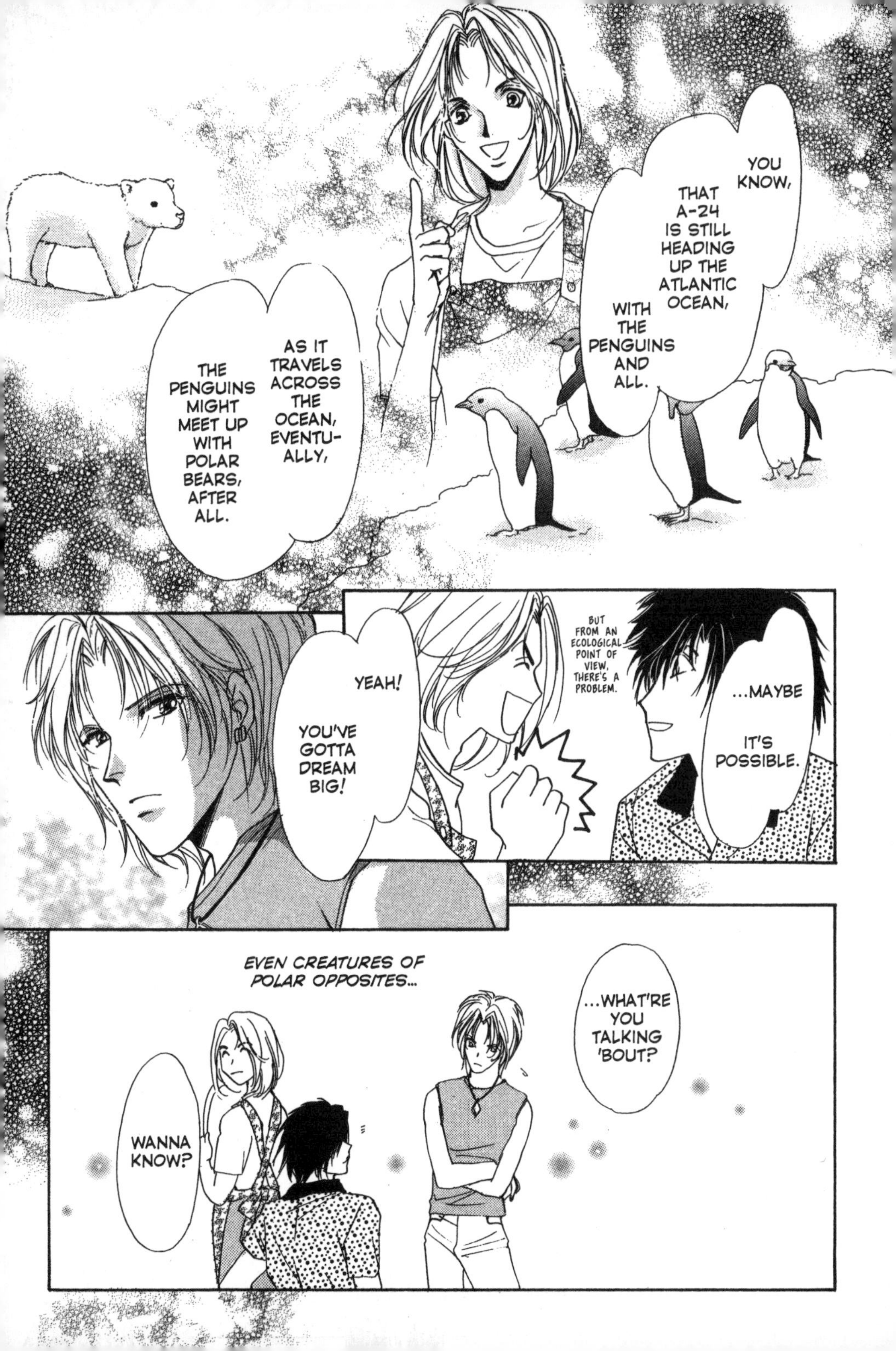
YOU KNOW,
THAT A-24 IS STILL HEADING UP THE ATLANTIC OCEAN,
WITH THE PENGUINS AND ALL.
AS IT TRAVELS ACROSS THE OCEAN, EVENTU-ALLY,
THE PENGUINS MIGHT MEET UP WITH POLAR BEARS, AFTER ALL.
...MAYBE
IT'S POSSIBLE.
BUT FROM AN ECOLOGICAL POINT OF VIEW, THERE'S A PROBLEM.
YEAH!
YOU'VE GOTTA DREAM BIG!
...WHAT'RE YOU TALKING 'BOUT?
EVEN CREATURES OF POLAR OPPOSITES...
WANNA KNOW?

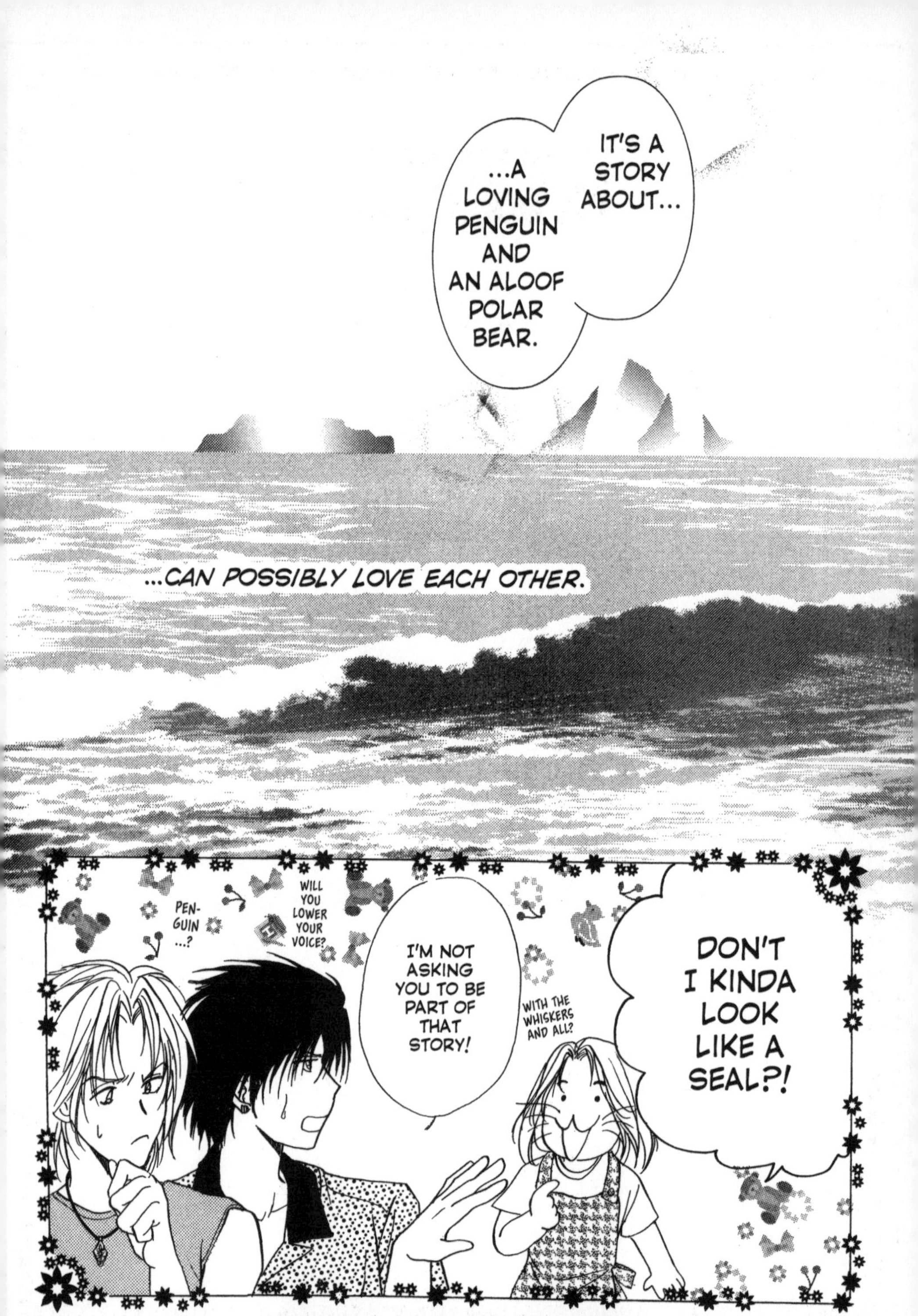
IT'S A STORY ABOUT...
...A LOVING PENGUIN AND AN ALOOF POLAR BEAR.
...CAN POSSIBLY LOVE EACH OTHER.
DON'T I KINDA LOOK LIKE A SEAL?!
WITH THE WHISKERS AND ALL?
I'M NOT ASKING YOU TO BE PART OF THAT STORY!
WILL YOU LOWER YOUR VOICE?
PEN-GUIN ...?

YELLOW ACT.4 / THE END

PROFILE

Suspect #2

name

TAKI

age

22

height and weight

182 CM / 70 KG

blood type

A

occupation

DRUG SNATCHER

special qualifications

AN EXCELLENT FIGHTER AND GOOD WITH MACHINES.

personality

DISPASSIONATE ON THE SURFACE, PASSIONATE INSIDE.

background

HIS IDENTITY IS A SECRET, EXCEPT THAT HE'S HETERO.

YELLOW

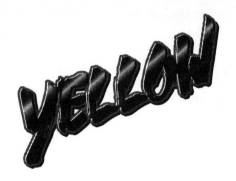

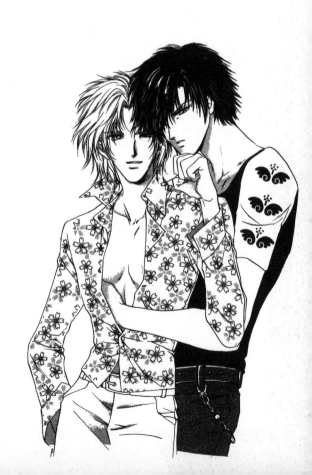

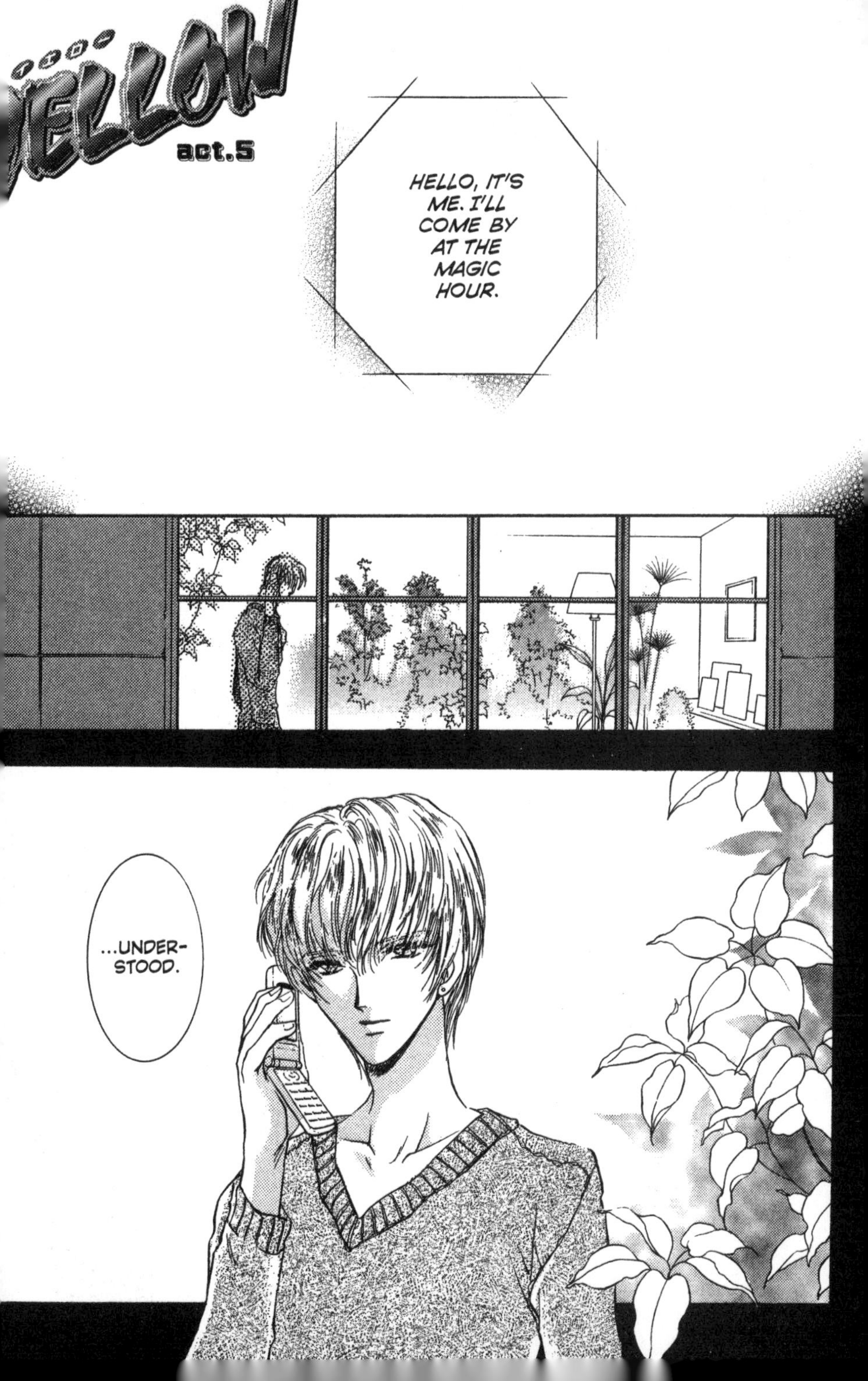
ELLOW
act.5
HELLO, IT'S ME. I'LL COME BY AT THE MAGIC HOUR.
...UNDER-STOOD.

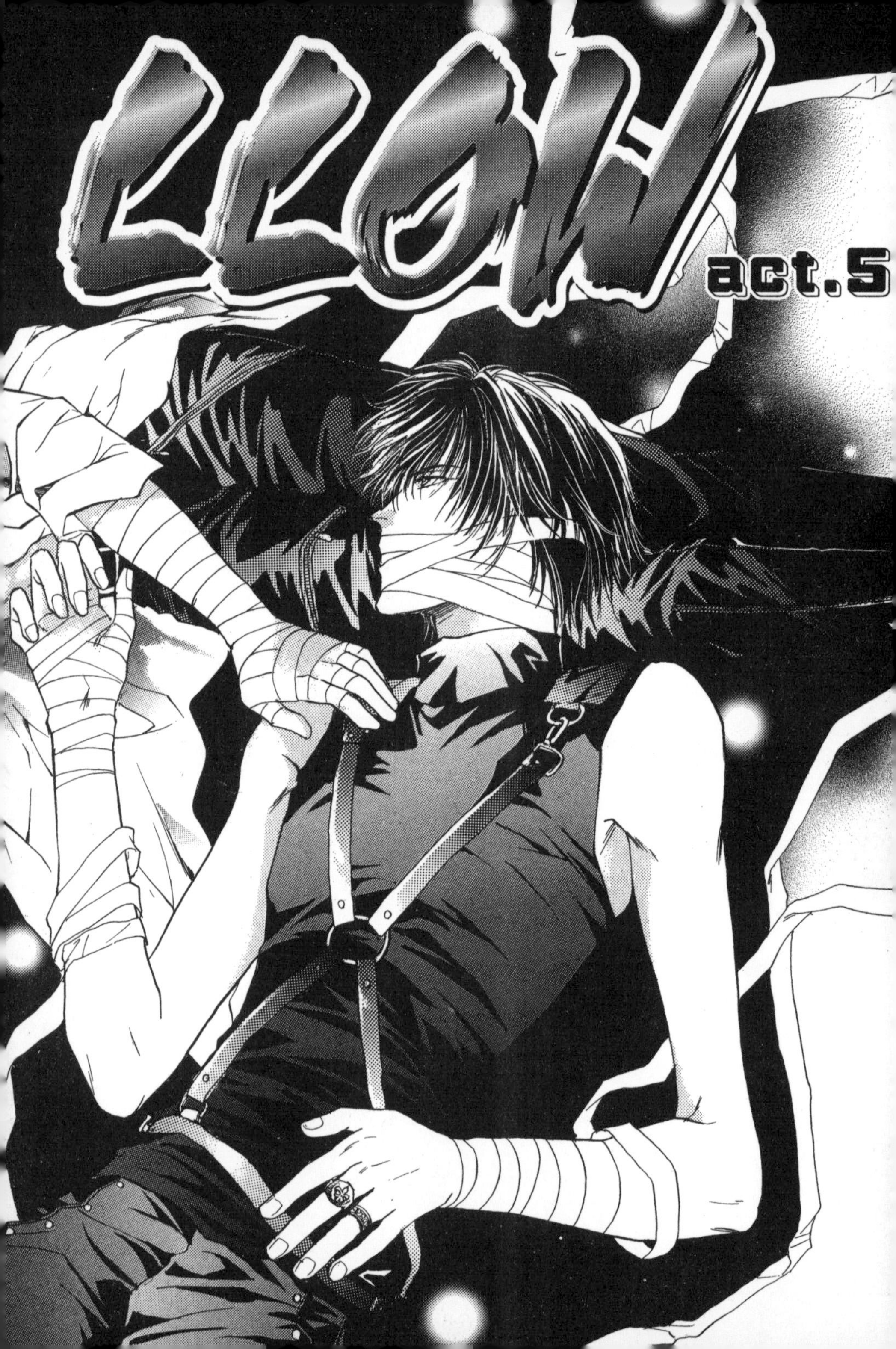
act.5

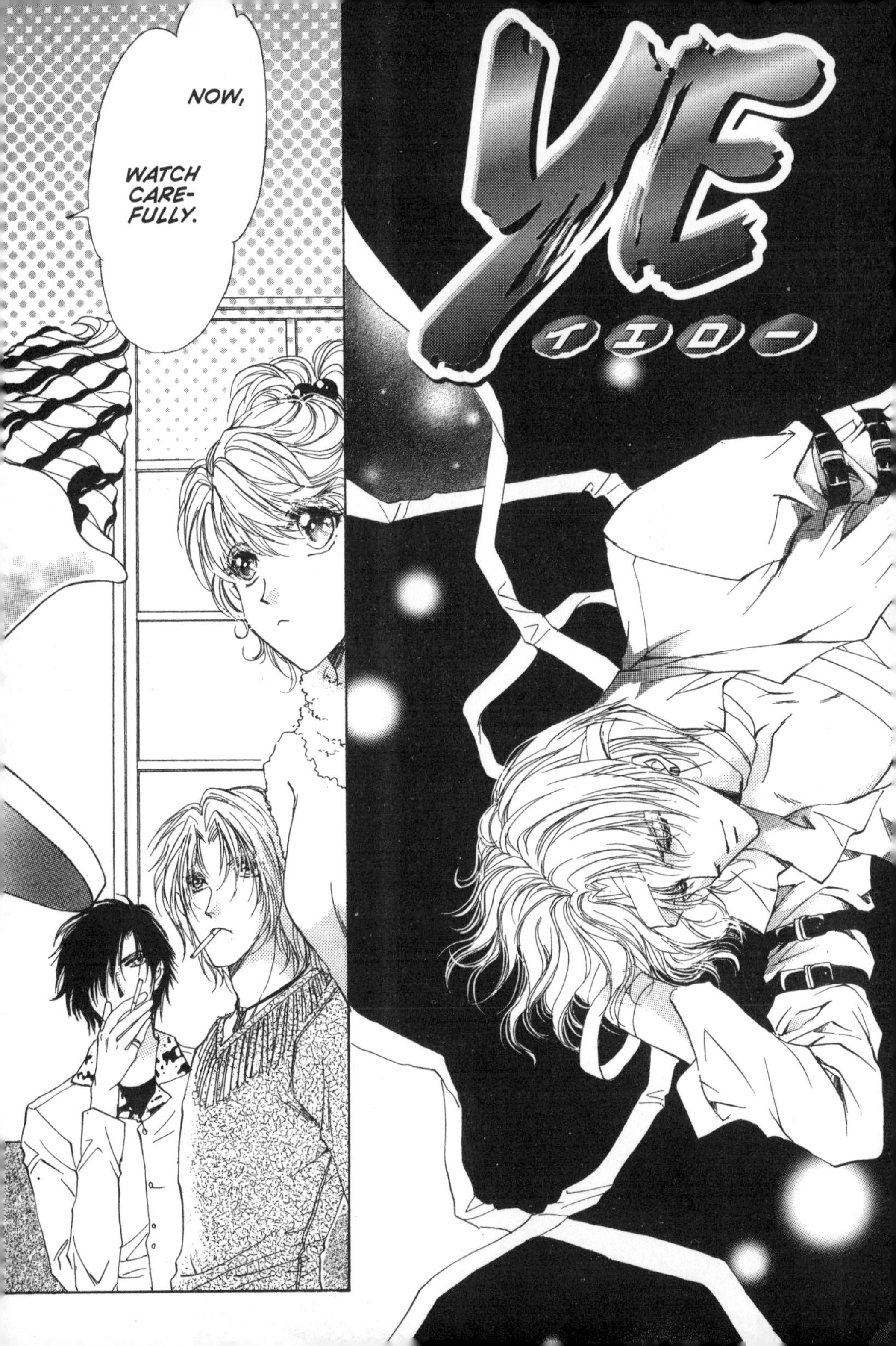
YE
イエロー
NOW, WATCH CARE-FULLY.

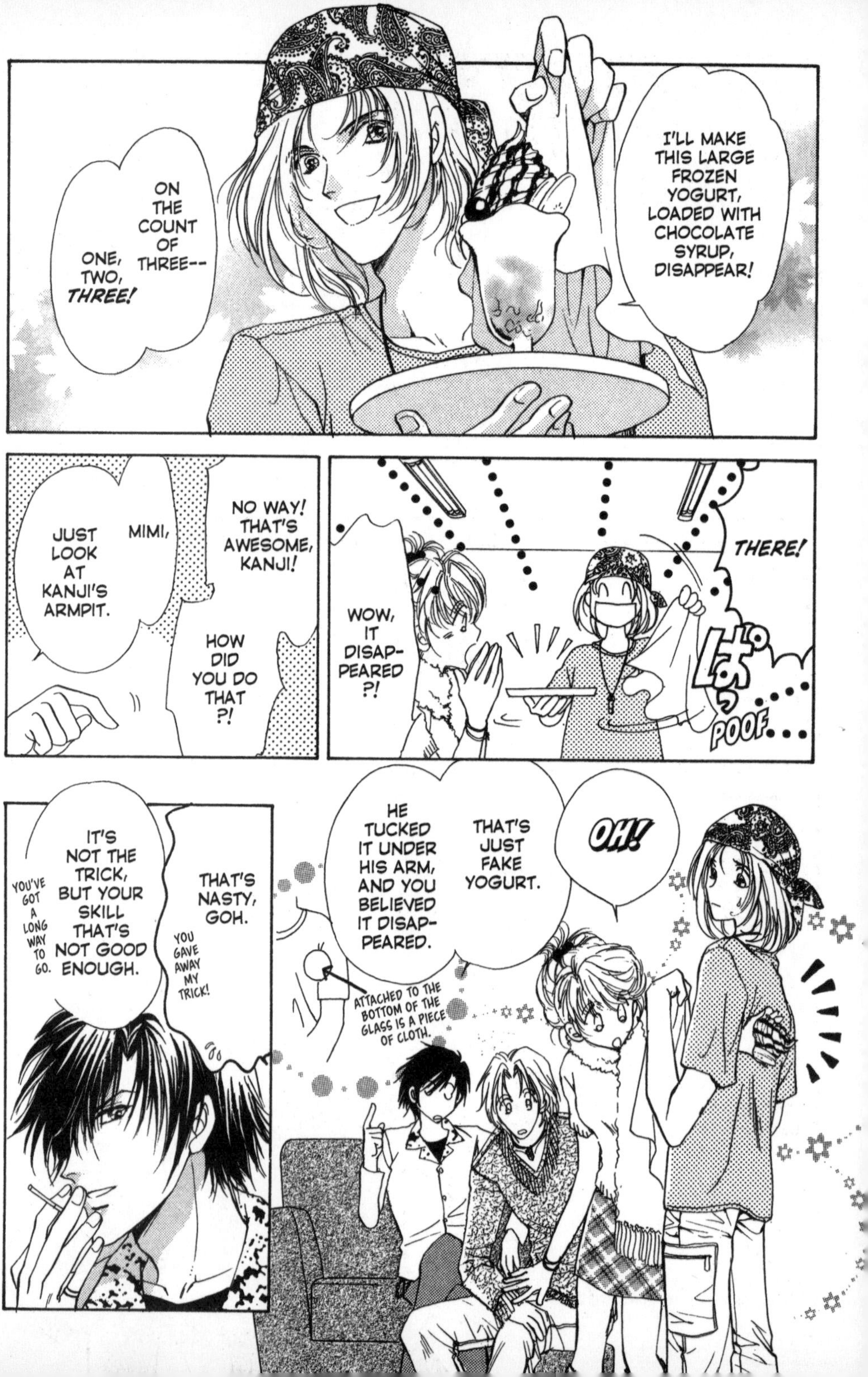
I'LL MAKE THIS LARGE FROZEN YOGURT, LOADED WITH CHOCOLATE SYRUP, DISAPPEAR!
ON THE COUNT OF THREE--
ONE, TWO, *THREE!*
THERE!
ぱっ
POOF...
WOW, IT DISAP-PEARED?!
NO WAY! THAT'S AWESOME, KANJI!
HOW DID YOU DO THAT?!
MIMI,
JUST LOOK AT KANJI'S ARMPIT.
OH!
THAT'S JUST FAKE YOGURT.
HE TUCKED IT UNDER HIS ARM, AND YOU BELIEVED IT DISAP-PEARED.
ATTACHED TO THE BOTTOM OF THE GLASS IS A PIECE OF CLOTH.
THAT'S NASTY, GOH.
YOU GAVE AWAY MY TRICK!
IT'S NOT THE TRICK, BUT YOUR SKILL THAT'S NOT GOOD ENOUGH.
YOU'VE GOT A LONG WAY TO GO.

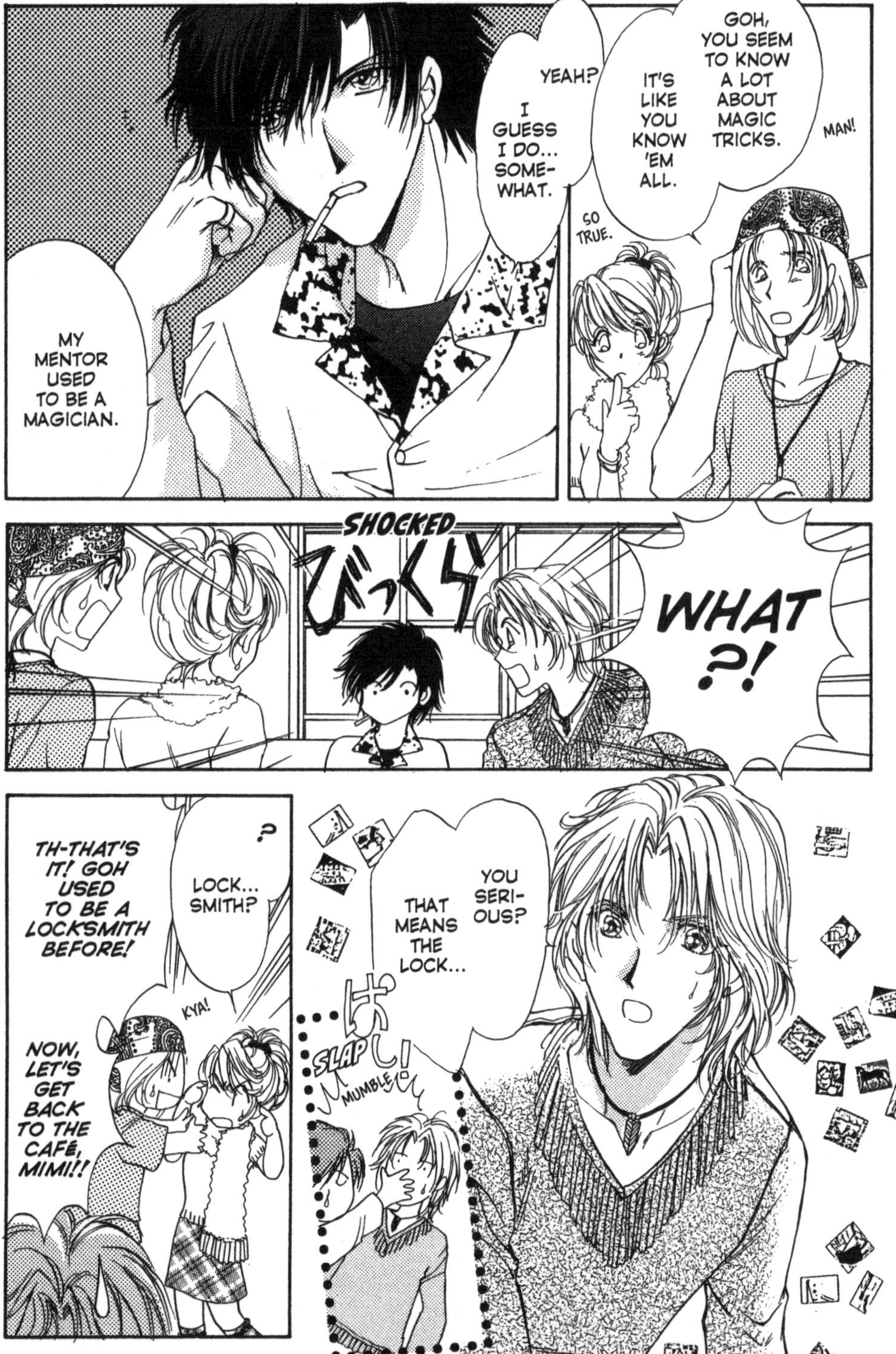

GOH, YOU SEEM TO KNOW A LOT ABOUT MAGIC TRICKS.
IT'S LIKE YOU KNOW 'EM ALL.
MAN!
SO TRUE.
YEAH?
I GUESS I DO... SOME-WHAT.
MY MENTOR USED TO BE A MAGICIAN.
WHAT?!
SHOCKED
びっくり
YOU SERI-OUS?
THAT MEANS THE LOCK...
SLAP
はし!
MUMBLE
?
LOCK... SMITH?
TH-THAT'S IT! GOH USED TO BE A LOCKSMITH BEFORE!
KYA!
NOW, LET'S GET BACK TO THE CAFÉ, MIMI!!

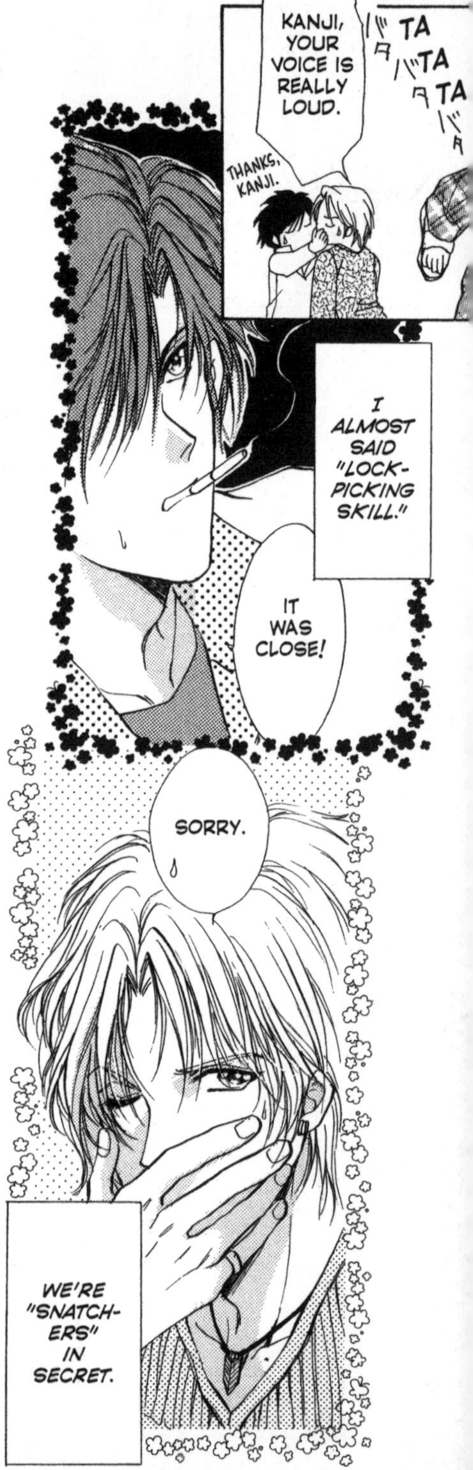
KANJI, YOUR VOICE IS REALLY LOUD.
TA TA TA
THANKS, KANJI.
I ALMOST SAID "LOCK-PICKING SKILL."
IT WAS CLOSE!
SORRY.
WE'RE "SNATCHERS" IN SECRET.

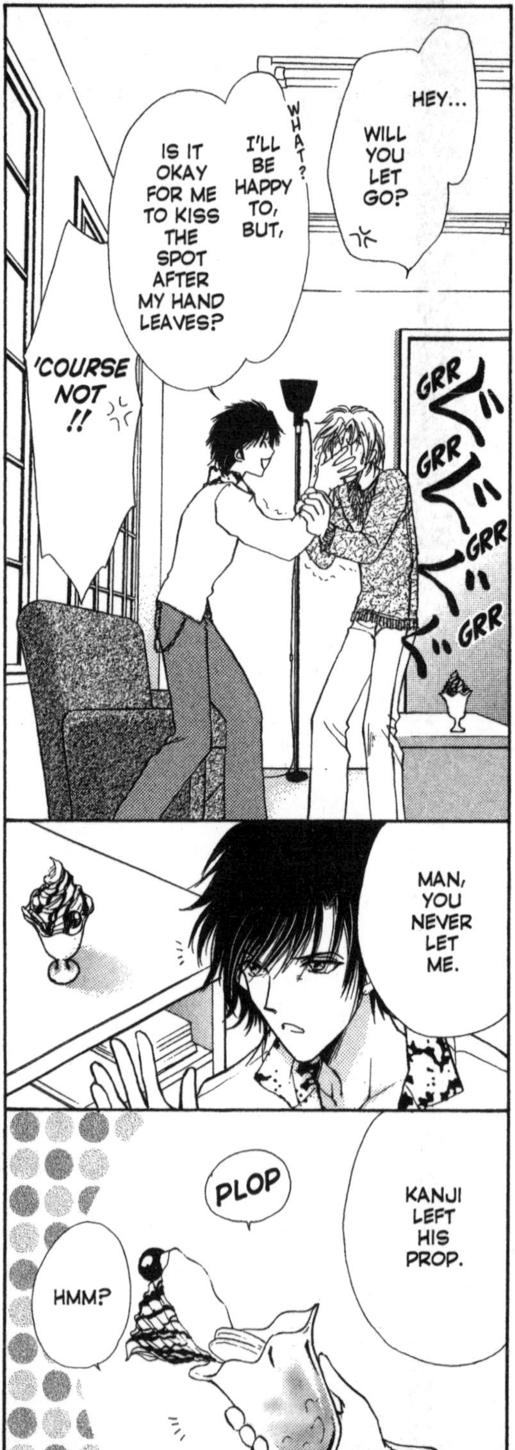
HEY... WILL YOU LET GO?
WHAT?
I'LL BE HAPPY TO, BUT,
IS IT OKAY FOR ME TO KISS THE SPOT AFTER MY HAND LEAVES?
'COURSE NOT!!
GRR GRR GRR GRR
MAN, YOU NEVER LET ME.
KANJI LEFT HIS PROP.
PLOP
HMM?

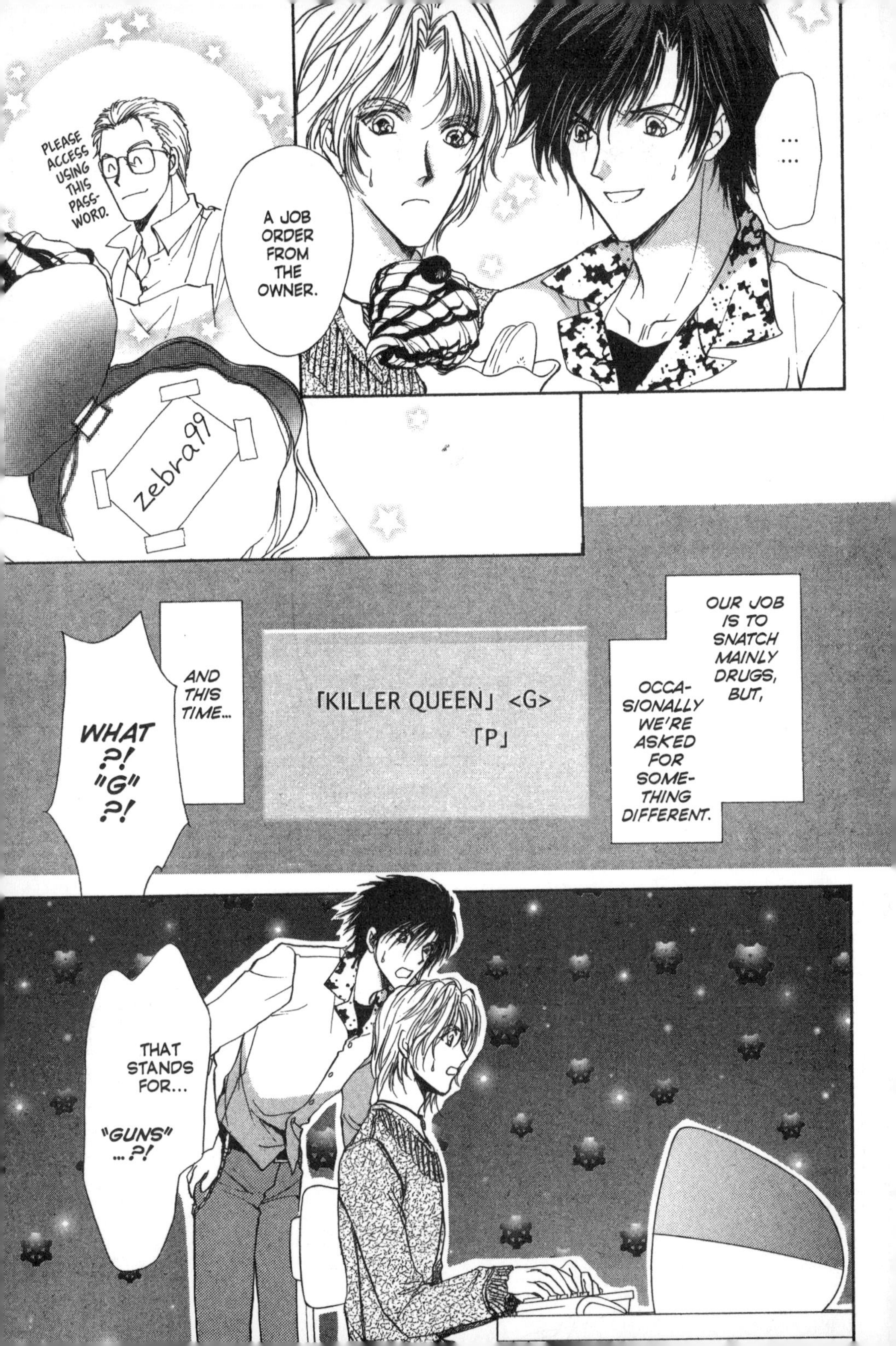

…
…
A JOB ORDER FROM THE OWNER.
PLEASE ACCESS USING THIS PASSWORD.
zebra99
OUR JOB IS TO SNATCH MAINLY DRUGS, BUT,
OCCASIONALLY WE'RE ASKED FOR SOMETHING DIFFERENT.
「KILLER QUEEN」 <G>
「P」
AND THIS TIME...
WHAT?! "G"?!
THAT STANDS FOR...
"GUNS" ...?!

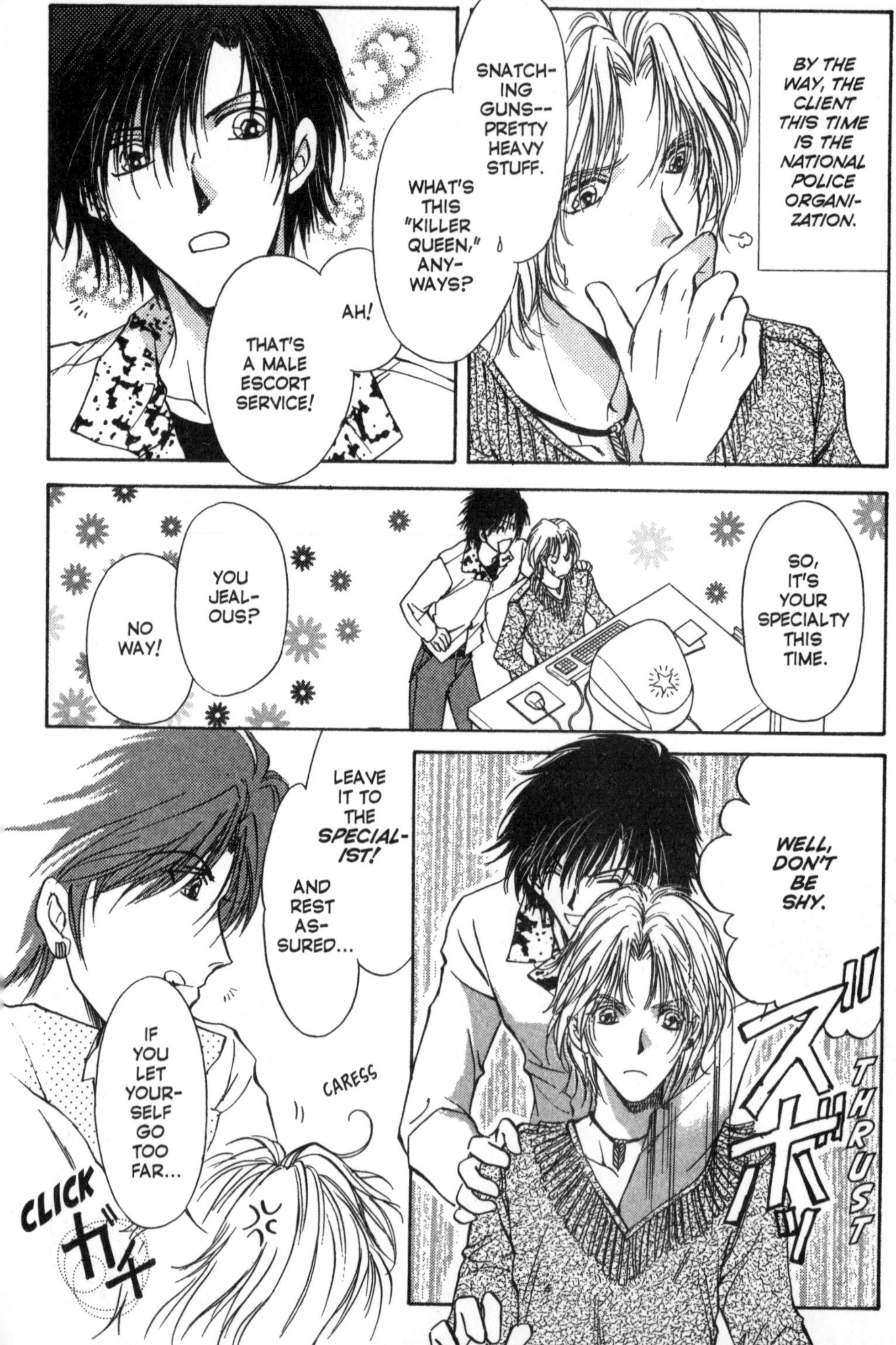
BY THE WAY, THE CLIENT THIS TIME IS THE NATIONAL POLICE ORGANIZATION.
SNATCHING GUNS--PRETTY HEAVY STUFF.
WHAT'S THIS "KILLER QUEEN," ANYWAYS?
AH!
THAT'S A MALE ESCORT SERVICE!
SO, IT'S YOUR SPECIALTY THIS TIME.
YOU JEALOUS?
NO WAY!
WELL, DON'T BE SHY.
THRUST
LEAVE IT TO THE *SPECIALIST!*
AND REST ASSURED...
CARESS
IF YOU LET YOURSELF GO TOO FAR...
CLICK

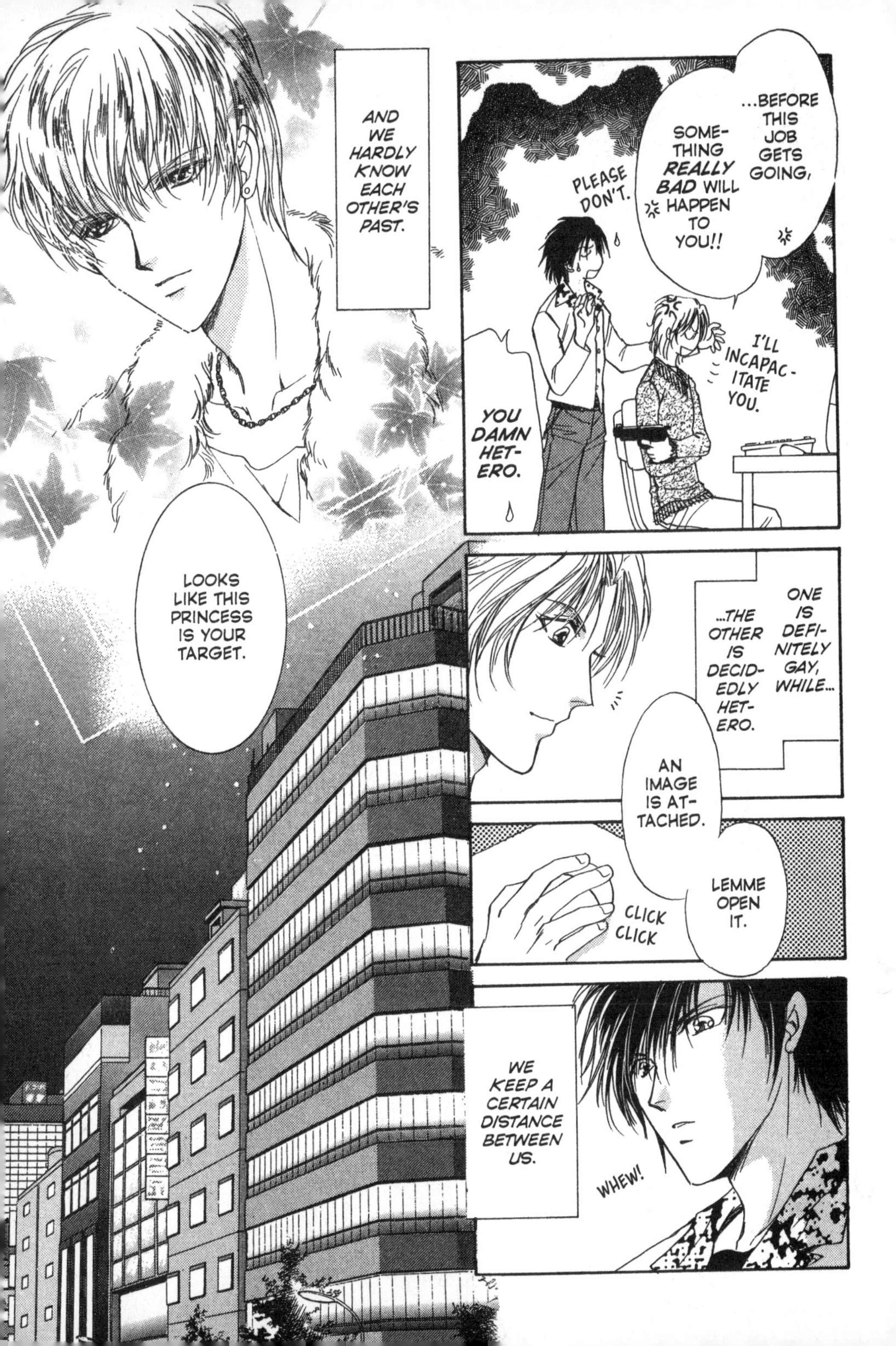

...BEFORE THIS JOB GETS GOING, SOMETHING *REALLY BAD* WILL HAPPEN TO YOU!!
PLEASE DON'T.
I'LL INCAPACITATE YOU.
YOU DAMN HETERO.
ONE IS DEFINITELY GAY, WHILE...
...THE OTHER IS DECIDEDLY HETERO.
AN IMAGE IS ATTACHED.
LEMME OPEN IT.
CLICK CLICK
WE KEEP A CERTAIN DISTANCE BETWEEN US.
WHEW!
AND WE HARDLY KNOW EACH OTHER'S PAST.
LOOKS LIKE THIS PRINCESS IS YOUR TARGET.

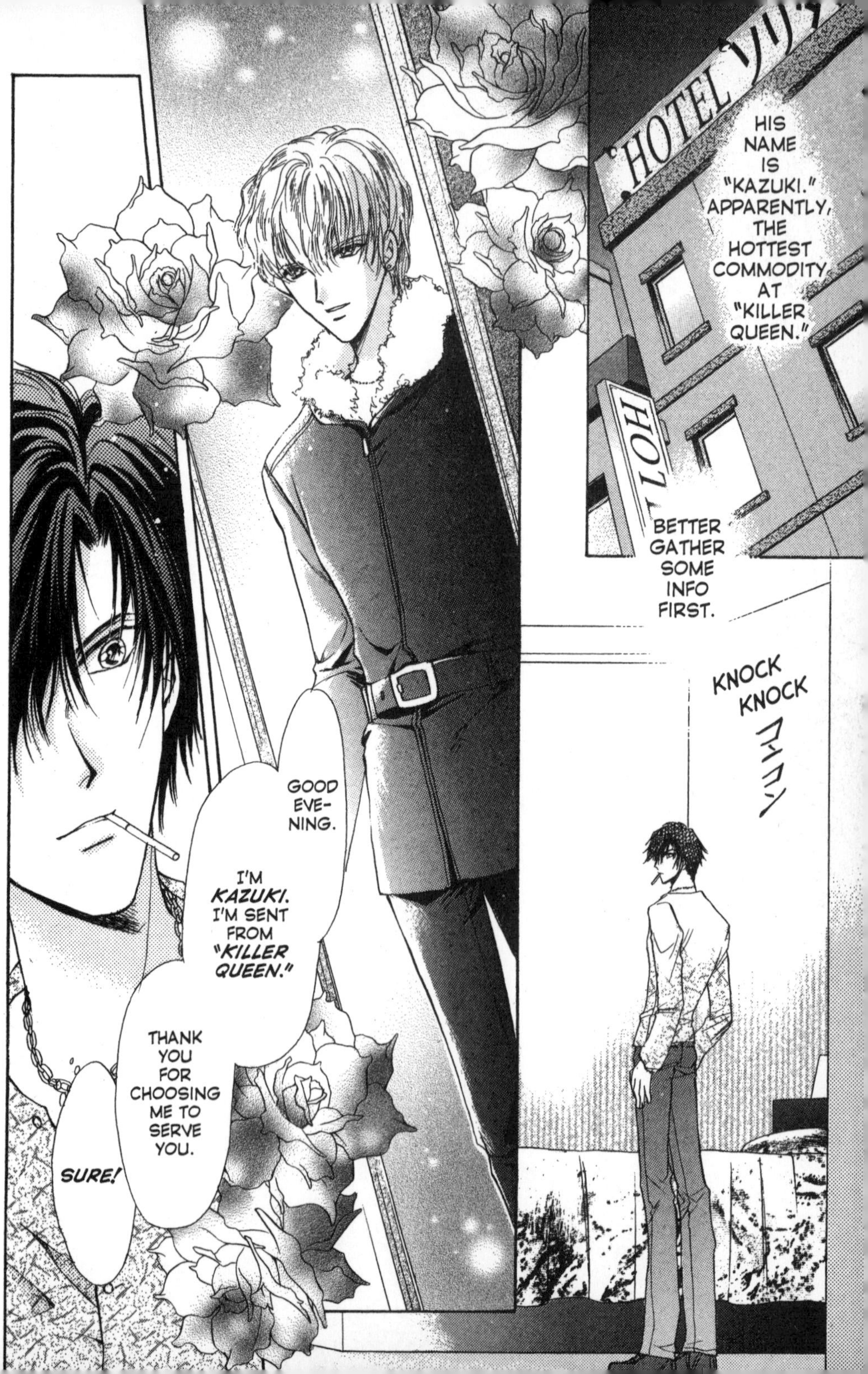
HOTEL
HIS NAME IS "KAZUKI." APPARENTLY, THE HOTTEST COMMODITY AT "KILLER QUEEN."
BETTER GATHER SOME INFO FIRST.
KNOCK KNOCK
GOOD EVE-NING.
I'M KAZUKI. I'M SENT FROM "KILLER QUEEN."
THANK YOU FOR CHOOSING ME TO SERVE YOU.
SURE!

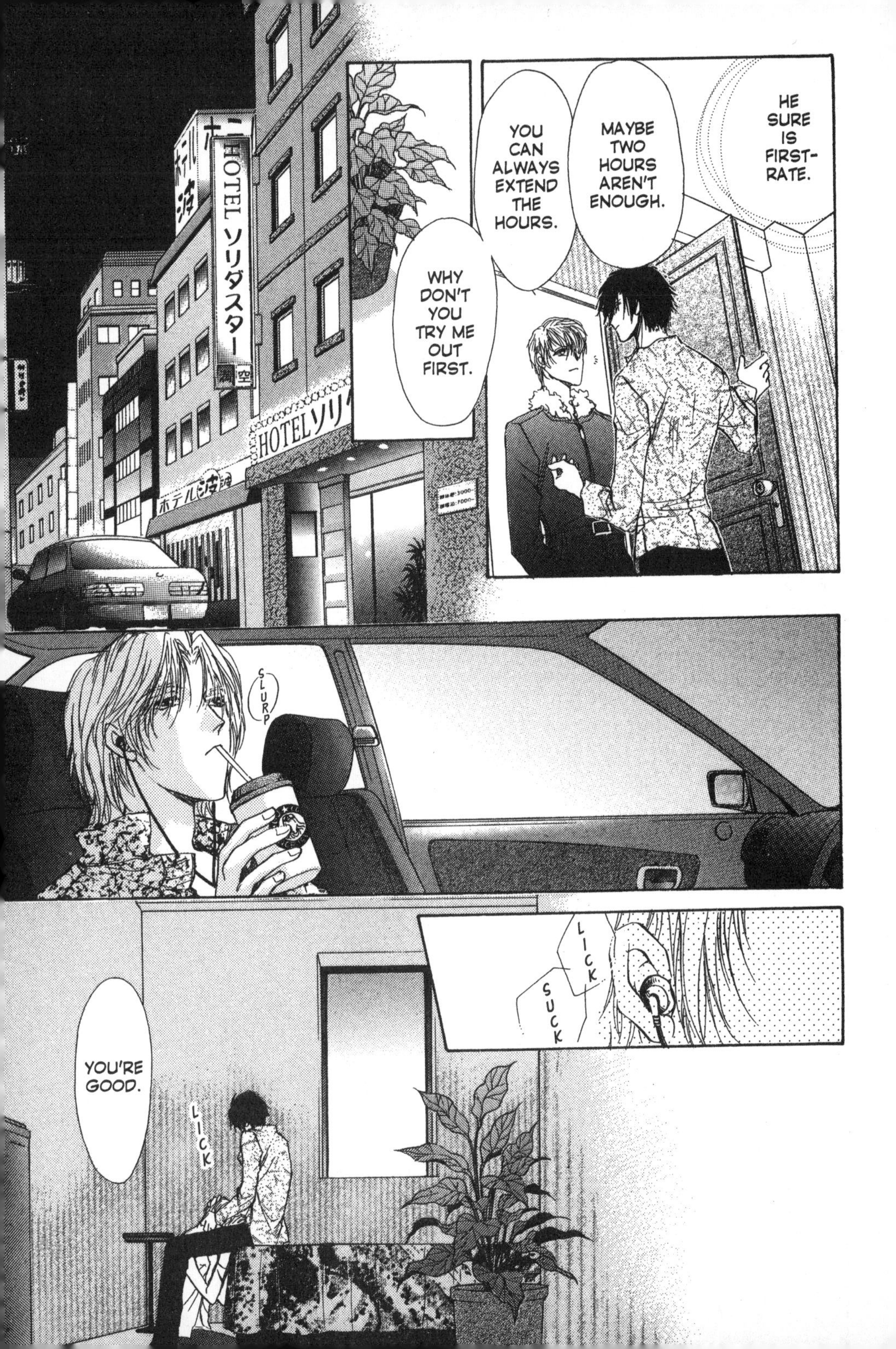
HE SURE IS FIRST-RATE.
MAYBE TWO HOURS AREN'T ENOUGH.
YOU CAN ALWAYS EXTEND THE HOURS.
WHY DON'T YOU TRY ME OUT FIRST.
HOTEL ソリダスター
HOTELソリ
SLURP
LICK
SUCK
YOU'RE GOOD.
LICK

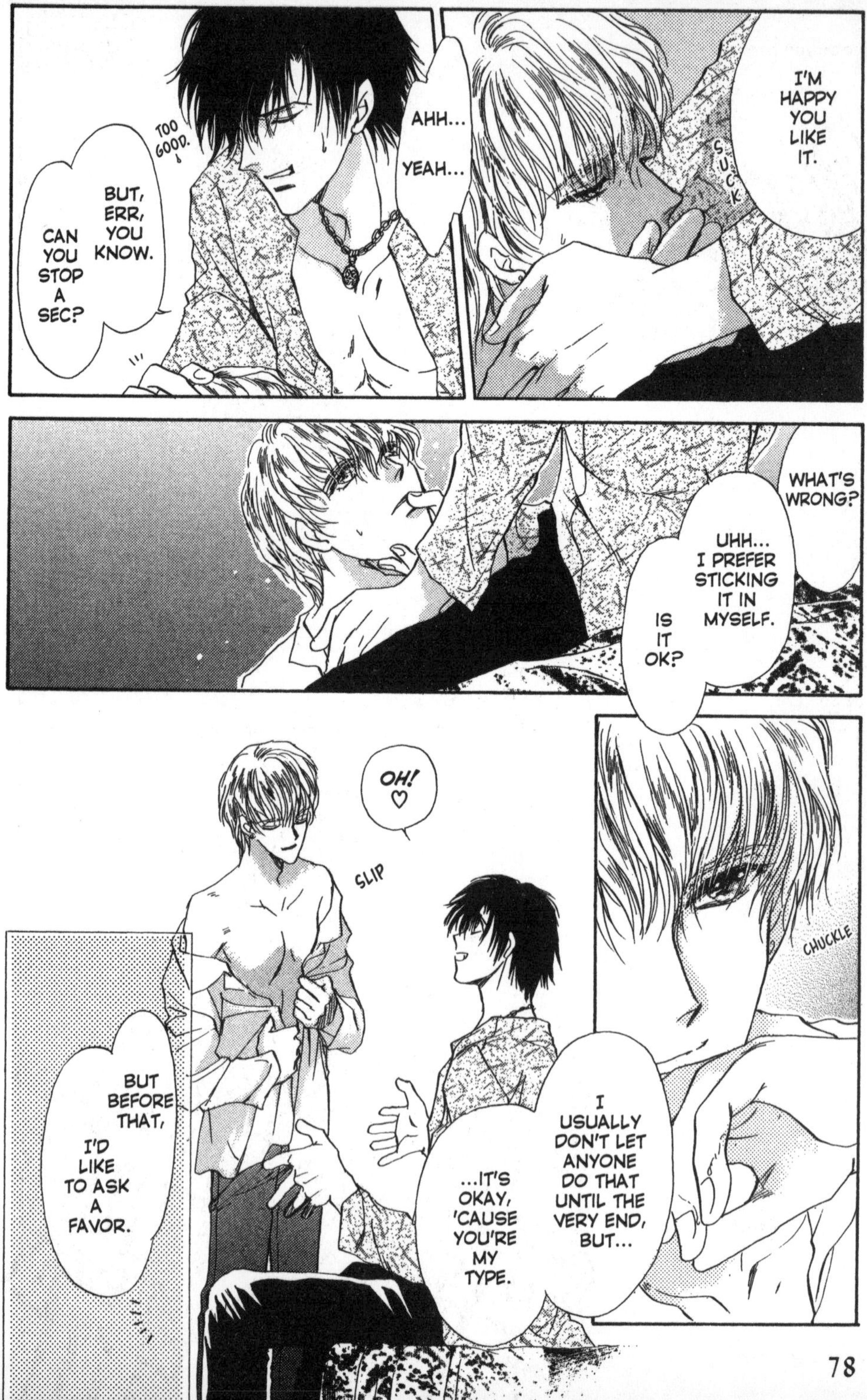
I'M HAPPY YOU LIKE IT.
SUCK
AHH...
YEAH...
TOO GOOD.
BUT, ERR, YOU KNOW.
CAN YOU STOP A SEC?
WHAT'S WRONG?
UHH... I PREFER STICKING IT IN MYSELF.
IS IT OK?
CHUCKLE
I USUALLY DON'T LET ANYONE DO THAT UNTIL THE VERY END, BUT...
...IT'S OKAY, 'CAUSE YOU'RE MY TYPE.
OH! ♡
SLIP
BUT BEFORE THAT,
I'D LIKE TO ASK A FAVOR.

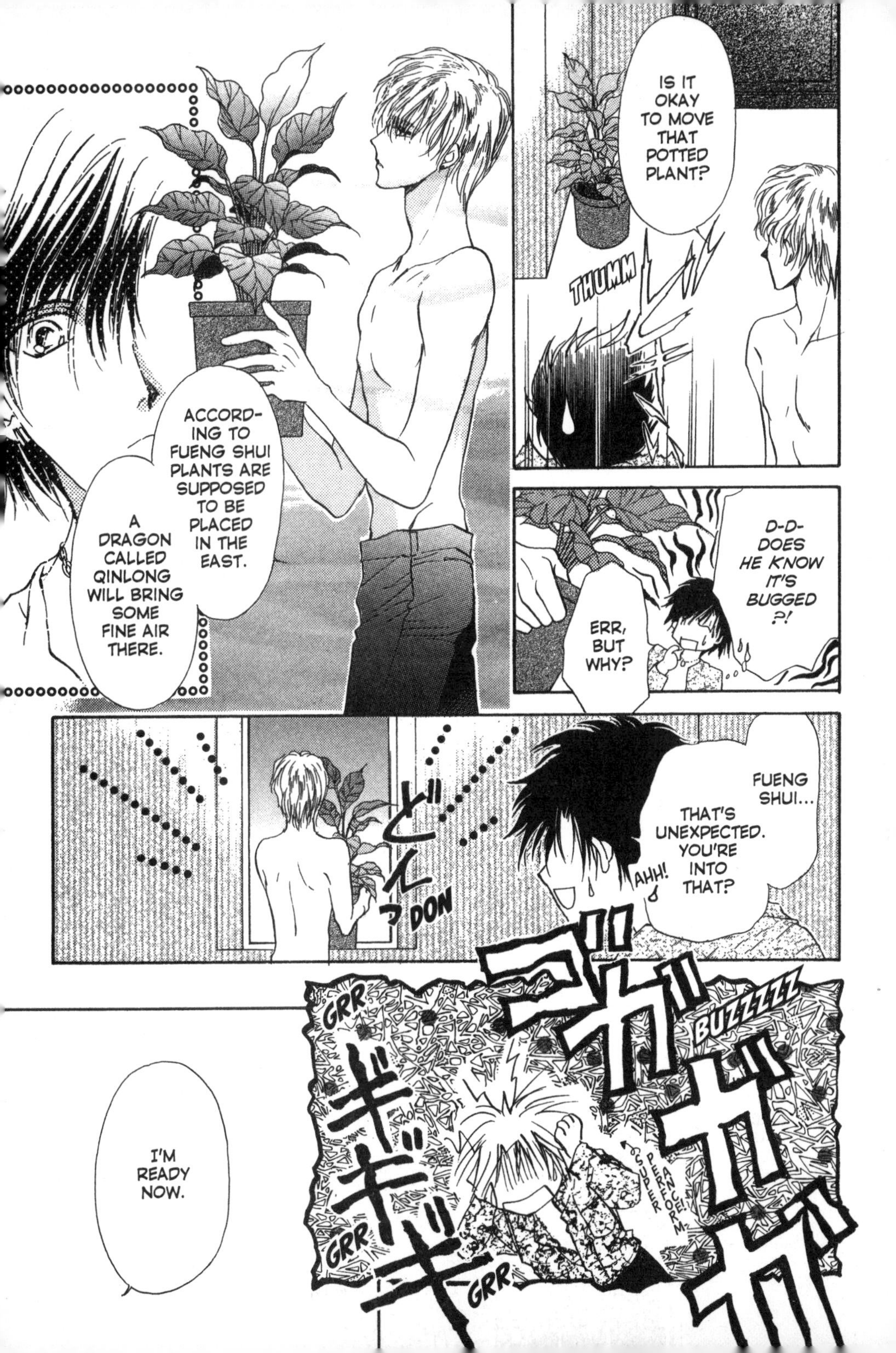
IS IT OKAY TO MOVE THAT POTTED PLANT?
THUMM
D-D-DOES HE KNOW IT'S BUGGED ?!
ERR, BUT WHY?
ACCORDING TO FUENG SHUI PLANTS ARE SUPPOSED TO BE PLACED IN THE EAST.
A DRAGON CALLED QINLONG WILL BRING SOME FINE AIR THERE.
FUENG SHUI...
THAT'S UNEXPECTED. YOU'RE INTO THAT?
AHH!
DON
BUZZZZZZ
GRR
SUPER PERFORMANCE!
GRR
GRR
I'M READY NOW.

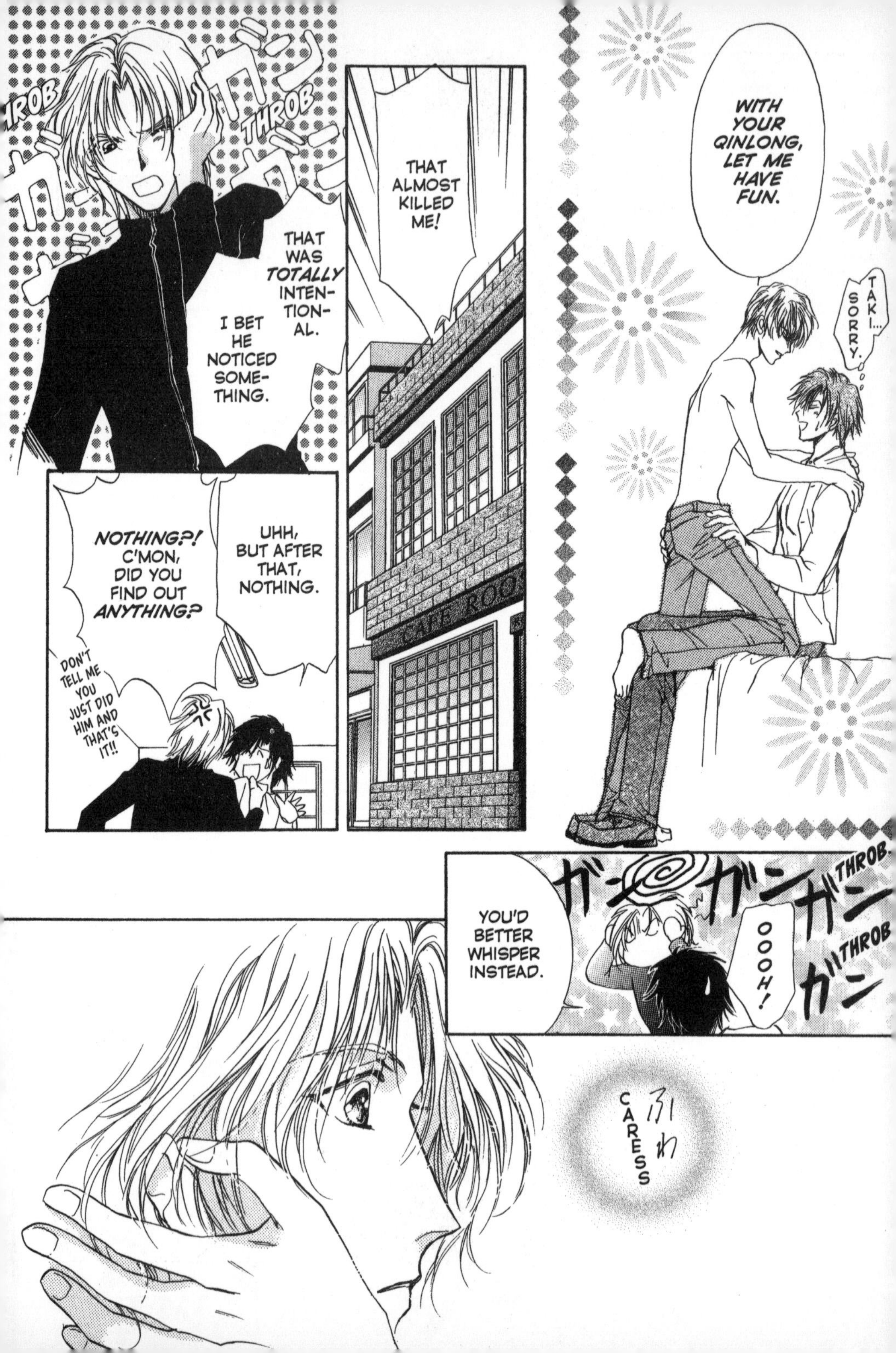

WITH YOUR QINLONG, LET ME HAVE FUN.
TAKI... SORRY.
THAT ALMOST KILLED ME!
THROB
THROB
THAT WAS *TOTALLY* INTENTIONAL.
I BET HE NOTICED SOMETHING.
UHH, BUT AFTER THAT, NOTHING.
NOTHING?! C'MON, DID YOU FIND OUT *ANYTHING?*
DON'T TELL ME YOU JUST DID HIM AND THAT'S IT!!
CAFE ROO
THROB
THROB
OOOOH!
YOU'D BETTER WHISPER INSTEAD.
CARESS

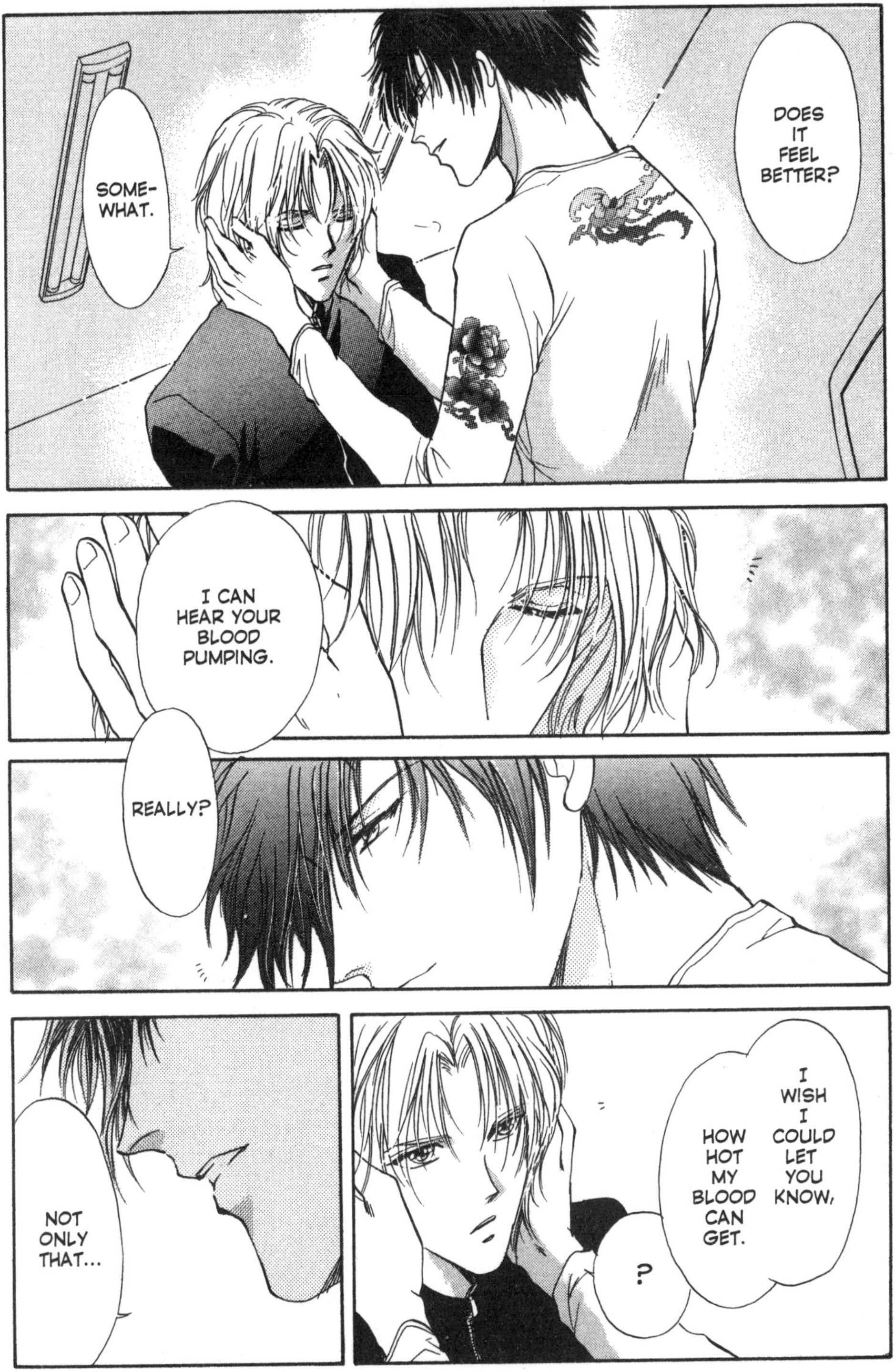
DOES IT FEEL BETTER?
SOME-WHAT.
I CAN HEAR YOUR BLOOD PUMPING.
REALLY?
I WISH I COULD LET YOU KNOW,
HOW HOT MY BLOOD CAN GET.
?
NOT ONLY THAT...

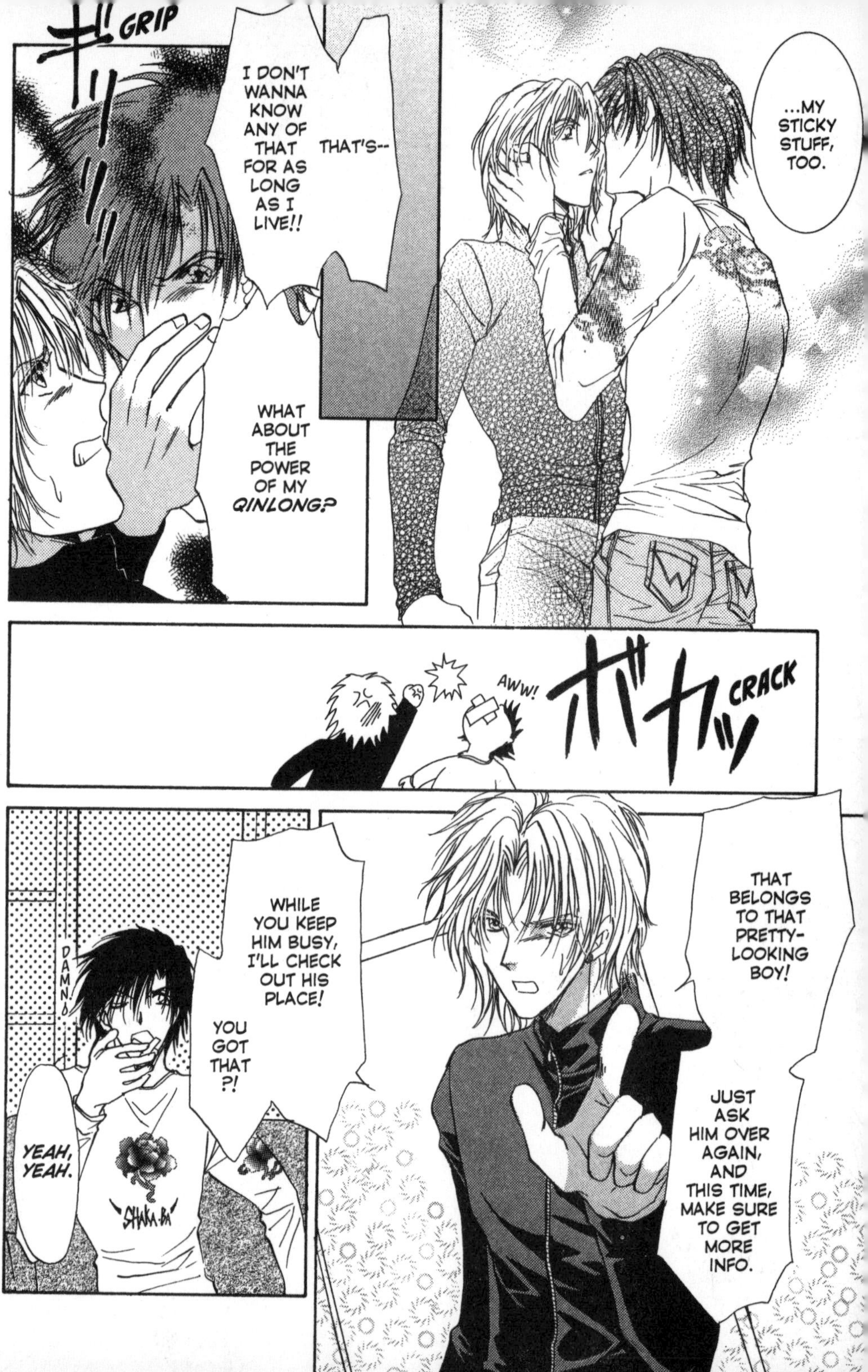
...MY STICKY STUFF, TOO.
THAT'S--
I DON'T WANNA KNOW ANY OF THAT FOR AS LONG AS I LIVE!!
GRIP
WHAT ABOUT THE POWER OF MY *QINLONG?*
CRACK
AWW!
THAT BELONGS TO THAT PRETTY-LOOKING BOY!
JUST ASK HIM OVER AGAIN, AND THIS TIME, MAKE SURE TO GET MORE INFO.
WHILE YOU KEEP HIM BUSY, I'LL CHECK OUT HIS PLACE!
YOU GOT THAT?!
DAMN.
YEAH, YEAH.
SHAKA-BA

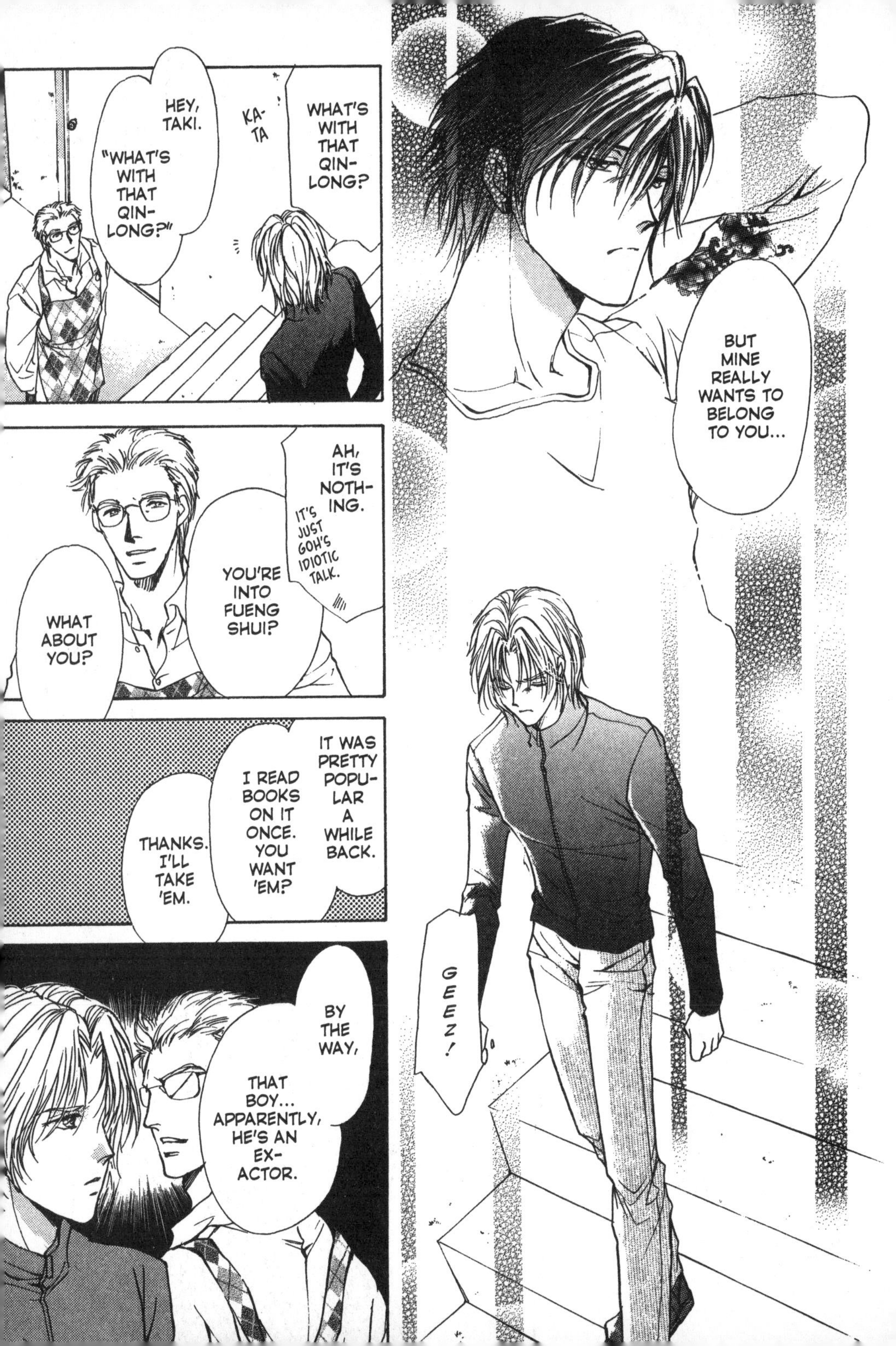
BUT MINE REALLY WANTS TO BELONG TO YOU...
GEEZ!
WHAT'S WITH THAT QIN-LONG?
KA-TA
HEY, TAKI.
"WHAT'S WITH THAT QIN-LONG?"
AH, IT'S NOTHING.
IT'S JUST GOH'S IDIOTIC TALK.
YOU'RE INTO FUENG SHUI?
WHAT ABOUT YOU?
IT WAS PRETTY POPULAR A WHILE BACK.
I READ BOOKS ON IT ONCE. YOU WANT 'EM?
THANKS. I'LL TAKE 'EM.
BY THE WAY,
THAT BOY... APPARENTLY, HE'S AN EX-ACTOR.

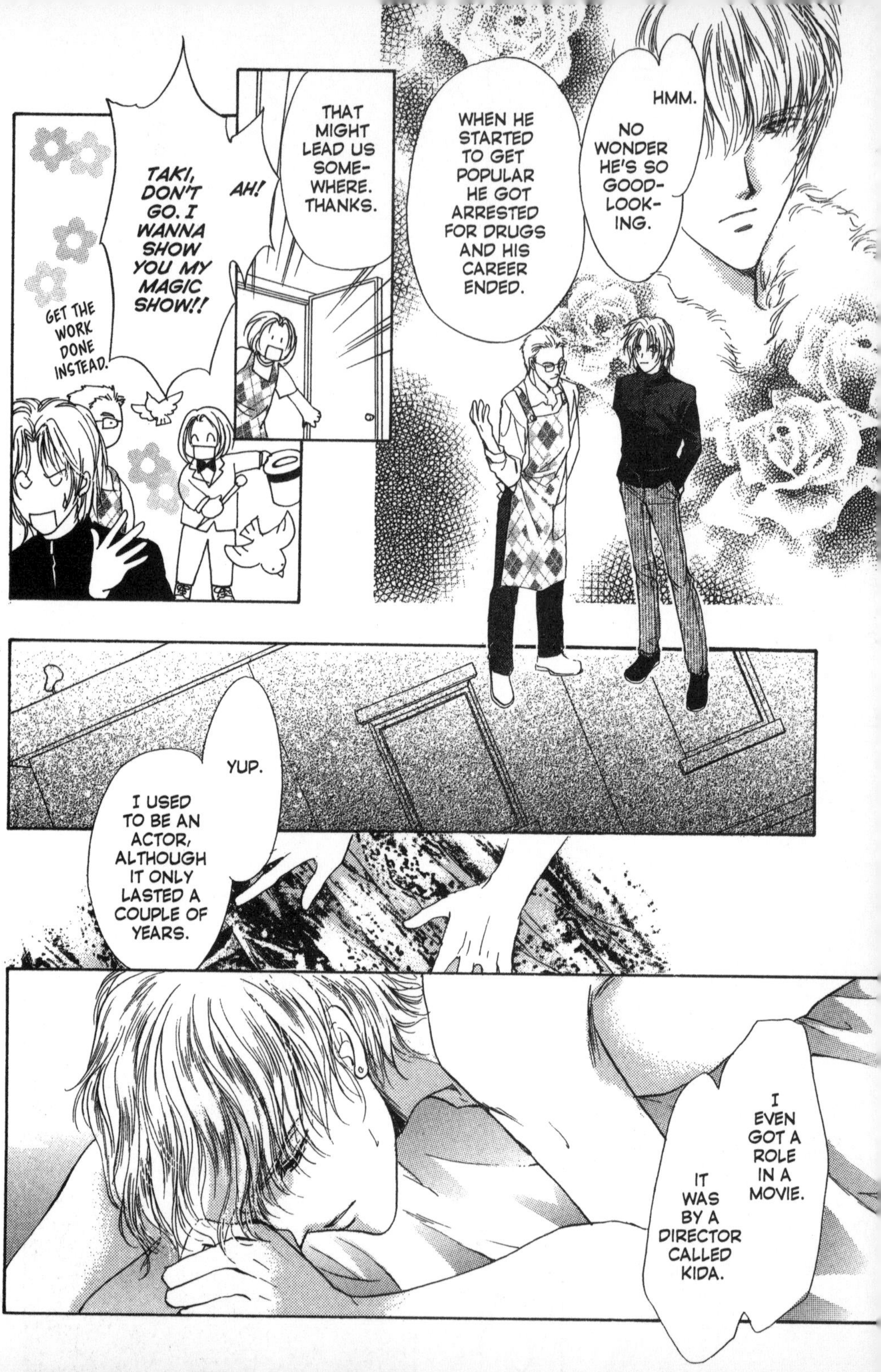
HMM.
NO WONDER HE'S SO GOOD-LOOKING.
WHEN HE STARTED TO GET POPULAR HE GOT ARRESTED FOR DRUGS AND HIS CAREER ENDED.
THAT MIGHT LEAD US SOME-WHERE. THANKS.
AH!
TAKI, DON'T GO. I WANNA SHOW YOU MY MAGIC SHOW!!
GET THE WORK DONE INSTEAD.
YUP.
I USED TO BE AN ACTOR, ALTHOUGH IT ONLY LASTED A COUPLE OF YEARS.
I EVEN GOT A ROLE IN A MOVIE.
IT WAS BY A DIRECTOR CALLED KIDA.

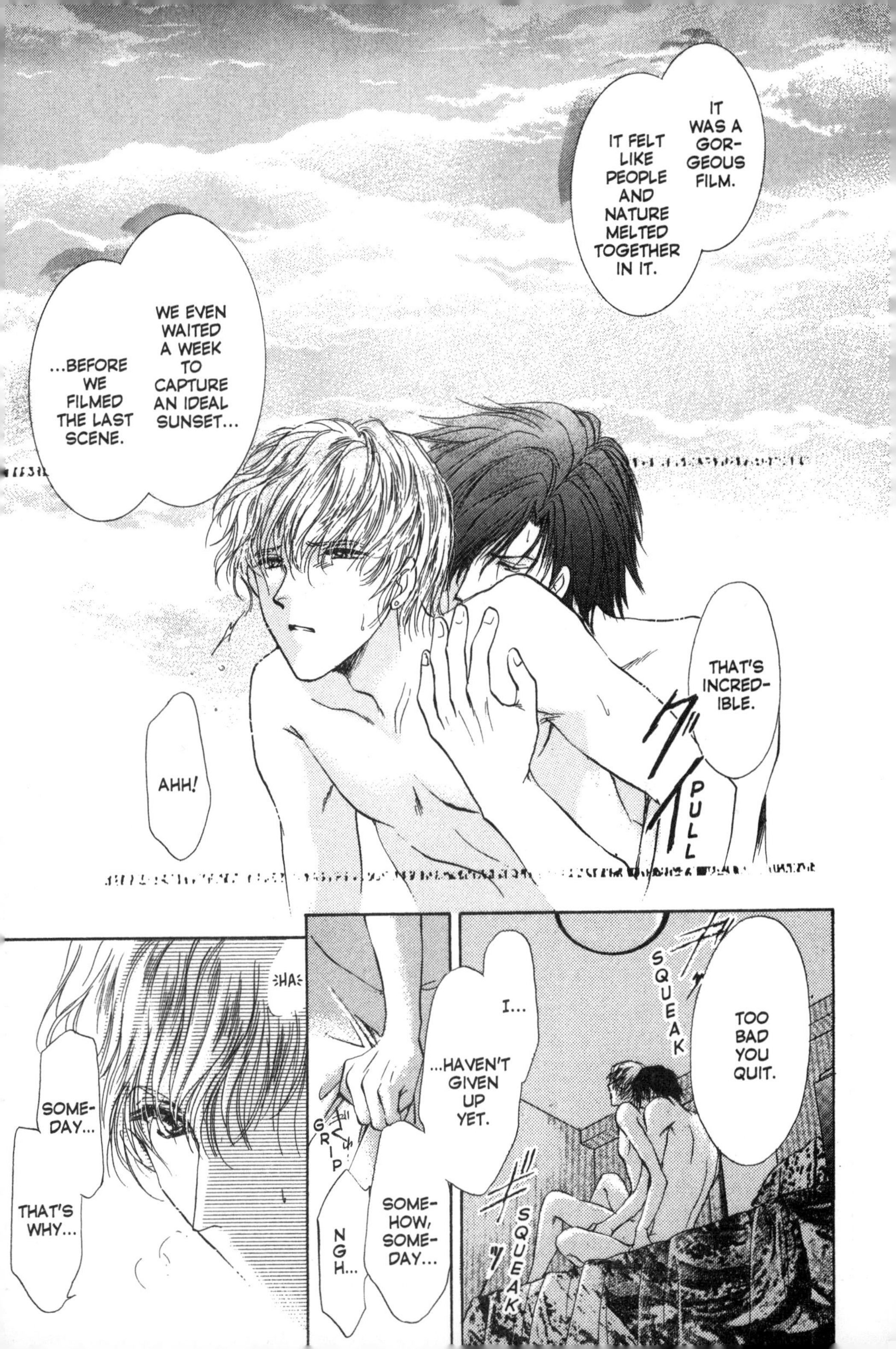
IT WAS A GORGEOUS FILM.
IT FELT LIKE PEOPLE AND NATURE MELTED TOGETHER IN IT.
WE EVEN WAITED A WEEK TO CAPTURE AN IDEAL SUNSET...
...BEFORE WE FILMED THE LAST SCENE.
THAT'S INCREDIBLE.
PULL
AHH!
SQUEAK
TOO BAD YOU QUIT.
I...
...HAVEN'T GIVEN UP YET.
SOMEHOW, SOMEDAY...
SQUEAK
GRIP
NGH...
HA
SOMEDAY...
THAT'S WHY...

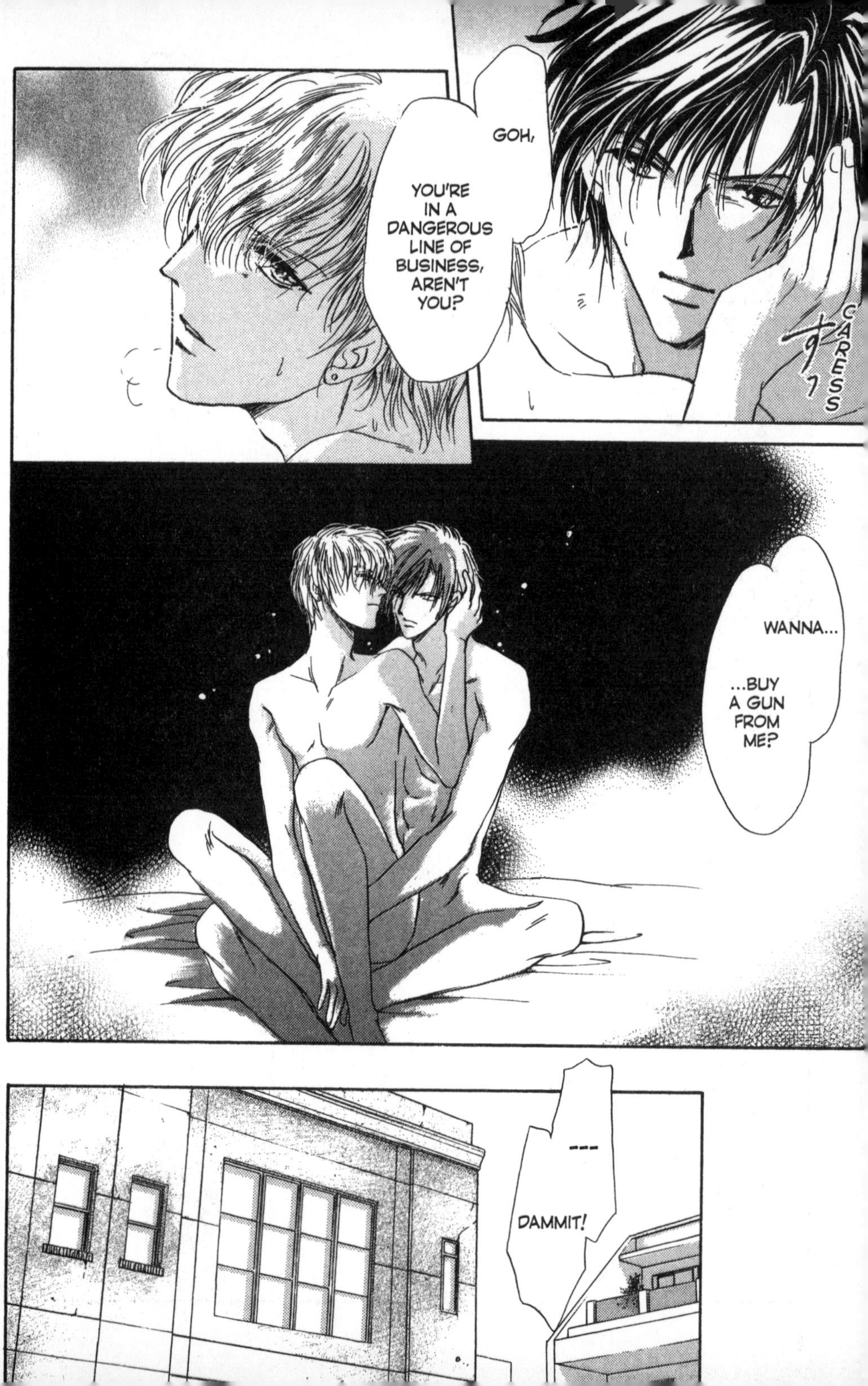
GOH,
YOU'RE IN A DANGEROUS LINE OF BUSINESS, AREN'T YOU?
CARESS
WANNA...
...BUY A GUN FROM ME?

DAMMIT!

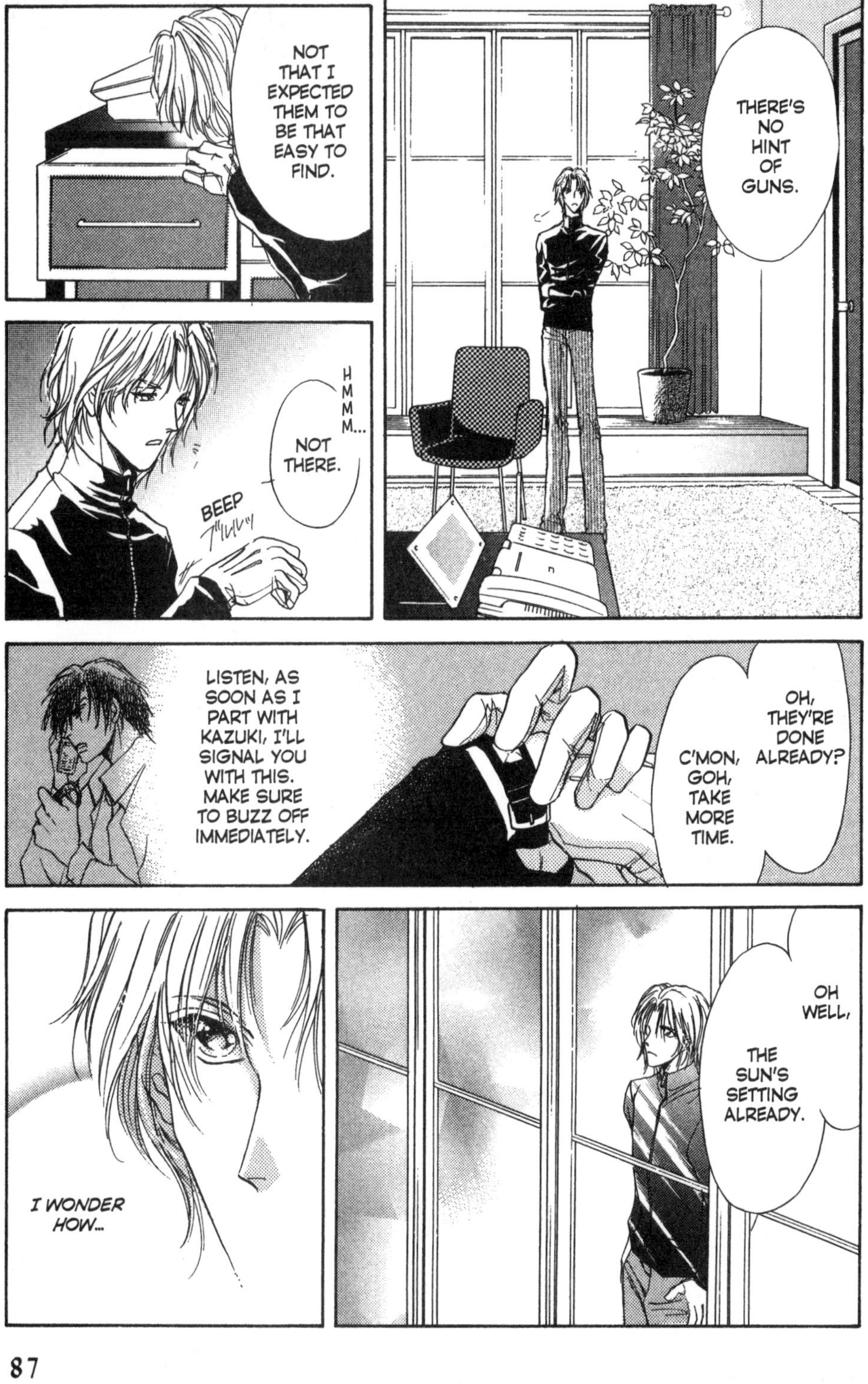
THERE'S NO HINT OF GUNS.
NOT THAT I EXPECTED THEM TO BE THAT EASY TO FIND.
HMMM... NOT THERE.
BEEP
ブルルッ
OH, THEY'RE DONE ALREADY?
C'MON, GOH, TAKE MORE TIME.
LISTEN, AS SOON AS I PART WITH KAZUKI, I'LL SIGNAL YOU WITH THIS. MAKE SURE TO BUZZ OFF IMMEDIATELY.
OH WELL,
THE SUN'S SETTING ALREADY.
I WONDER HOW...

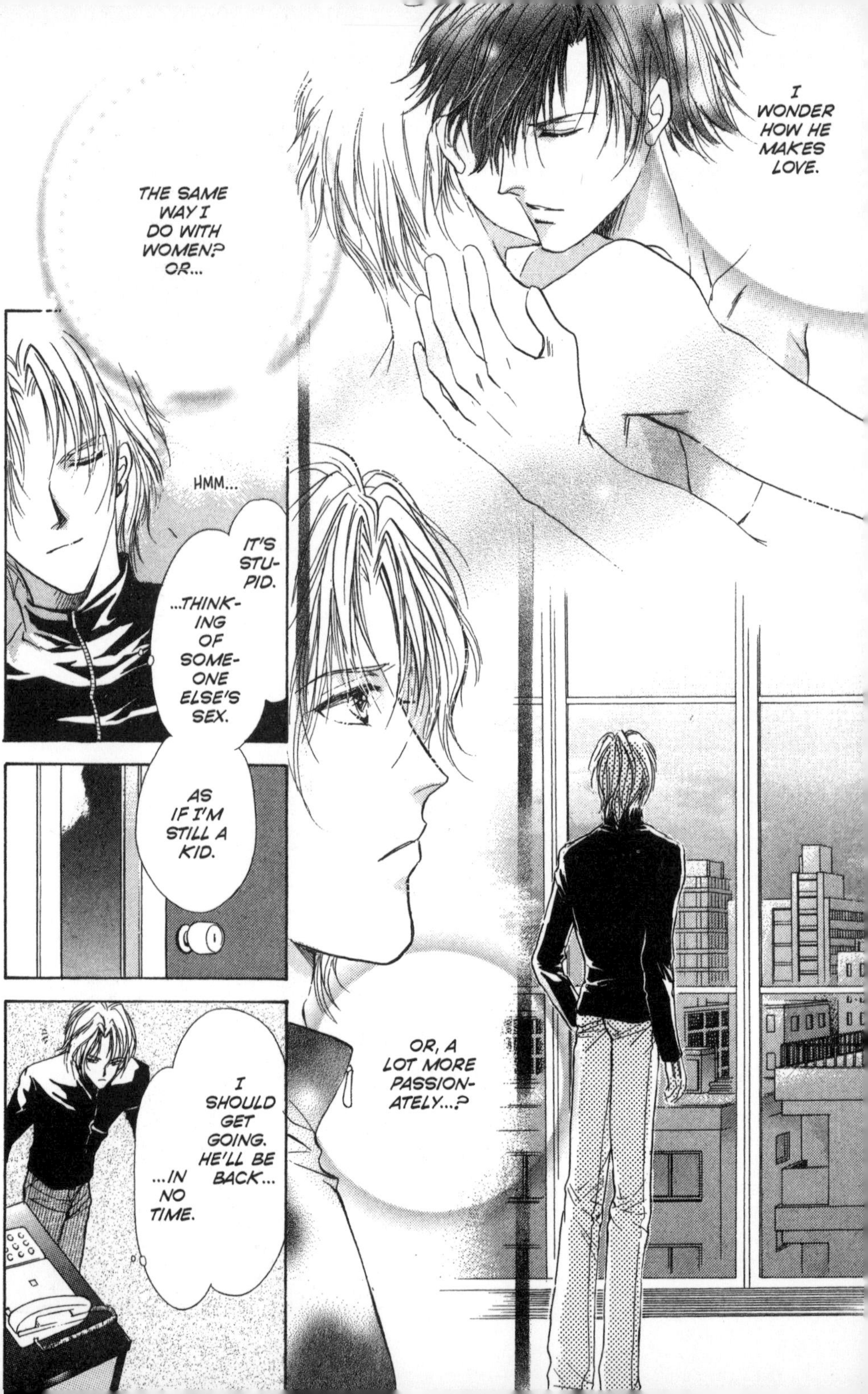
I WONDER HOW HE MAKES LOVE.
THE SAME WAY I DO WITH WOMEN? OR...
OR, A LOT MORE PASSION-ATELY...?
HMM...
IT'S STU-PID.
...THINK-ING OF SOME-ONE ELSE'S SEX.
AS IF I'M STILL A KID.
I SHOULD GET GOING. HE'LL BE BACK...
...IN NO TIME.

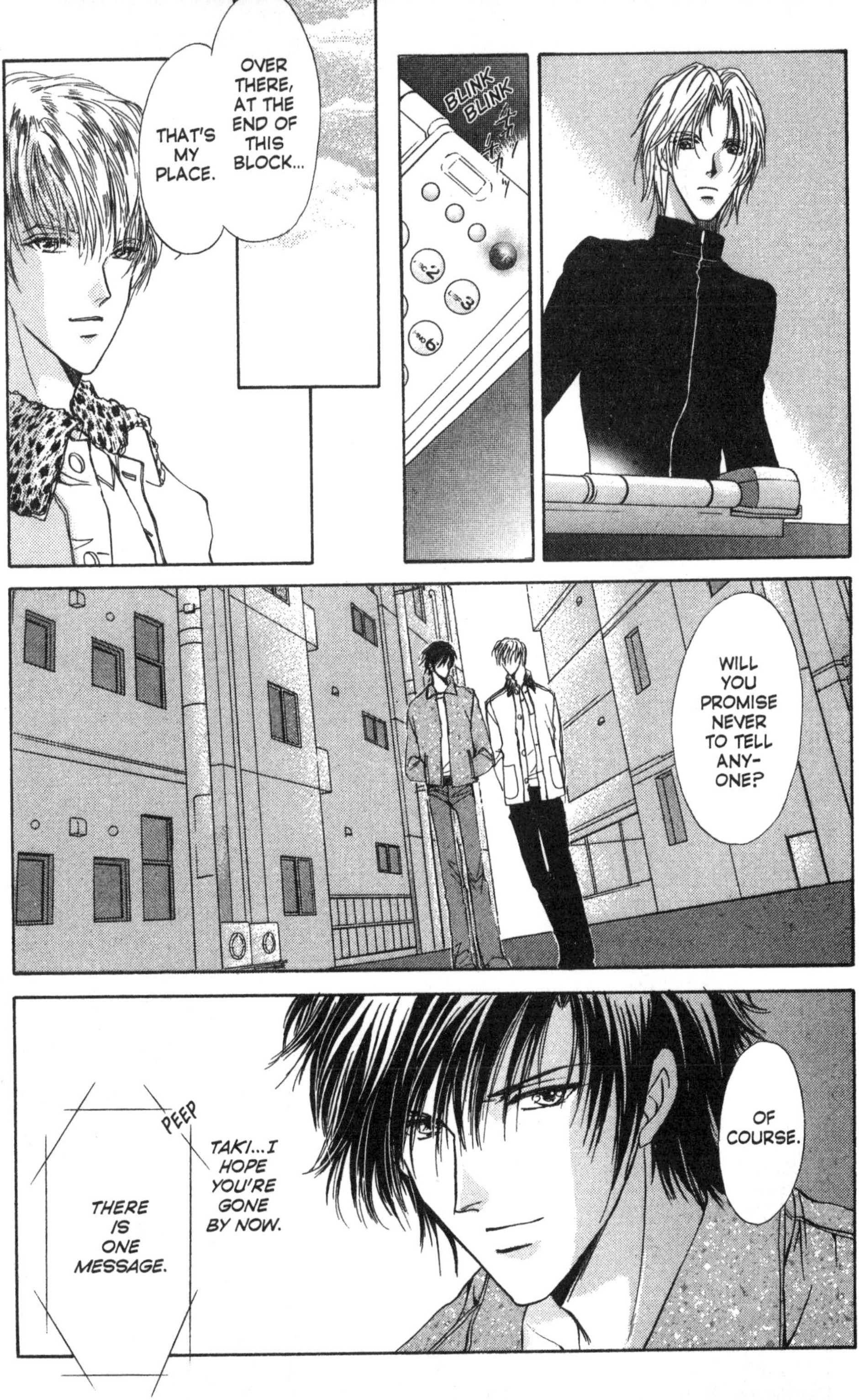
BLINK BLINK
OVER THERE, AT THE END OF THIS BLOCK...
THAT'S MY PLACE.
WILL YOU PROMISE NEVER TO TELL ANY-ONE?
OF COURSE.
PEEP
TAKI...I HOPE YOU'RE GONE BY NOW.
THERE IS ONE MESSAGE.

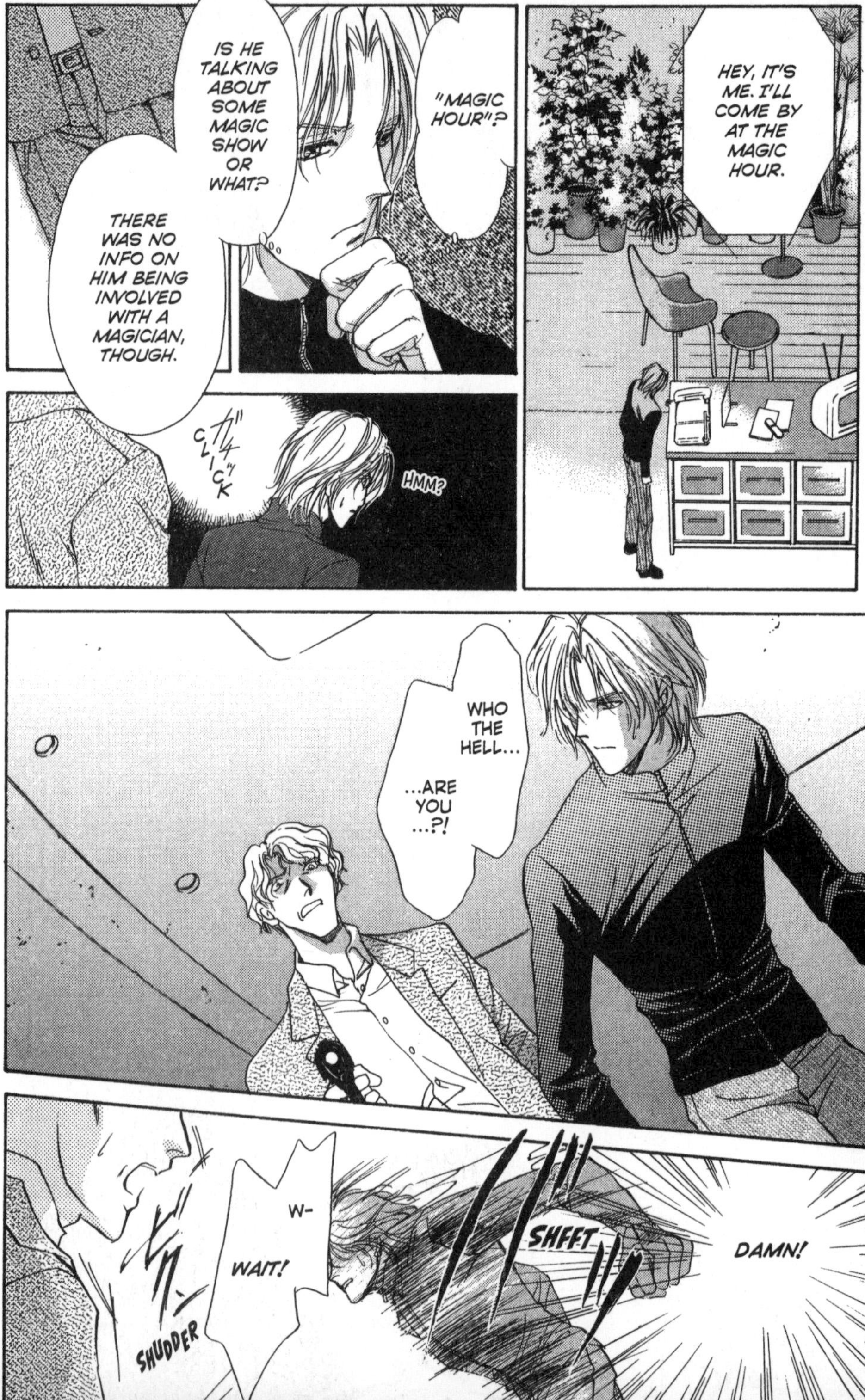
HEY, IT'S ME. I'LL COME BY AT THE MAGIC HOUR.
"MAGIC HOUR"?
IS HE TALKING ABOUT SOME MAGIC SHOW OR WHAT?
THERE WAS NO INFO ON HIM BEING INVOLVED WITH A MAGICIAN, THOUGH.
HMM?
CLICK
WHO THE HELL...
...ARE YOU ...?!
DAMN!
SHFFT
W-
WAIT!
SHUDDER

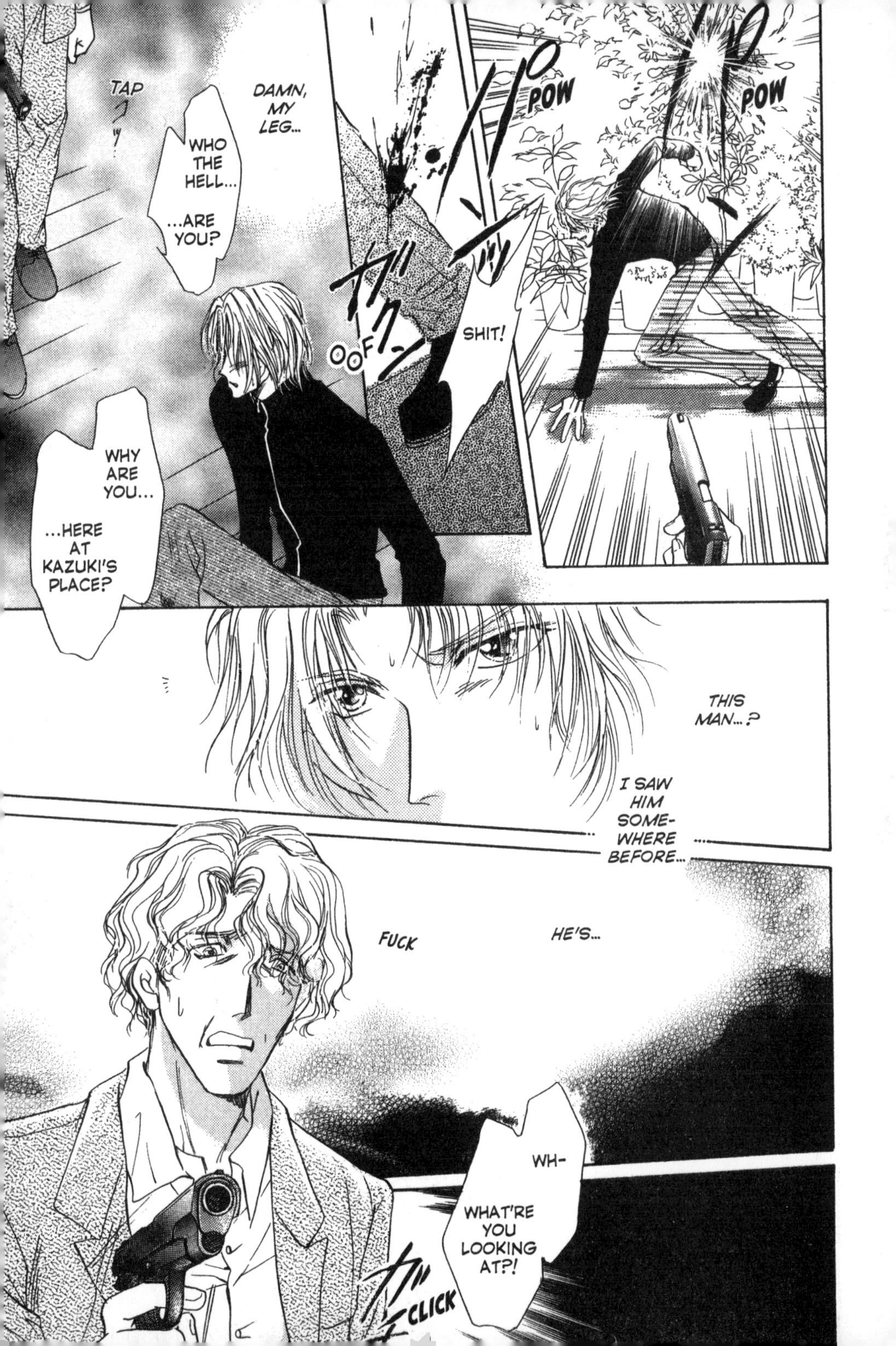
POW
POW
SHIT!
OOF
DAMN, MY LEG...
WHO THE HELL... ...ARE YOU?
TAP
WHY ARE YOU... ...HERE AT KAZUKI'S PLACE?
THIS MAN...?
I SAW HIM SOMEWHERE BEFORE...
HE'S...
FUCK
WH- WHAT'RE YOU LOOKING AT?!
CLICK

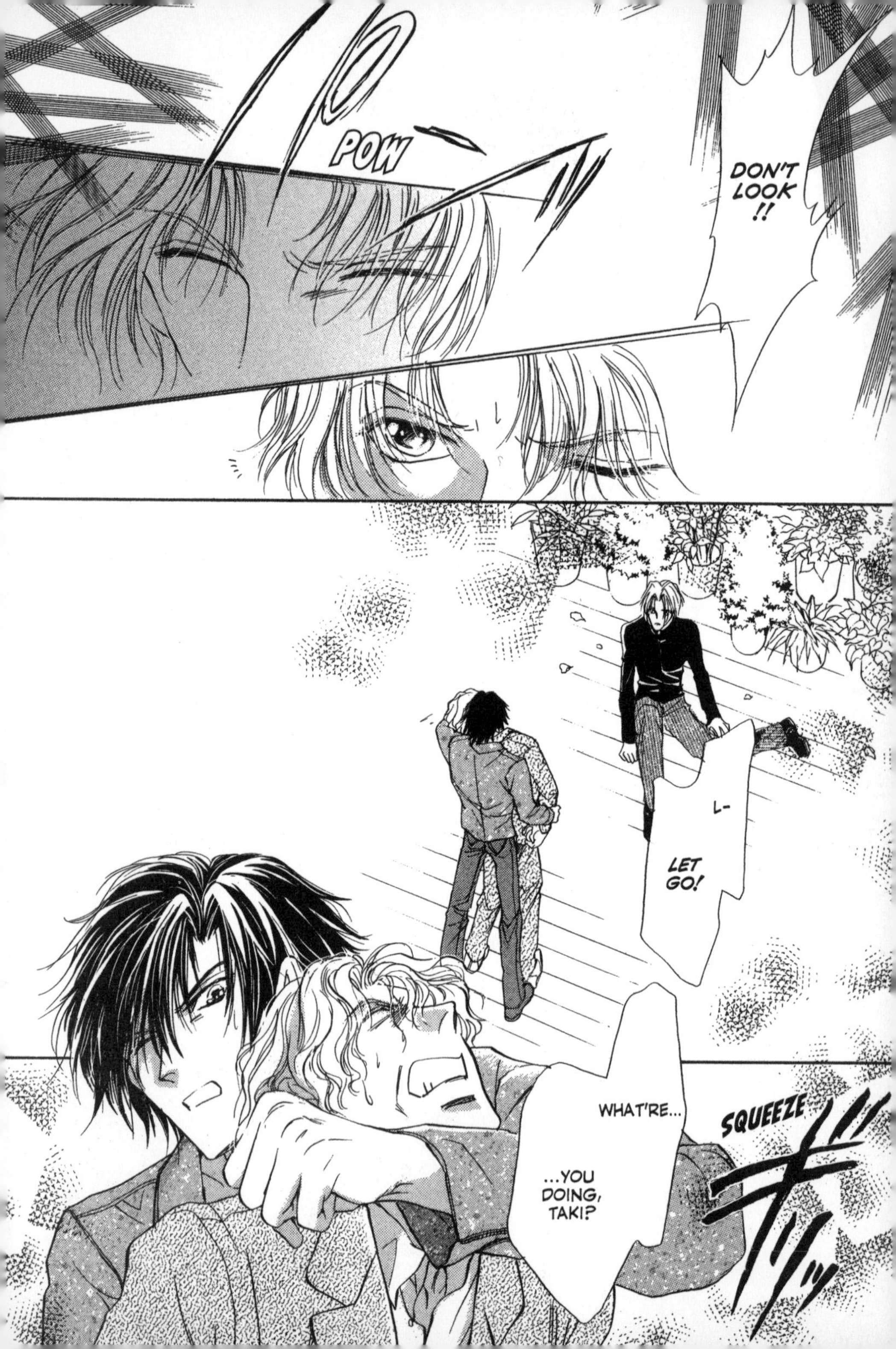
DON'T LOOK!!
POW
L-
LET GO!
SQUEEZE
WHAT'RE...
...YOU DOING, TAKI?

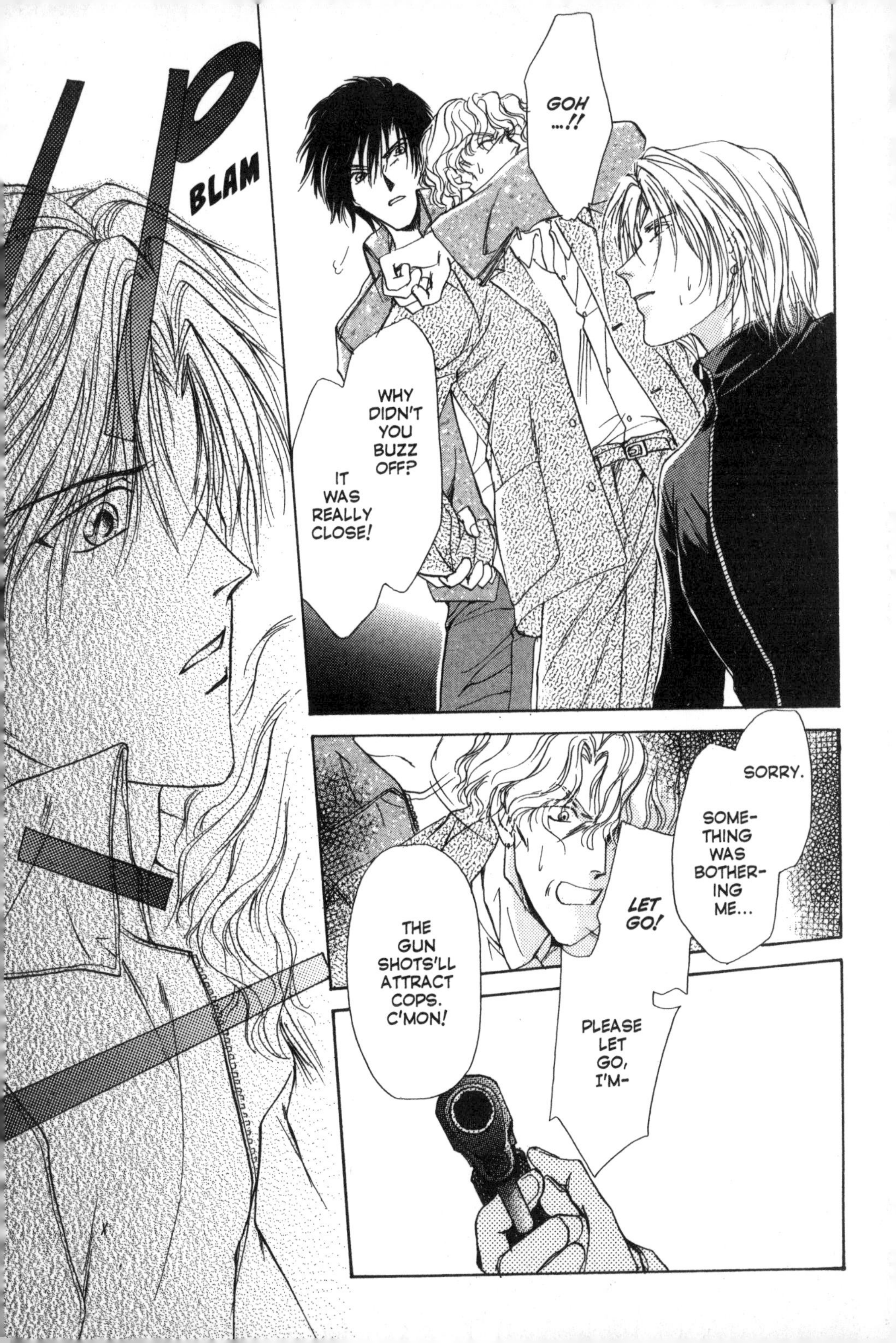
GOH ...!!
WHY DIDN'T YOU BUZZ OFF?
IT WAS REALLY CLOSE!
SORRY.
SOME-THING WAS BOTHER-ING ME...
LET GO!
THE GUN SHOTS'LL ATTRACT COPS. C'MON!
PLEASE LET GO, I'M-
BLAM

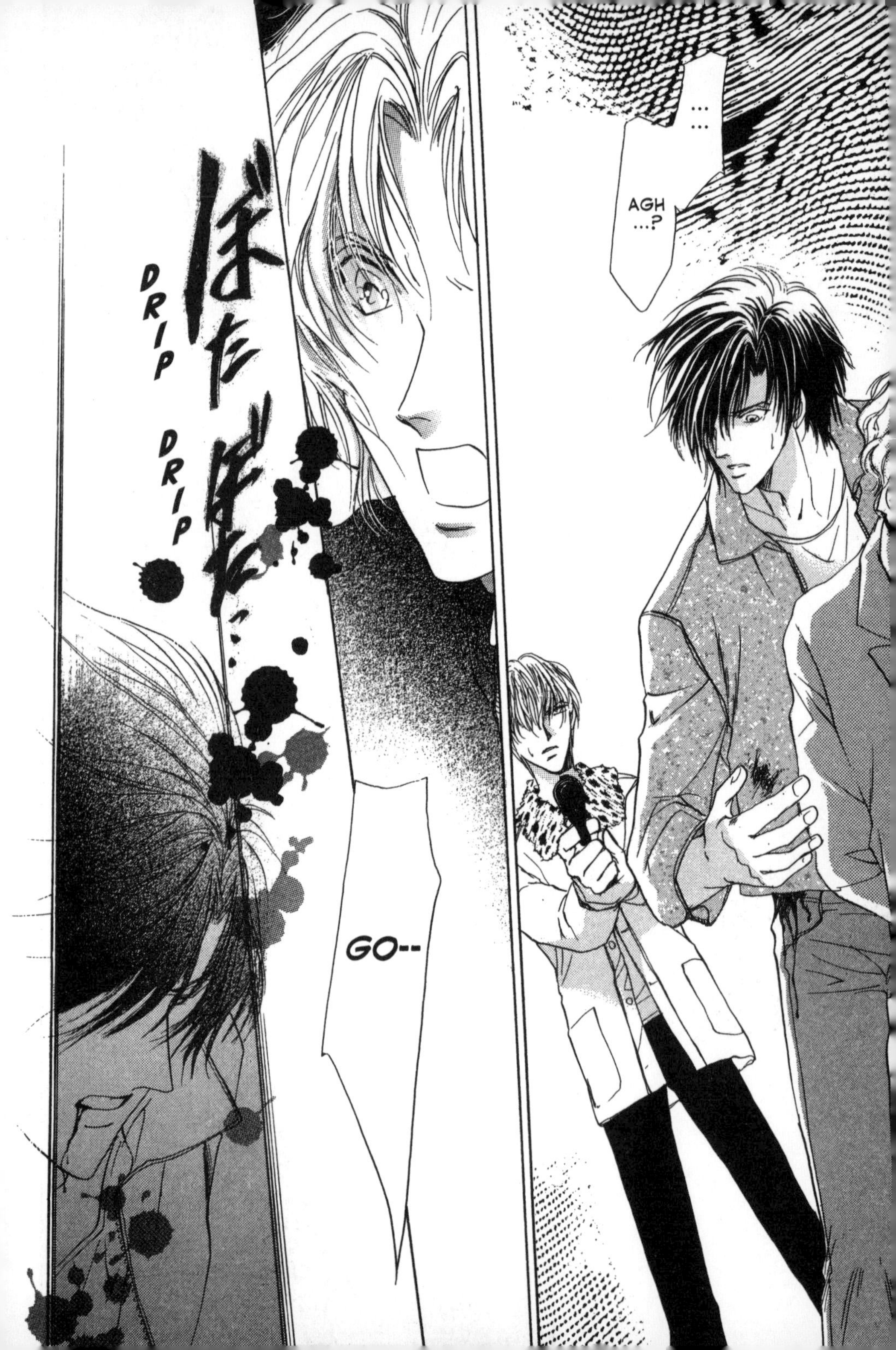
... ...
AGH ...?
GO--
ぼたぼたっ
DRIP DRIP DRIP

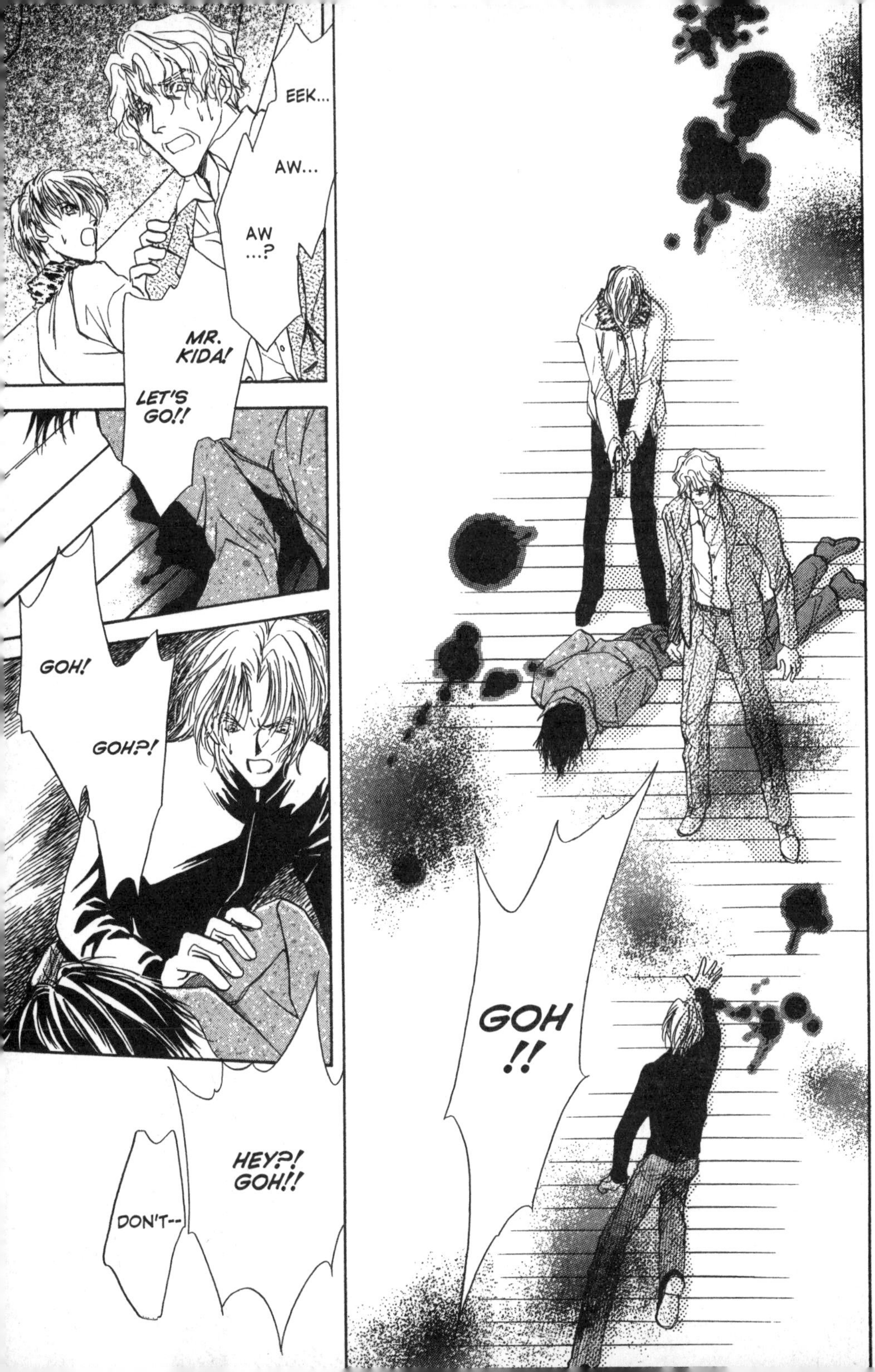
GOH !!
EEK...
AW...
AW ...?
MR. KIDA!
LET'S GO!!
GOH!
GOH?!
HEY?! GOH!!
DON'T--

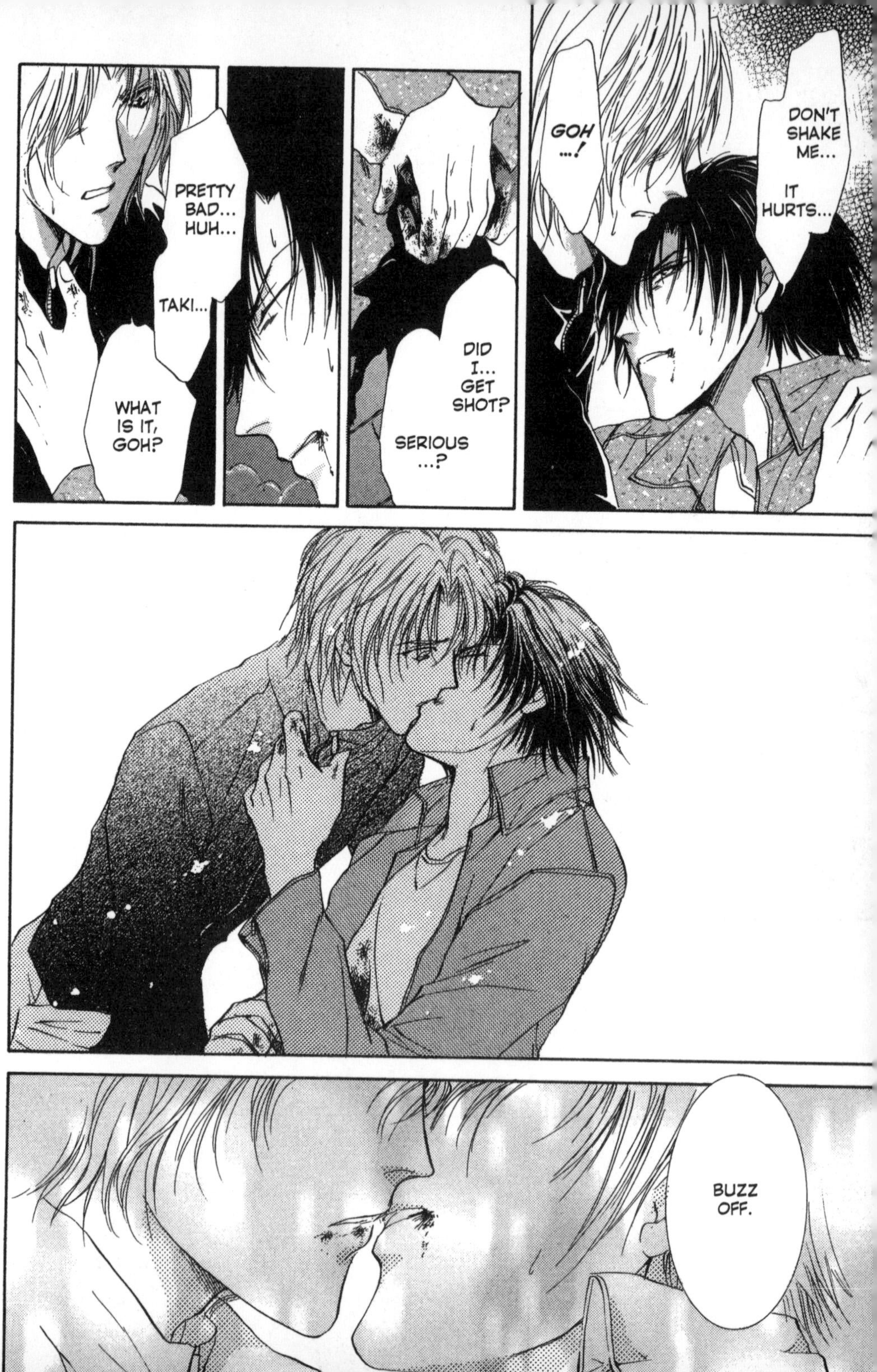
DON'T SHAKE ME...
IT HURTS...
GOH ...!
DID I... GET SHOT?
SERIOUS ...?
PRETTY BAD... HUH...
TAKI...
WHAT IS IT, GOH?
BUZZ OFF.

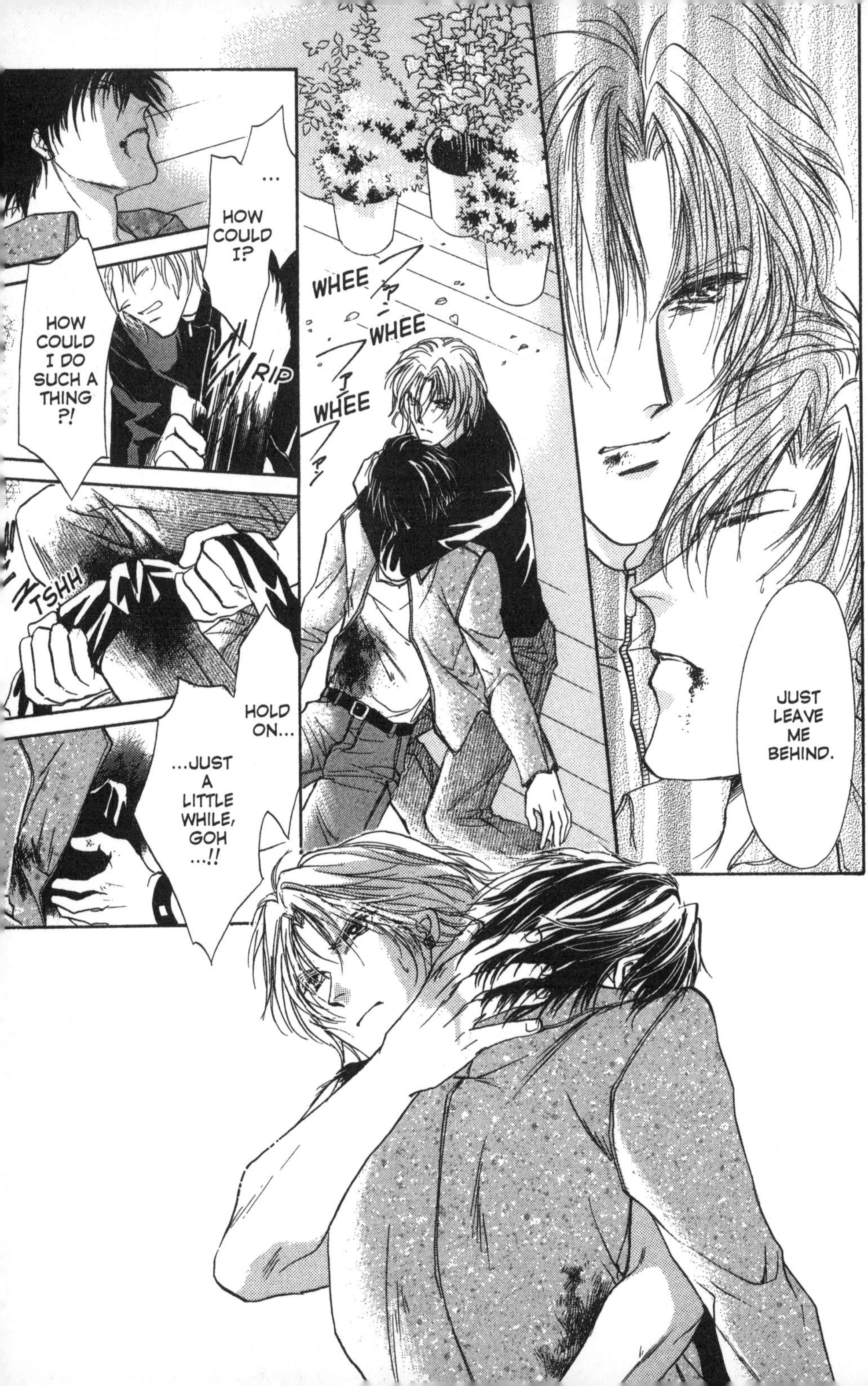
JUST LEAVE ME BEHIND.
WHEE
WHEE
WHEE
...
HOW COULD I?
HOW COULD I DO SUCH A THING ?!
RIP
TSHH
HOLD ON...
...JUST A LITTLE WHILE, GOH ...!!

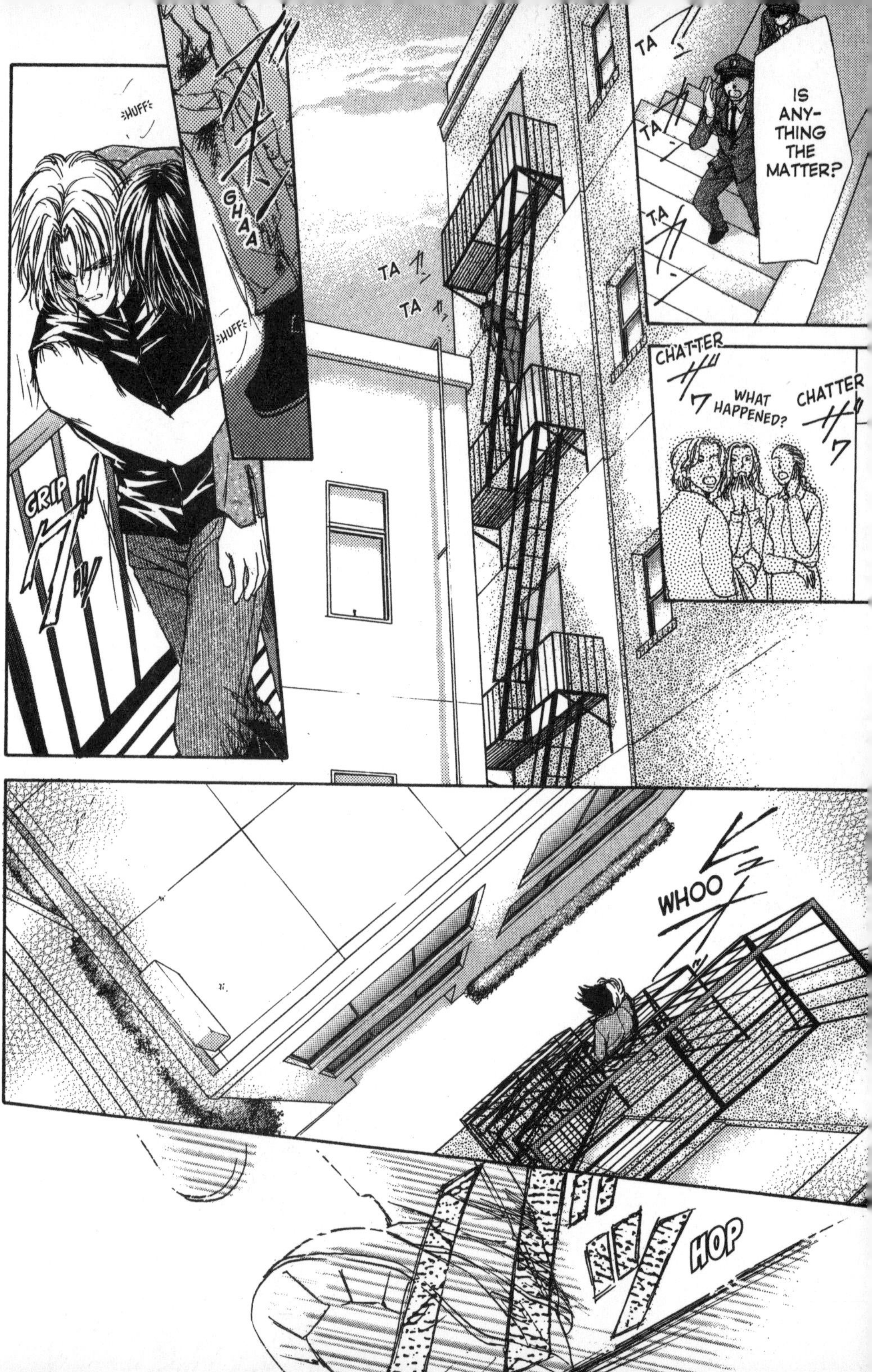
TA
TA
TA
IS ANYTHING THE MATTER?
CHATTER
CHATTER
WHAT HAPPENED?
TA
TA
GHAA
HUFF
HUFF
GRIP
WHOO
HOP

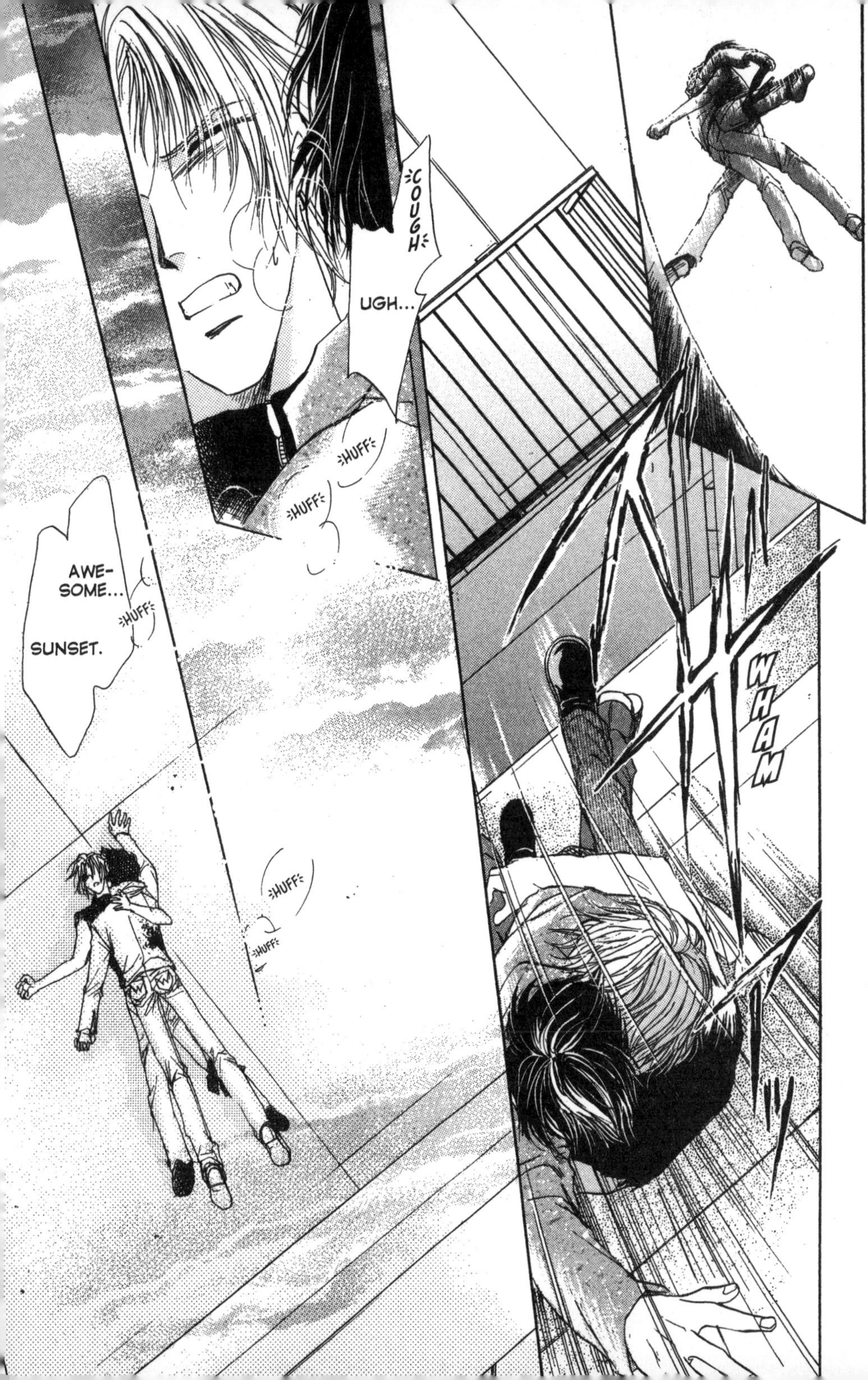
WHAM
COUGH
UGH...
HUFF
HUFF
AWESOME... HUFF SUNSET.
HUFF
HUFF

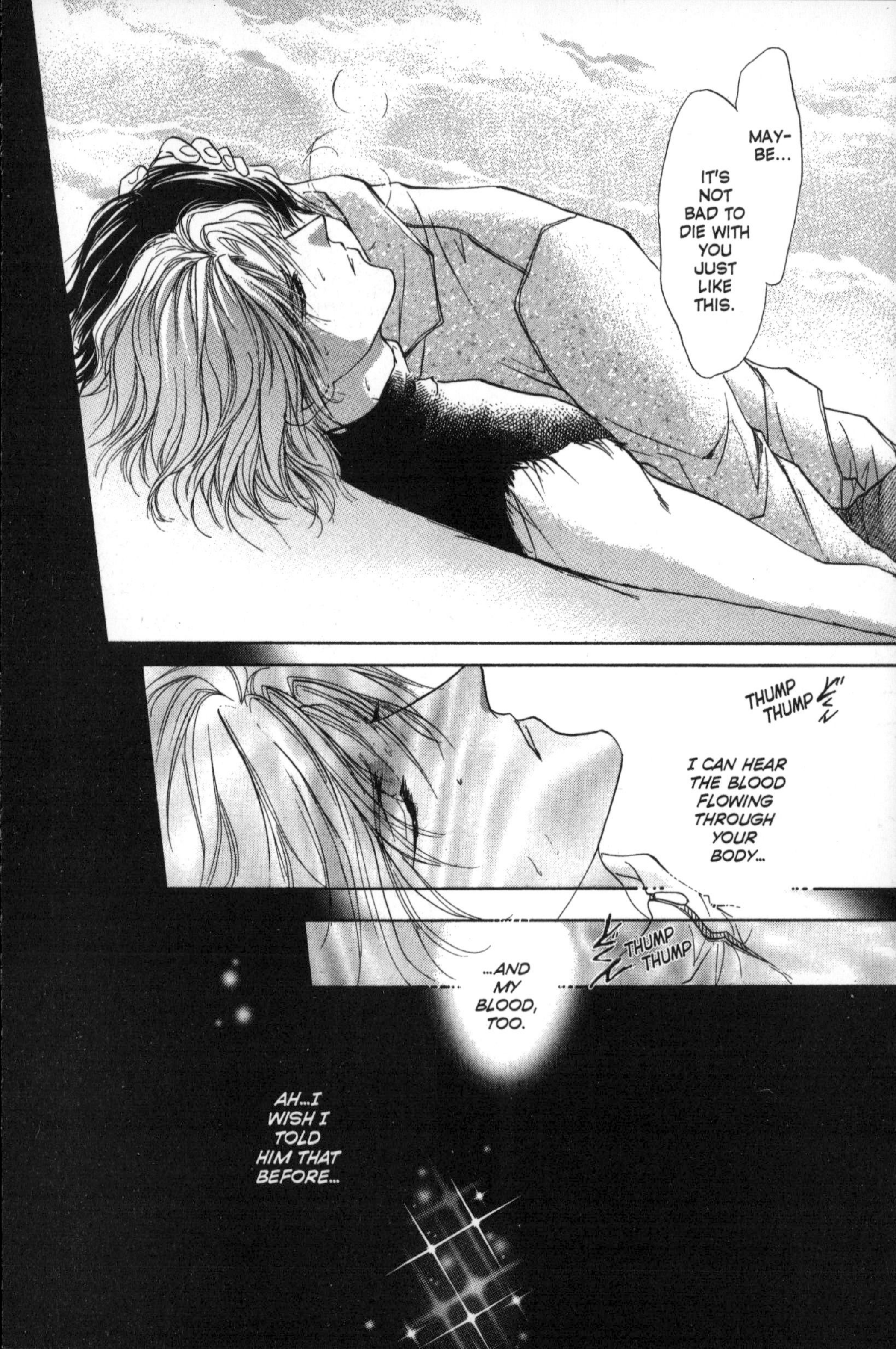
MAY-BE... IT'S NOT BAD TO DIE WITH YOU JUST LIKE THIS.
THUMP THUMP
I CAN HEAR THE BLOOD FLOWING THROUGH YOUR BODY...
THUMP THUMP
...AND MY BLOOD, TOO.
AH...I WISH I TOLD HIM THAT BEFORE...

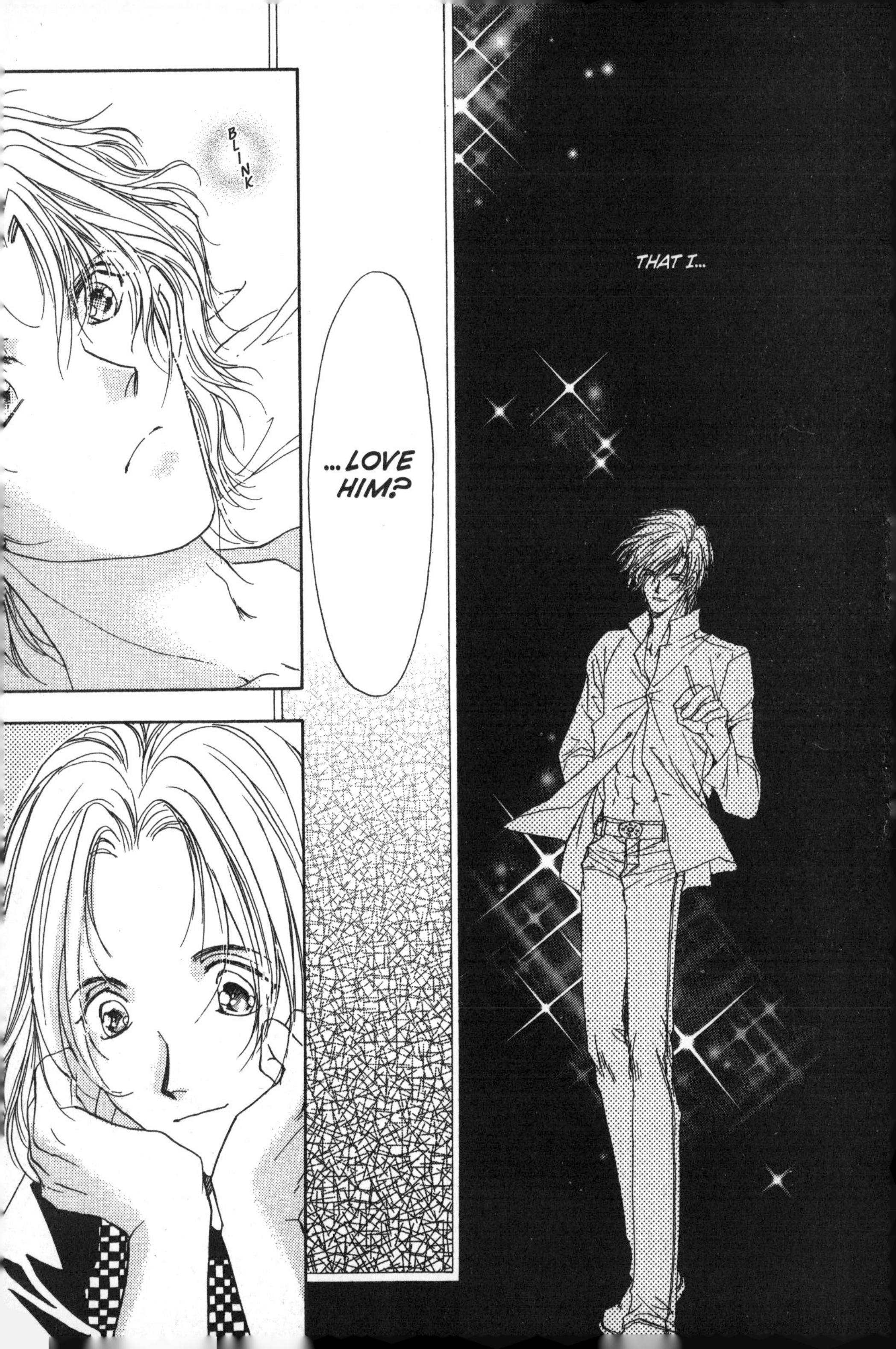
THAT I...
...LOVE HIM?
BLINK

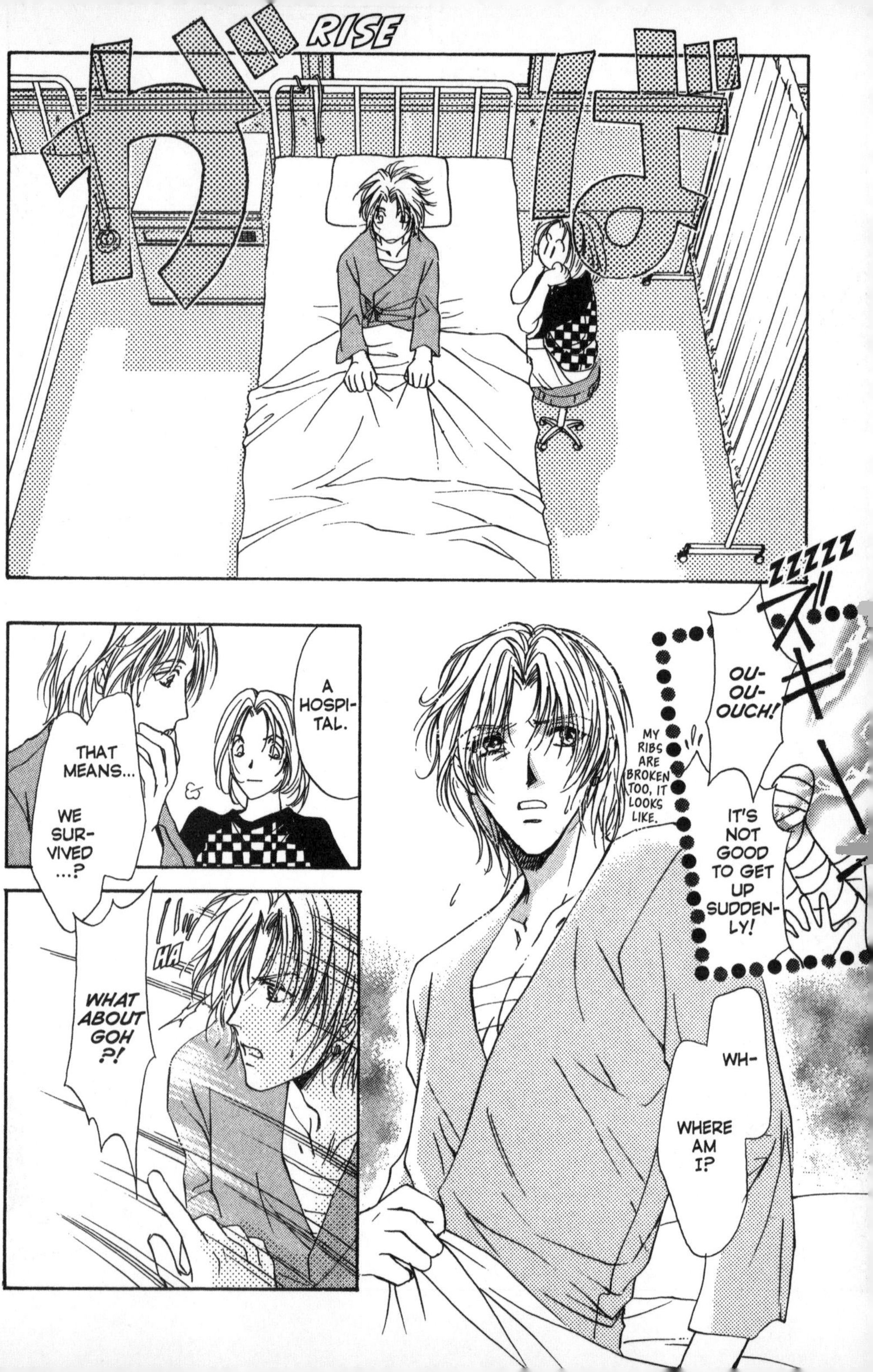
RISE
ZZZZZ
OU-OU-OUCH!
IT'S NOT GOOD TO GET UP SUDDENLY!
MY RIBS ARE BROKEN TOO, IT LOOKS LIKE.
WH-
WHERE AM I?
A HOSPITAL.
THAT MEANS...
WE SURVIVED ...?
HA
WHAT ABOUT GOH ?!

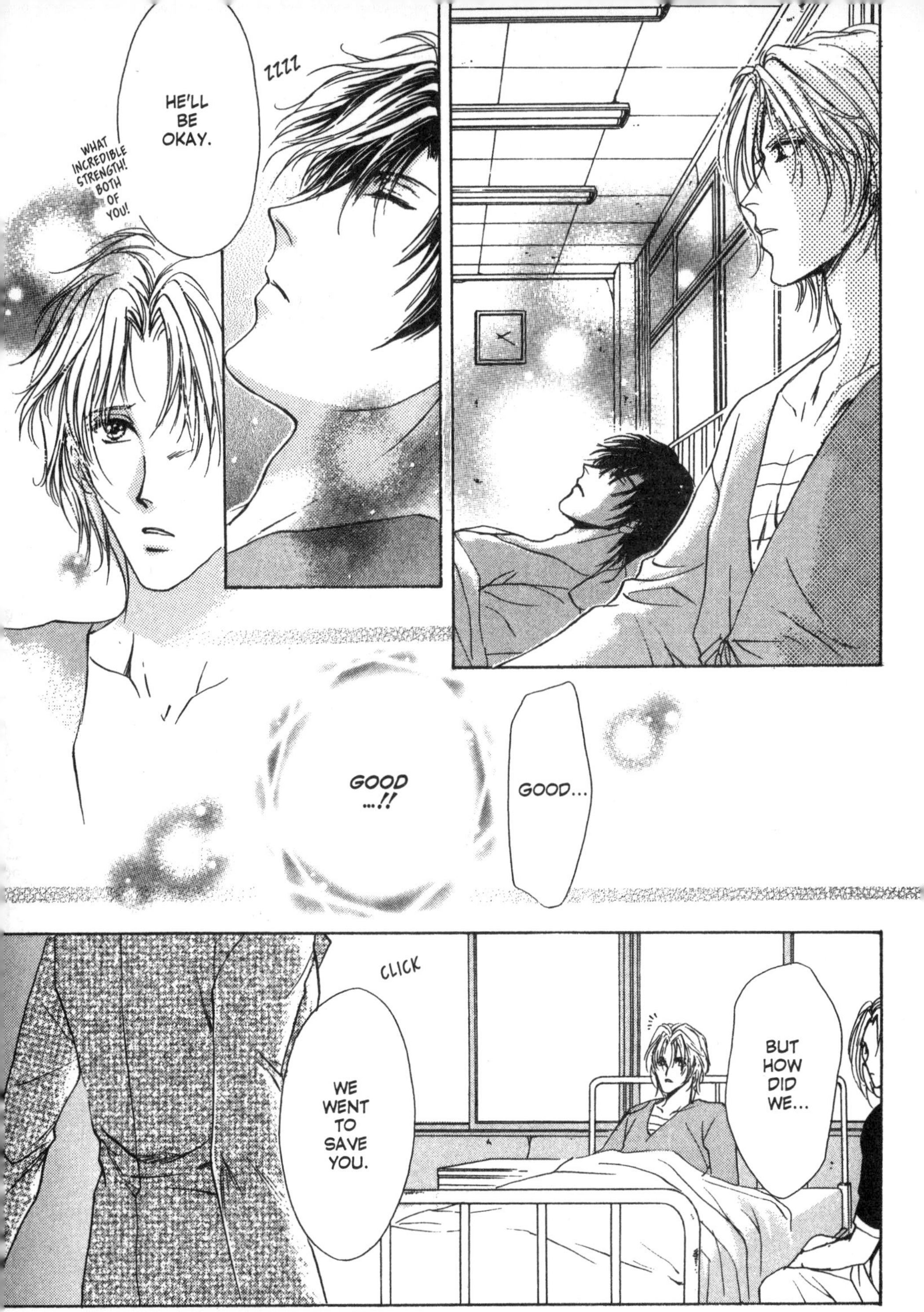
ZZZZ
HE'LL BE OKAY.
WHAT INCREDIBLE STRENGTH! BOTH OF YOU!
GOOD...
GOOD ...!!
BUT HOW DID WE...
CLICK
WE WENT TO SAVE YOU.

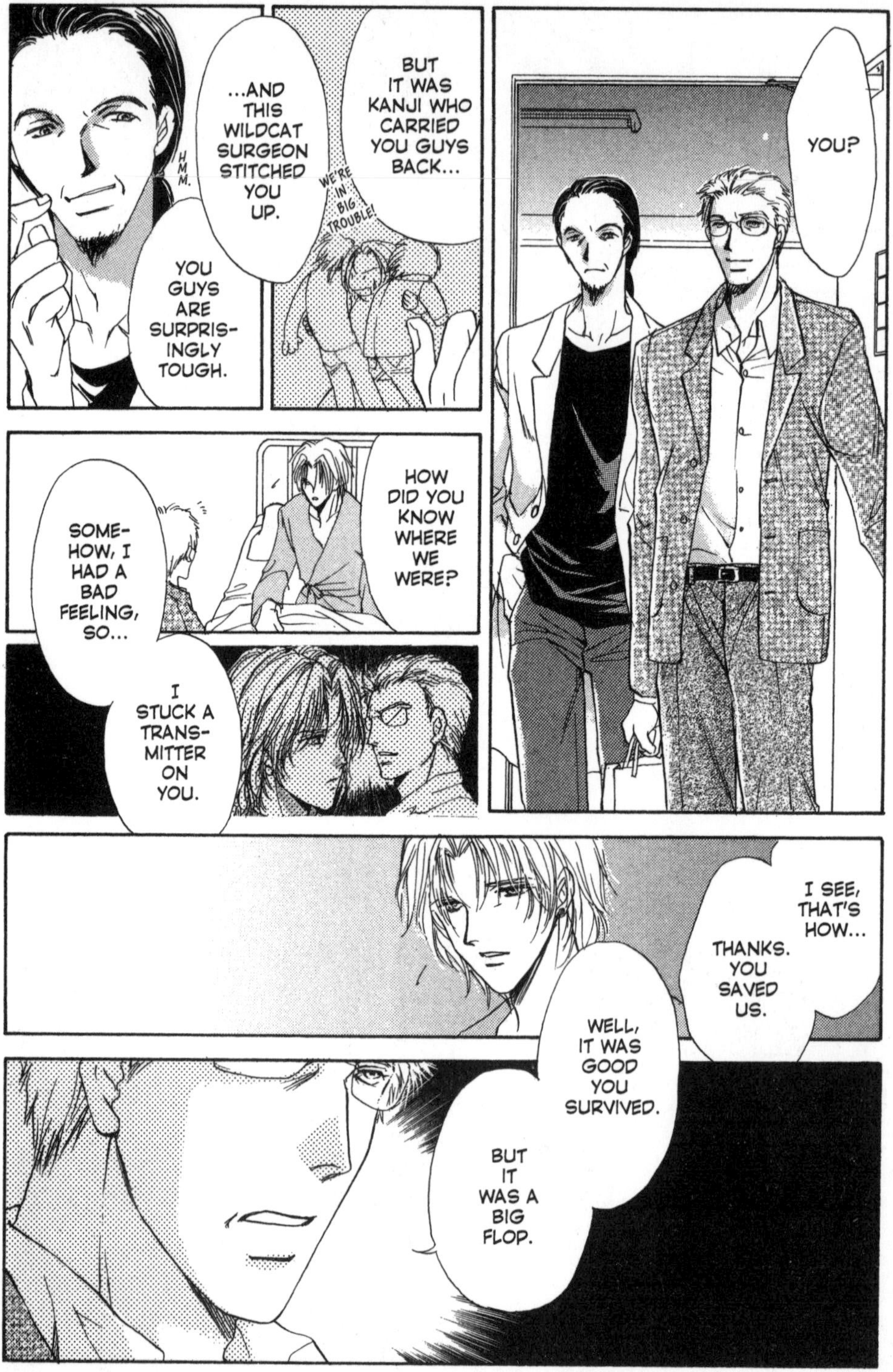
YOU?
BUT IT WAS KANJI WHO CARRIED YOU GUYS BACK...
WE'RE IN BIG TROUBLE!
...AND THIS WILDCAT SURGEON STITCHED YOU UP.
HMM.
YOU GUYS ARE SURPRISINGLY TOUGH.
HOW DID YOU KNOW WHERE WE WERE?
SOMEHOW, I HAD A BAD FEELING, SO...
I STUCK A TRANSMITTER ON YOU.
I SEE, THAT'S HOW...
THANKS. YOU SAVED US.
WELL, IT WAS GOOD YOU SURVIVED.
BUT IT WAS A BIG FLOP.

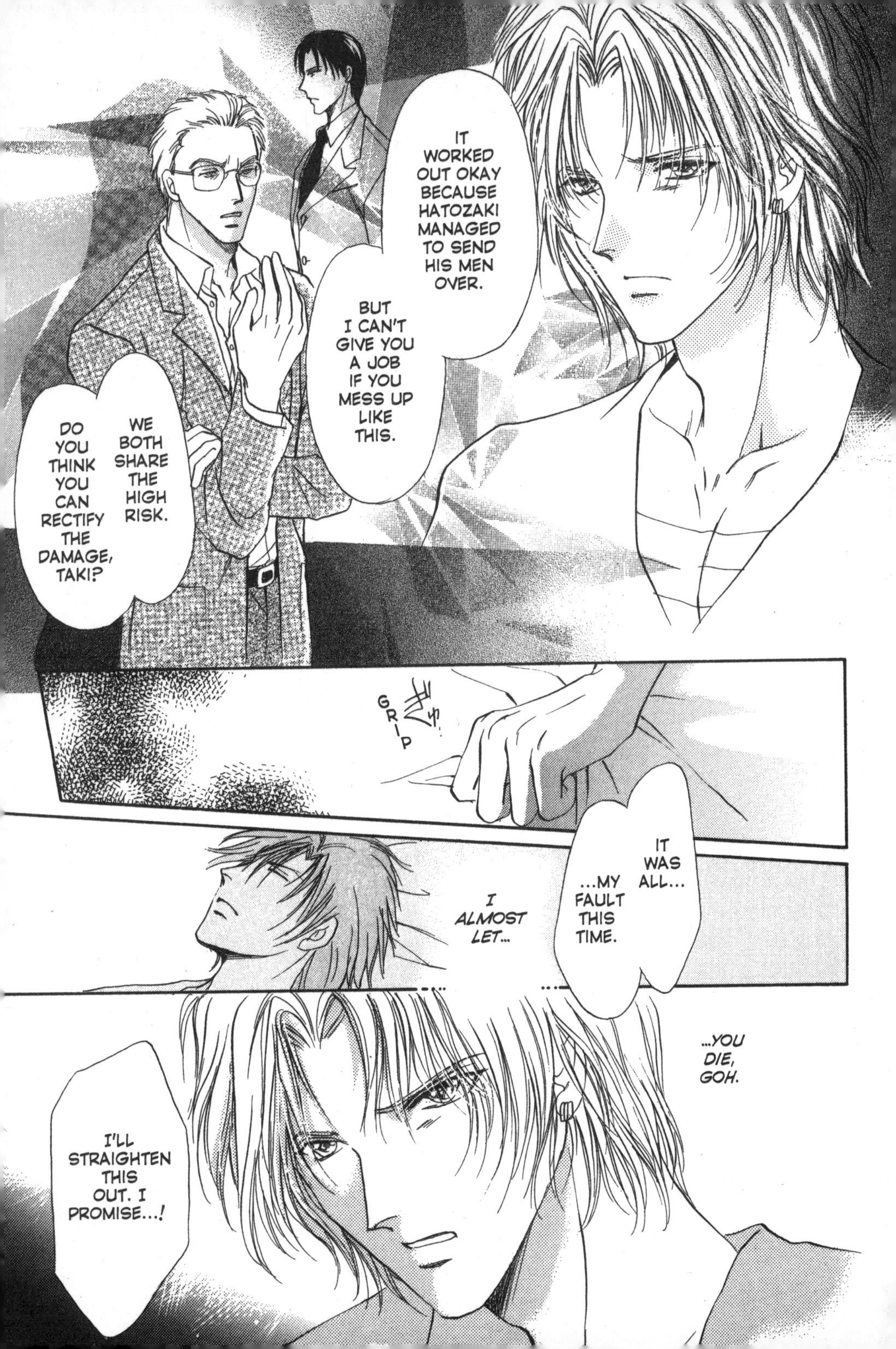
IT WORKED OUT OKAY BECAUSE HATOZAKI MANAGED TO SEND HIS MEN OVER.
BUT I CAN'T GIVE YOU A JOB IF YOU MESS UP LIKE THIS.
WE BOTH SHARE THE HIGH RISK.
DO YOU THINK YOU CAN RECTIFY THE DAMAGE, TAKI?
GRIP
IT WAS ALL...
...MY FAULT THIS TIME.
I ALMOST LET...
...YOU DIE, GOH.
I'LL STRAIGHTEN THIS OUT. I PROMISE...!

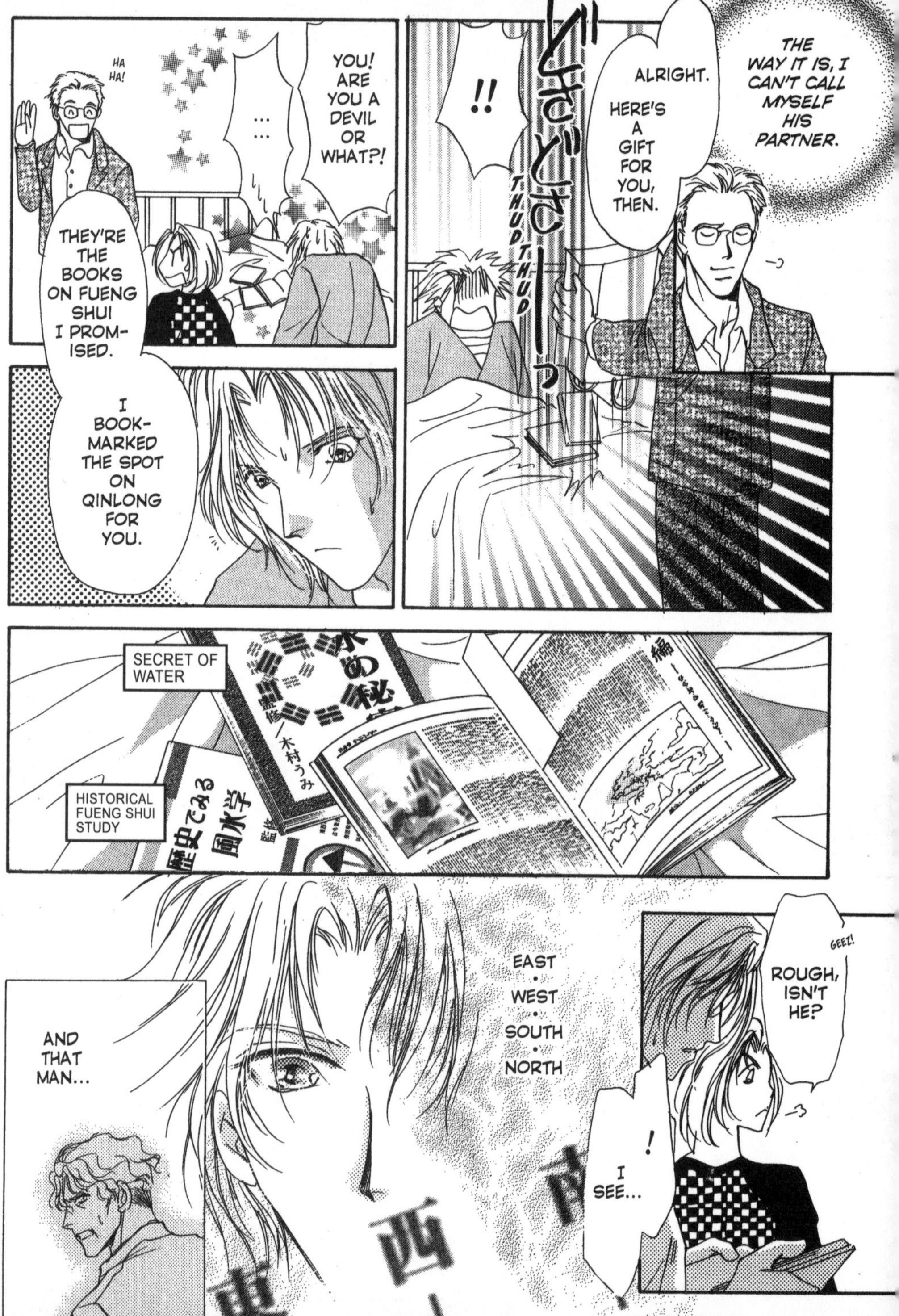
THE WAY IT IS, I CAN'T CALL MYSELF HIS PARTNER.
ALRIGHT.
HERE'S A GIFT FOR YOU, THEN.
THUD THUD
!!
HA HA!
YOU! ARE YOU A DEVIL OR WHAT?!
… …
THEY'RE THE BOOKS ON FUENG SHUI I PROMISED.
I BOOKMARKED THE SPOT ON QINLONG FOR YOU.
SECRET OF WATER
HISTORICAL FUENG SHUI STUDY
GEEZ!
ROUGH, ISN'T HE?
!
I SEE…
EAST • WEST • SOUTH • NORTH
AND THAT MAN…

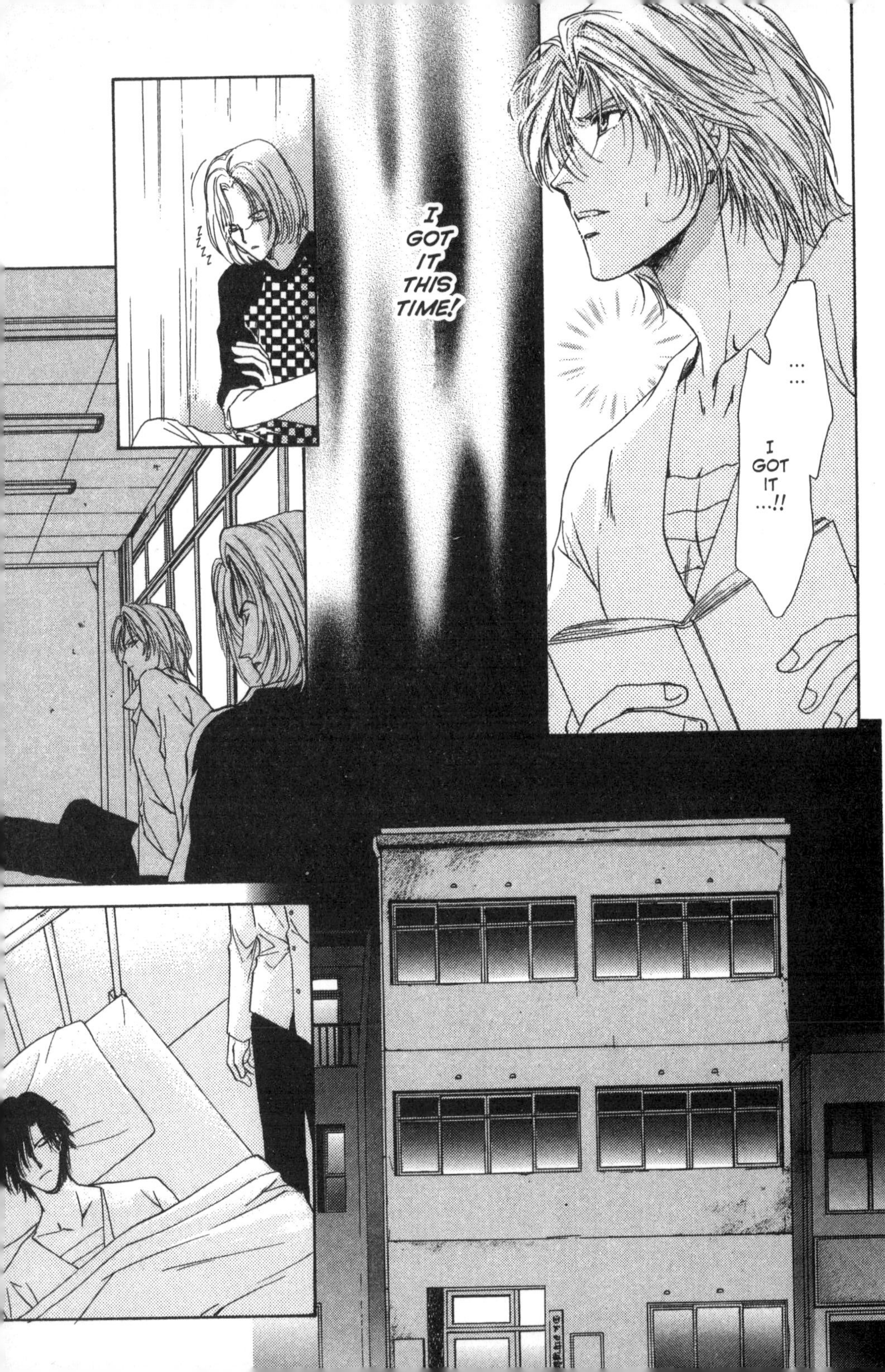
... ...
I GOT IT ...!!
I GOT IT THIS TIME!
ZZZ

...I'LL BE RIGHT BACK, PARTNER.

SORRY ABOUT LETTING YOU GET SHOT.

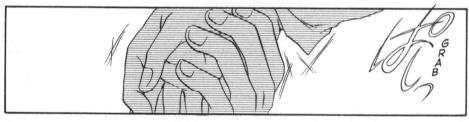

GRAB

WHERE?

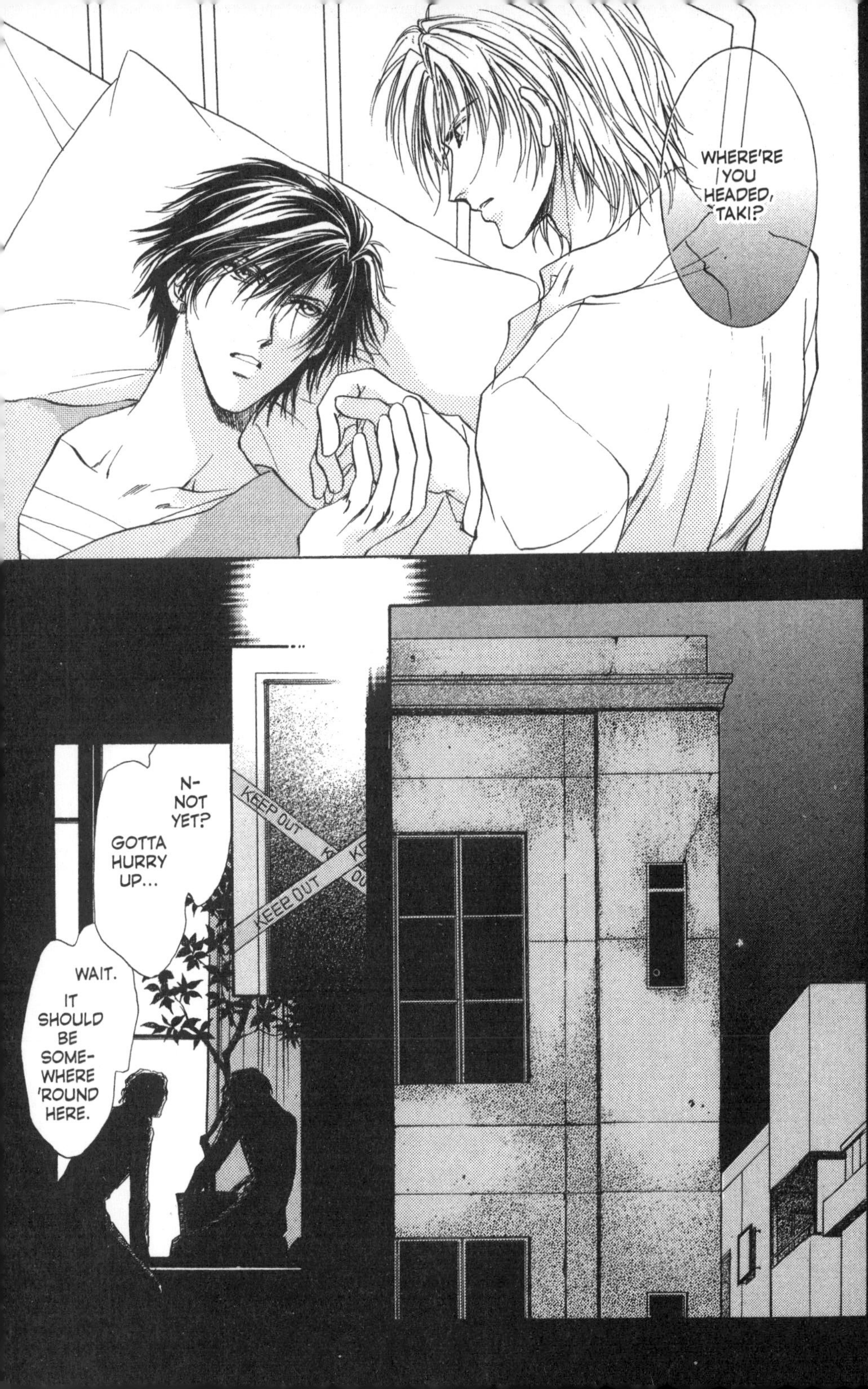
WHERE'RE YOU HEADED, TAKI?
KEEP OUT
N-NOT YET? GOTTA HURRY UP...
WAIT. IT SHOULD BE SOMEWHERE 'ROUND HERE.

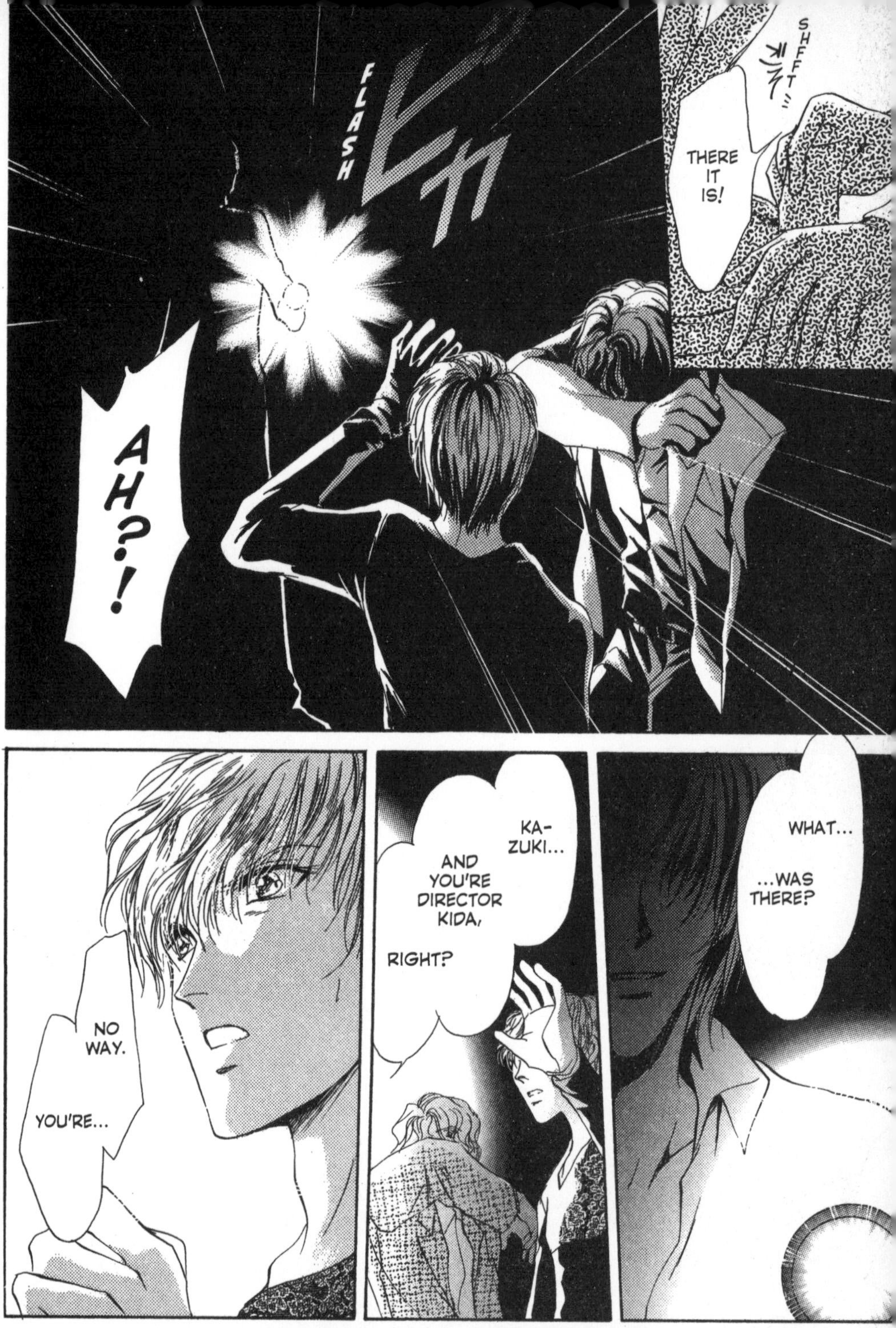
SHFFT!!
THERE IT IS!
FLASH
AH?!
WHAT...
...WAS THERE?
KA-ZUKI...
AND YOU'RE DIRECTOR KIDA,
RIGHT?
NO WAY.
YOU'RE...

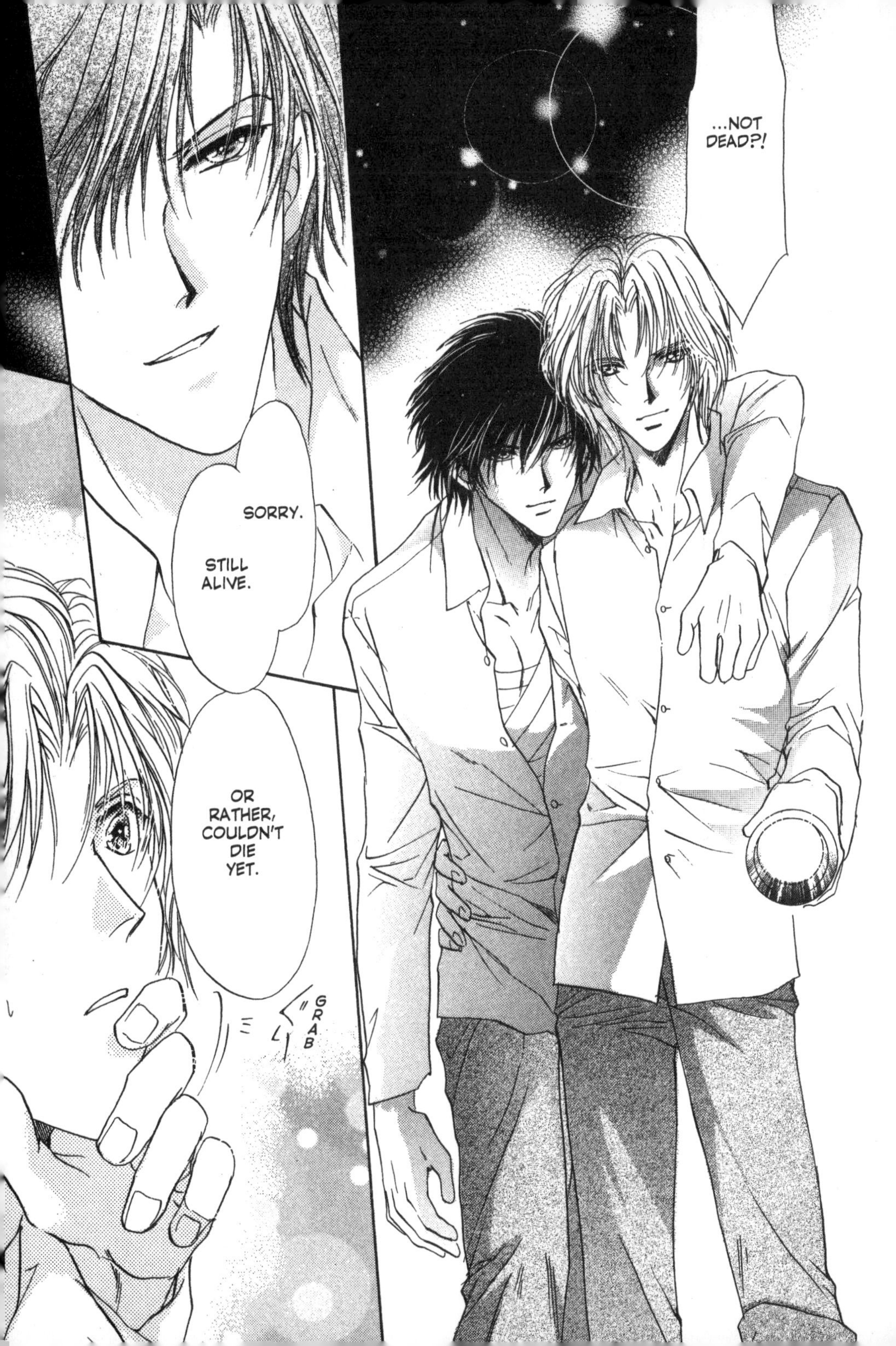
...NOT DEAD?!
SORRY.
STILL ALIVE.
OR RATHER, COULDN'T DIE YET.
GRAB

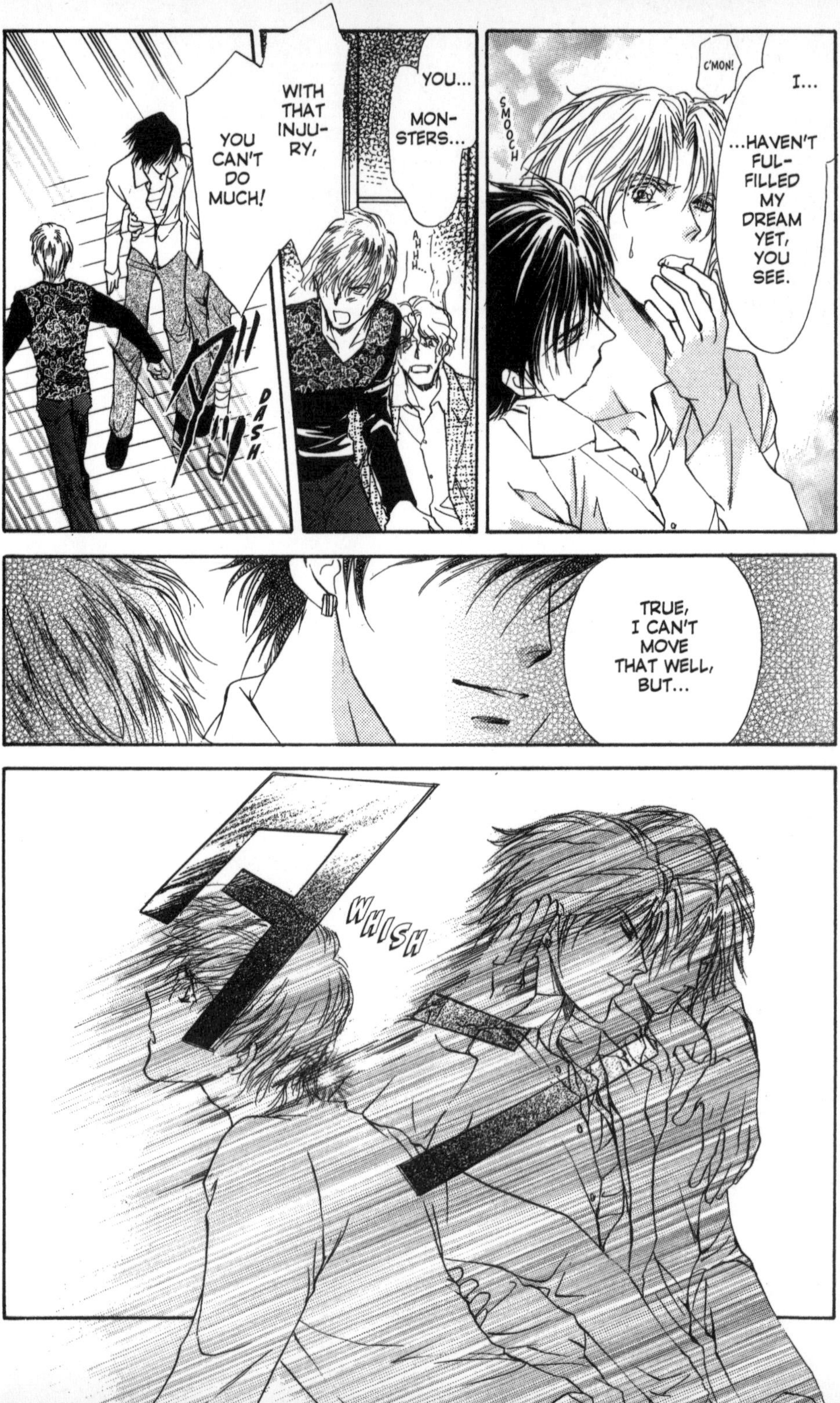
I...
C'MON!
SMOOCH
...HAVEN'T FUL-FILLED MY DREAM YET, YOU SEE.
YOU...
MON-STERS...
AHHH...
WITH THAT INJU-RY,
YOU CAN'T DO MUCH!
DASH
TRUE, I CAN'T MOVE THAT WELL, BUT...
WHISH

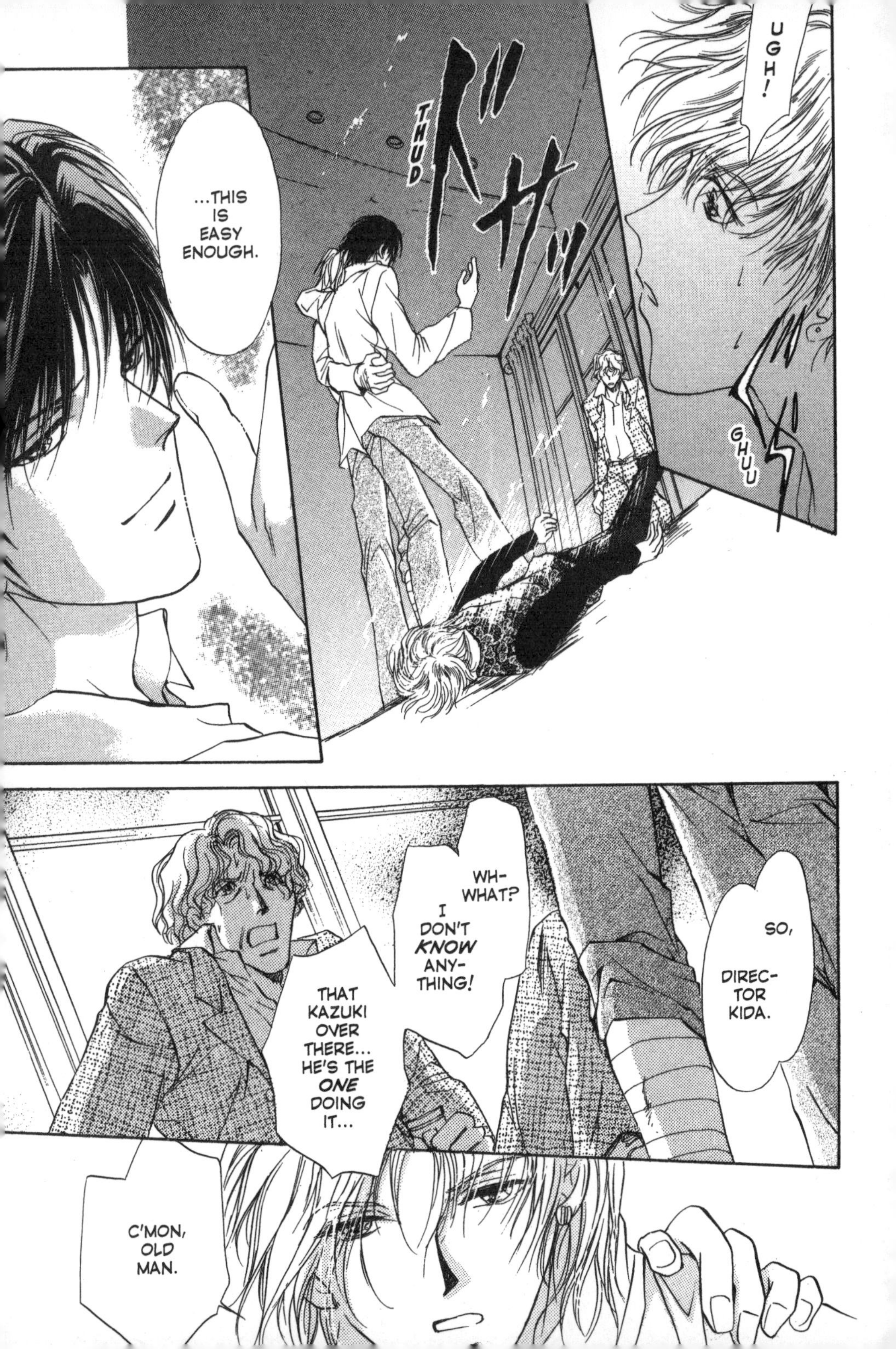
UGH!
GHUU
THUD
...THIS IS EASY ENOUGH.
SO, DIRECTOR KIDA.
WH-WHAT? I DON'T *KNOW* ANYTHING!
THAT KAZUKI OVER THERE... HE'S THE *ONE* DOING IT...
C'MON, OLD MAN.

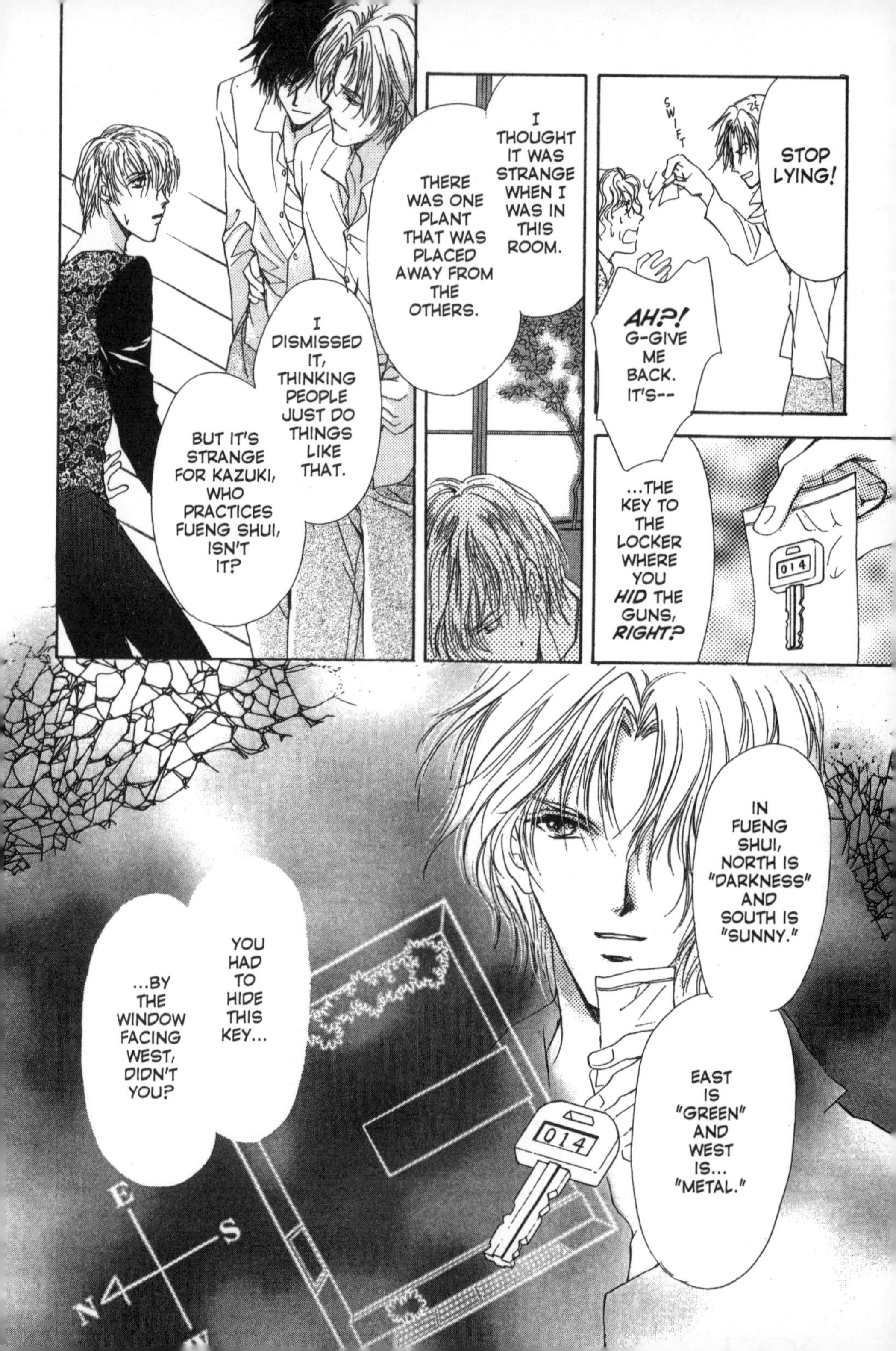
STOP LYING!
SWIFT
AH?! G-GIVE ME BACK. IT'S--
...THE KEY TO THE LOCKER WHERE YOU HID THE GUNS, RIGHT?
I THOUGHT IT WAS STRANGE WHEN I WAS IN THIS ROOM.
THERE WAS ONE PLANT THAT WAS PLACED AWAY FROM THE OTHERS.
I DISMISSED IT, THINKING PEOPLE JUST DO THINGS LIKE THAT.
BUT IT'S STRANGE FOR KAZUKI, WHO PRACTICES FUENG SHUI, ISN'T IT?
IN FUENG SHUI, NORTH IS "DARKNESS" AND SOUTH IS "SUNNY."
EAST IS "GREEN" AND WEST IS... "METAL."
YOU HAD TO HIDE THIS KEY...
...BY THE WINDOW FACING WEST, DIDN'T YOU?

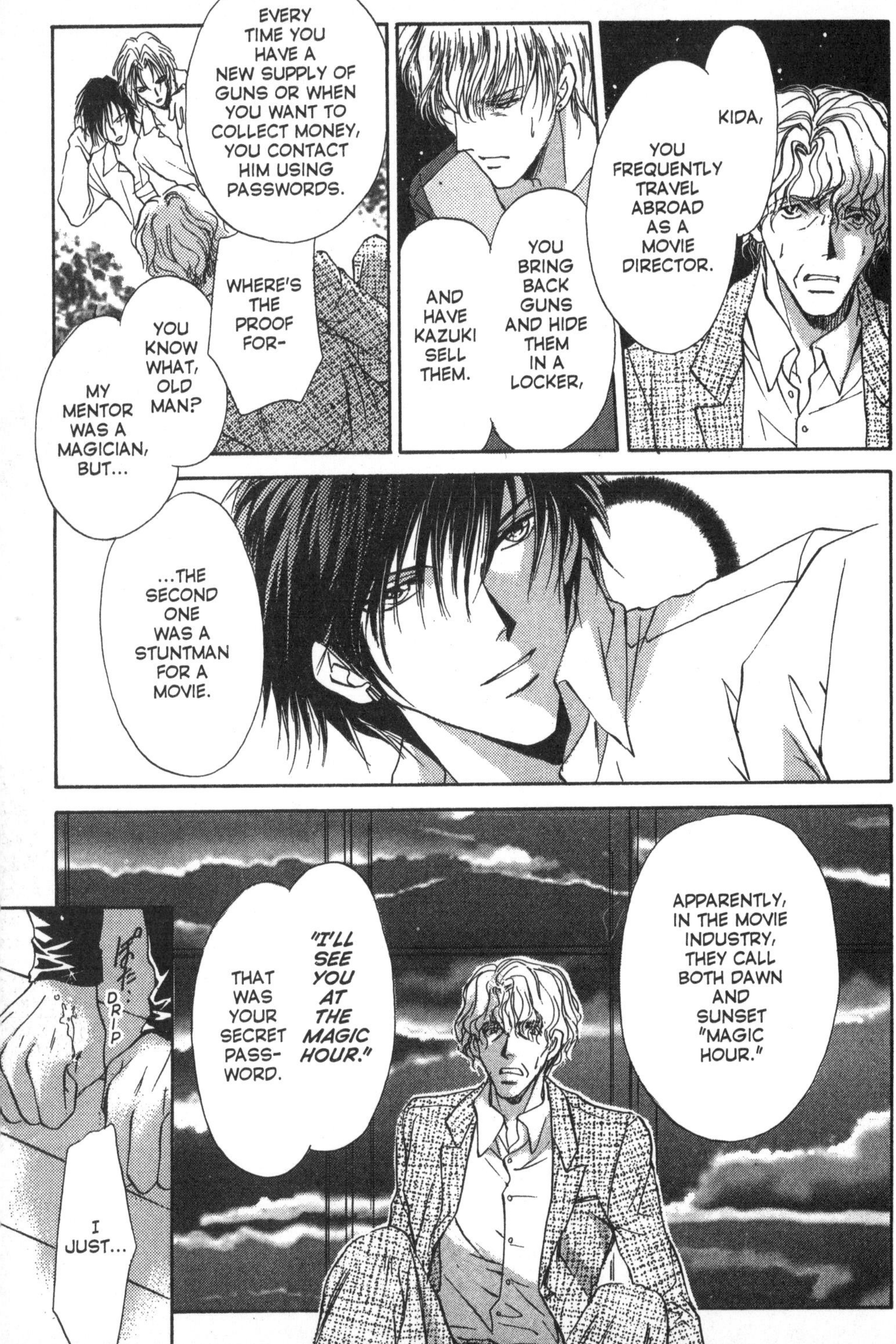
KIDA,
YOU FREQUENTLY TRAVEL ABROAD AS A MOVIE DIRECTOR.
YOU BRING BACK GUNS AND HIDE THEM IN A LOCKER,
AND HAVE KAZUKI SELL THEM.
EVERY TIME YOU HAVE A NEW SUPPLY OF GUNS OR WHEN YOU WANT TO COLLECT MONEY, YOU CONTACT HIM USING PASSWORDS.
WHERE'S THE PROOF FOR-
YOU KNOW WHAT, OLD MAN?
MY MENTOR WAS A MAGICIAN, BUT...
...THE SECOND ONE WAS A STUNTMAN FOR A MOVIE.
APPARENTLY, IN THE MOVIE INDUSTRY, THEY CALL BOTH DAWN AND SUNSET "MAGIC HOUR."
"I'LL SEE YOU AT THE MAGIC HOUR."
THAT WAS YOUR SECRET PASS-WORD.
DRIP
I JUST...

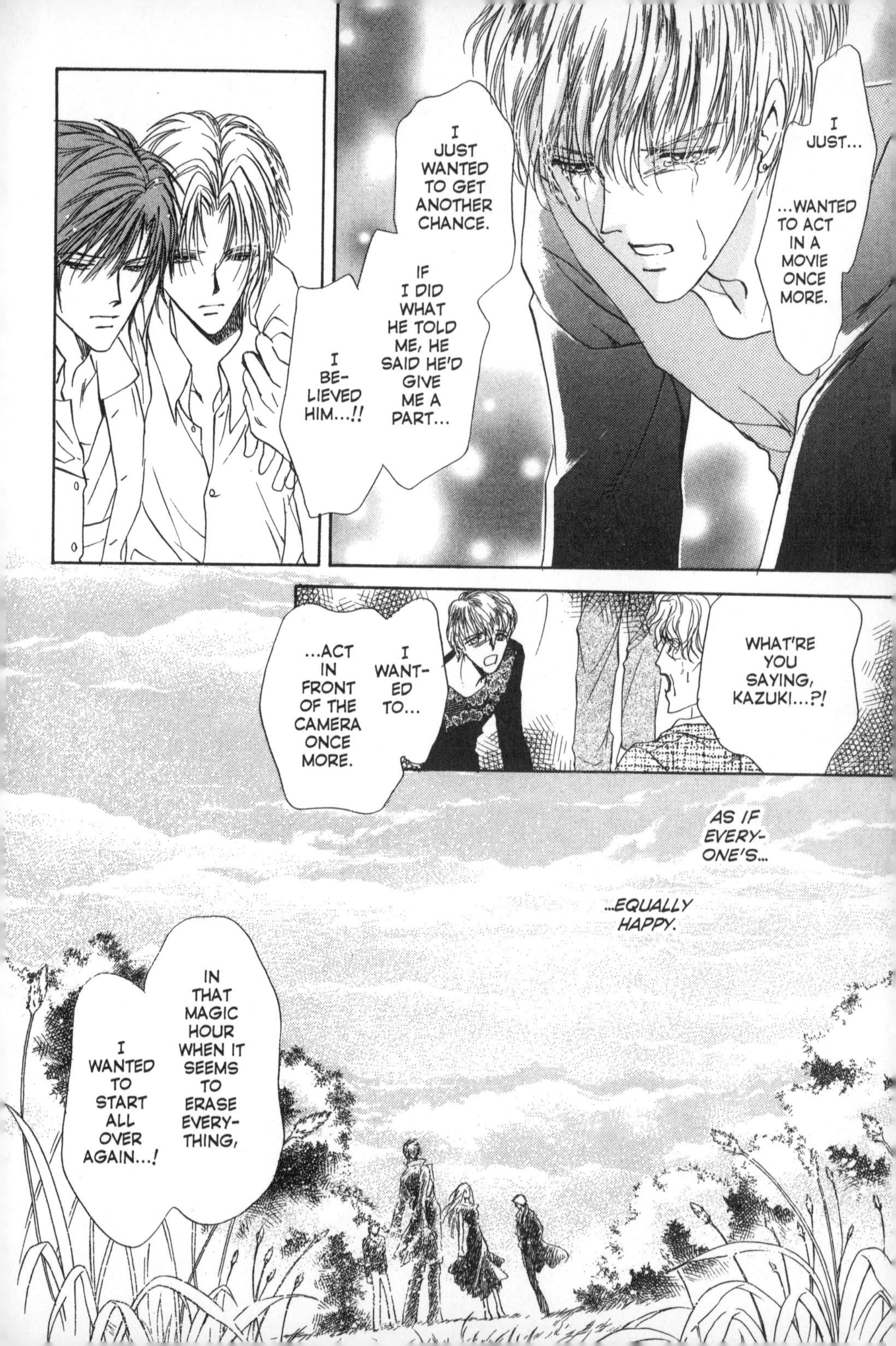
I JUST...
...WANTED TO ACT IN A MOVIE ONCE MORE.
I JUST WANTED TO GET ANOTHER CHANCE.
IF I DID WHAT HE TOLD ME, HE SAID HE'D GIVE ME A PART...
I BE-LIEVED HIM...!!
WHAT'RE YOU SAYING, KAZUKI...?!
I WANT-ED TO...
...ACT IN FRONT OF THE CAMERA ONCE MORE.
AS IF EVERY-ONE'S...
...EQUALLY HAPPY.
IN THAT MAGIC HOUR WHEN IT SEEMS TO ERASE EVERY-THING,
I WANTED TO START ALL OVER AGAIN...!

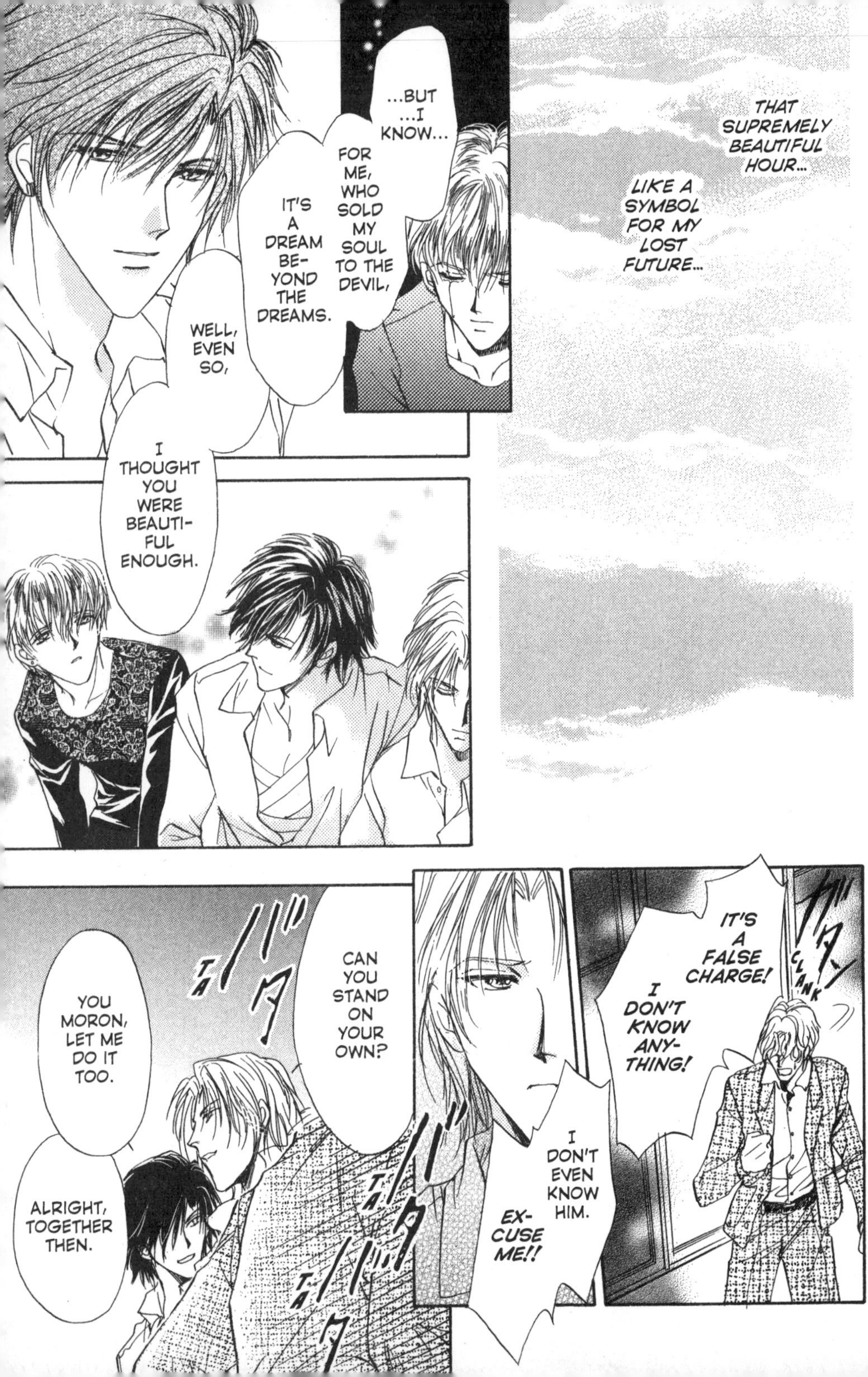

THAT SUPREMELY BEAUTIFUL HOUR...
LIKE A SYMBOL FOR MY LOST FUTURE...
...BUT ...I KNOW...
FOR ME, WHO SOLD MY SOUL TO THE DEVIL,
IT'S A DREAM BE-YOND THE DREAMS.
WELL, EVEN SO,
I THOUGHT YOU WERE BEAUTI-FUL ENOUGH.
IT'S A FALSE CHARGE!
I DON'T KNOW ANY-THING!
CLANK
I DON'T EVEN KNOW HIM.
EX-CUSE ME!!
TA
TA
CAN YOU STAND ON YOUR OWN?
TA
YOU MORON, LET ME DO IT TOO.
ALRIGHT, TOGETHER THEN.

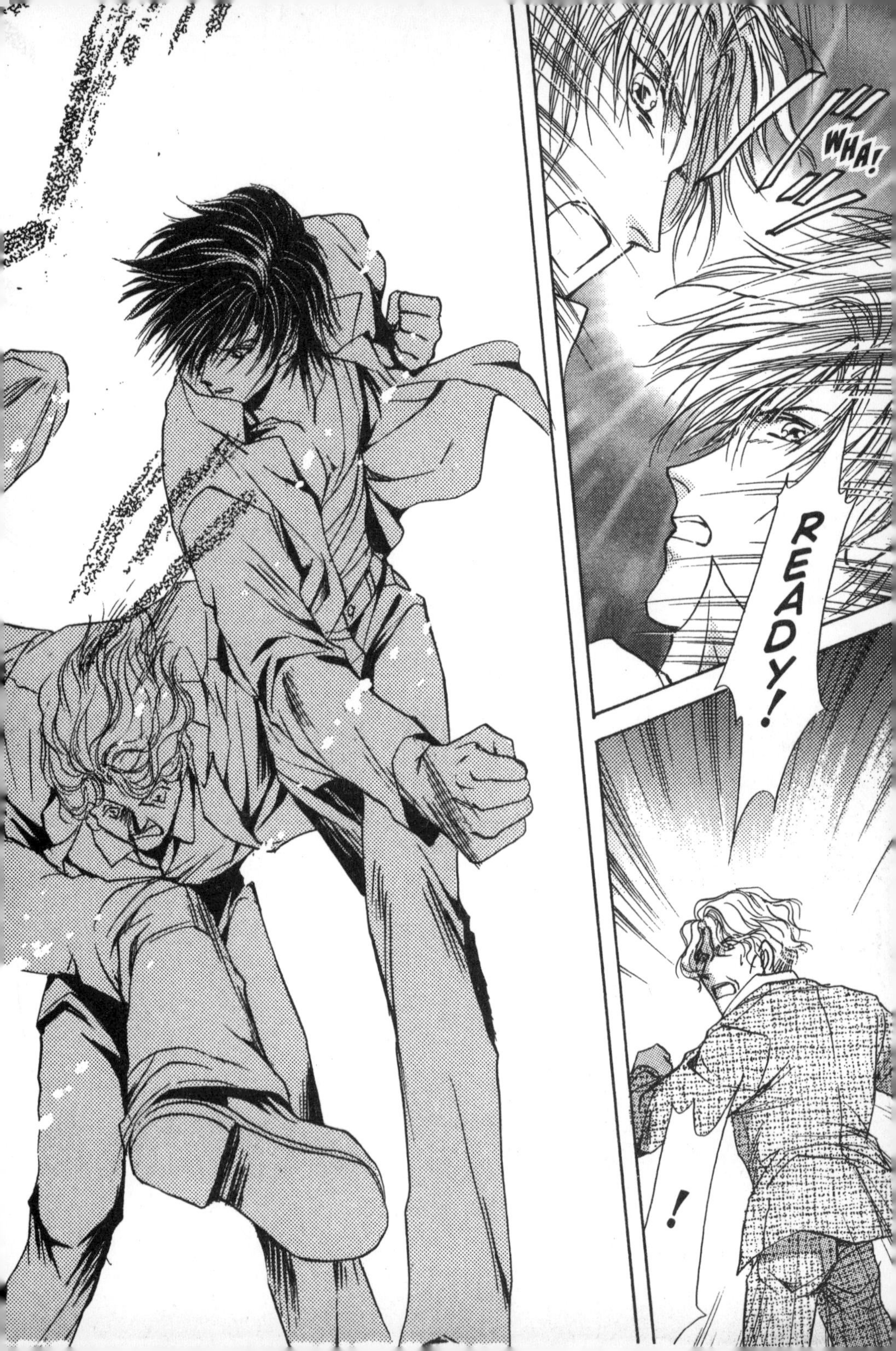
WHA!
READY!
!

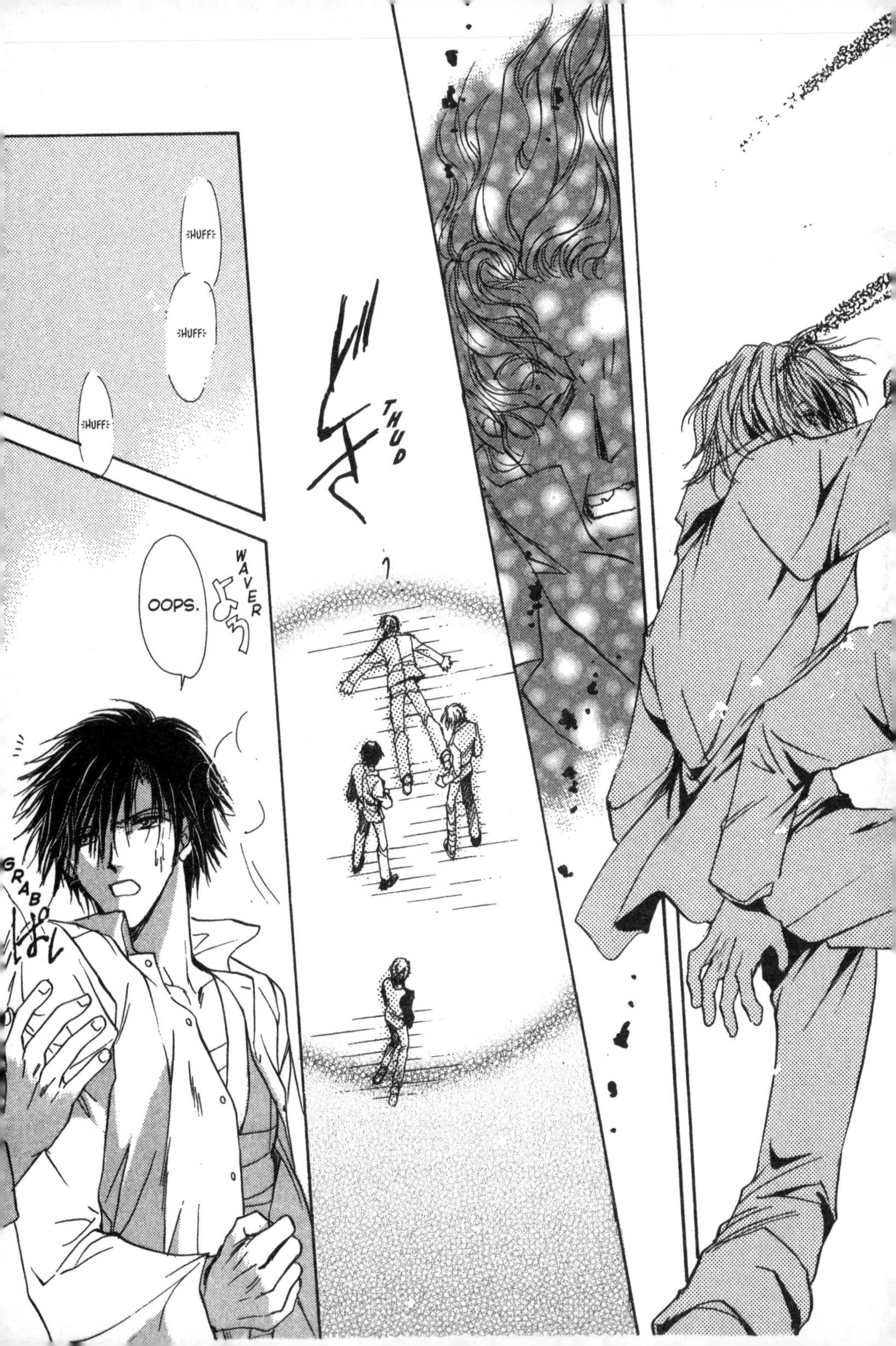
THUD
HUFF
HUFF
HUFF
OOPS.
WAVER
GRAB

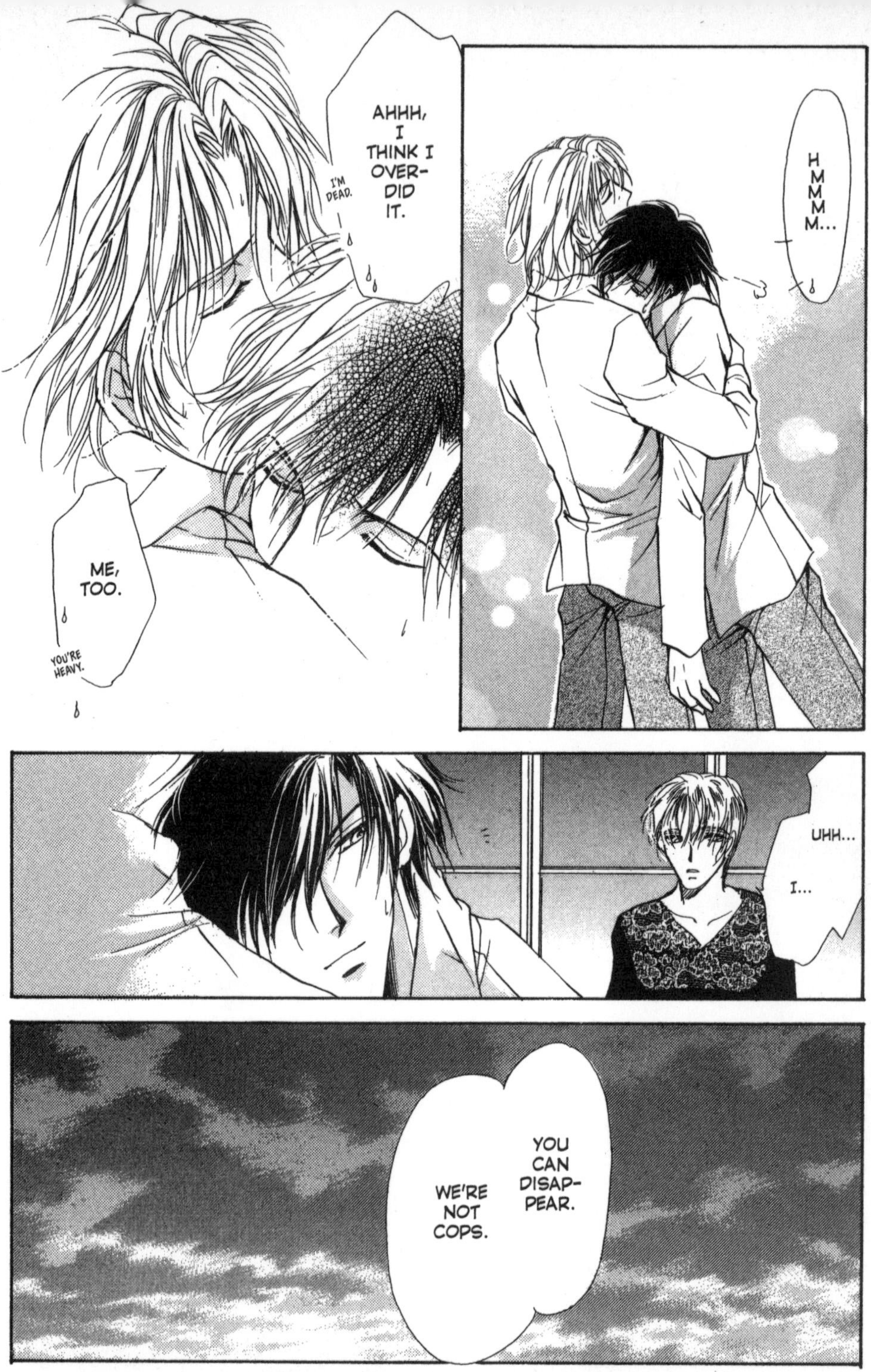
HMMMM...
AHHH, I THINK I OVER-DID IT.
I'M DEAD.
ME, TOO.
YOU'RE HEAVY.
UHH...
I...
YOU CAN DISAP-PEAR.
WE'RE NOT COPS.

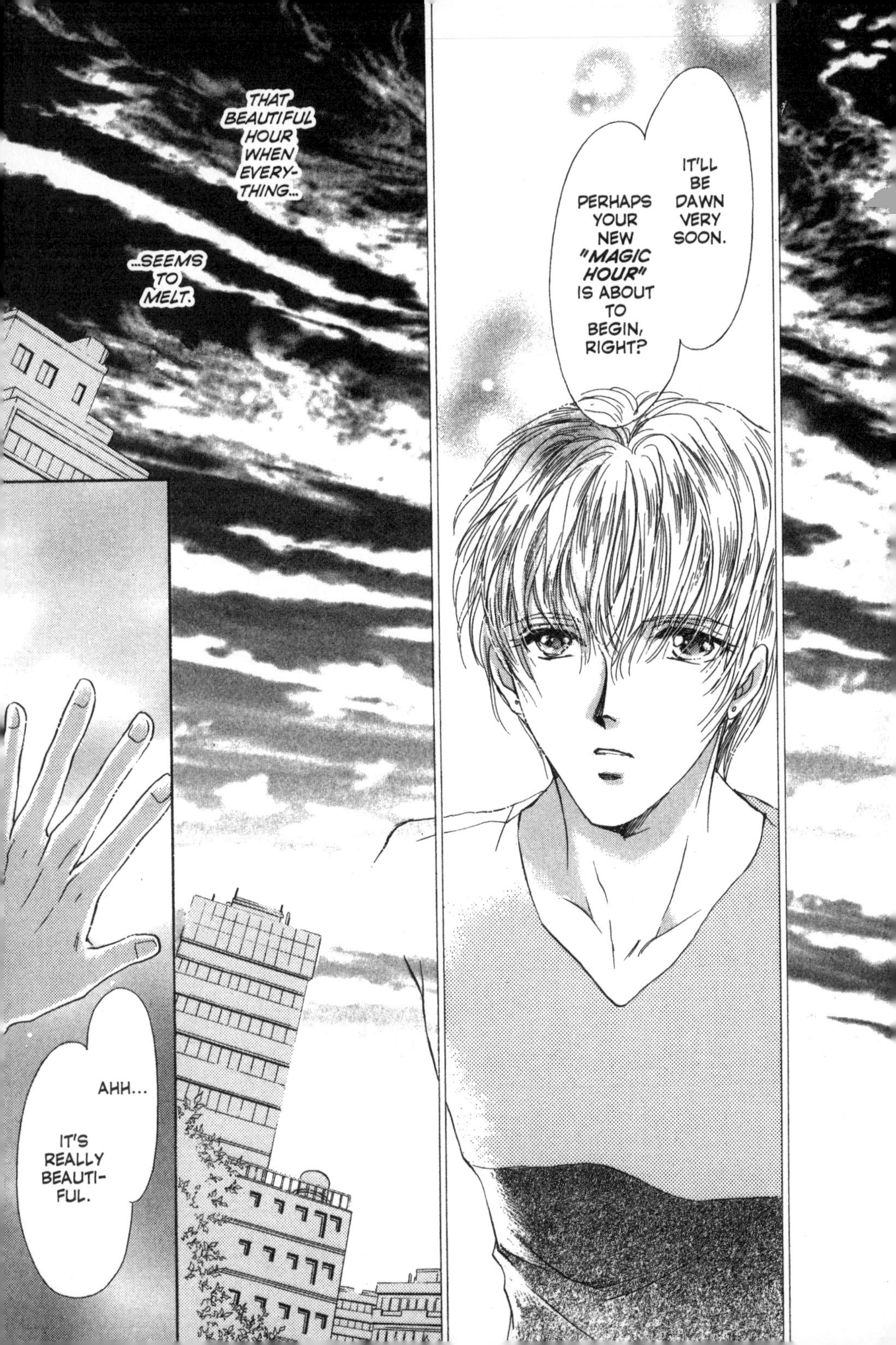
THAT BEAUTIFUL HOUR WHEN EVERY-THING...
...SEEMS TO MELT.
IT'LL BE DAWN VERY SOON.
PERHAPS YOUR NEW "MAGIC HOUR" IS ABOUT TO BEGIN, RIGHT?
AHH...
IT'S REALLY BEAUTI-FUL.

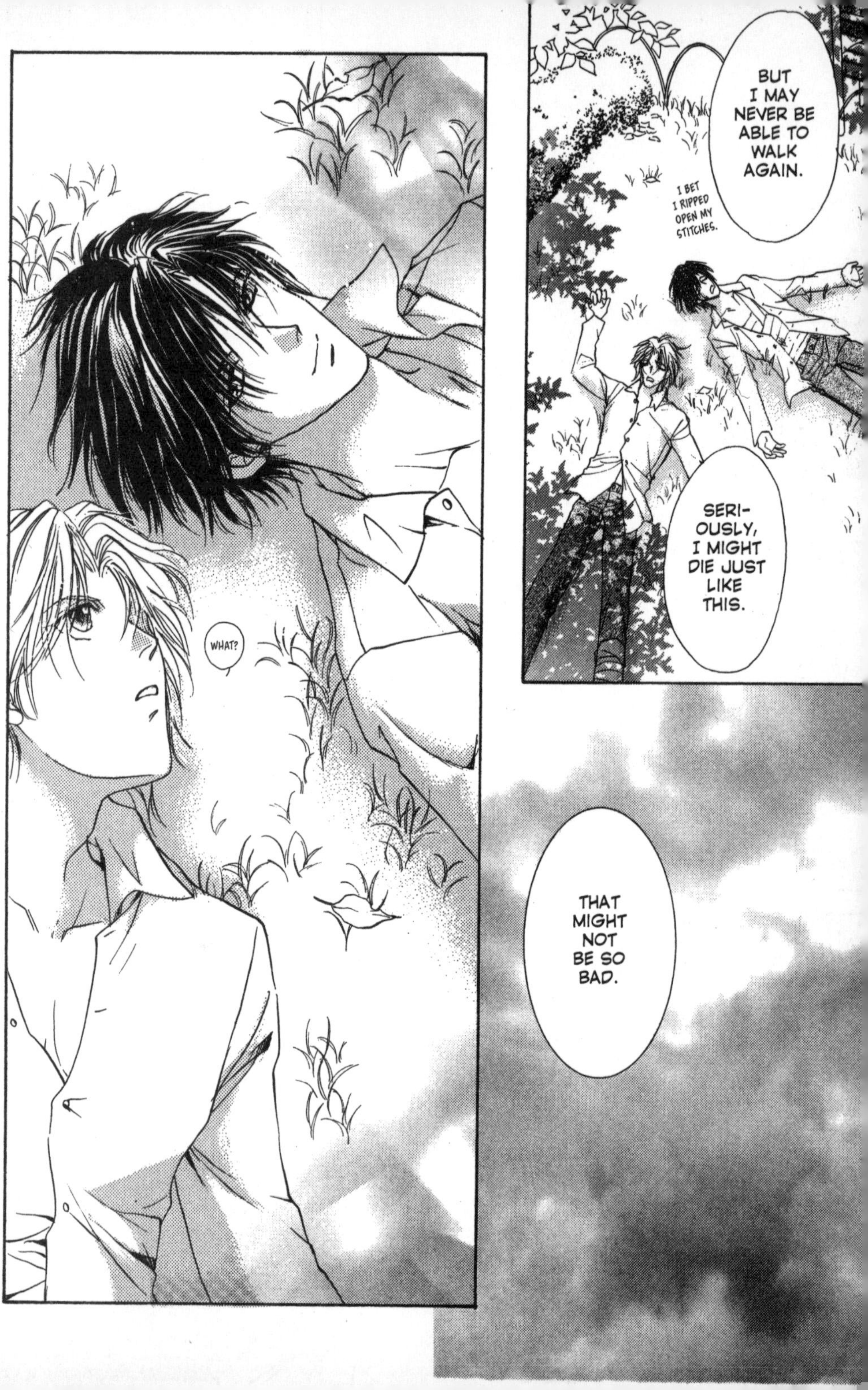
BUT I MAY NEVER BE ABLE TO WALK AGAIN.
I BET I RIPPED OPEN MY STITCHES.
SERIOUSLY, I MIGHT DIE JUST LIKE THIS.
THAT MIGHT NOT BE SO BAD.
WHAT?

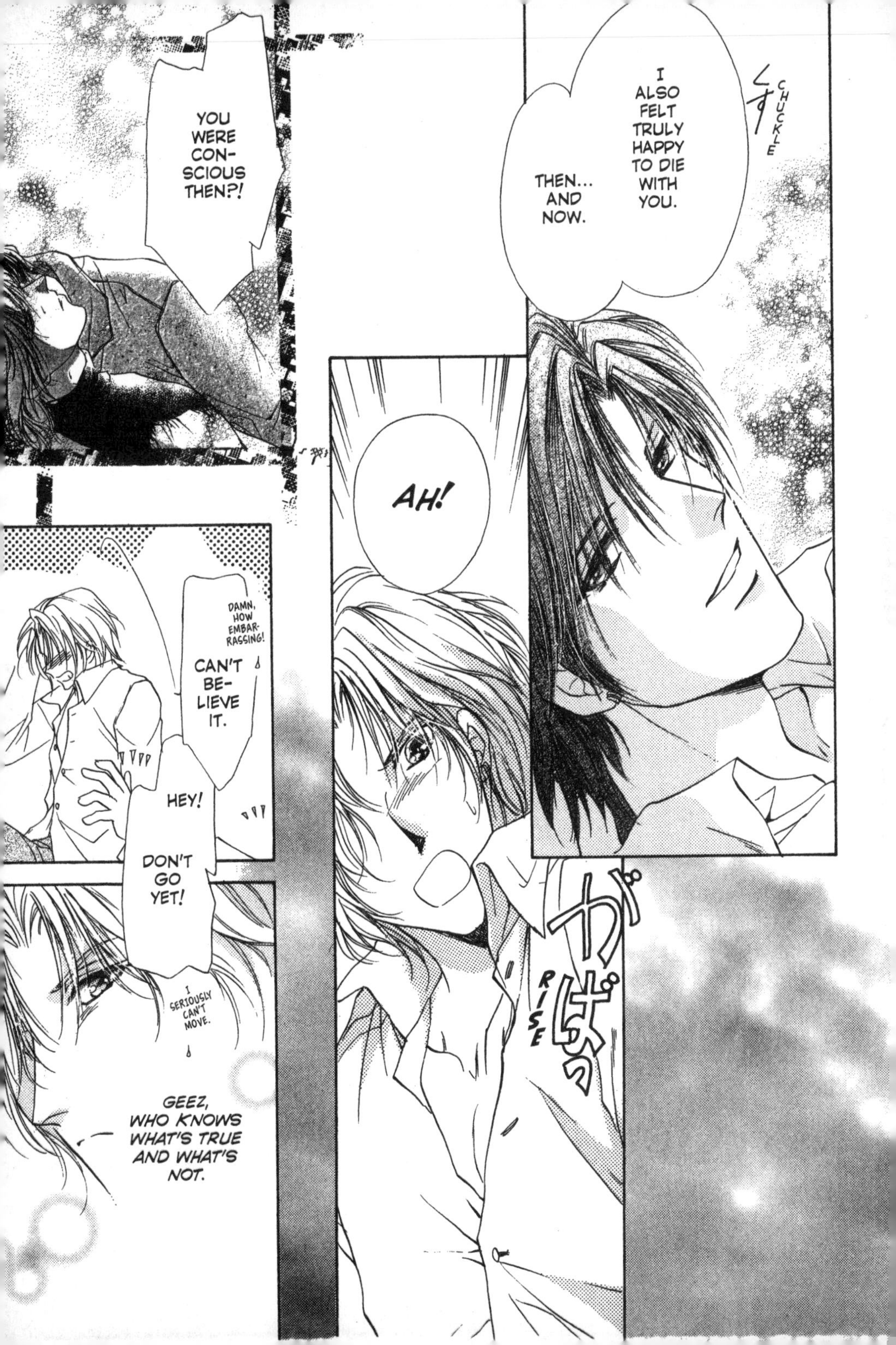

くす CHUCKLE
I ALSO FELT TRULY HAPPY TO DIE WITH YOU.
THEN... AND NOW.
YOU WERE CON-SCIOUS THEN?!
AH!
がばっ RISE
CAN'T BE-LIEVE IT.
DAMN, HOW EMBAR-RASSING!
HEY!
DON'T GO YET!
I SERIOUSLY CAN'T MOVE.
GEEZ, WHO KNOWS WHAT'S TRUE AND WHAT'S NOT.

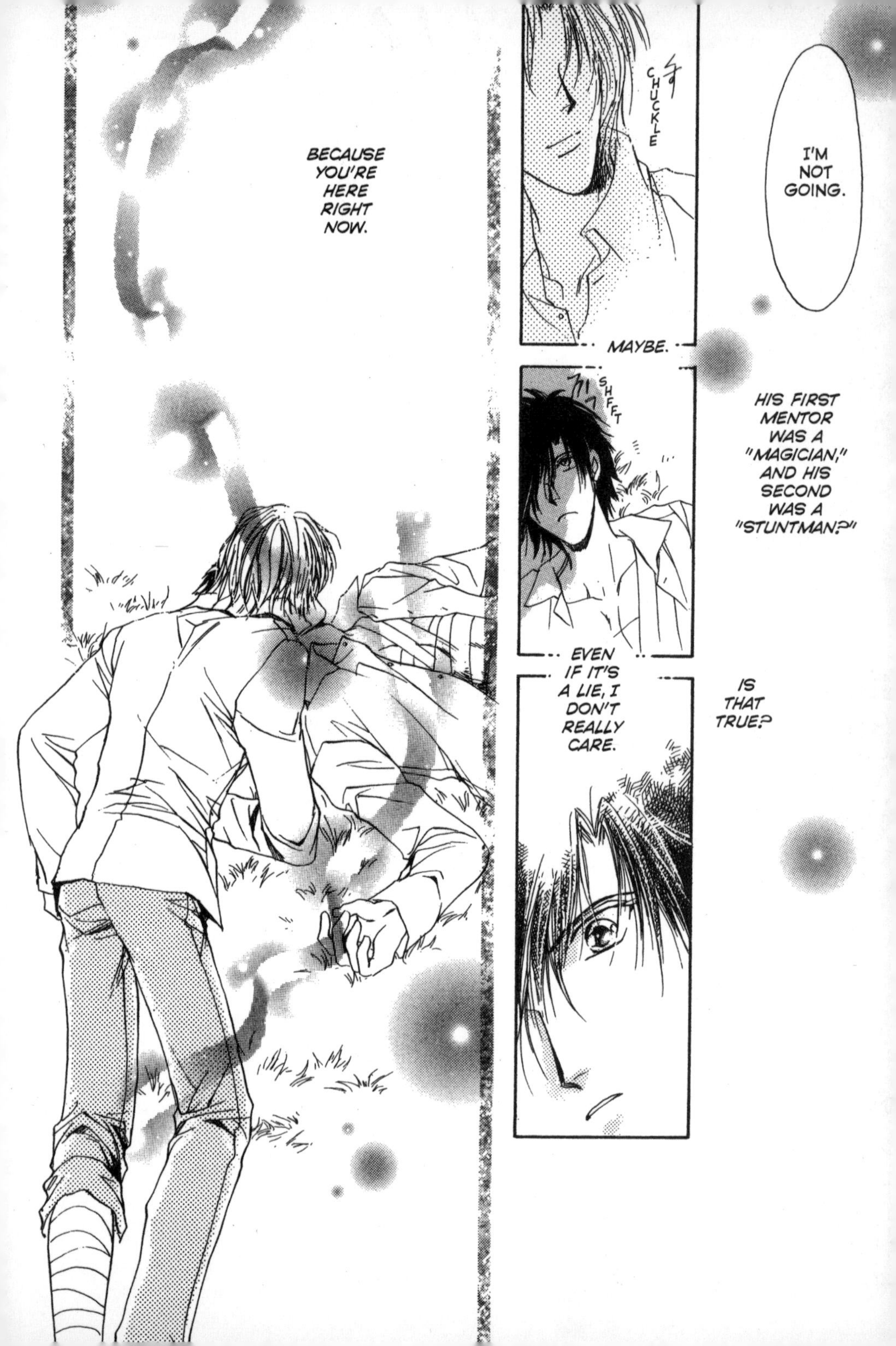
I'M NOT GOING.
CHUCKLE
MAYBE.
HIS FIRST MENTOR WAS A "MAGICIAN," AND HIS SECOND WAS A "STUNTMAN?"
SHFFT
IS THAT TRUE?
EVEN IF IT'S A LIE, I DON'T REALLY CARE.
BECAUSE YOU'RE HERE RIGHT NOW.

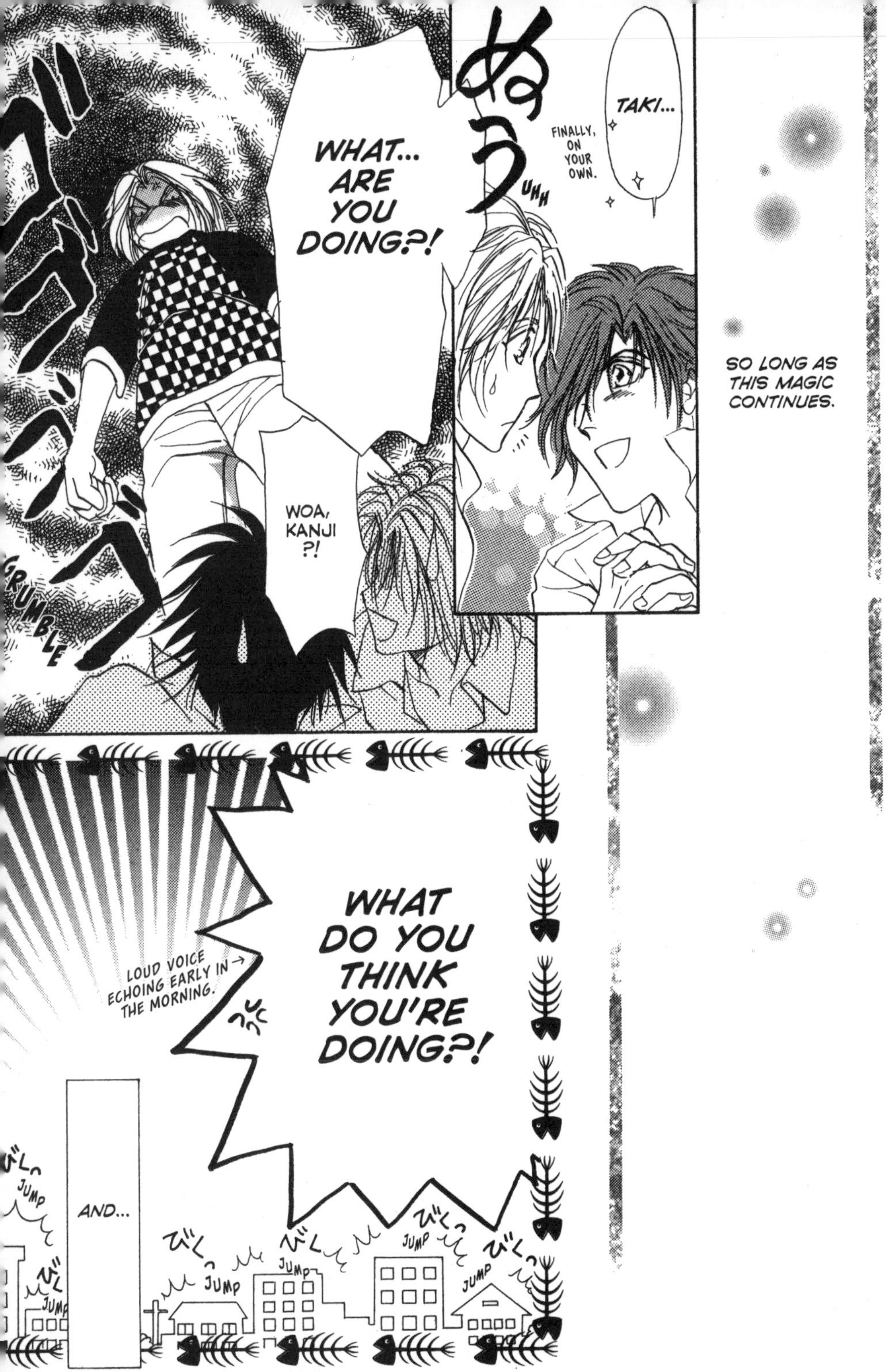
SO LONG AS THIS MAGIC CONTINUES.
TAKI...
FINALLY, ON YOUR OWN.
ぬう
UHH
WHAT... ARE YOU DOING?!
WOA, KANJI ?!
GRUMBLE
WHAT DO YOU THINK YOU'RE DOING?!
LOUD VOICE ECHOING EARLY IN THE MORNING.
JUMP
JUMP
JUMP
JUMP
JUMP
JUMP
AND...

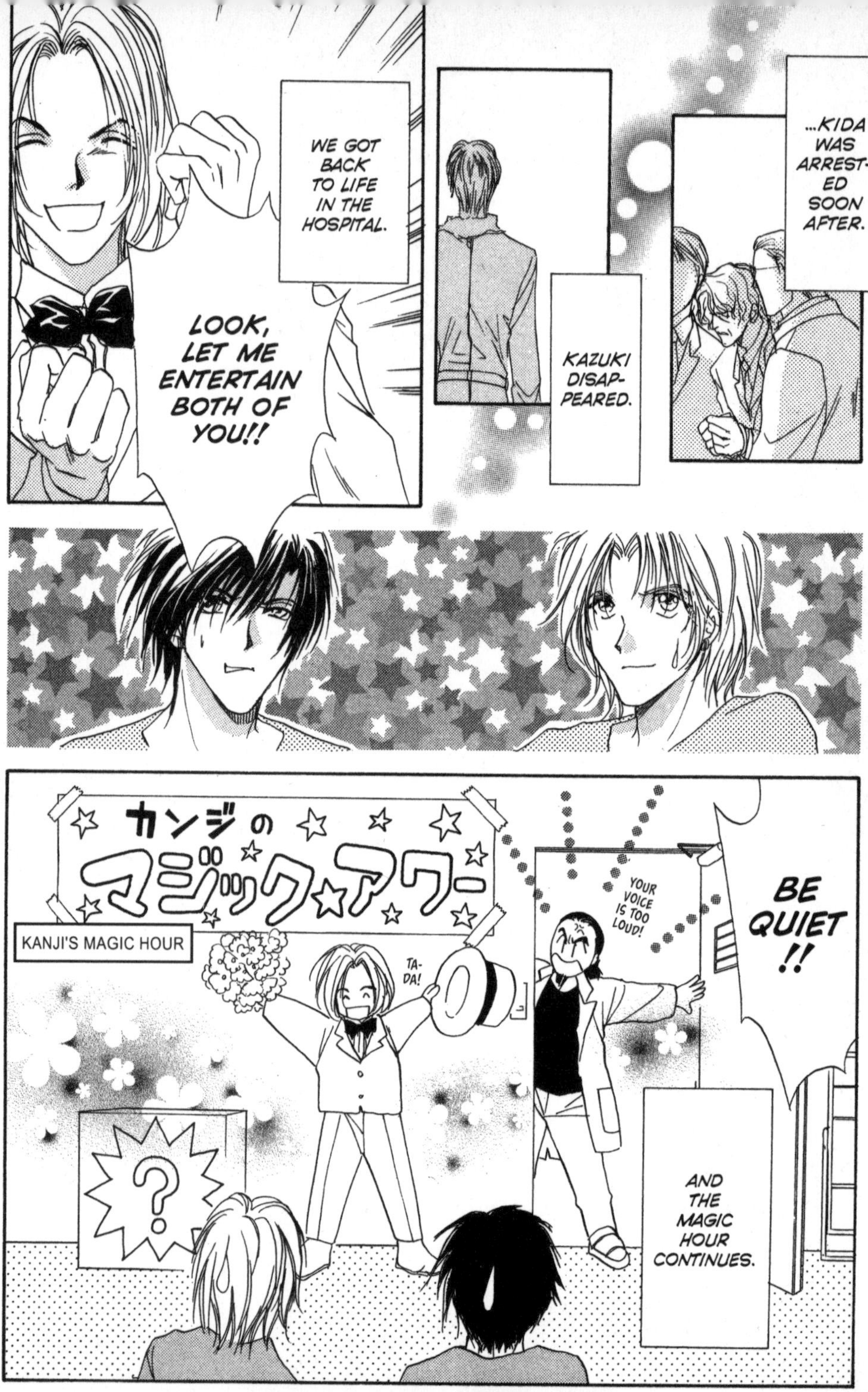
...KIDA WAS ARRESTED SOON AFTER.
KAZUKI DISAPPEARED.
WE GOT BACK TO LIFE IN THE HOSPITAL.
LOOK, LET ME ENTERTAIN BOTH OF YOU!!
BE QUIET!!
YOUR VOICE IS TOO LOUD!
カンジのマジック☆アワー
KANJI'S MAGIC HOUR
TA-DA!
AND THE MAGIC HOUR CONTINUES.

YELLOW ACT.5 / THE END

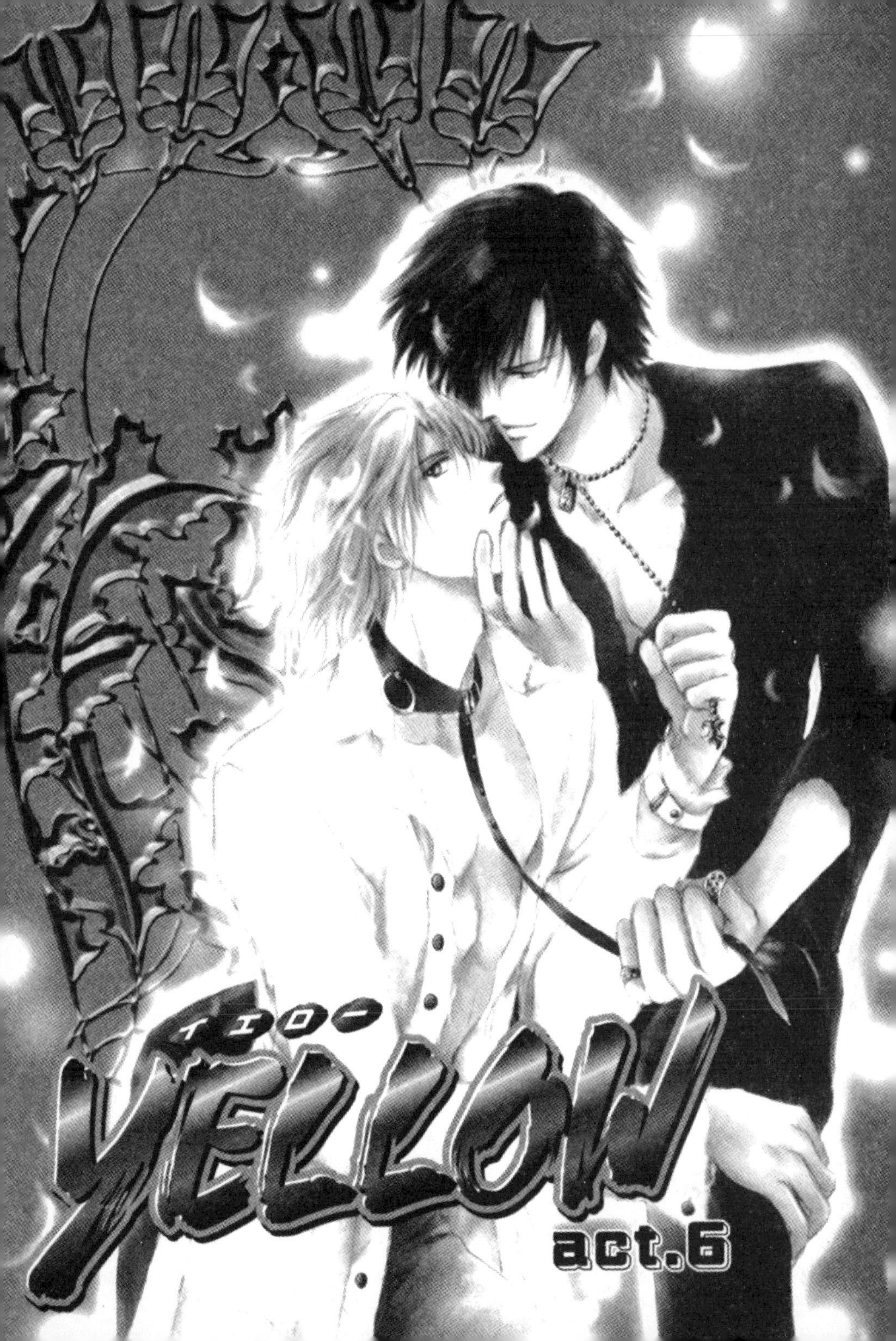
イエロー
YELLOW
act.6

PROFILE

Suspect #3

name

SHIGEYUKI TSUNUGA

background

HIS IDENTITY IS A SECRET, EXCEPT THAT HE PROBABLY IS AN EX-DETECTIVE.

Suspect #4

name

RYUICHI HATOZAKI

background

HE'S ON A CAREER TRACK AT THE METROPOLITAN POLICE BOARD AND IS TSUNUGA'S EX-COLLEAGUE.

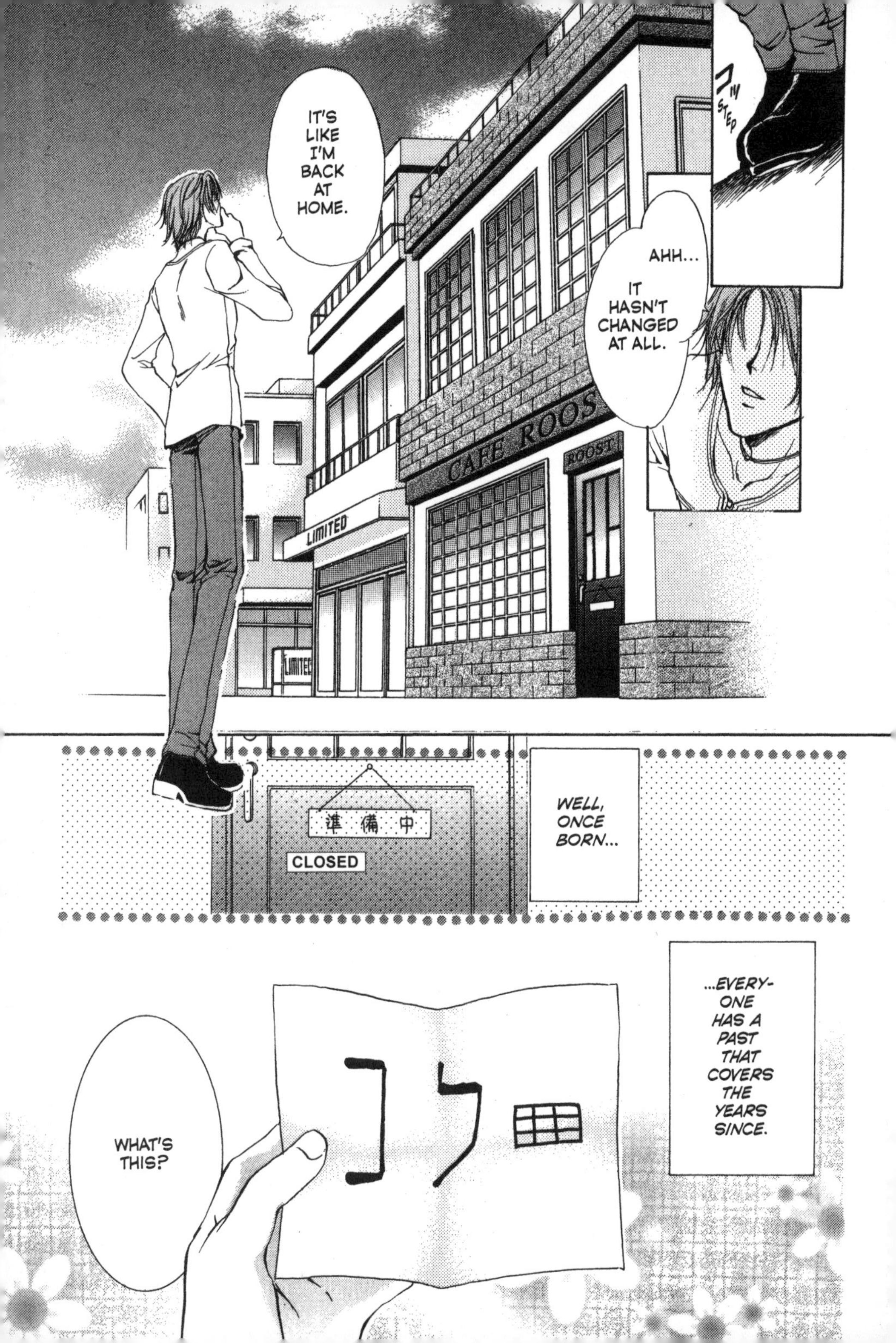

STEP
AHH...
IT HASN'T CHANGED AT ALL.
IT'S LIKE I'M BACK AT HOME.
CAFE ROOS
ROOST
LIMITED
LIMITED
WELL, ONCE BORN...
準備中
CLOSED
...EVERY-ONE HAS A PAST THAT COVERS THE YEARS SINCE.
WHAT'S THIS?

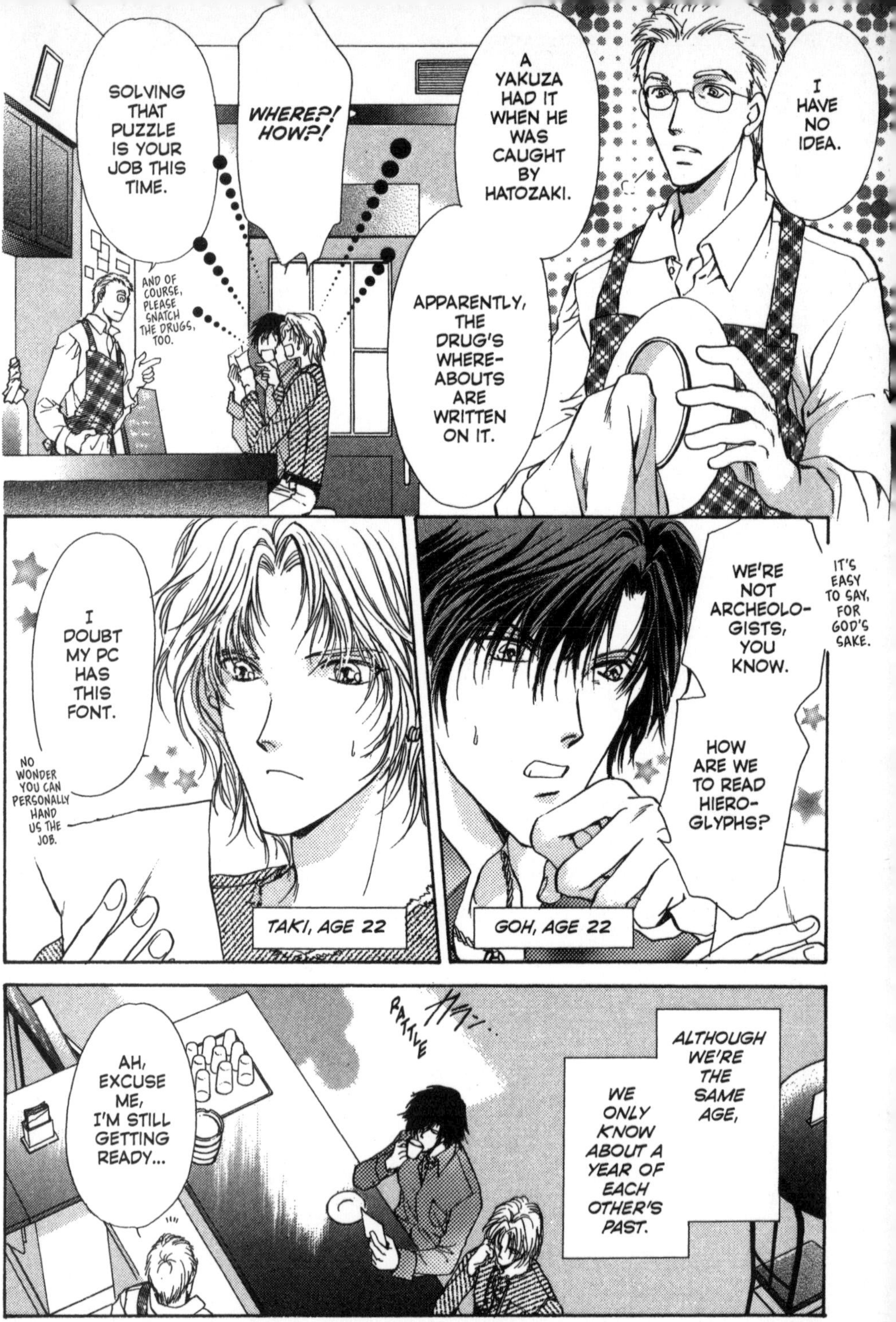
I HAVE NO IDEA.
A YAKUZA HAD IT WHEN HE WAS CAUGHT BY HATOZAKI.
APPARENTLY, THE DRUG'S WHERE-ABOUTS ARE WRITTEN ON IT.
WHERE?! HOW?!
SOLVING THAT PUZZLE IS YOUR JOB THIS TIME.
AND OF COURSE, PLEASE SNATCH THE DRUGS, TOO.
IT'S EASY TO SAY, FOR GOD'S SAKE.
WE'RE NOT ARCHEOLO-GISTS, YOU KNOW.
HOW ARE WE TO READ HIERO-GLYPHS?
GOH, AGE 22
I DOUBT MY PC HAS THIS FONT.
NO WONDER YOU CAN PERSONALLY HAND US THE JOB.
TAKI, AGE 22
ALTHOUGH WE'RE THE SAME AGE,
WE ONLY KNOW ABOUT A YEAR OF EACH OTHER'S PAST.
RATTTLE
AH, EXCUSE ME, I'M STILL GETTING READY...

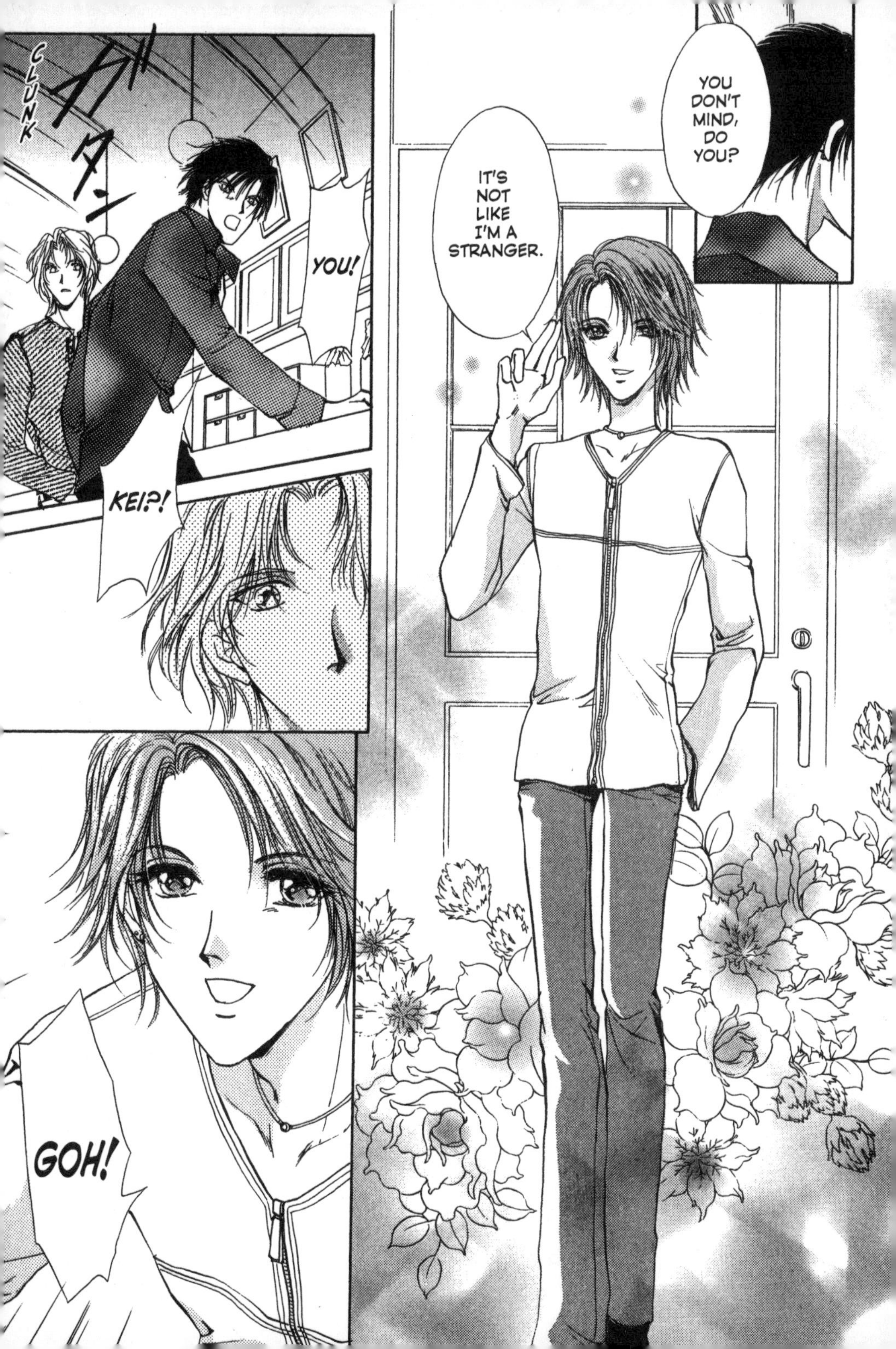
YOU DON'T MIND, DO YOU?
IT'S NOT LIKE I'M A STRANGER.
CLUNK
YOU!
KEI?!
GOH!

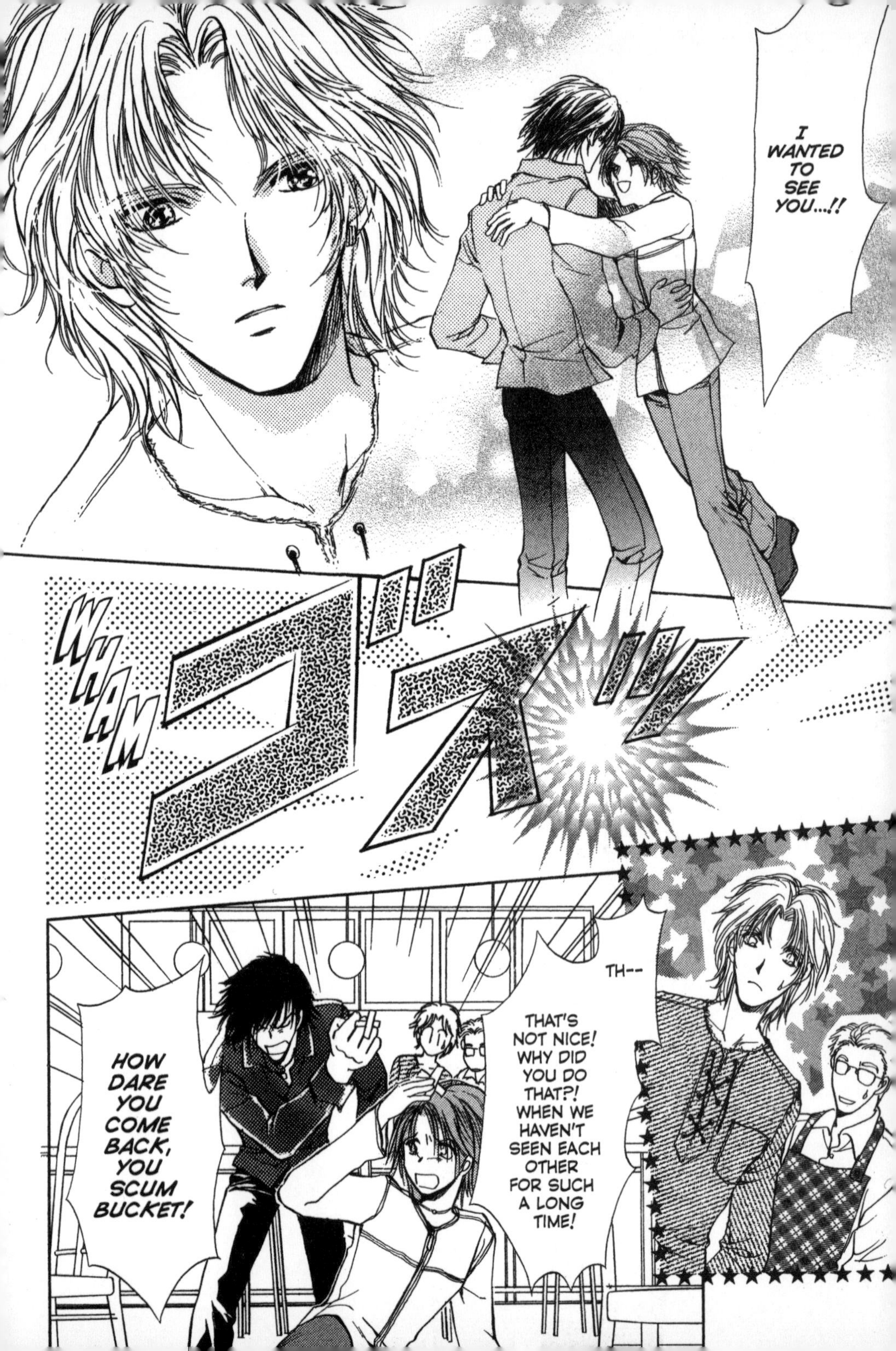
I WANTED TO SEE YOU...!!
WHAM
ゴズッ
TH--
THAT'S NOT NICE! WHY DID YOU DO THAT?! WHEN WE HAVEN'T SEEN EACH OTHER FOR SUCH A LONG TIME!
HOW DARE YOU COME BACK, YOU SCUM BUCKET!

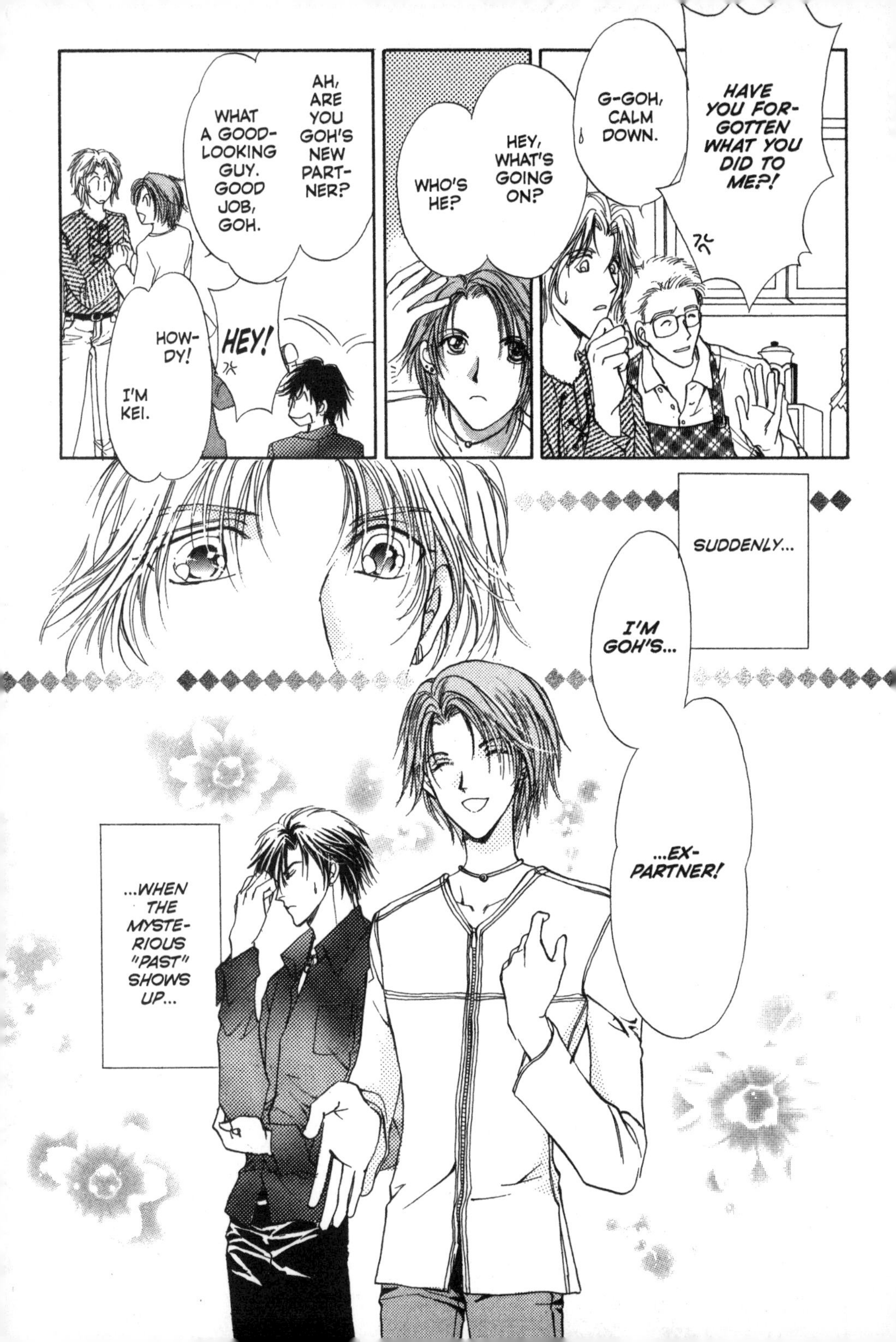
HAVE YOU FOR-GOTTEN WHAT YOU DID TO ME?!
G-GOH, CALM DOWN.
HEY, WHAT'S GOING ON?
WHO'S HE?
AH, ARE YOU GOH'S NEW PART-NER?
WHAT A GOOD-LOOKING GUY. GOOD JOB, GOH.
HEY!
HOW-DY!
I'M KEI.
SUDDENLY...
I'M GOH'S...
...EX-PARTNER!
...WHEN THE MYSTE-RIOUS "PAST" SHOWS UP...

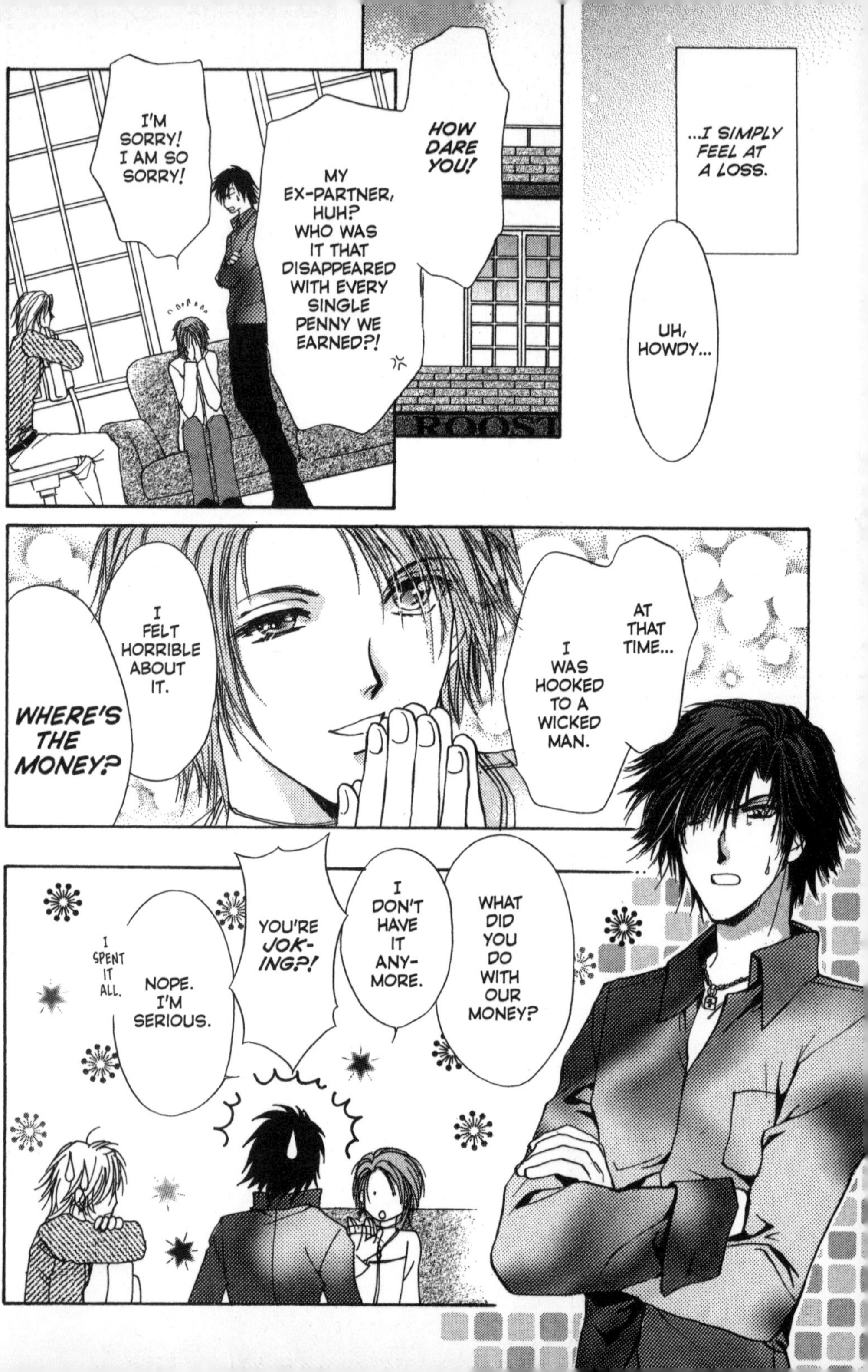
...I SIMPLY FEEL AT A LOSS.
UH, HOWDY...
HOW DARE YOU!
MY EX-PARTNER, HUH? WHO WAS IT THAT DISAPPEARED WITH EVERY SINGLE PENNY WE EARNED?!
I'M SORRY! I AM SO SORRY!
AT THAT TIME... I WAS HOOKED TO A WICKED MAN.
I FELT HORRIBLE ABOUT IT.
WHERE'S THE MONEY?
WHAT DID YOU DO WITH OUR MONEY?
I DON'T HAVE IT ANY-MORE.
YOU'RE JOKING?!
NOPE. I'M SERIOUS.
I SPENT IT ALL.

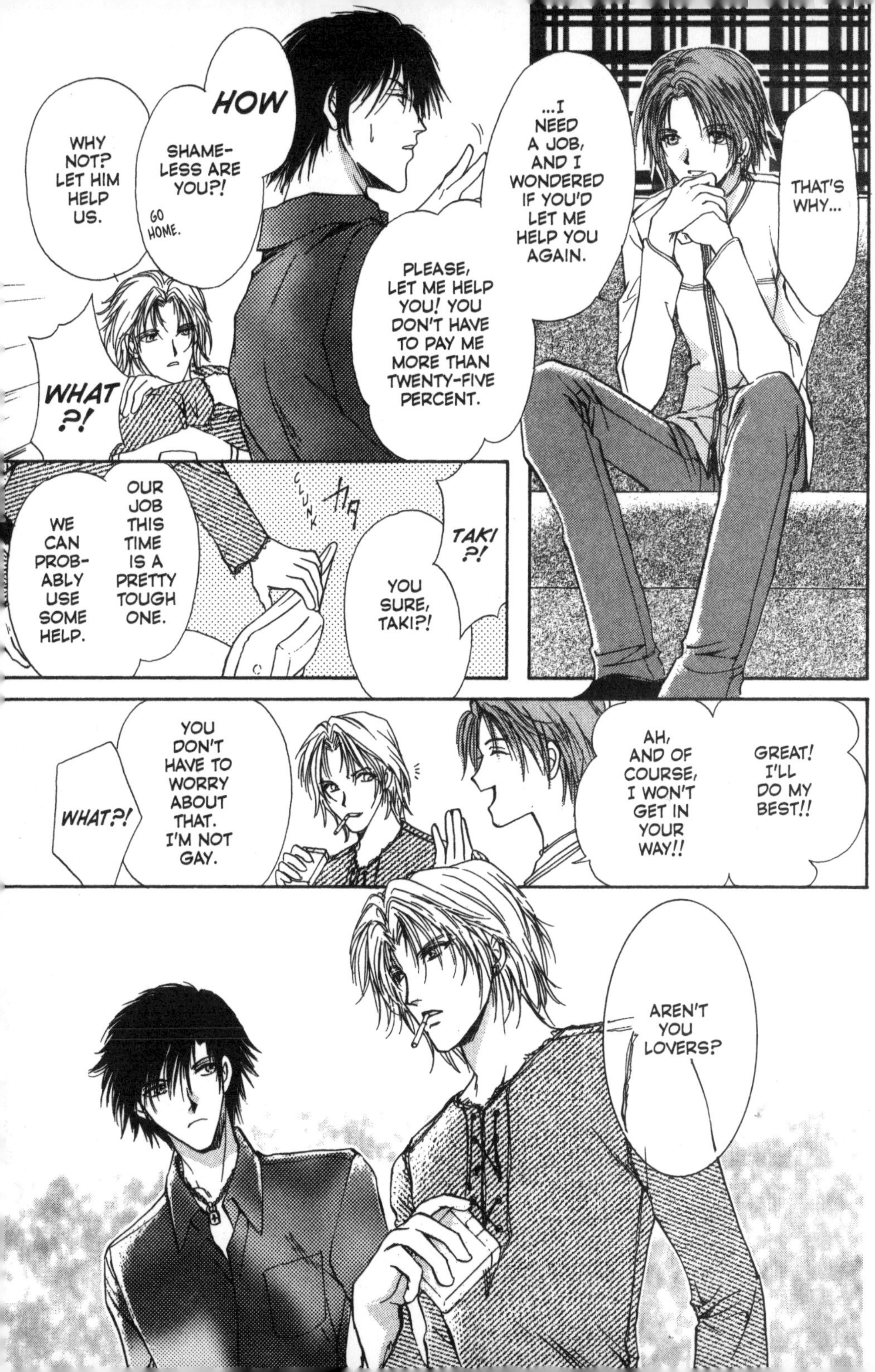
THAT'S WHY...
...I NEED A JOB, AND I WONDERED IF YOU'D LET ME HELP YOU AGAIN.
PLEASE, LET ME HELP YOU! YOU DON'T HAVE TO PAY ME MORE THAN TWENTY-FIVE PERCENT.
HOW SHAMELESS ARE YOU?!
GO HOME.
WHY NOT? LET HIM HELP US.
WHAT?!
TAKI?!
YOU SURE, TAKI?!
CLUNK
OUR JOB THIS TIME IS A PRETTY TOUGH ONE.
WE CAN PROBABLY USE SOME HELP.
GREAT! I'LL DO MY BEST!!
AH, AND OF COURSE, I WON'T GET IN YOUR WAY!!
YOU DON'T HAVE TO WORRY ABOUT THAT. I'M NOT GAY.
WHAT?!
AREN'T YOU LOVERS?

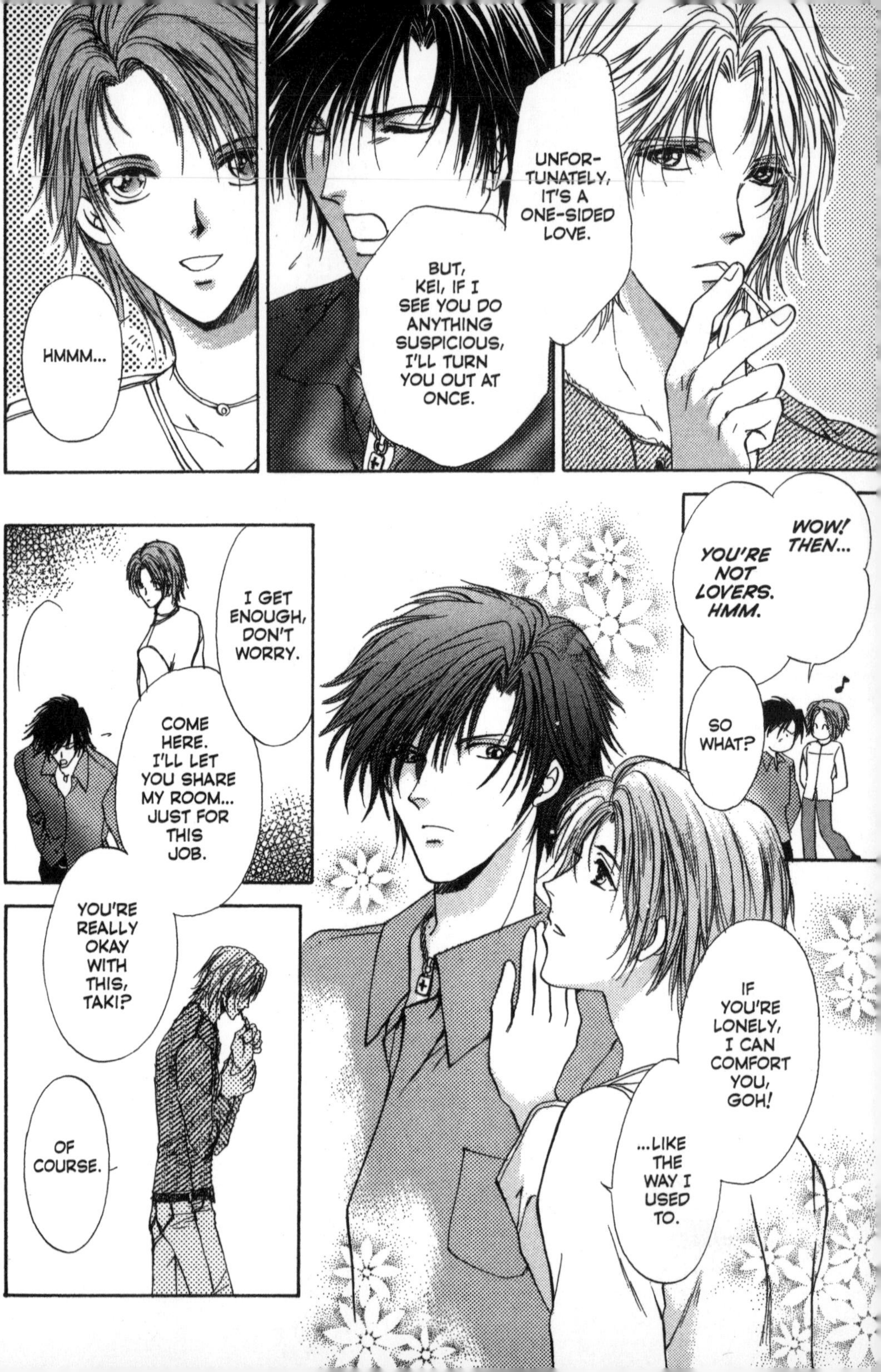
UNFOR-TUNATELY, IT'S A ONE-SIDED LOVE.
BUT, KEI, IF I SEE YOU DO ANYTHING SUSPICIOUS, I'LL TURN YOU OUT AT ONCE.
HMMM...
WOW! THEN...
YOU'RE NOT LOVERS. HMM.
SO WHAT?
IF YOU'RE LONELY, I CAN COMFORT YOU, GOH!
...LIKE THE WAY I USED TO.
I GET ENOUGH, DON'T WORRY.
COME HERE. I'LL LET YOU SHARE MY ROOM... JUST FOR THIS JOB.
YOU'RE REALLY OKAY WITH THIS, TAKI?
OF COURSE.

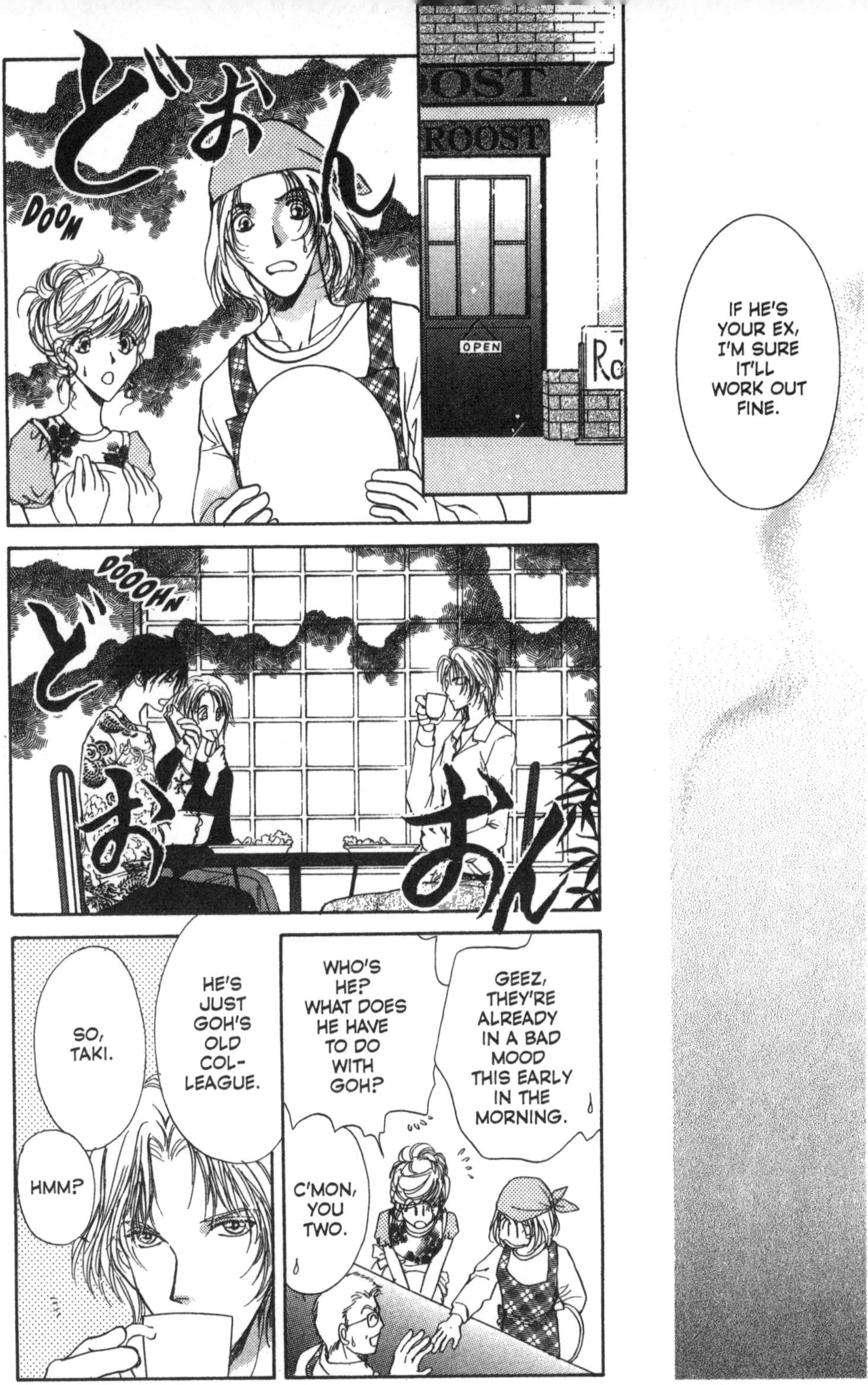
IF HE'S YOUR EX, I'M SURE IT'LL WORK OUT FINE.
どおん
DOOM
ROOST
ROOST
OPEN
DOOOHN
どおん
GEEZ, THEY'RE ALREADY IN A BAD MOOD THIS EARLY IN THE MORNING.
WHO'S HE? WHAT DOES HE HAVE TO DO WITH GOH?
C'MON, YOU TWO.
HE'S JUST GOH'S OLD COL-LEAGUE.
SO, TAKI.
HMM?

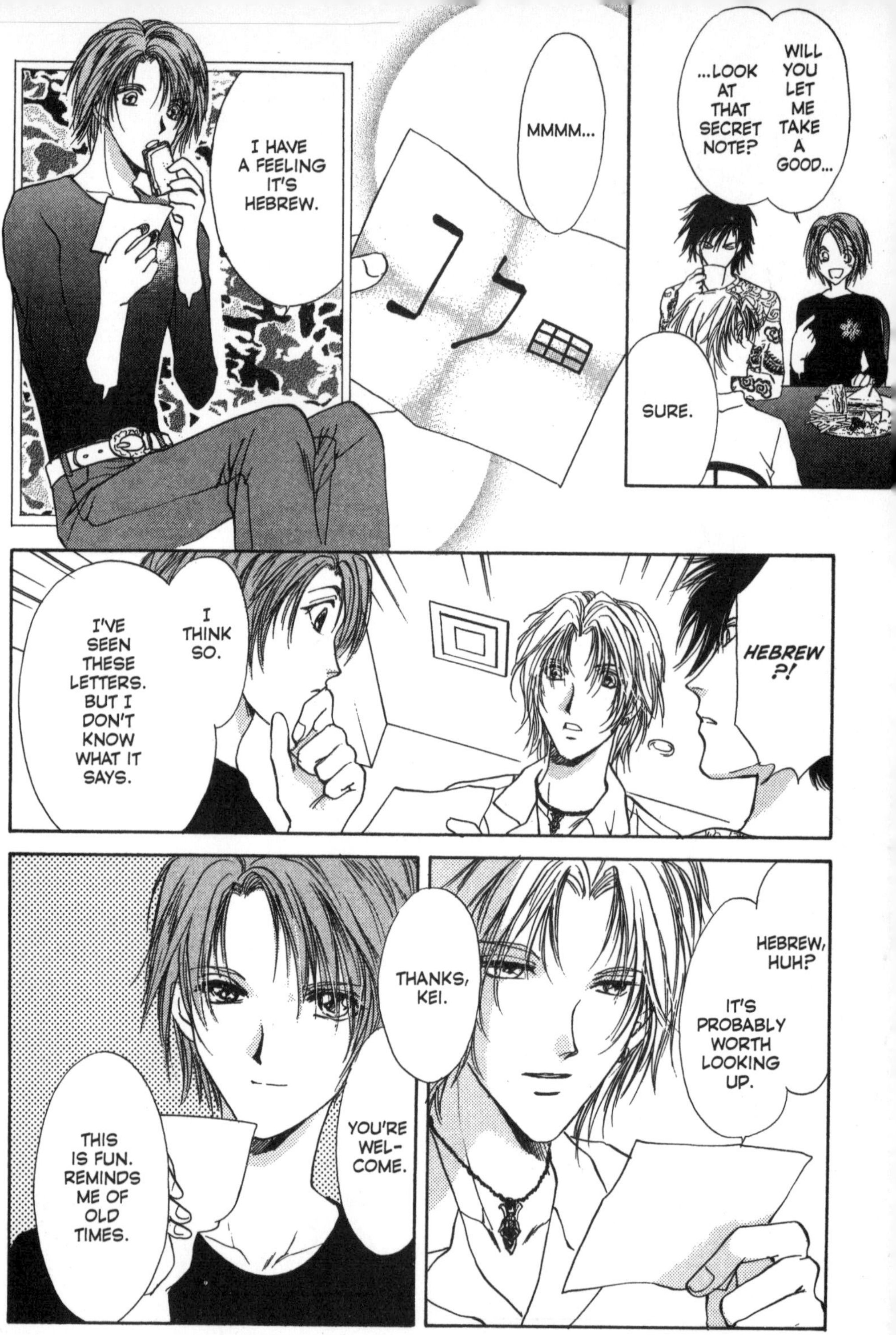
WILL YOU LET ME TAKE A GOOD...
...LOOK AT THAT SECRET NOTE?
SURE.
MMMM...
I HAVE A FEELING IT'S HEBREW.
HEBREW ?!
I THINK SO.
I'VE SEEN THESE LETTERS. BUT I DON'T KNOW WHAT IT SAYS.
HEBREW, HUH?
IT'S PROBABLY WORTH LOOKING UP.
THANKS, KEI.
YOU'RE WEL-COME.
THIS IS FUN. REMINDS ME OF OLD TIMES.

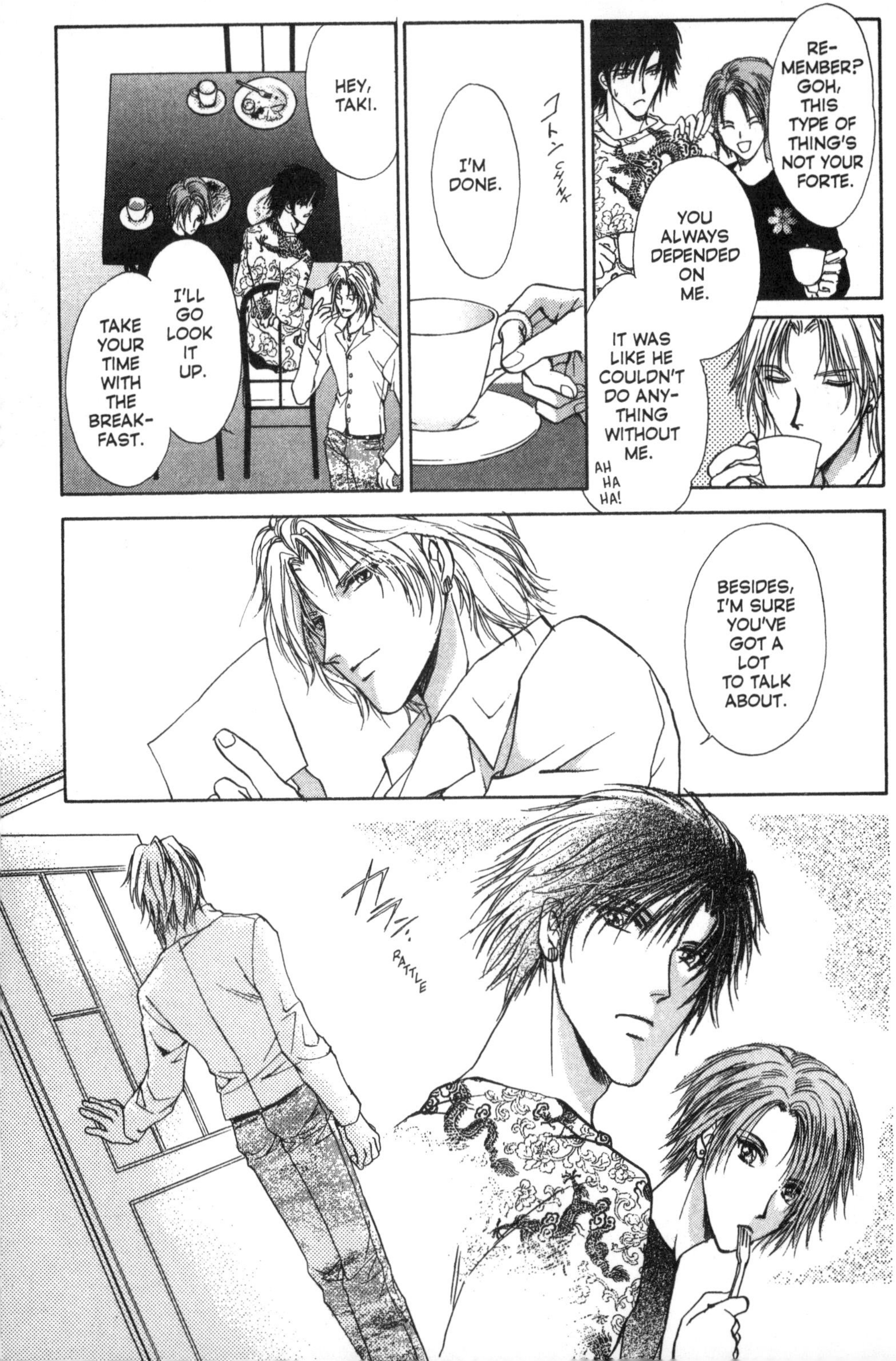
RE-MEMBER? GOH, THIS TYPE OF THING'S NOT YOUR FORTE.
YOU ALWAYS DEPENDED ON ME.
IT WAS LIKE HE COULDN'T DO ANYTHING WITHOUT ME.
AH HA HA!
I'M DONE.
コトン
CHINK
HEY, TAKI.
I'LL GO LOOK IT UP.
TAKE YOUR TIME WITH THE BREAKFAST.
BESIDES, I'M SURE YOU'VE GOT A LOT TO TALK ABOUT.
RATTLE

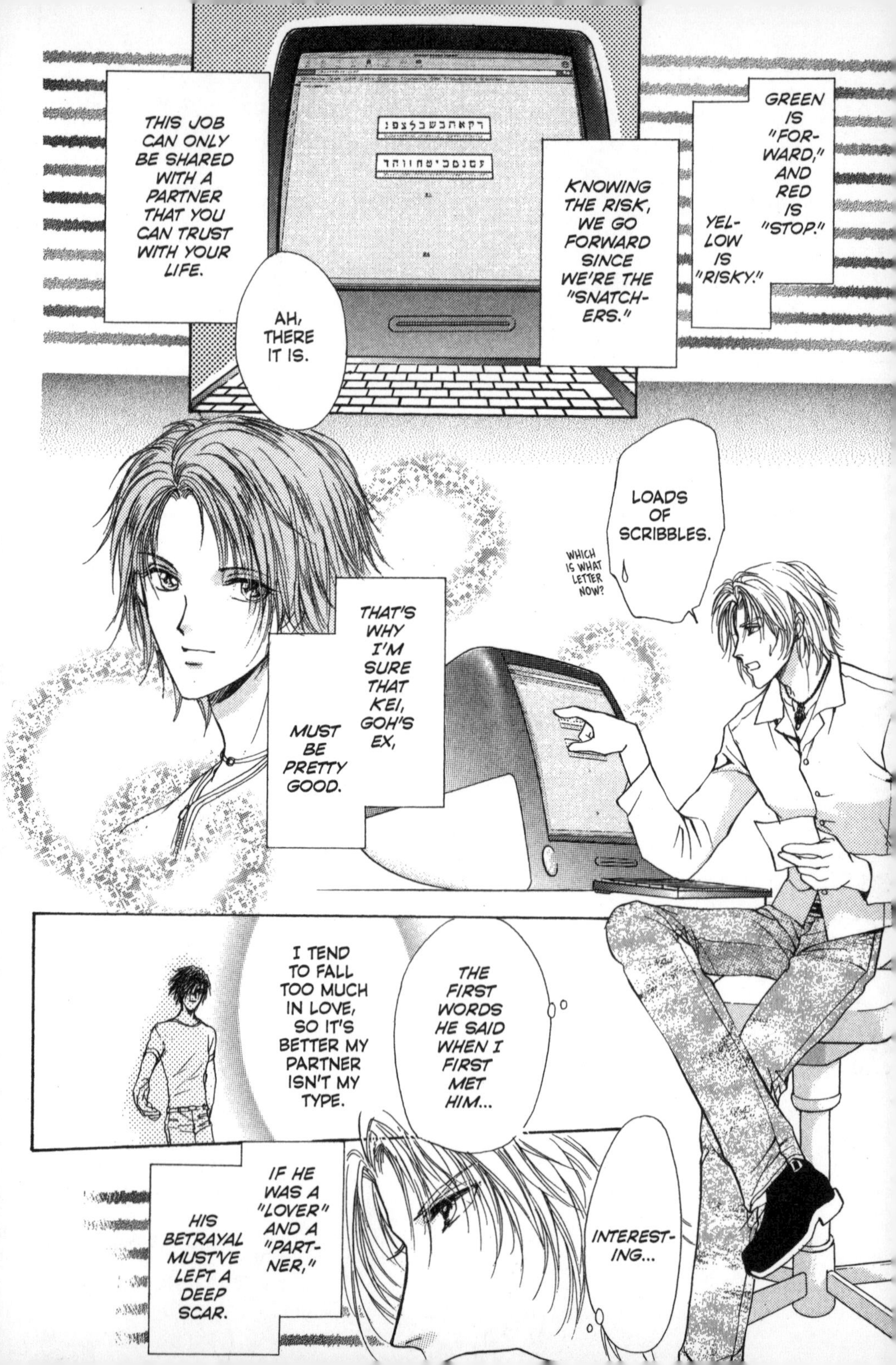
GREEN IS "FORWARD," AND RED IS "STOP."
YELLOW IS "RISKY."
KNOWING THE RISK, WE GO FORWARD SINCE WE'RE THE "SNATCHERS."
THIS JOB CAN ONLY BE SHARED WITH A PARTNER THAT YOU CAN TRUST WITH YOUR LIFE.
AH, THERE IT IS.
LOADS OF SCRIBBLES.
WHICH IS WHAT LETTER NOW?
THAT'S WHY I'M SURE THAT KEI, GOH'S EX,
MUST BE PRETTY GOOD.
THE FIRST WORDS HE SAID WHEN I FIRST MET HIM...
I TEND TO FALL TOO MUCH IN LOVE, SO IT'S BETTER MY PARTNER ISN'T MY TYPE.
INTERESTING...
IF HE WAS A "LOVER" AND A "PARTNER,"
HIS BETRAYAL MUST'VE LEFT A DEEP SCAR.

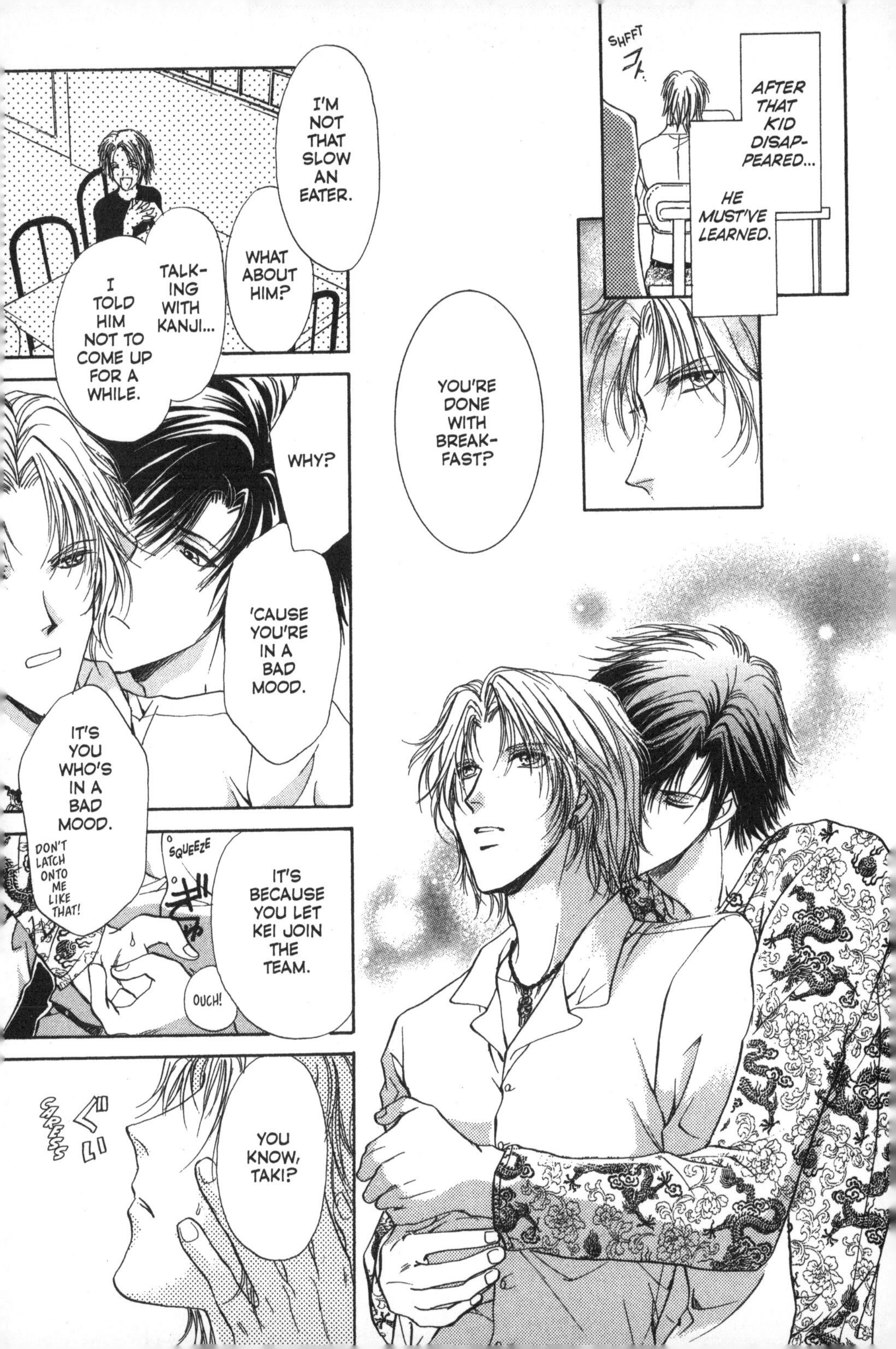
SHFFT
AFTER THAT KID DISAPPEARED...
HE MUST'VE LEARNED.
YOU'RE DONE WITH BREAKFAST?
I'M NOT THAT SLOW AN EATER.
WHAT ABOUT HIM?
TALKING WITH KANJI...
I TOLD HIM NOT TO COME UP FOR A WHILE.
WHY?
'CAUSE YOU'RE IN A BAD MOOD.
IT'S YOU WHO'S IN A BAD MOOD.
SQUEEZE
IT'S BECAUSE YOU LET KEI JOIN THE TEAM.
DON'T LATCH ONTO ME LIKE THAT!
OUCH!
CARESS
YOU KNOW, TAKI?

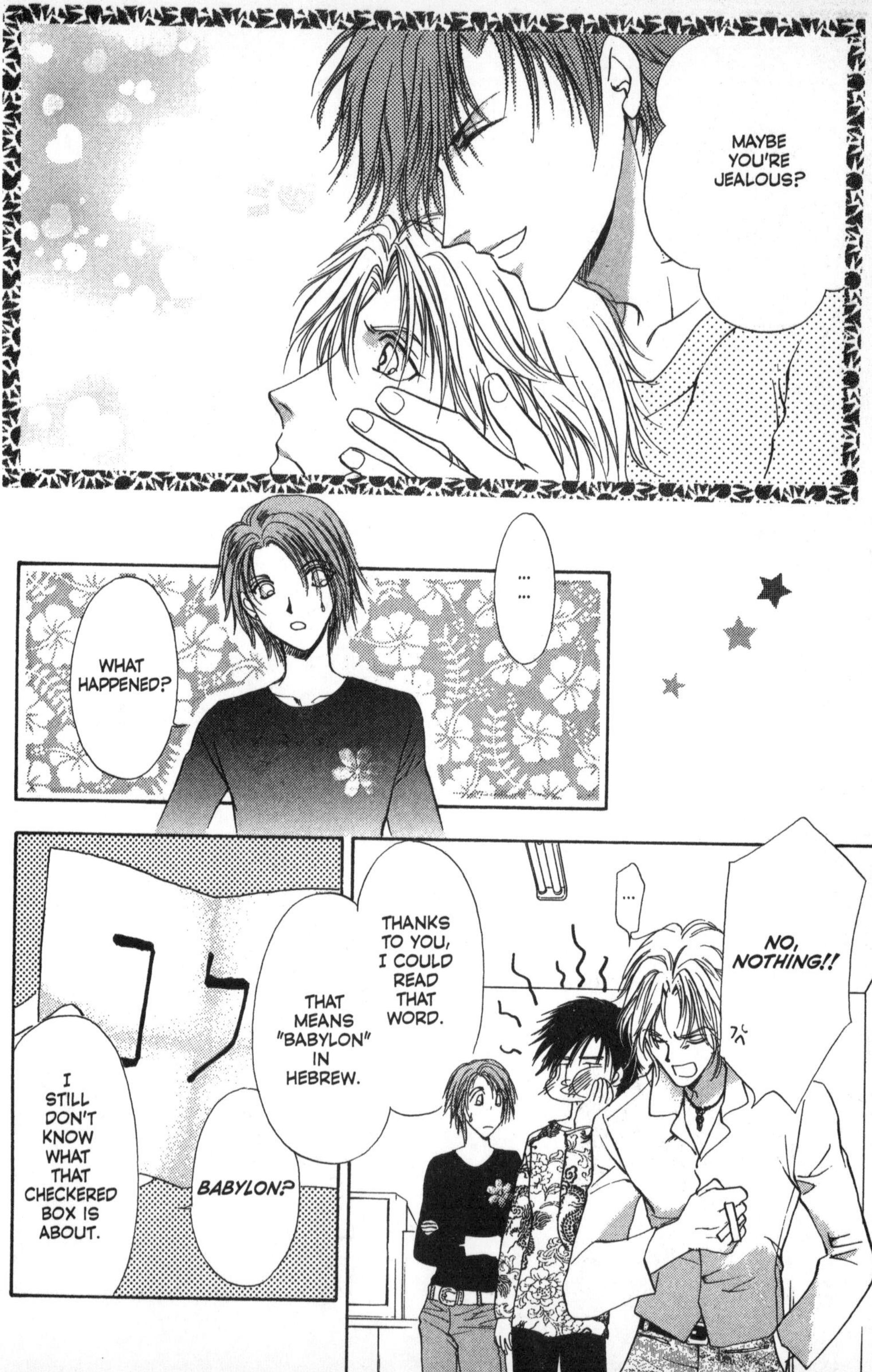
MAYBE YOU'RE JEALOUS?
......
WHAT HAPPENED?
NO, NOTHING!!
...
THANKS TO YOU, I COULD READ THAT WORD.
THAT MEANS "BABYLON" IN HEBREW.
BABYLON?
I STILL DON'T KNOW WHAT THAT CHECKERED BOX IS ABOUT.

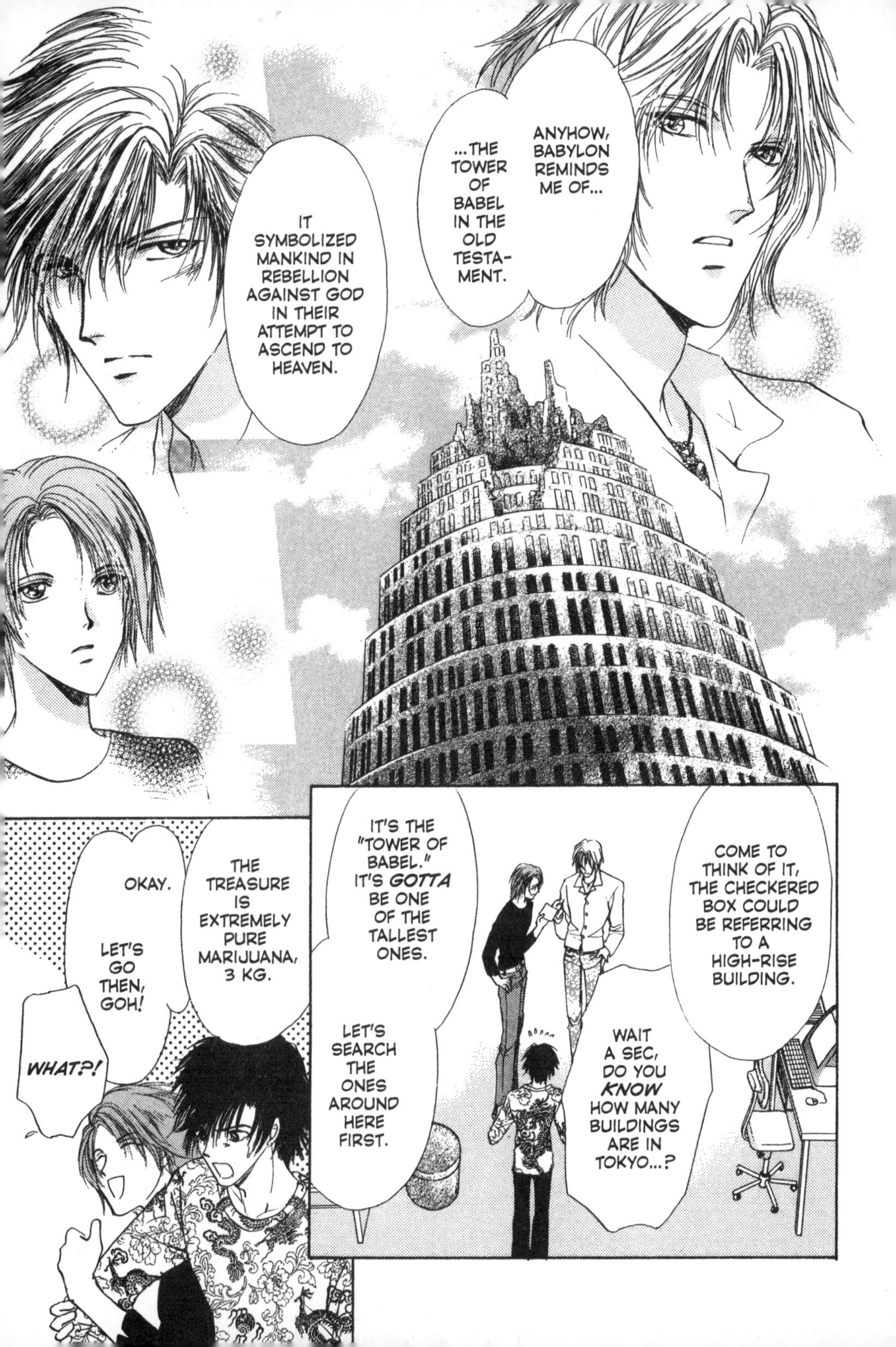
ANYHOW, BABYLON REMINDS ME OF...
...THE TOWER OF BABEL IN THE OLD TESTAMENT.
IT SYMBOLIZED MANKIND IN REBELLION AGAINST GOD IN THEIR ATTEMPT TO ASCEND TO HEAVEN.
COME TO THINK OF IT, THE CHECKERED BOX COULD BE REFERRING TO A HIGH-RISE BUILDING.
IT'S THE "TOWER OF BABEL." IT'S *GOTTA* BE ONE OF THE TALLEST ONES.
WAIT A SEC, DO YOU *KNOW* HOW MANY BUILDINGS ARE IN TOKYO...?
LET'S SEARCH THE ONES AROUND HERE FIRST.
THE TREASURE IS EXTREMELY PURE MARIJUANA, 3 KG.
OKAY.
LET'S GO THEN, GOH!
WHAT?!

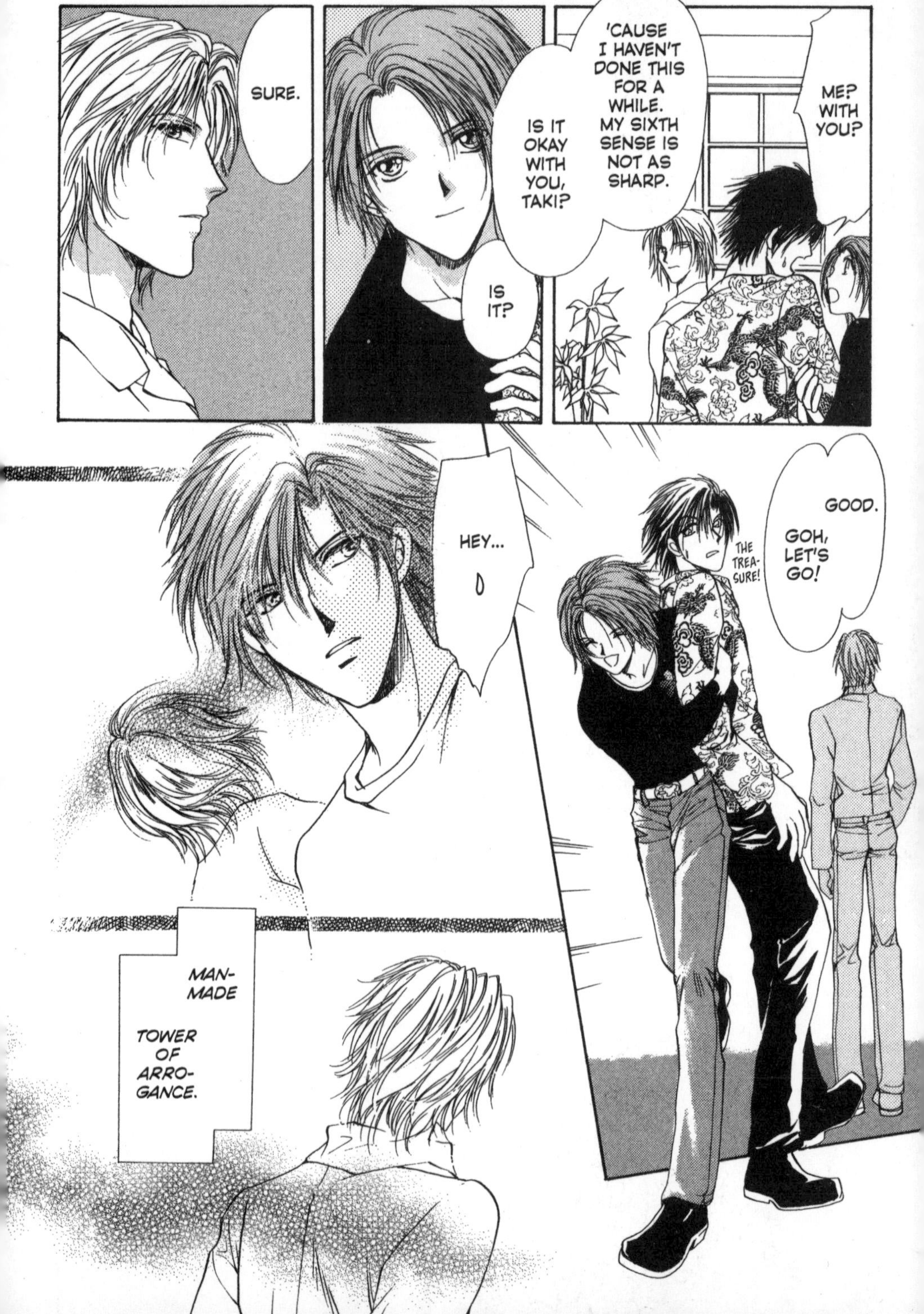
ME? WITH YOU?
'CAUSE I HAVEN'T DONE THIS FOR A WHILE. MY SIXTH SENSE IS NOT AS SHARP.
IS IT OKAY WITH YOU, TAKI?
IS IT?
SURE.
GOOD.
GOH, LET'S GO!
THE TREA-SURE!
HEY...
MAN-MADE
TOWER OF ARRO-GANCE.

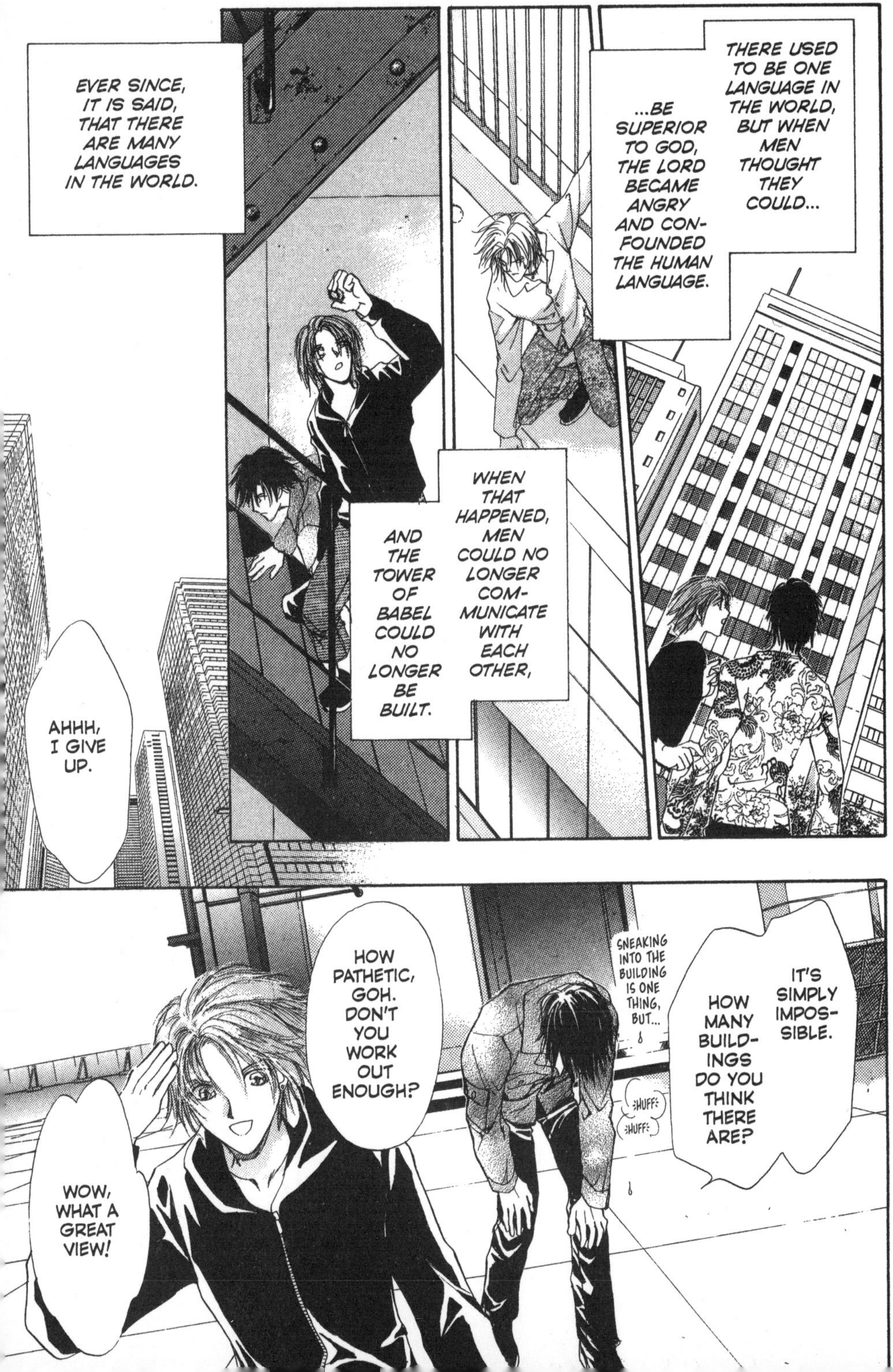
THERE USED TO BE ONE LANGUAGE IN THE WORLD, BUT WHEN MEN THOUGHT THEY COULD...
...BE SUPERIOR TO GOD, THE LORD BECAME ANGRY AND CON-FOUNDED THE HUMAN LANGUAGE.
WHEN THAT HAPPENED, MEN COULD NO LONGER COM-MUNICATE WITH EACH OTHER,
AND THE TOWER OF BABEL COULD NO LONGER BE BUILT.
EVER SINCE, IT IS SAID, THAT THERE ARE MANY LANGUAGES IN THE WORLD.
AHHH, I GIVE UP.
IT'S SIMPLY IMPOS-SIBLE.
HOW MANY BUILD-INGS DO YOU THINK THERE ARE?
SNEAKING INTO THE BUILDING IS ONE THING, BUT...
HUFF
HUFF
HOW PATHETIC, GOH. DON'T YOU WORK OUT ENOUGH?
WOW, WHAT A GREAT VIEW!

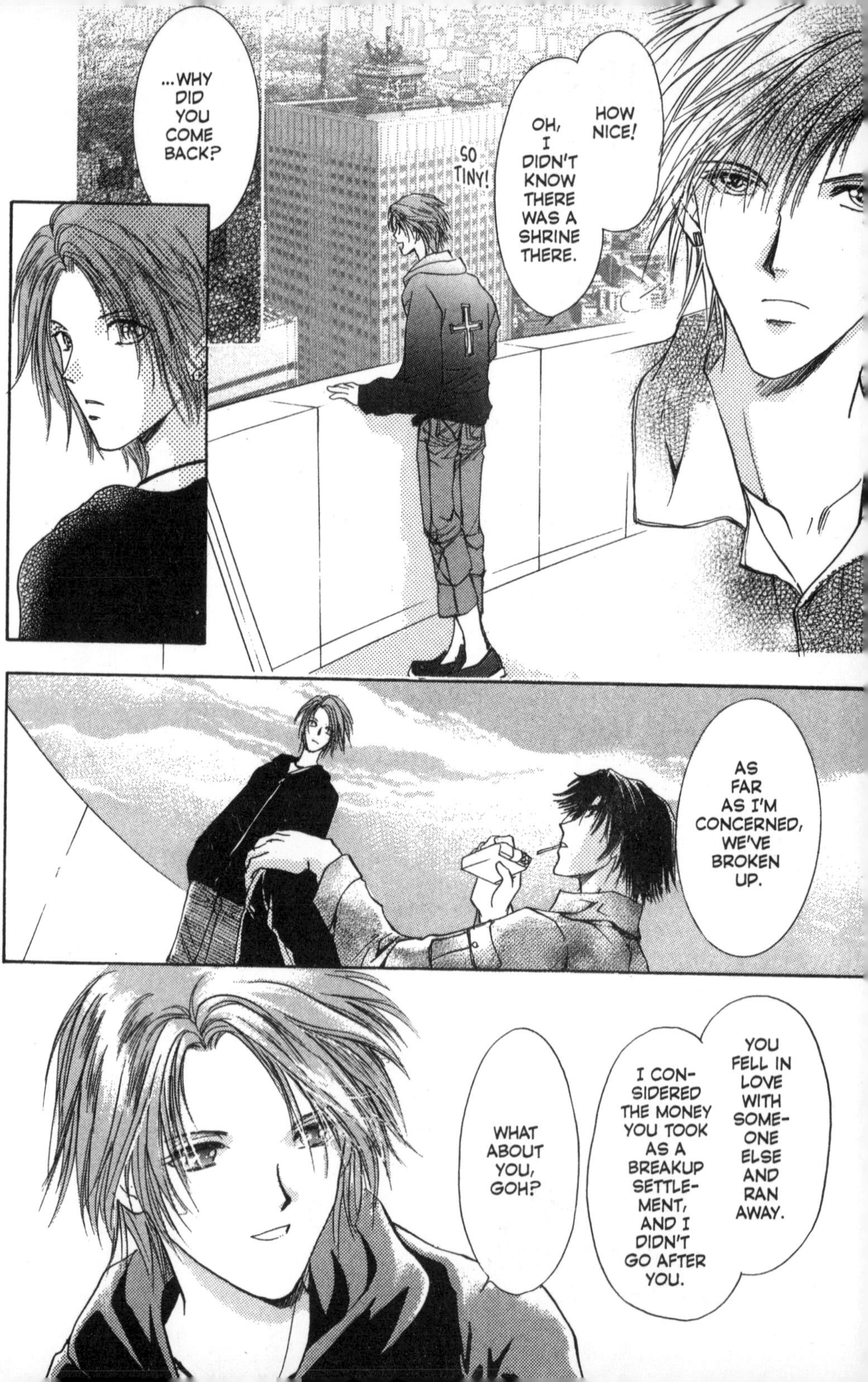
HOW NICE!
OH, I DIDN'T KNOW THERE WAS A SHRINE THERE.
SO TINY!
...WHY DID YOU COME BACK?
AS FAR AS I'M CONCERNED, WE'VE BROKEN UP.
YOU FELL IN LOVE WITH SOME-ONE ELSE AND RAN AWAY.
I CON-SIDERED THE MONEY YOU TOOK AS A BREAKUP SETTLE-MENT, AND I DIDN'T GO AFTER YOU.
WHAT ABOUT YOU, GOH?

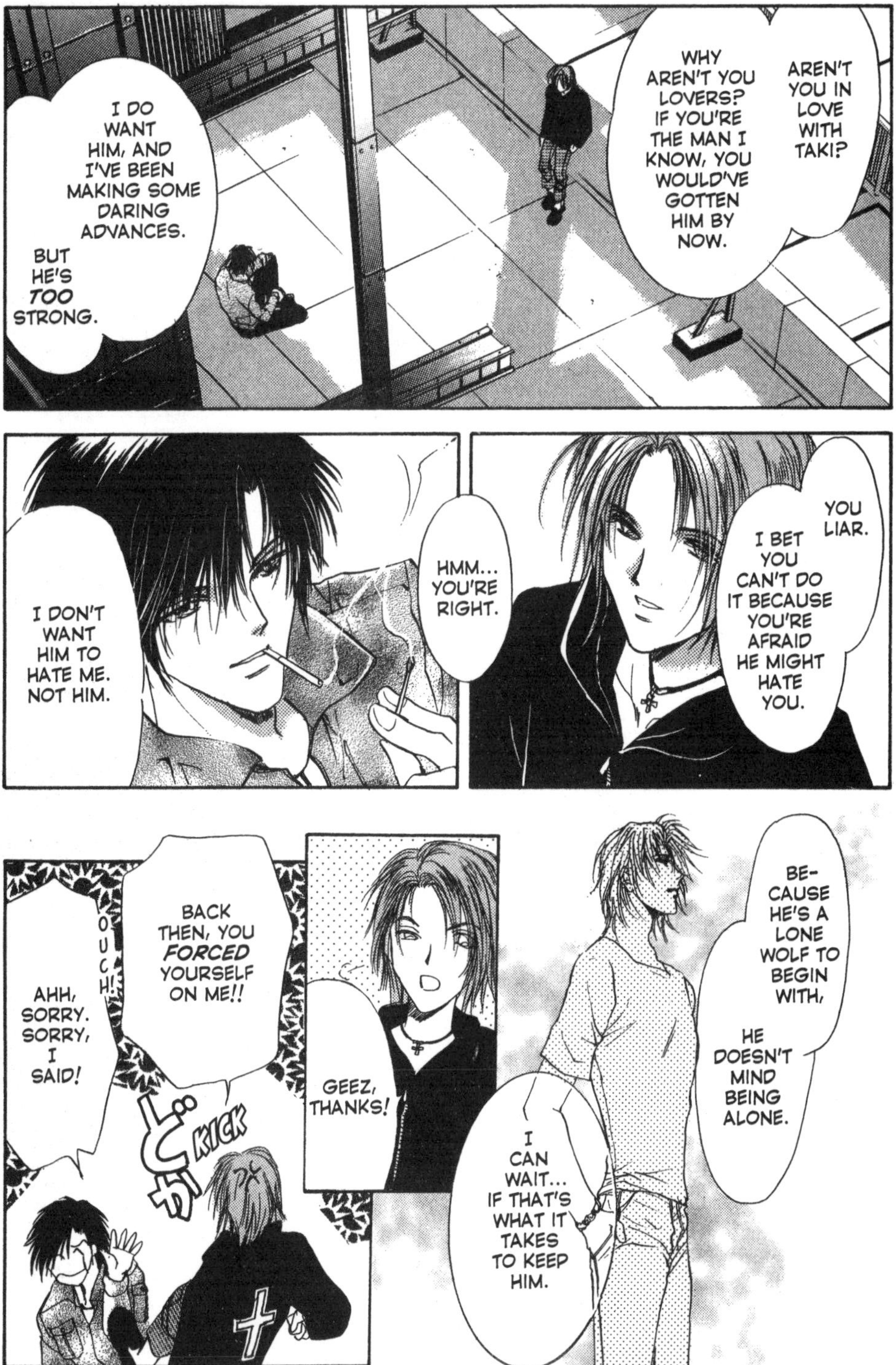
AREN'T YOU IN LOVE WITH TAKI?
WHY AREN'T YOU LOVERS? IF YOU'RE THE MAN I KNOW, YOU WOULD'VE GOTTEN HIM BY NOW.
I DO WANT HIM, AND I'VE BEEN MAKING SOME DARING ADVANCES.
BUT HE'S *TOO* STRONG.
YOU LIAR.
I BET YOU CAN'T DO IT BECAUSE YOU'RE AFRAID HE MIGHT HATE YOU.
HMM... YOU'RE RIGHT.
I DON'T WANT HIM TO HATE ME. NOT HIM.
BE- CAUSE HE'S A LONE WOLF TO BEGIN WITH,
HE DOESN'T MIND BEING ALONE.
I CAN WAIT... IF THAT'S WHAT IT TAKES TO KEEP HIM.
GEEZ, THANKS!
BACK THEN, YOU *FORCED* YOURSELF ON ME!!
OUCH!
AHH, SORRY. SORRY, I SAID!
KICK

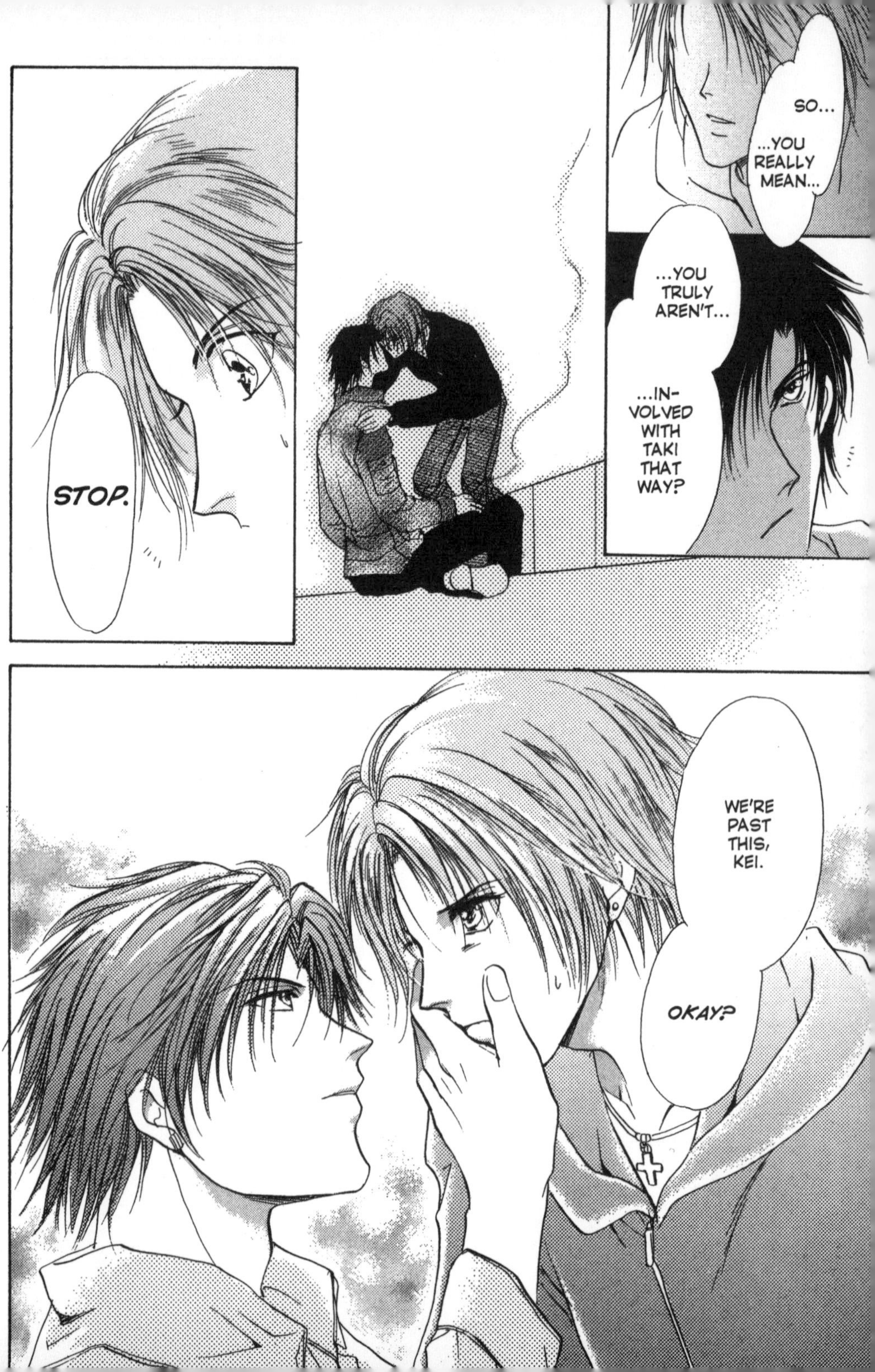
SO... ...YOU REALLY MEAN...
...YOU TRULY AREN'T... ...IN-VOLVED WITH TAKI THAT WAY?
STOP.
WE'RE PAST THIS, KEI.
OKAY?

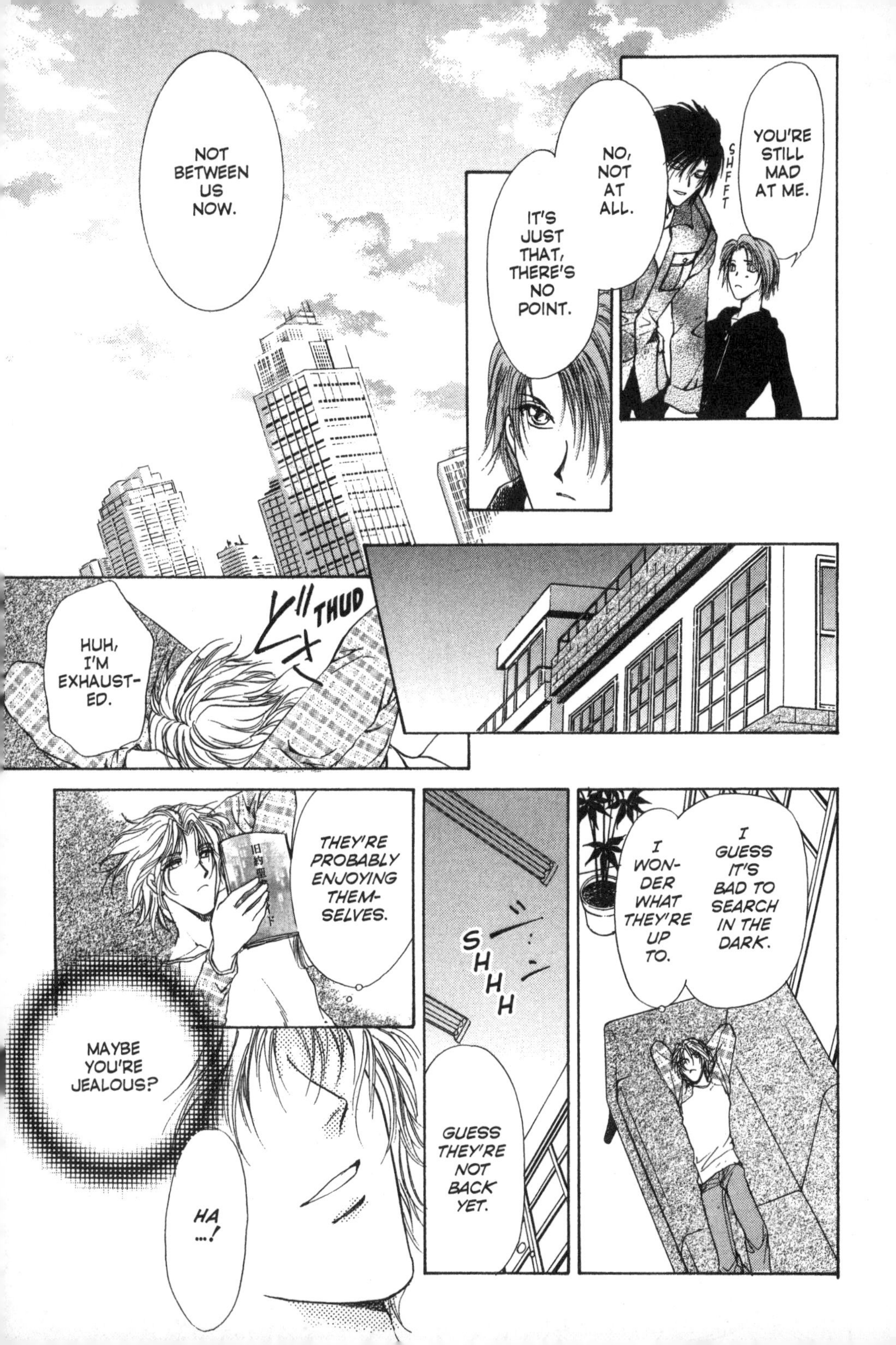
YOU'RE STILL MAD AT ME.
SHFFT
NO, NOT AT ALL.
IT'S JUST THAT, THERE'S NO POINT.
NOT BETWEEN US NOW.
THUD
HUH, I'M EXHAUST-ED.
I GUESS IT'S BAD TO SEARCH IN THE DARK.
I WON-DER WHAT THEY'RE UP TO.
SHHH
GUESS THEY'RE NOT BACK YET.
THEY'RE PROBABLY ENJOYING THEM-SELVES.
MAYBE YOU'RE JEALOUS?
HA...!

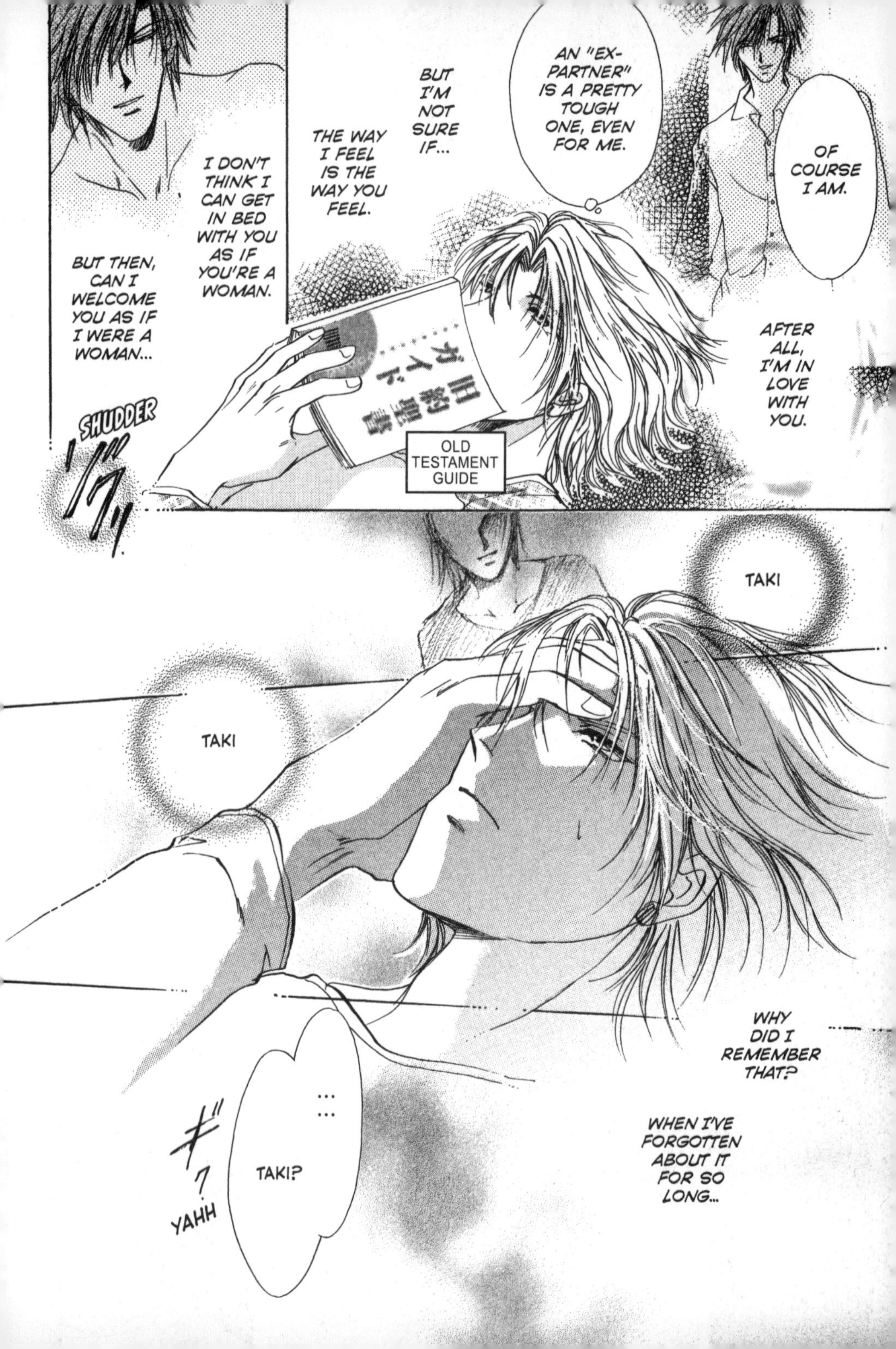
OF COURSE I AM.
AFTER ALL, I'M IN LOVE WITH YOU.
AN "EX-PARTNER" IS A PRETTY TOUGH ONE, EVEN FOR ME.
BUT I'M NOT SURE IF...
THE WAY I FEEL IS THE WAY YOU FEEL.
旧約聖書ガイド
OLD TESTAMENT GUIDE
I DON'T THINK I CAN GET IN BED WITH YOU AS IF YOU'RE A WOMAN.
BUT THEN, CAN I WELCOME YOU AS IF I WERE A WOMAN...
SHUDDER
TAKI
TAKI
WHY DID I REMEMBER THAT?
WHEN I'VE FORGOTTEN ABOUT IT FOR SO LONG...
......
TAKI?
YAHH

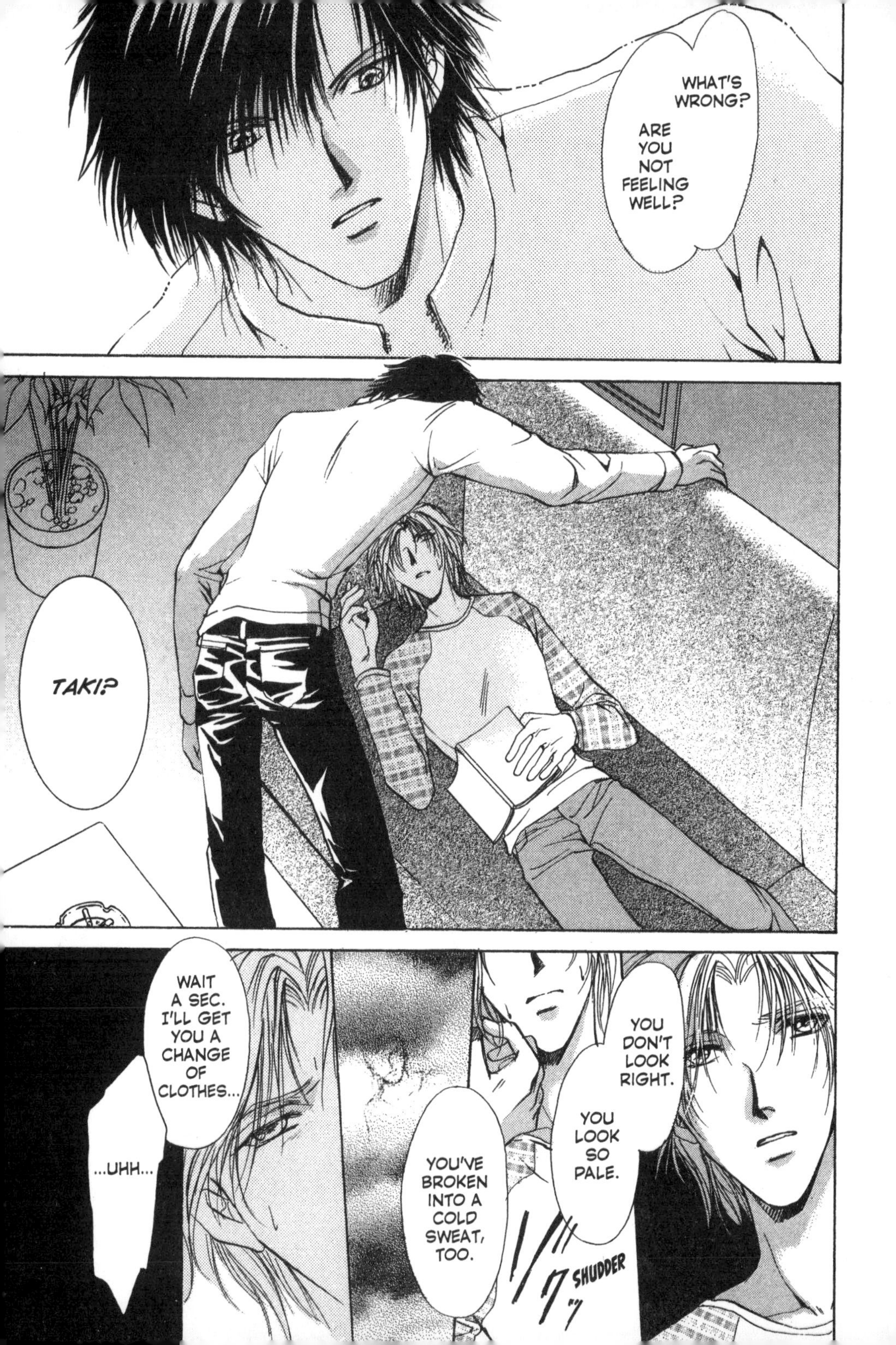
WHAT'S WRONG?
ARE YOU NOT FEELING WELL?
TAKI?
YOU DON'T LOOK RIGHT.
YOU LOOK SO PALE.
YOU'VE BROKEN INTO A COLD SWEAT, TOO.
SHUDDER
WAIT A SEC. I'LL GET YOU A CHANGE OF CLOTHES...
...UHH...

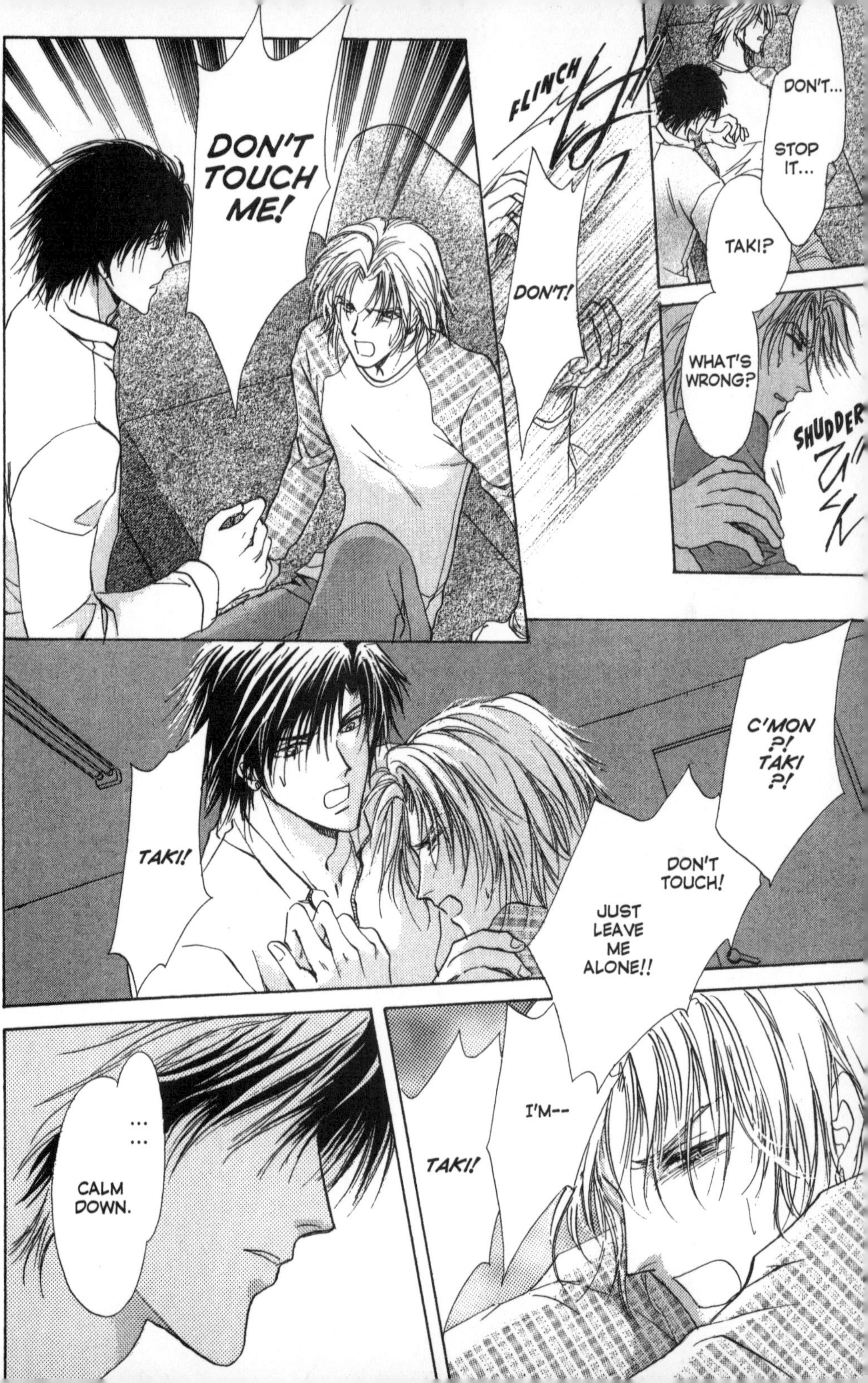
DON'T...
STOP IT...
TAKI?
WHAT'S WRONG?
SHUDDER
FLINCH
DON'T!
DON'T TOUCH ME!
C'MON ?! TAKI ?!
DON'T TOUCH!
JUST LEAVE ME ALONE!!
TAKI!
I'M--
TAKI!
... ...
CALM DOWN.

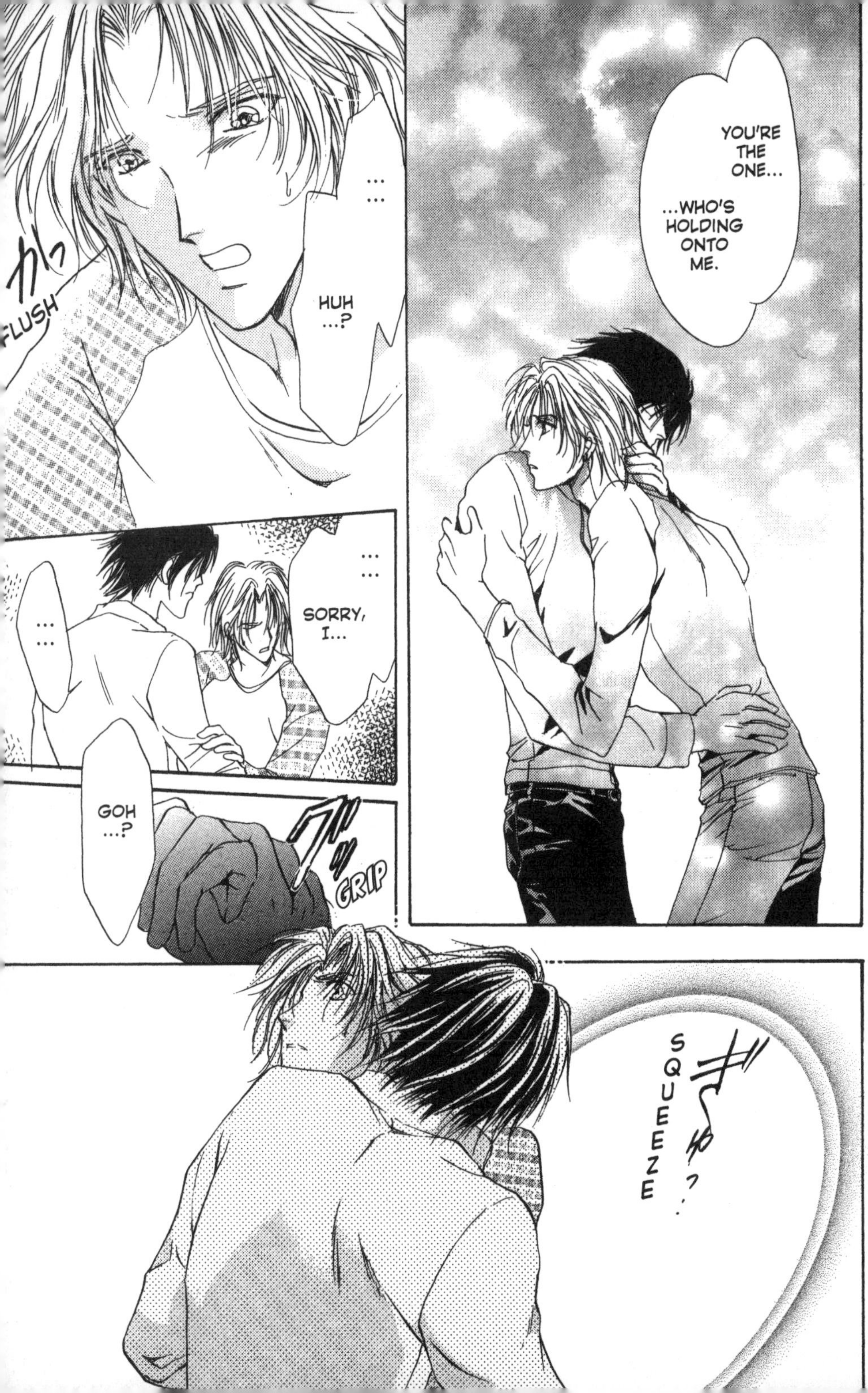
YOU'RE THE ONE...
...WHO'S HOLDING ONTO ME.
... ...
HUH ...?
FLUSH
... ...
SORRY, I...
... ...
GOH ...?
GRIP
SQUEEZE

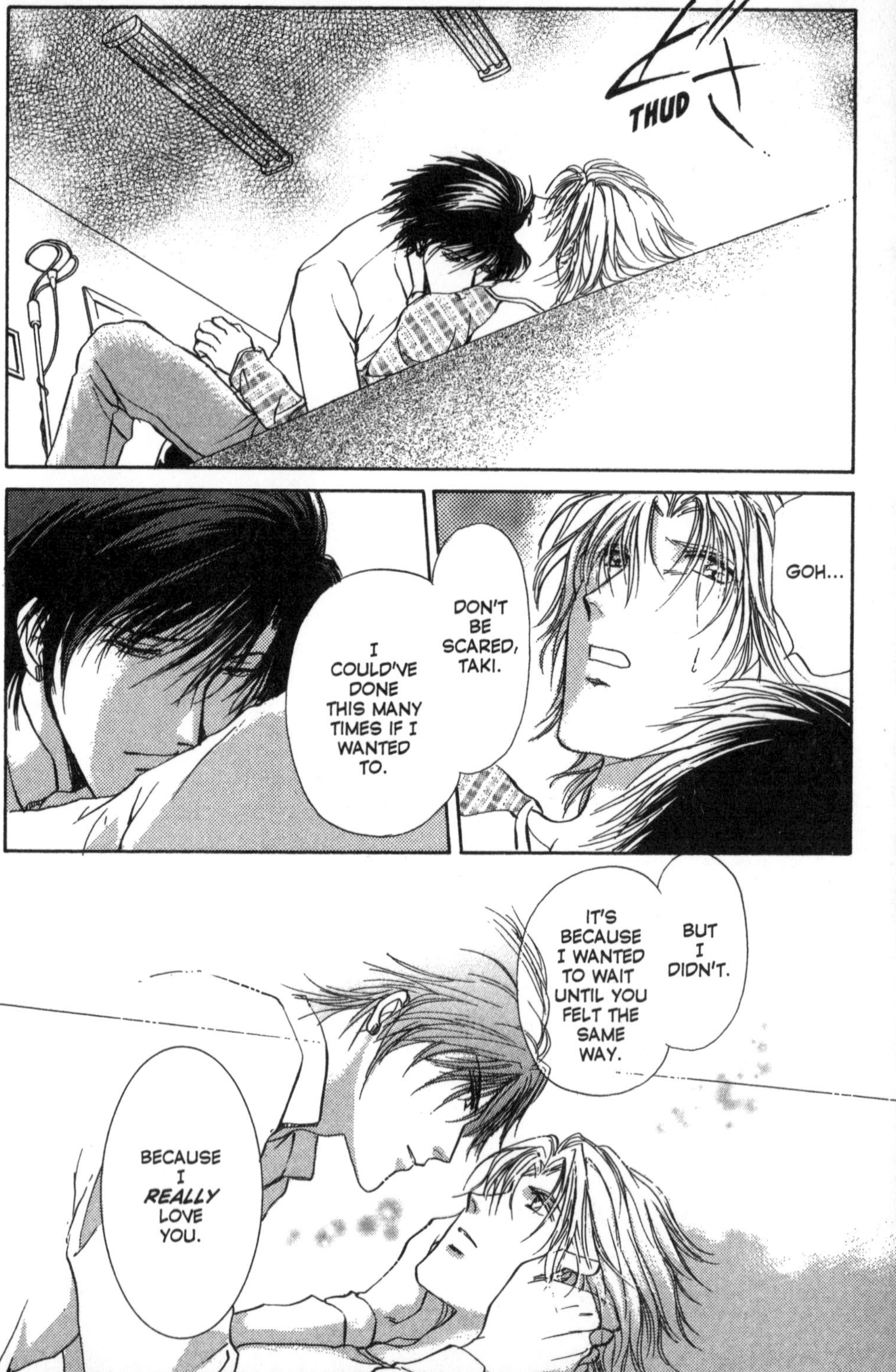
THUD
GOH...
DON'T BE SCARED, TAKI.
I COULD'VE DONE THIS MANY TIMES IF I WANTED TO.
BUT I DIDN'T.
IT'S BECAUSE I WANTED TO WAIT UNTIL YOU FELT THE SAME WAY.
BECAUSE I *REALLY* LOVE YOU.

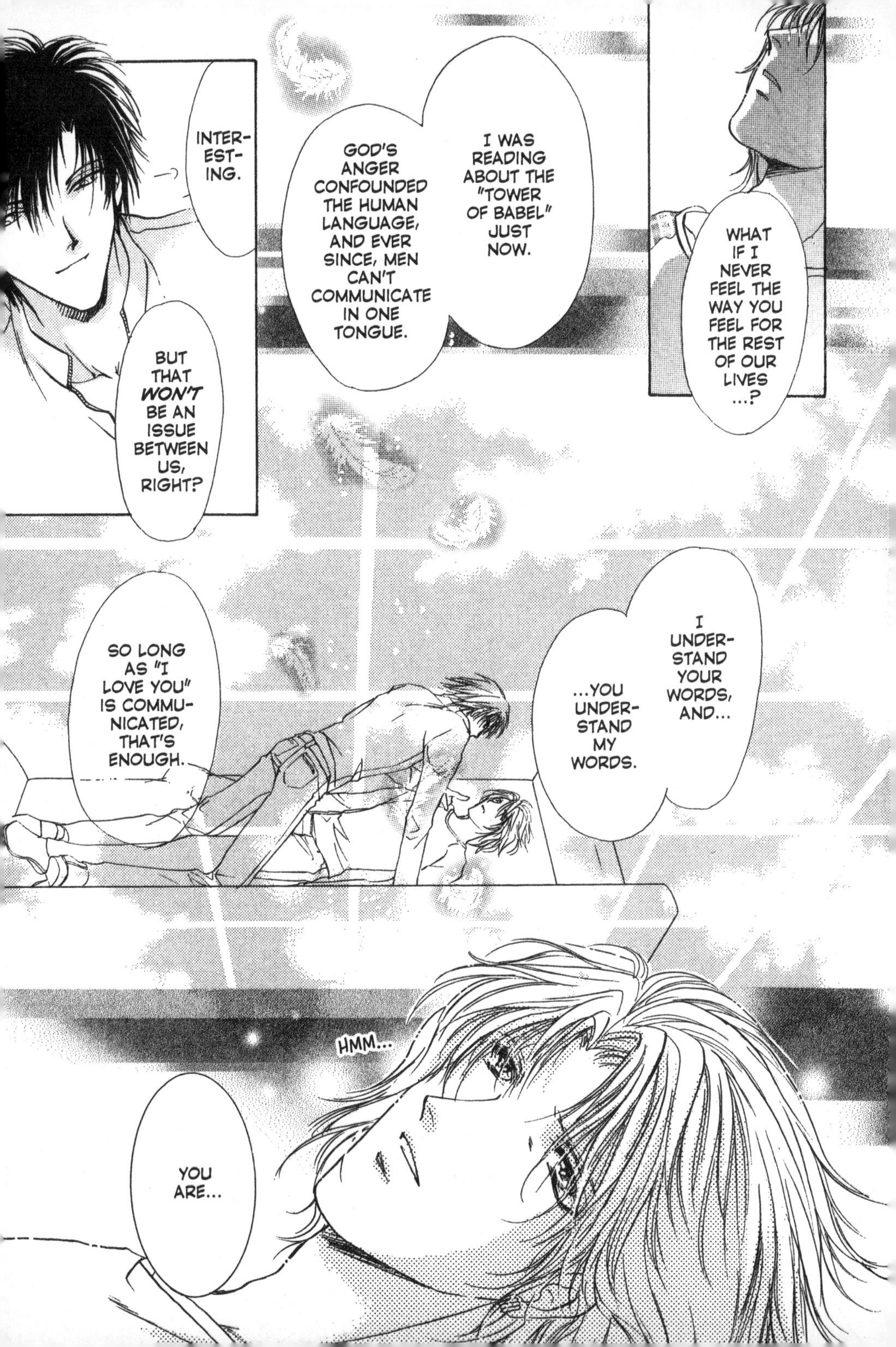
WHAT IF I NEVER FEEL THE WAY YOU FEEL FOR THE REST OF OUR LIVES ...?
I WAS READING ABOUT THE "TOWER OF BABEL" JUST NOW.
GOD'S ANGER CONFOUNDED THE HUMAN LANGUAGE, AND EVER SINCE, MEN CAN'T COMMUNICATE IN ONE TONGUE.
INTER-EST-ING.
BUT THAT ***WON'T*** BE AN ISSUE BETWEEN US, RIGHT?
I UNDER-STAND YOUR WORDS, AND...
...YOU UNDER-STAND MY WORDS.
SO LONG AS "I LOVE YOU" IS COMMU-NICATED, THAT'S ENOUGH.
HMM...
YOU ARE...

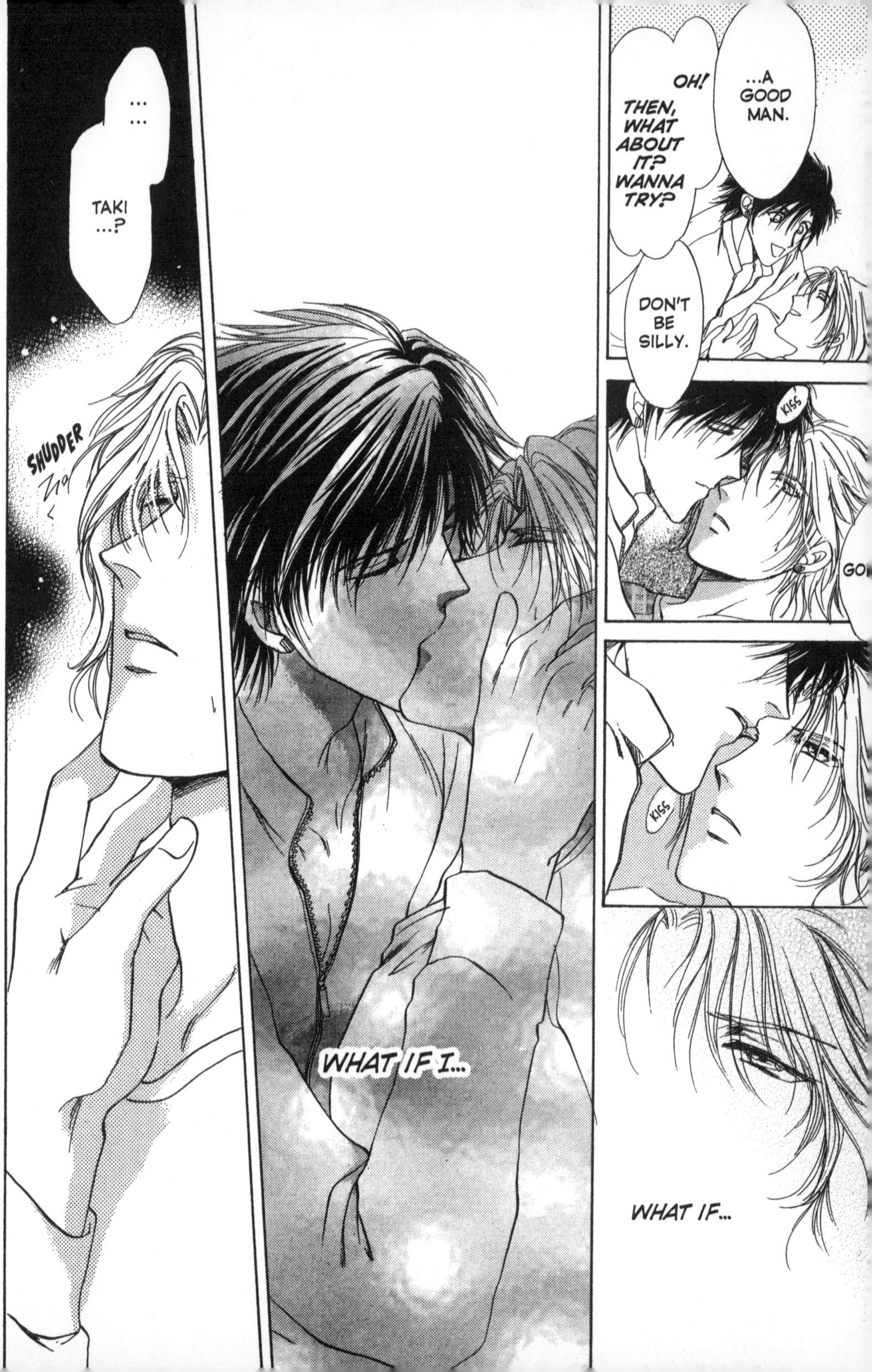
...A GOOD MAN.
OH! THEN, WHAT ABOUT IT? WANNA TRY?
DON'T BE SILLY.
KISS
KISS
WHAT IF...
WHAT IF I...
...
...
TAKI ...?
SHUDDER

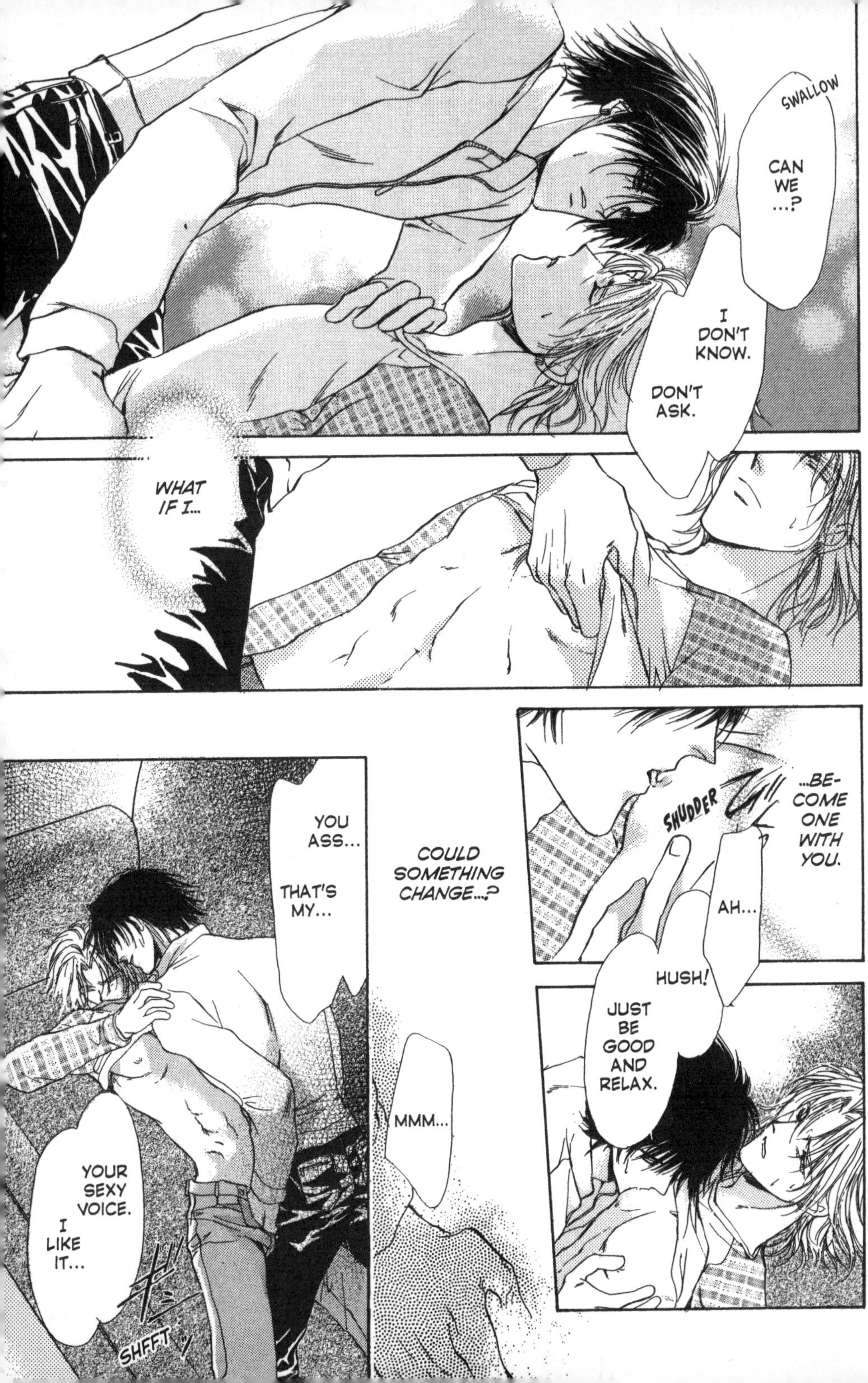
SWALLOW
CAN WE ...?
I DON'T KNOW.
DON'T ASK.
WHAT IF I...
...BE-COME ONE WITH YOU.
SHUDDER
AH...
HUSH!
JUST BE GOOD AND RELAX.
COULD SOMETHING CHANGE...?
YOU ASS...
THAT'S MY...
MMM...
YOUR SEXY VOICE.
I LIKE IT...
SHFFT

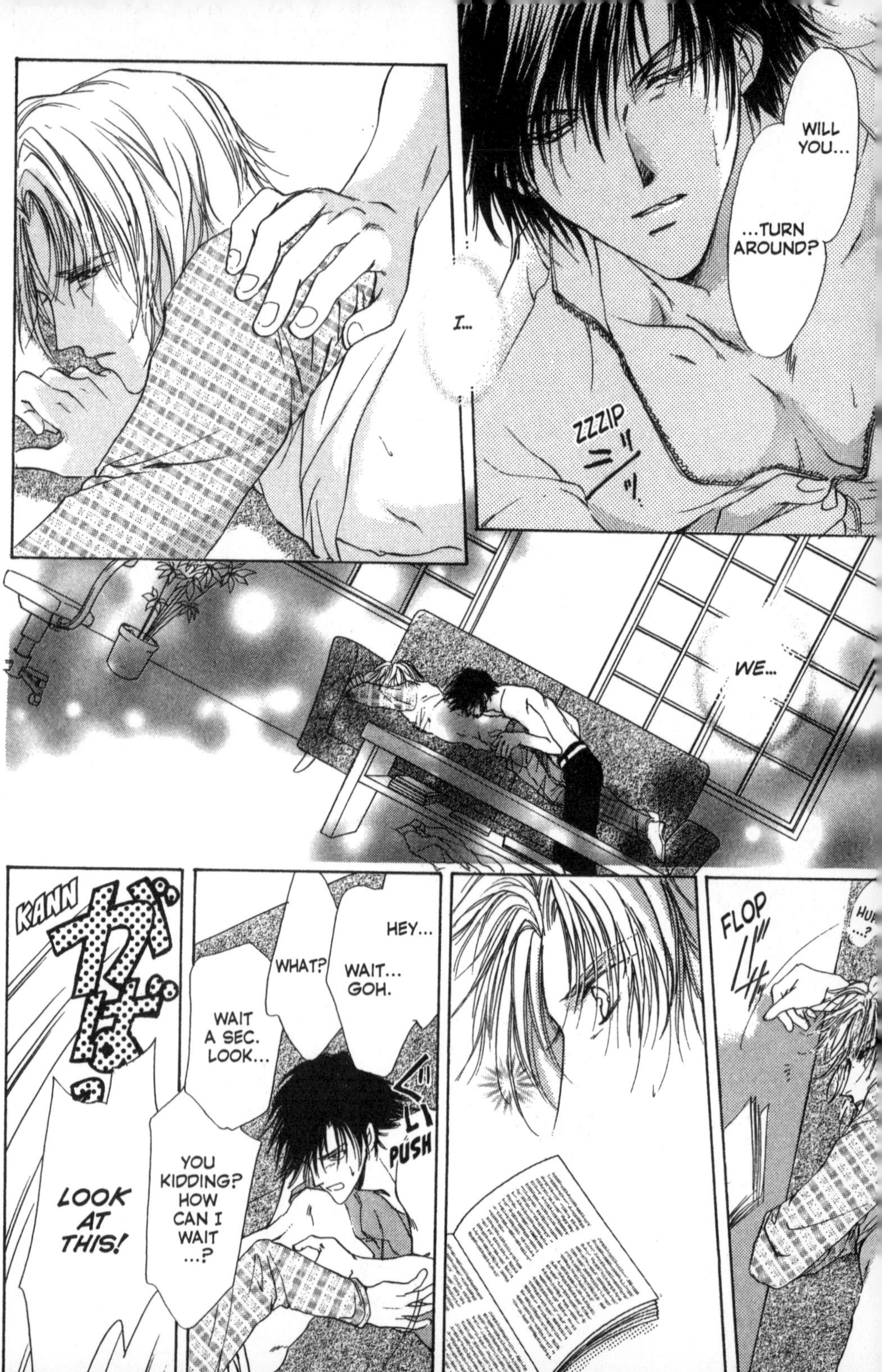

WILL YOU...
...TURN AROUND?
I...
ZZZIP
WE...
FLOP
HU...?
HEY...
WAIT... GOH.
WHAT?
WAIT A SEC. LOOK...
PUSH
YOU KIDDING? HOW CAN I WAIT...?
KANN
LOOK AT THIS!

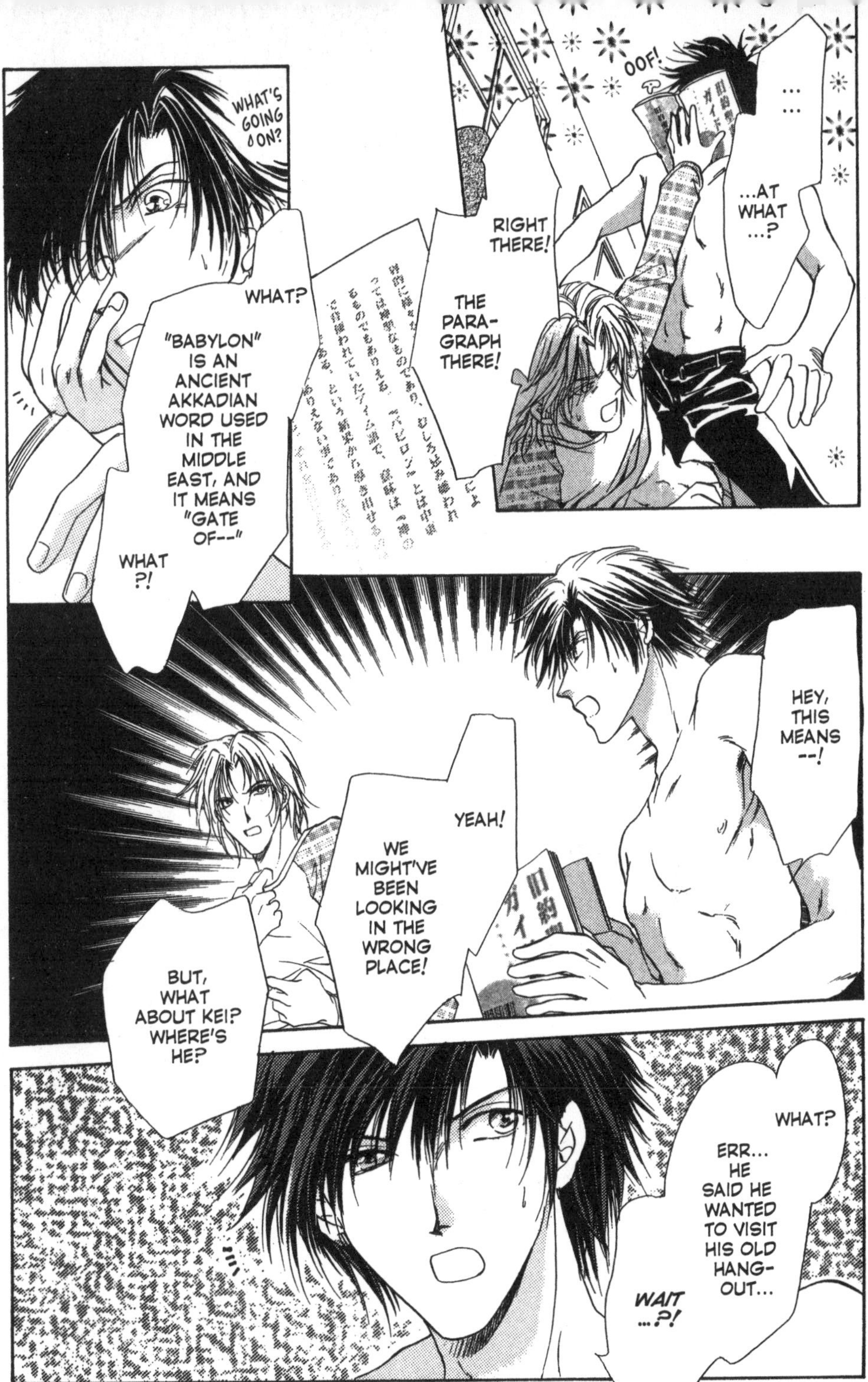
OOF!
...
...
...AT WHAT ...?
RIGHT THERE!
THE PARA-GRAPH THERE!
WHAT'S GOING ON?
WHAT?
"BABYLON" IS AN ANCIENT AKKADIAN WORD USED IN THE MIDDLE EAST, AND IT MEANS "GATE OF--"
WHAT ?!
HEY, THIS MEANS --!
YEAH!
WE MIGHT'VE BEEN LOOKING IN THE WRONG PLACE!
BUT, WHAT ABOUT KEI? WHERE'S HE?
WHAT?
ERR... HE SAID HE WANTED TO VISIT HIS OLD HANG-OUT...
WAIT ...?!

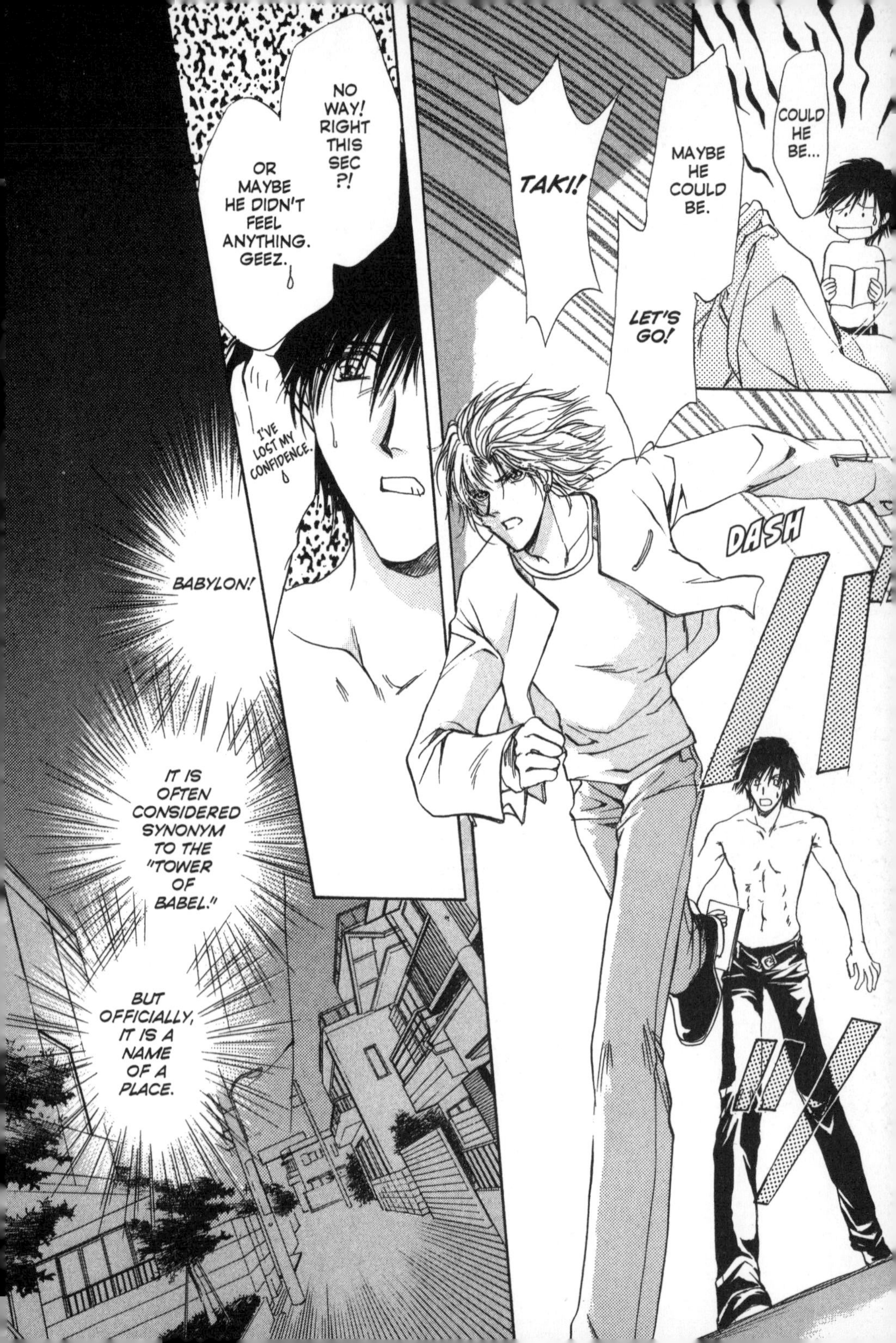

COULD HE BE...
MAYBE HE COULD BE.
TAKI!
LET'S GO!
DASH
NO WAY! RIGHT THIS SEC?!
OR MAYBE HE DIDN'T FEEL ANYTHING. GEEZ.
I'VE LOST MY CONFIDENCE.
BABYLON!
IT IS OFTEN CONSIDERED SYNONYM TO THE "TOWER OF BABEL."
BUT OFFICIALLY, IT IS A NAME OF A PLACE.

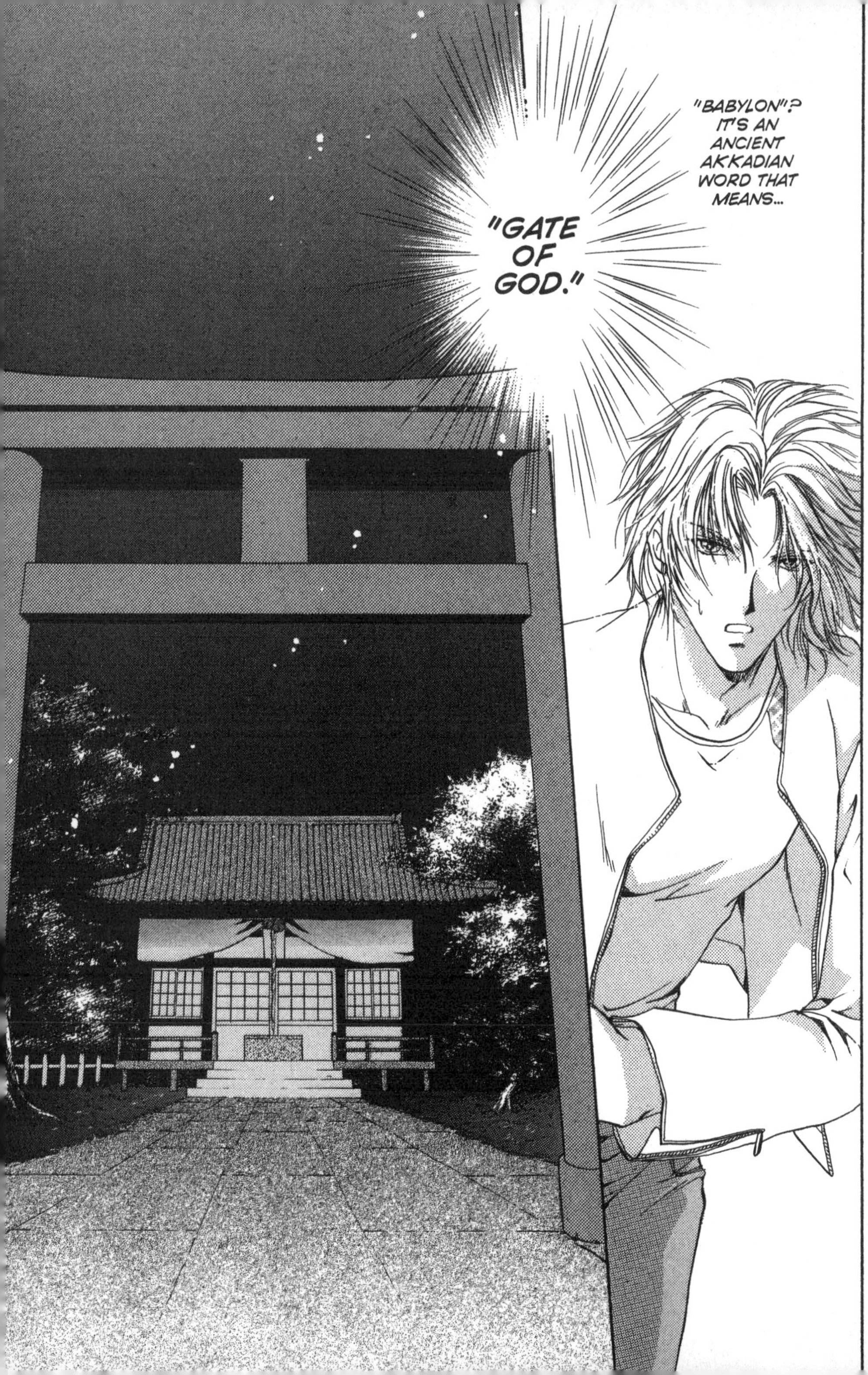
"BABYLON"? IT'S AN ANCIENT AKKADIAN WORD THAT MEANS...
"GATE OF GOD."

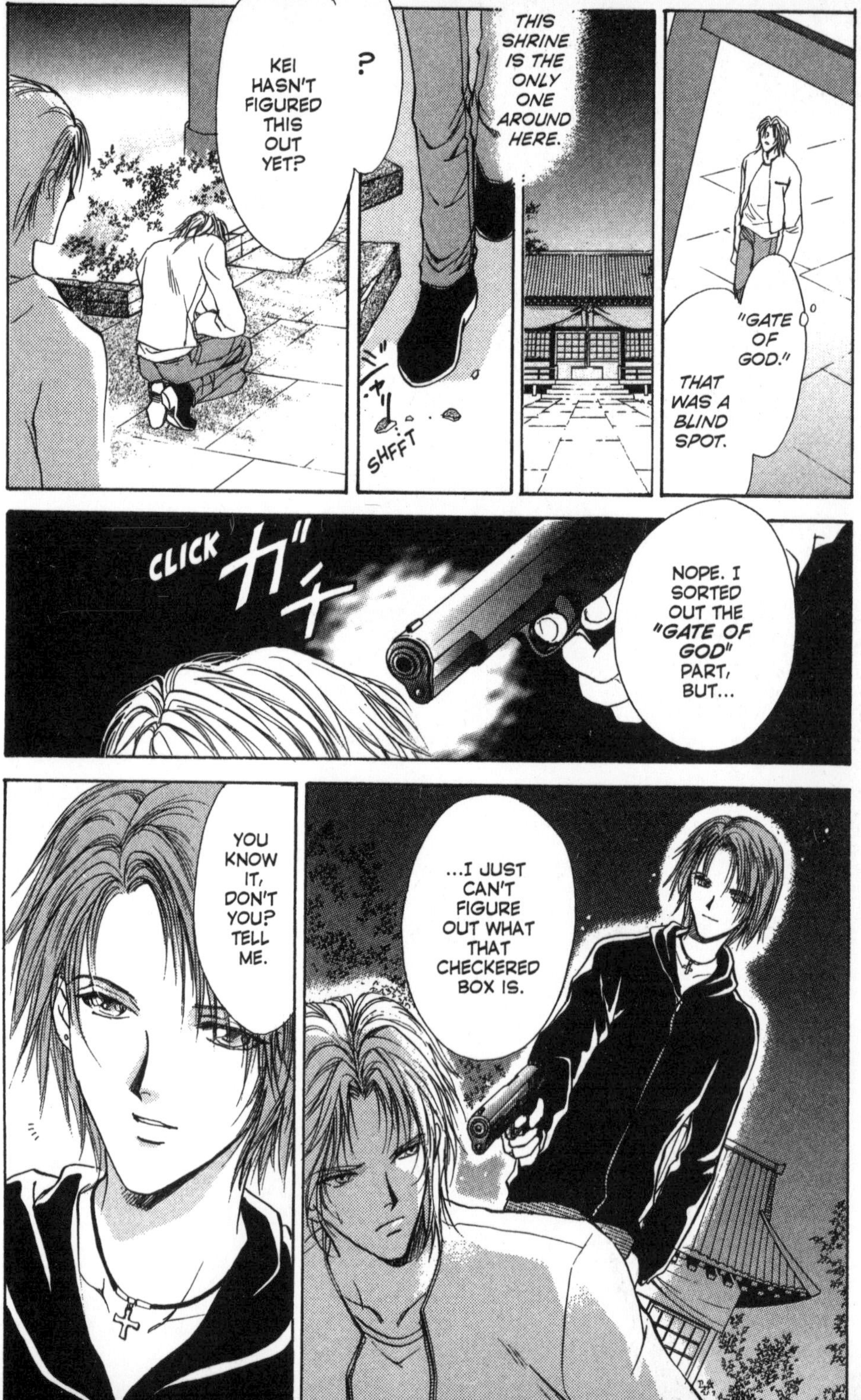
"GATE OF GOD."
THAT WAS A BLIND SPOT.
THIS SHRINE IS THE ONLY ONE AROUND HERE.
SHFFT
?
KEI HASN'T FIGURED THIS OUT YET?
NOPE. I SORTED OUT THE "GATE OF GOD" PART, BUT...
CLICK ガチ
...I JUST CAN'T FIGURE OUT WHAT THAT CHECKERED BOX IS.
YOU KNOW IT, DON'T YOU? TELL ME.

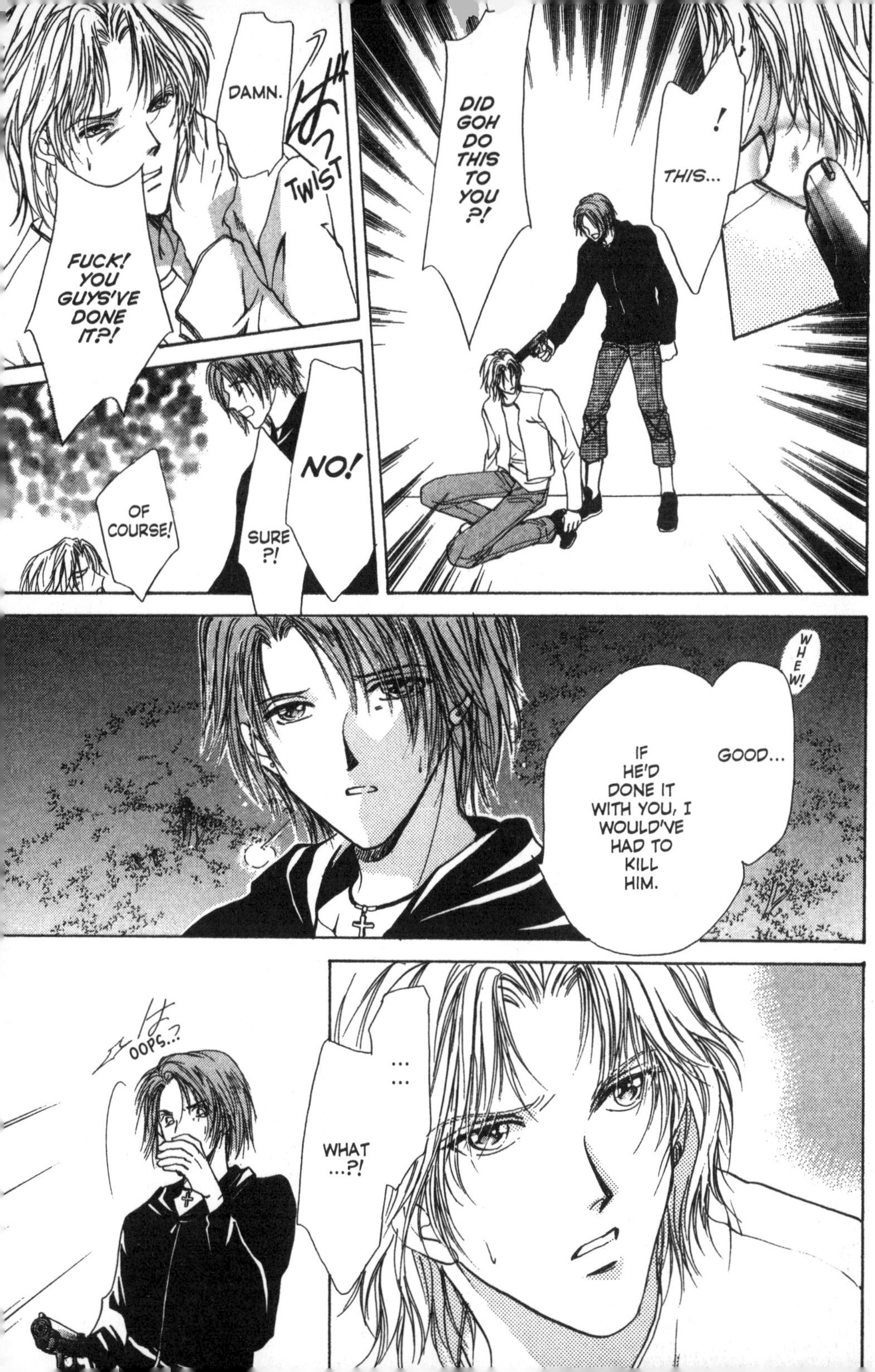
!
THIS...
DID GOH DO THIS TO YOU ?!
DAMN.
ばっ
TWIST
FUCK! YOU GUYS'VE DONE IT?!
NO!
SURE ?!
OF COURSE!
WHEW!
GOOD...
IF HE'D DONE IT WITH YOU, I WOULD'VE HAD TO KILL HIM.
... ...
WHAT ...?!
はっ
OOPS..?

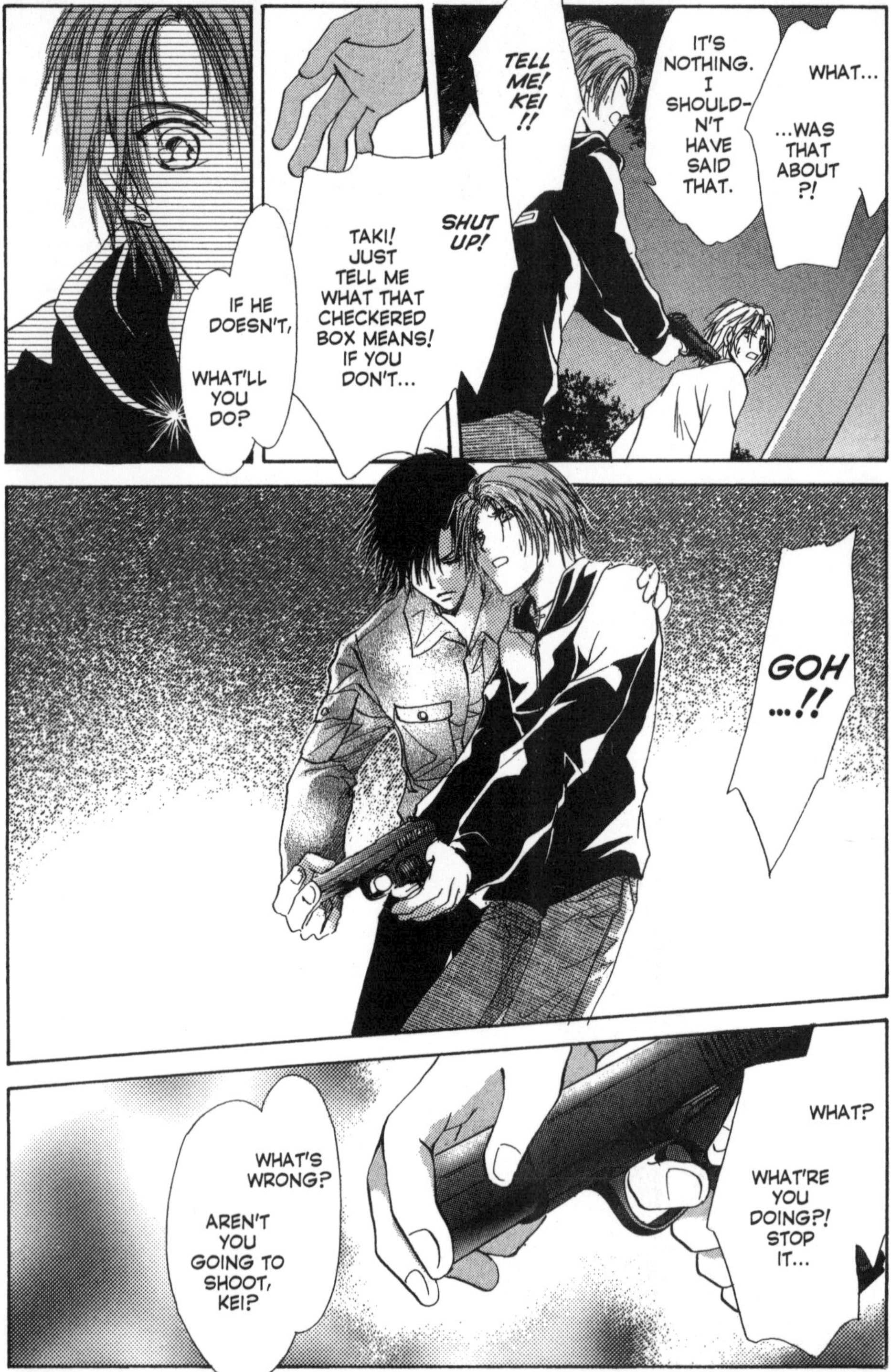
WHAT...
...WAS THAT ABOUT?!
IT'S NOTHING. I SHOULDN'T HAVE SAID THAT.
TELL ME! KEI!!
SHUT UP!
TAKI! JUST TELL ME WHAT THAT CHECKERED BOX MEANS! IF YOU DON'T...
IF HE DOESN'T,
WHAT'LL YOU DO?
GOH...!!
WHAT?
WHAT'RE YOU DOING?! STOP IT...
WHAT'S WRONG?
AREN'T YOU GOING TO SHOOT, KEI?

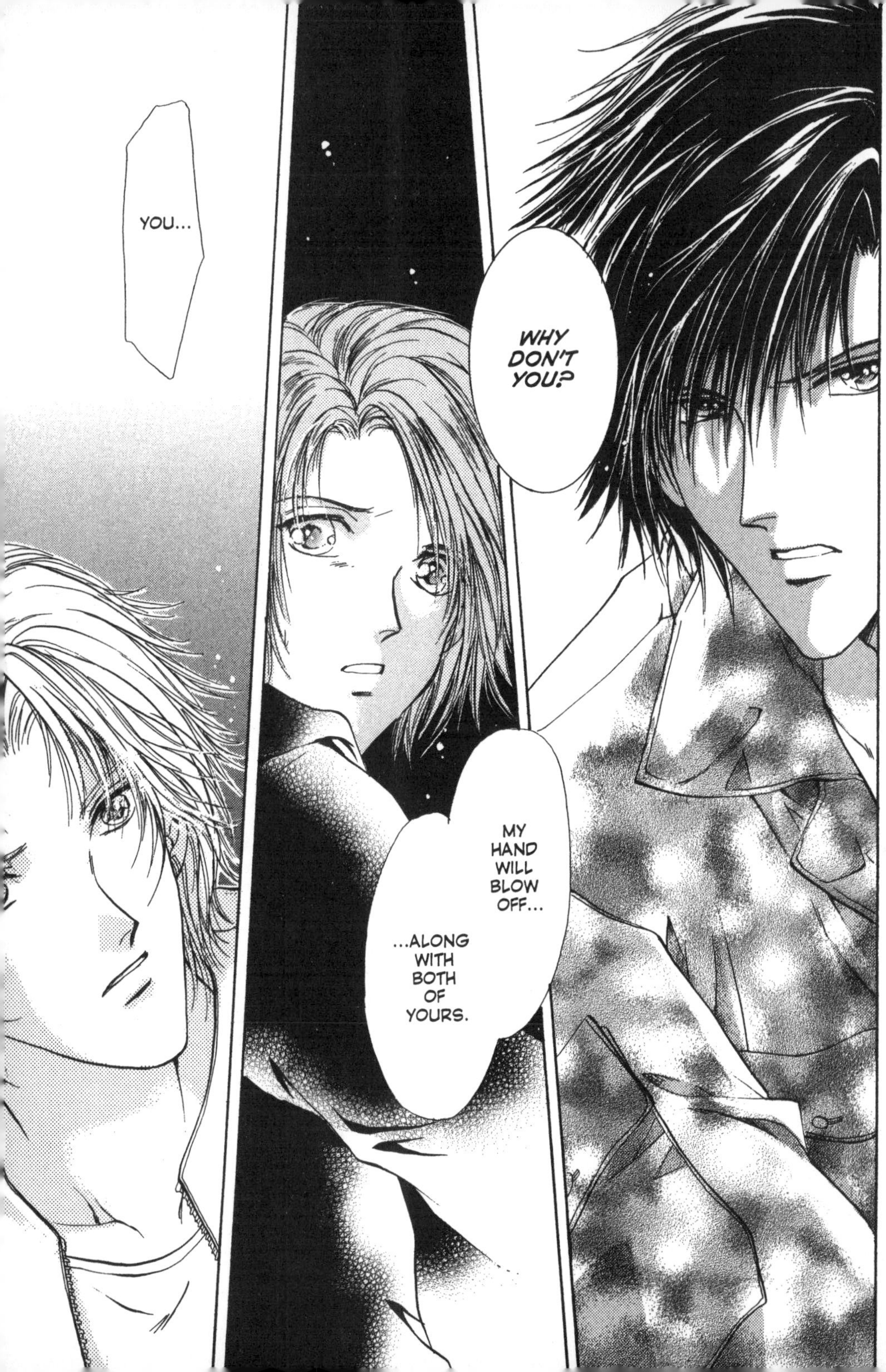
WHY DON'T YOU?
MY HAND WILL BLOW OFF...
...ALONG WITH BOTH OF YOURS.
YOU...

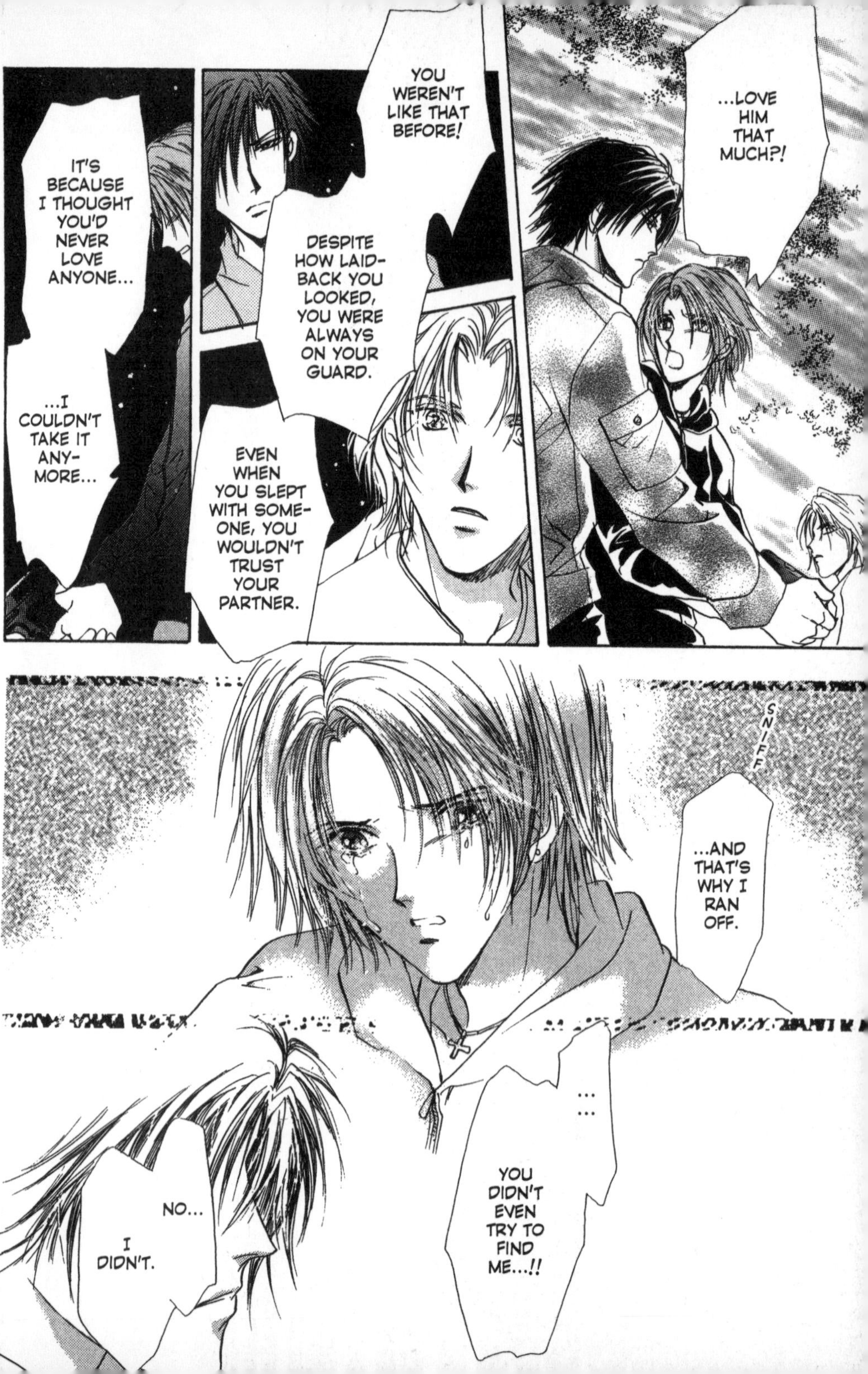
...LOVE HIM THAT MUCH?!
YOU WEREN'T LIKE THAT BEFORE!
DESPITE HOW LAID-BACK YOU LOOKED, YOU WERE ALWAYS ON YOUR GUARD.
EVEN WHEN YOU SLEPT WITH SOMEONE, YOU WOULDN'T TRUST YOUR PARTNER.
IT'S BECAUSE I THOUGHT YOU'D NEVER LOVE ANYONE...
...I COULDN'T TAKE IT ANYMORE...
SNIFF
...AND THAT'S WHY I RAN OFF.
......
YOU DIDN'T EVEN TRY TO FIND ME...!!
NO...
I DIDN'T.

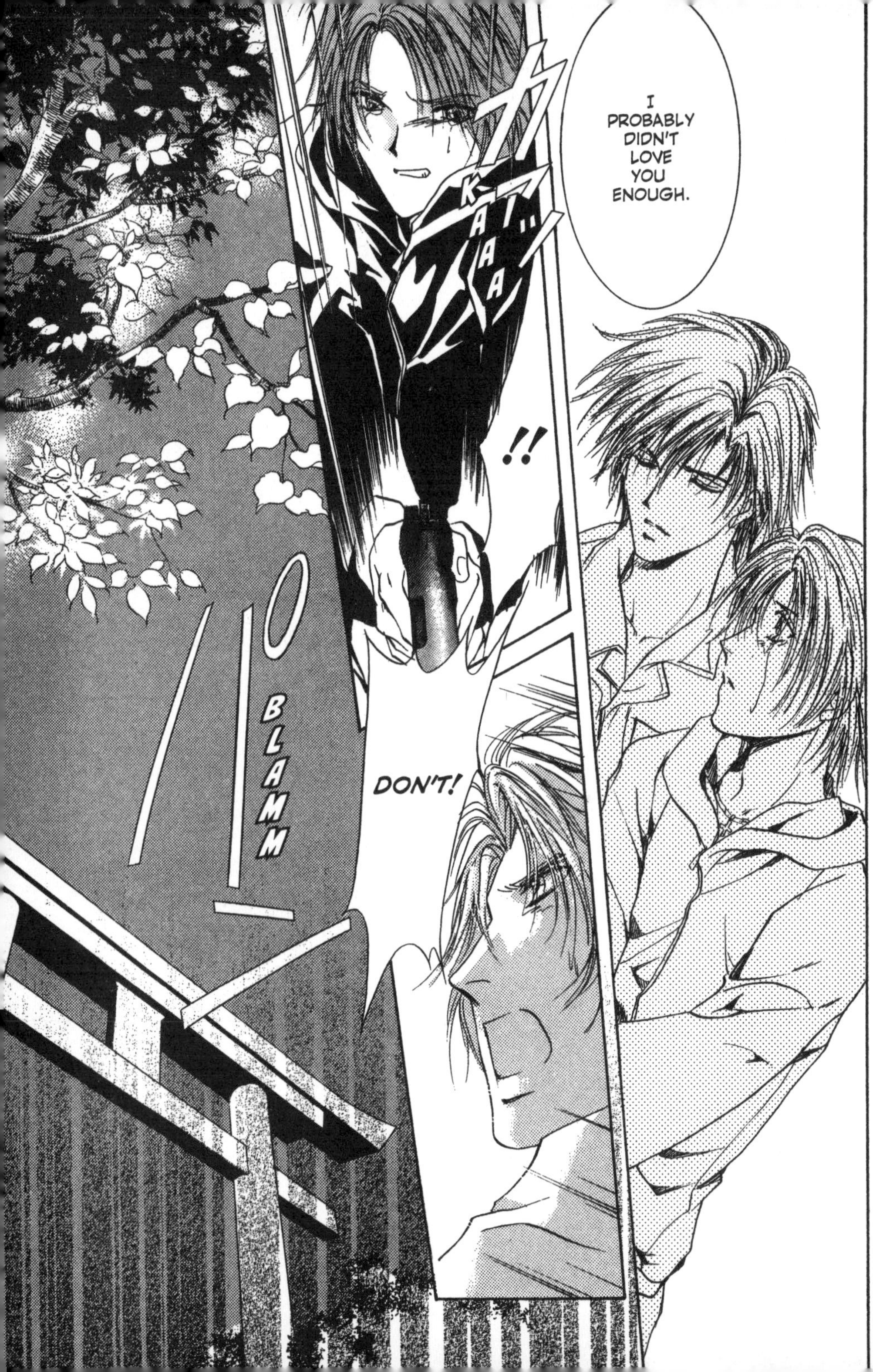
I PROBABLY DIDN'T LOVE YOU ENOUGH.
KATAAA!!
!!
DON'T!
BLAMM

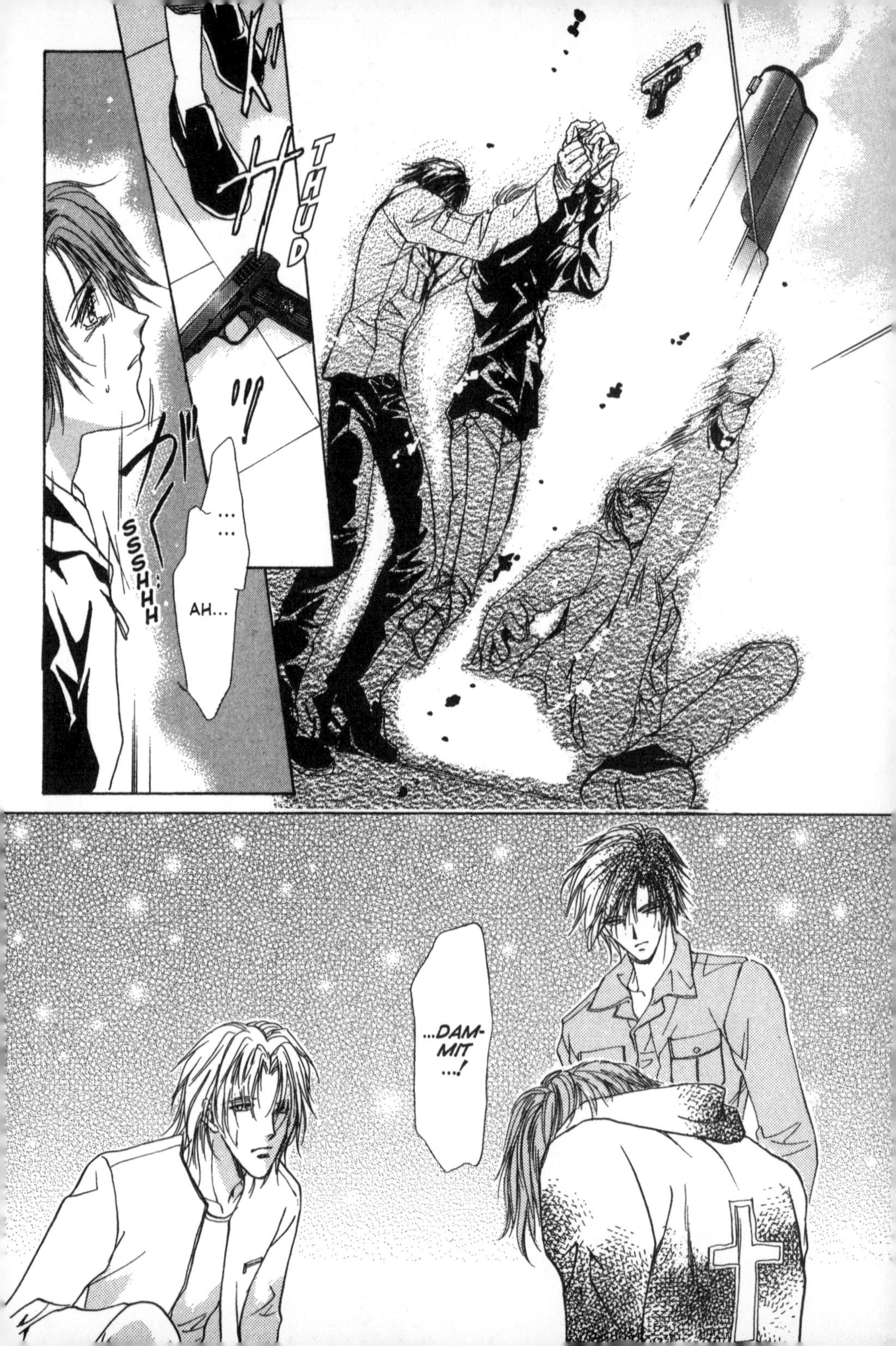
THUD
SSSHHH
......
AH...
...DAM-MIT ...!

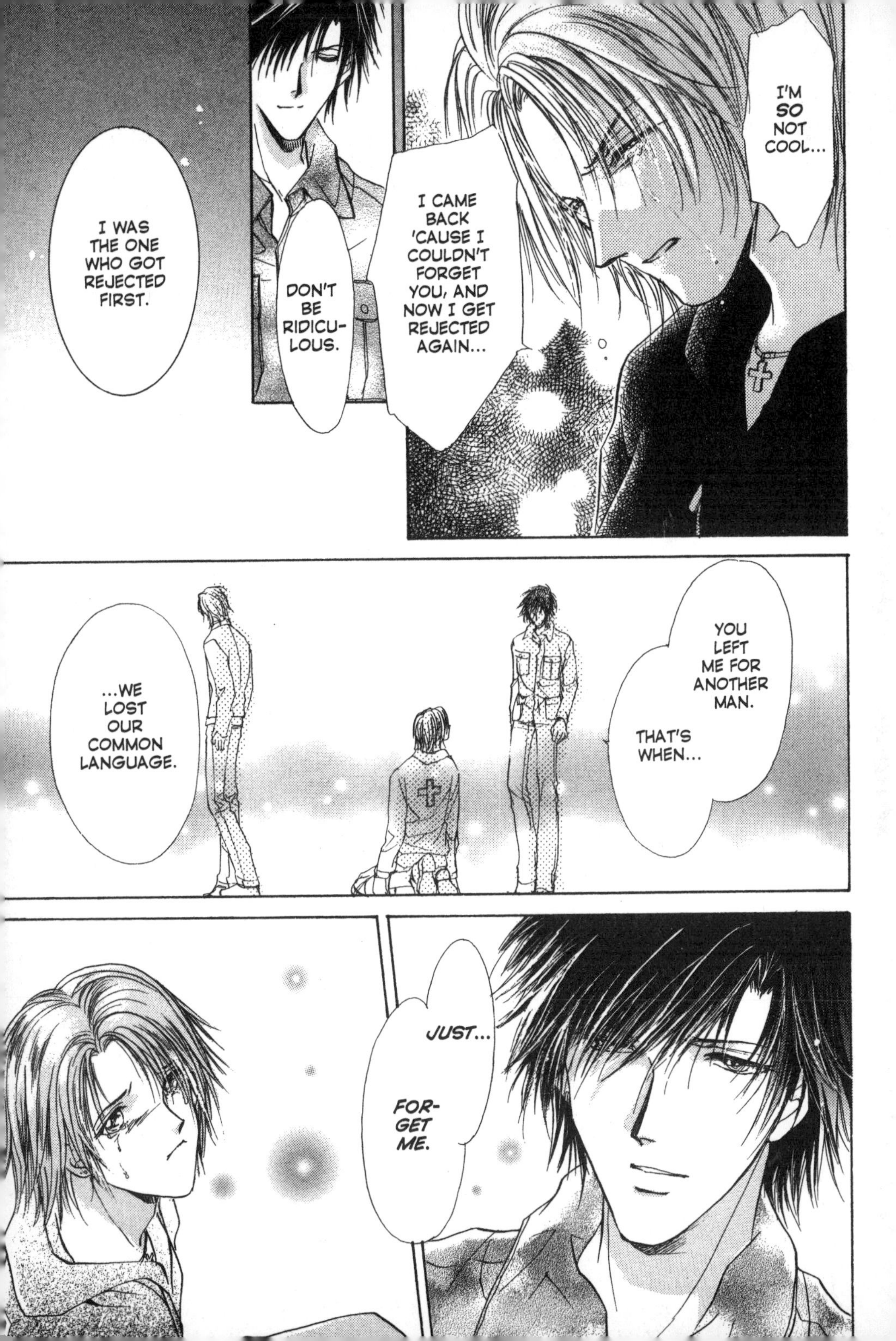
I'M SO NOT COOL...
I CAME BACK 'CAUSE I COULDN'T FORGET YOU, AND NOW I GET REJECTED AGAIN...
DON'T BE RIDICULOUS.
I WAS THE ONE WHO GOT REJECTED FIRST.
YOU LEFT ME FOR ANOTHER MAN.
THAT'S WHEN...
...WE LOST OUR COMMON LANGUAGE.
JUST...
FOR-GET ME.

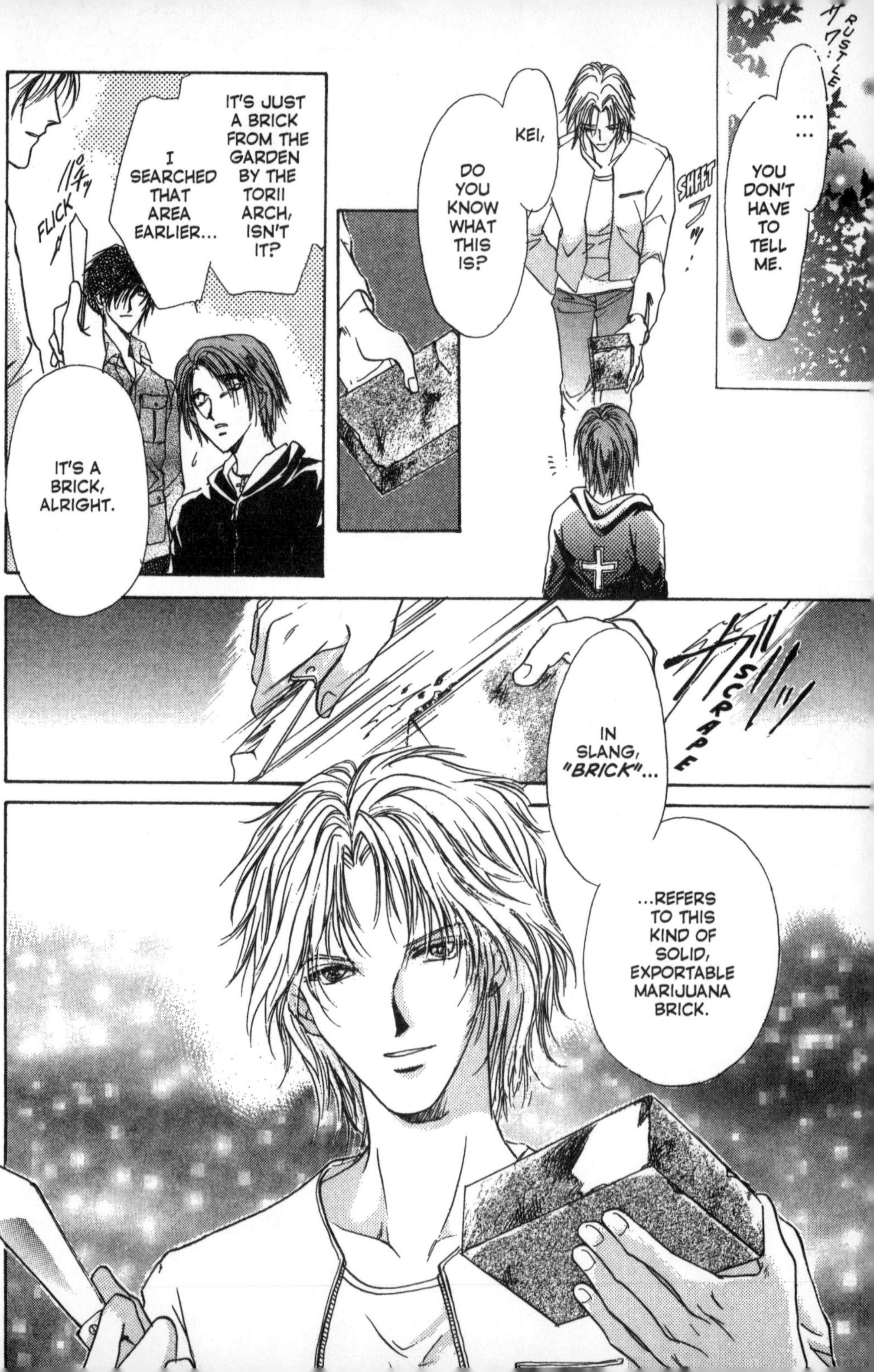

RUSTLE
……
YOU DON'T HAVE TO TELL ME.
SHFFT
KEI,
DO YOU KNOW WHAT THIS IS?
IT'S JUST A BRICK FROM THE GARDEN BY THE TORII ARCH, ISN'T IT?
I SEARCHED THAT AREA EARLIER…
FLICK
IT'S A BRICK, ALRIGHT.
SCRAPE
IN SLANG, "BRICK"…
…REFERS TO THIS KIND OF SOLID, EXPORTABLE MARIJUANA BRICK.

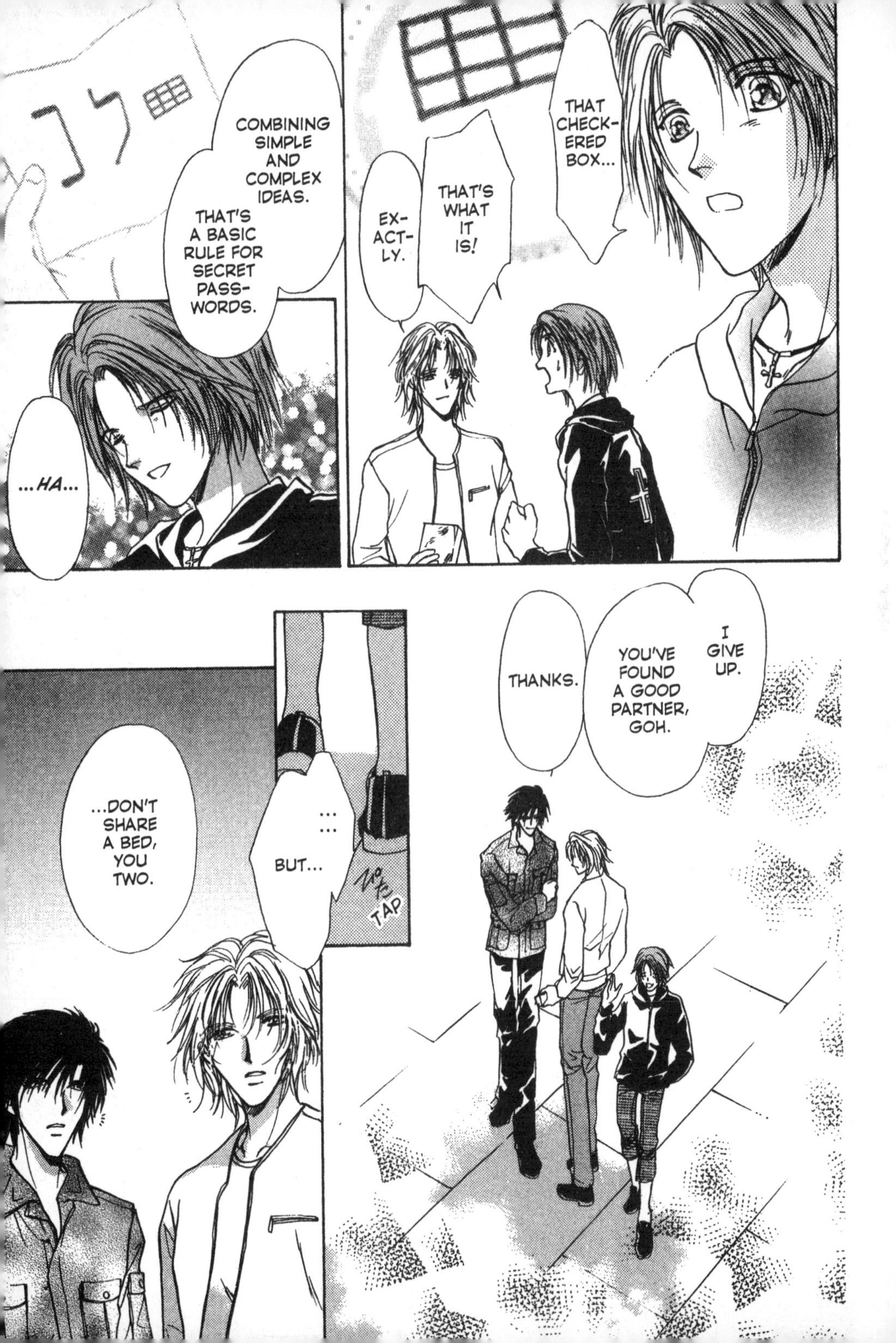
THAT CHECKERED BOX...
THAT'S WHAT IT IS!
EXACTLY.
COMBINING SIMPLE AND COMPLEX IDEAS.
THAT'S A BASIC RULE FOR SECRET PASSWORDS.
...HA...
I GIVE UP.
YOU'VE FOUND A GOOD PARTNER, GOH.
THANKS.
......
BUT...
TAP
...DON'T SHARE A BED, YOU TWO.

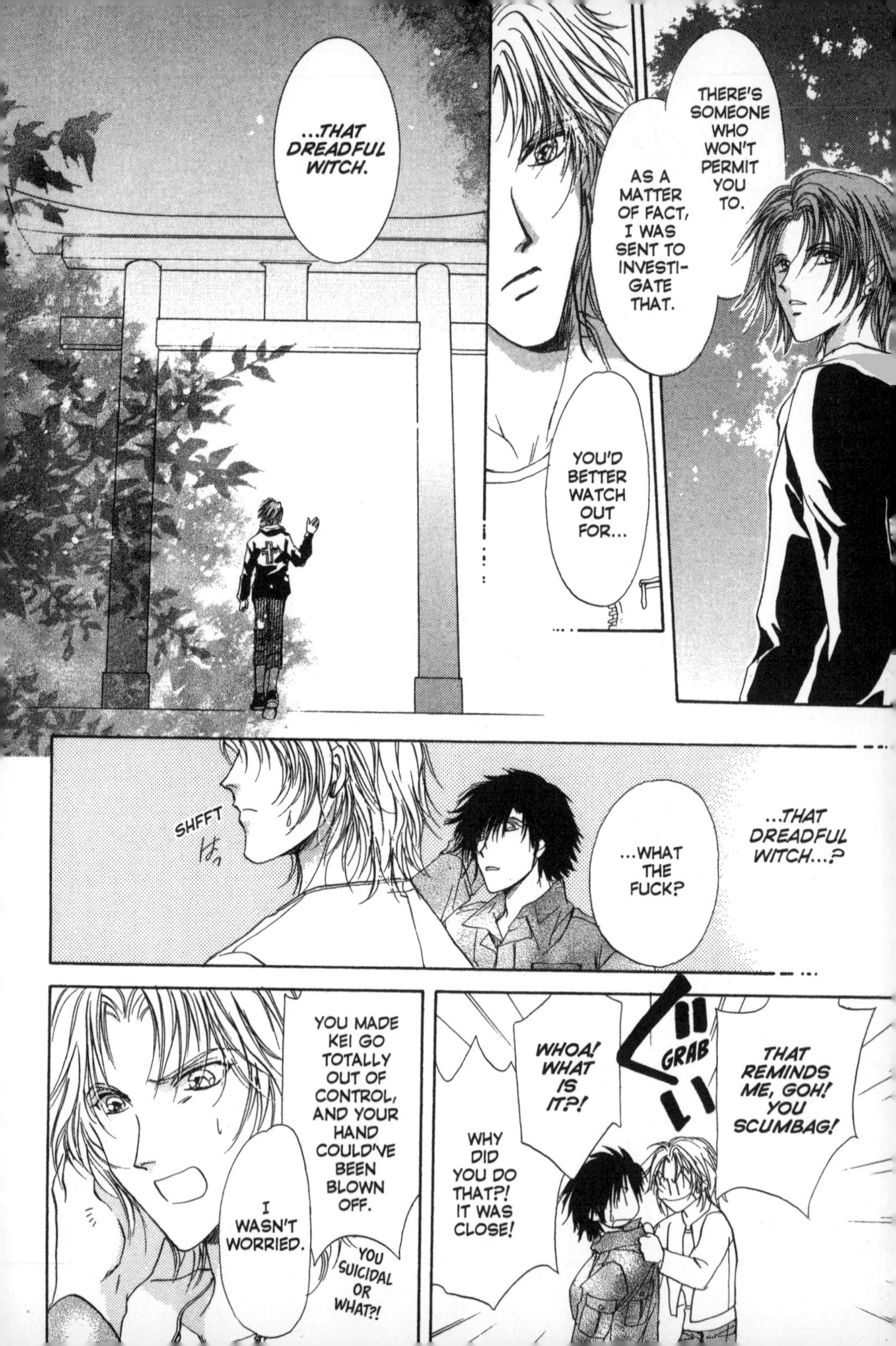
THERE'S SOMEONE WHO WON'T PERMIT YOU TO.
AS A MATTER OF FACT, I WAS SENT TO INVESTIGATE THAT.
YOU'D BETTER WATCH OUT FOR...
...THAT DREADFUL WITCH.
...THAT DREADFUL WITCH...?
...WHAT THE FUCK?
SHFFT
はっ
THAT REMINDS ME, GOH! YOU SCUMBAG!
GRAB
WHOA! WHAT IS IT?!
WHY DID YOU DO THAT?! IT WAS CLOSE!
YOU MADE KEI GO TOTALLY OUT OF CONTROL, AND YOUR HAND COULD'VE BEEN BLOWN OFF.
YOU SUICIDAL OR WHAT?!
I WASN'T WORRIED.

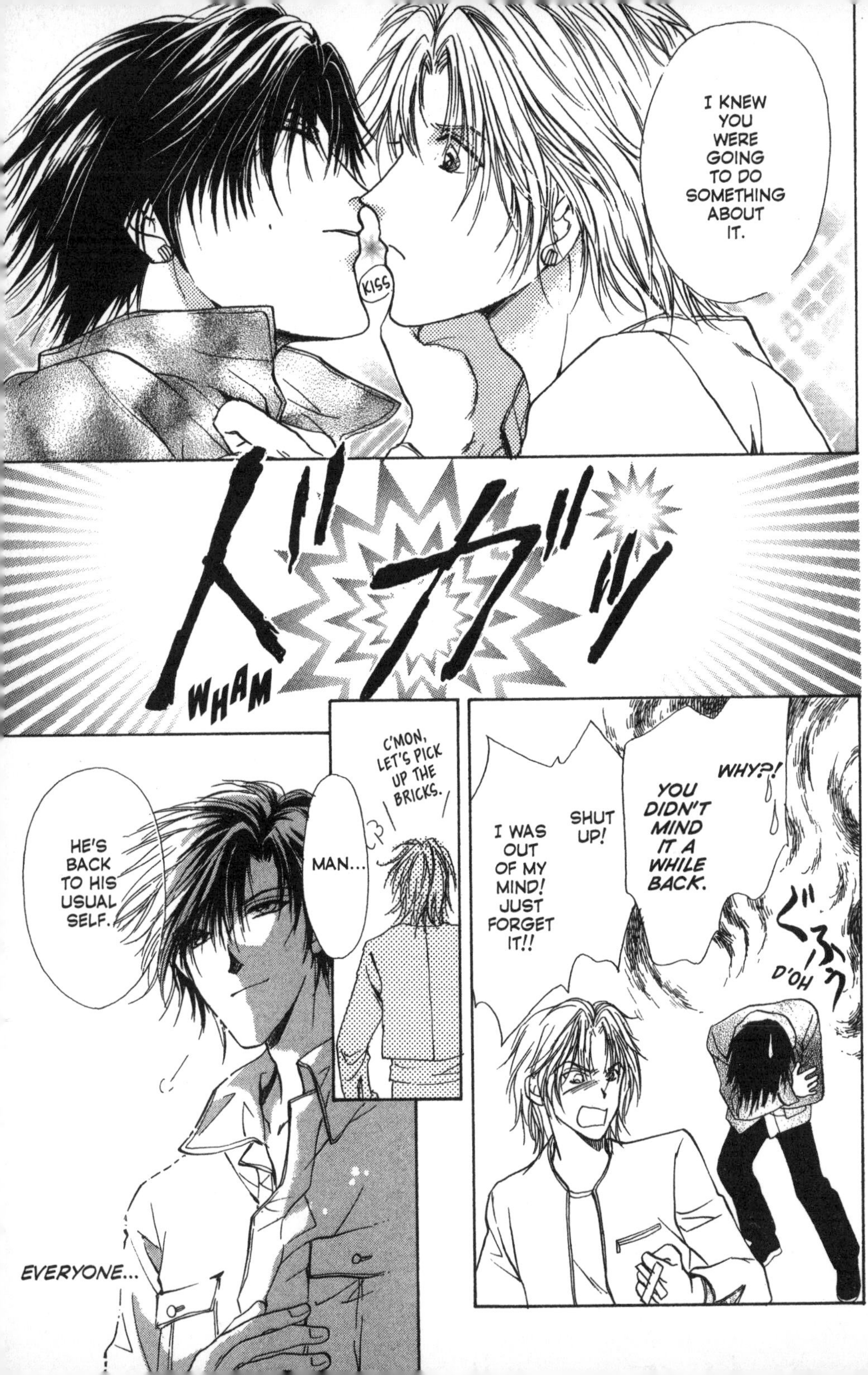
I KNEW YOU WERE GOING TO DO SOMETHING ABOUT IT.
KISS
ドガッ
WHAM
WHY?!
YOU DIDN'T MIND IT A WHILE BACK.
SHUT UP!
I WAS OUT OF MY MIND! JUST FORGET IT!!
ぐふっ
D'OH
C'MON, LET'S PICK UP THE BRICKS.
MAN...
HE'S BACK TO HIS USUAL SELF.
EVERYONE...

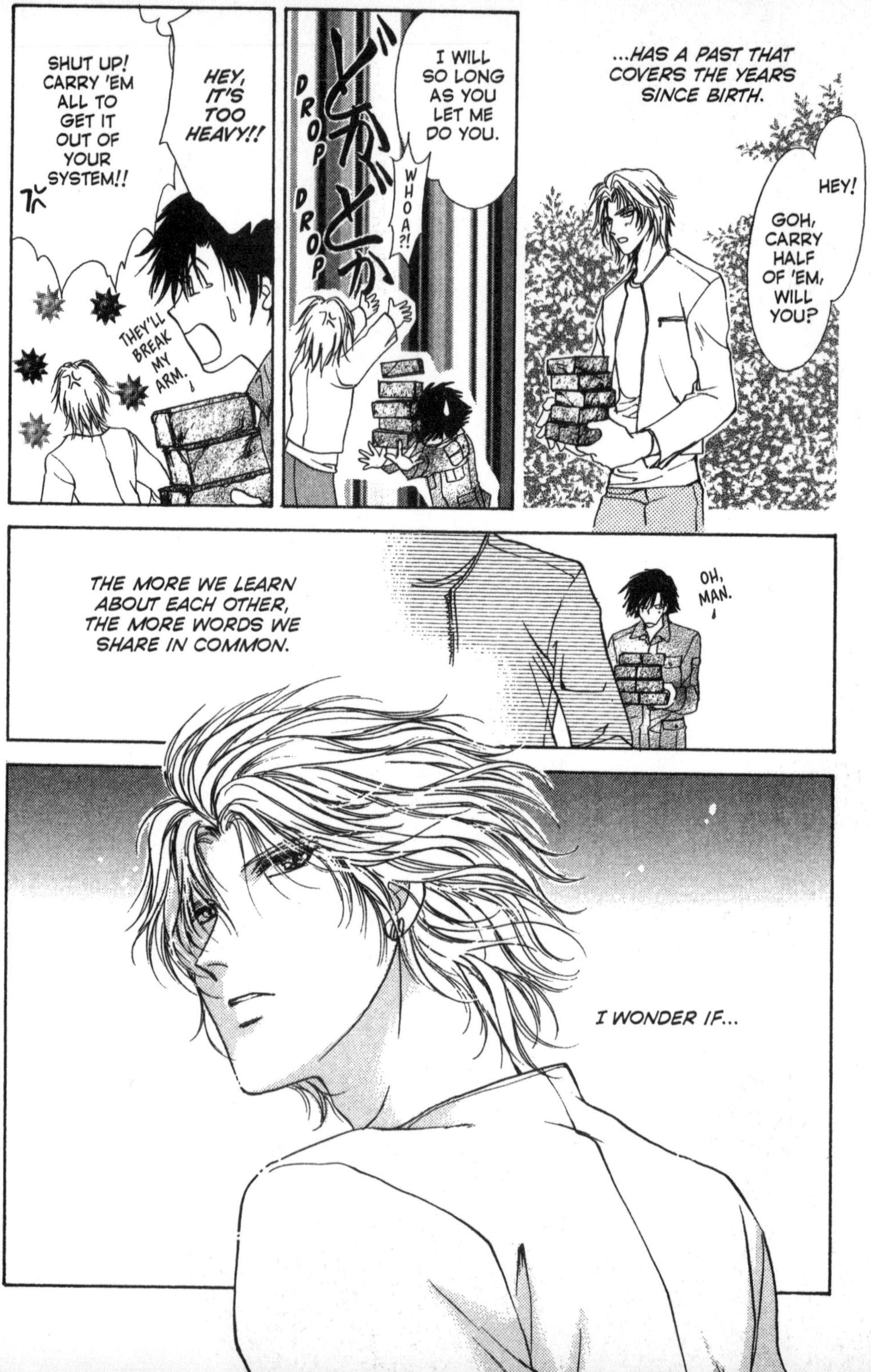
...HAS A PAST THAT COVERS THE YEARS SINCE BIRTH.
HEY!
GOH, CARRY HALF OF 'EM, WILL YOU?
I WILL SO LONG AS YOU LET ME DO YOU.
WHOA?!
DROP DROP
HEY, IT'S TOO HEAVY!!
SHUT UP! CARRY 'EM ALL TO GET IT OUT OF YOUR SYSTEM!!
THEY'LL BREAK MY ARM.
OH, MAN.
THE MORE WE LEARN ABOUT EACH OTHER, THE MORE WORDS WE SHARE IN COMMON.
I WONDER IF...

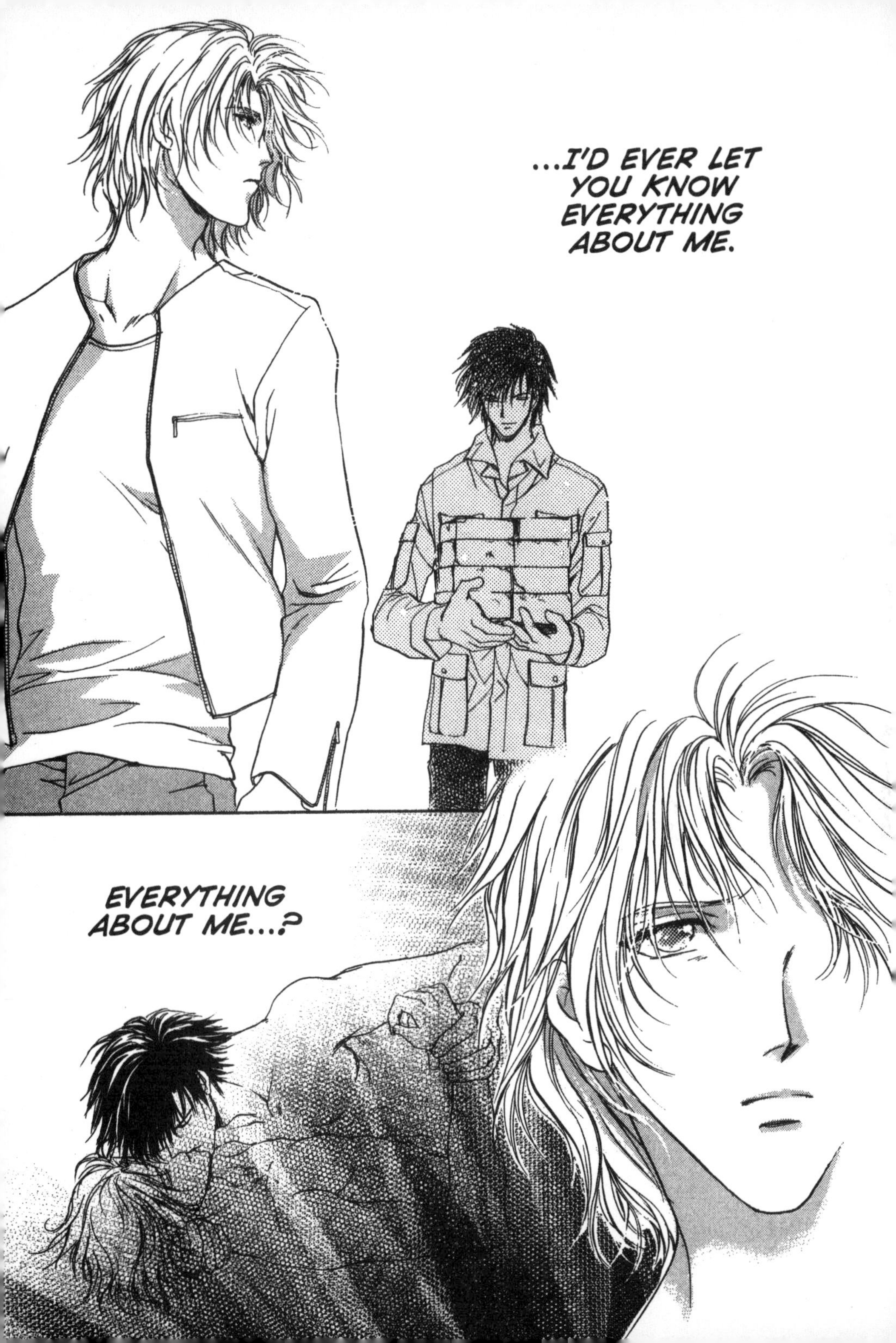
...I'D EVER LET YOU KNOW EVERYTHING ABOUT ME.
EVERYTHING ABOUT ME...?

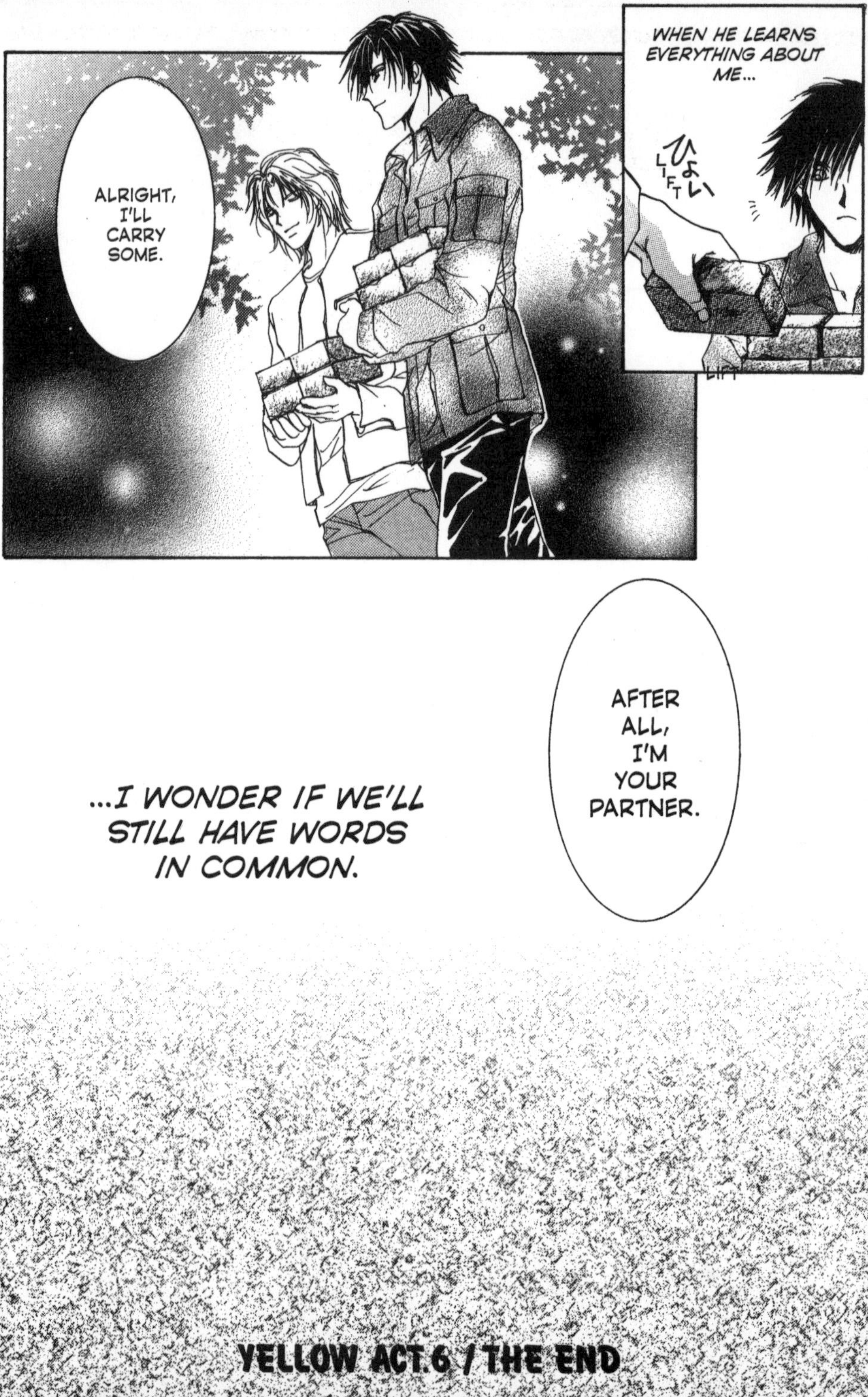
WHEN HE LEARNS EVERYTHING ABOUT ME...
ひょい
LIFT
LIFT
ALRIGHT, I'LL CARRY SOME.
AFTER ALL, I'M YOUR PARTNER.
...I WONDER IF WE'LL STILL HAVE WORDS IN COMMON.
YELLOW ACT.6 / THE END

PROFILE

Suspect #5

name

MIMI

background

18 YEARS OLD, WHO WORKS
AT THE "ROOST." SHE DOESN'T
KNOW ANYTHING ABOUT
THE SNATCHING BUSINESS.

Suspect #6

name

KANJI

background

EX-CUSTOMER FROM THE SNATCHING
BUSINESS, WHO WOUND UP
WORKING AT THE "ROOST." HE GETS
YELLED AT FOR HIS LOUD VOICE.

YELLOW

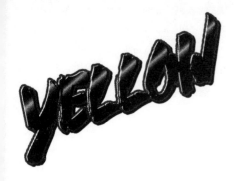

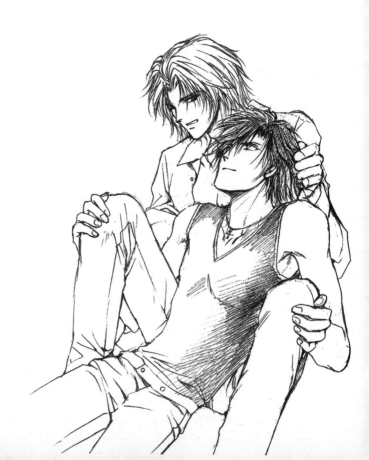

KISS & GIN & CIGARETTE

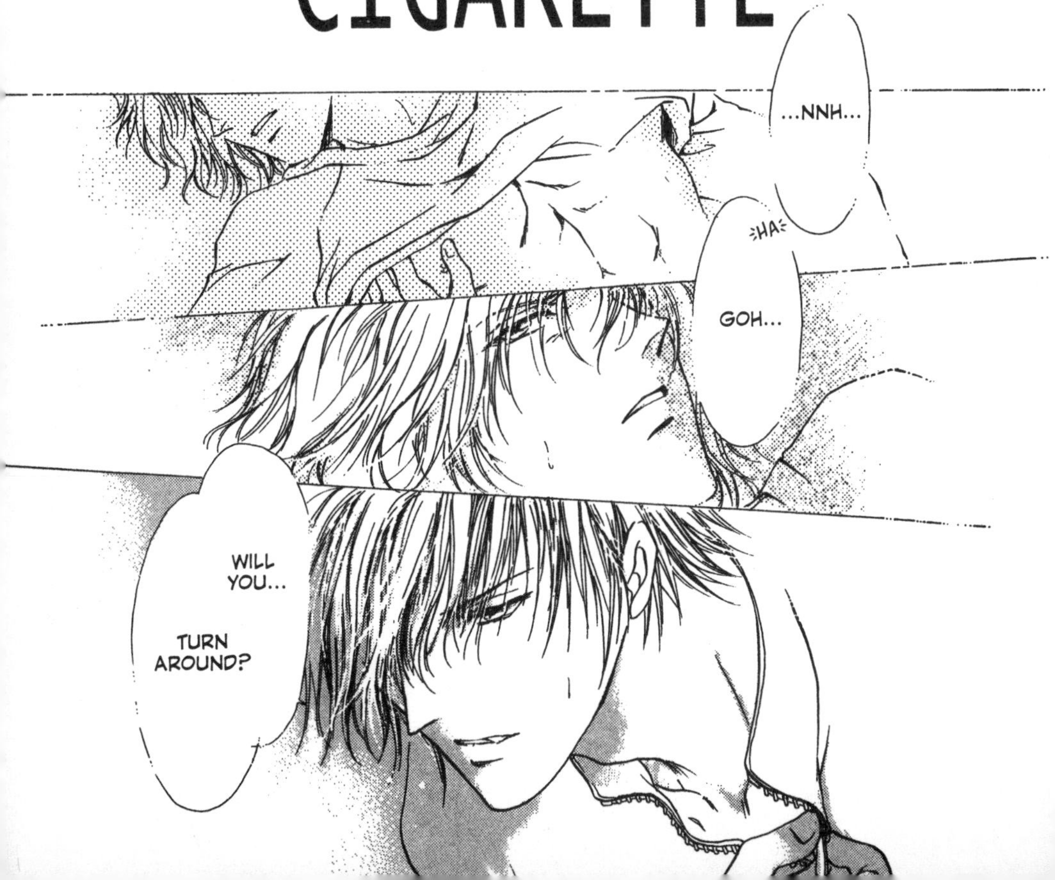
...NNH...
HA
GOH...
WILL YOU... TURN AROUND?

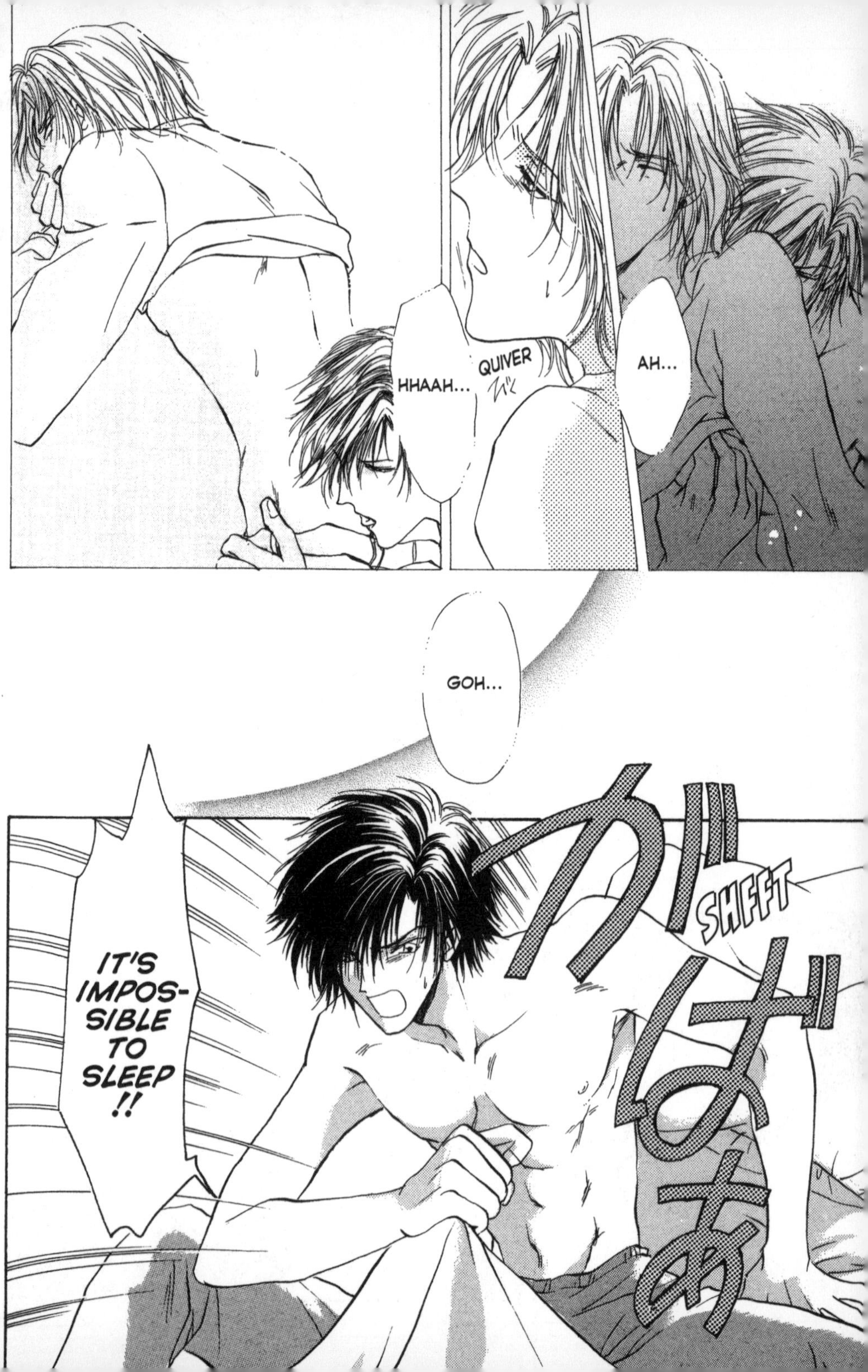
AH...
QUIVER
びく
HHAAH...
GOH...
SHFFT
IT'S IMPOSSIBLE TO SLEEP!!

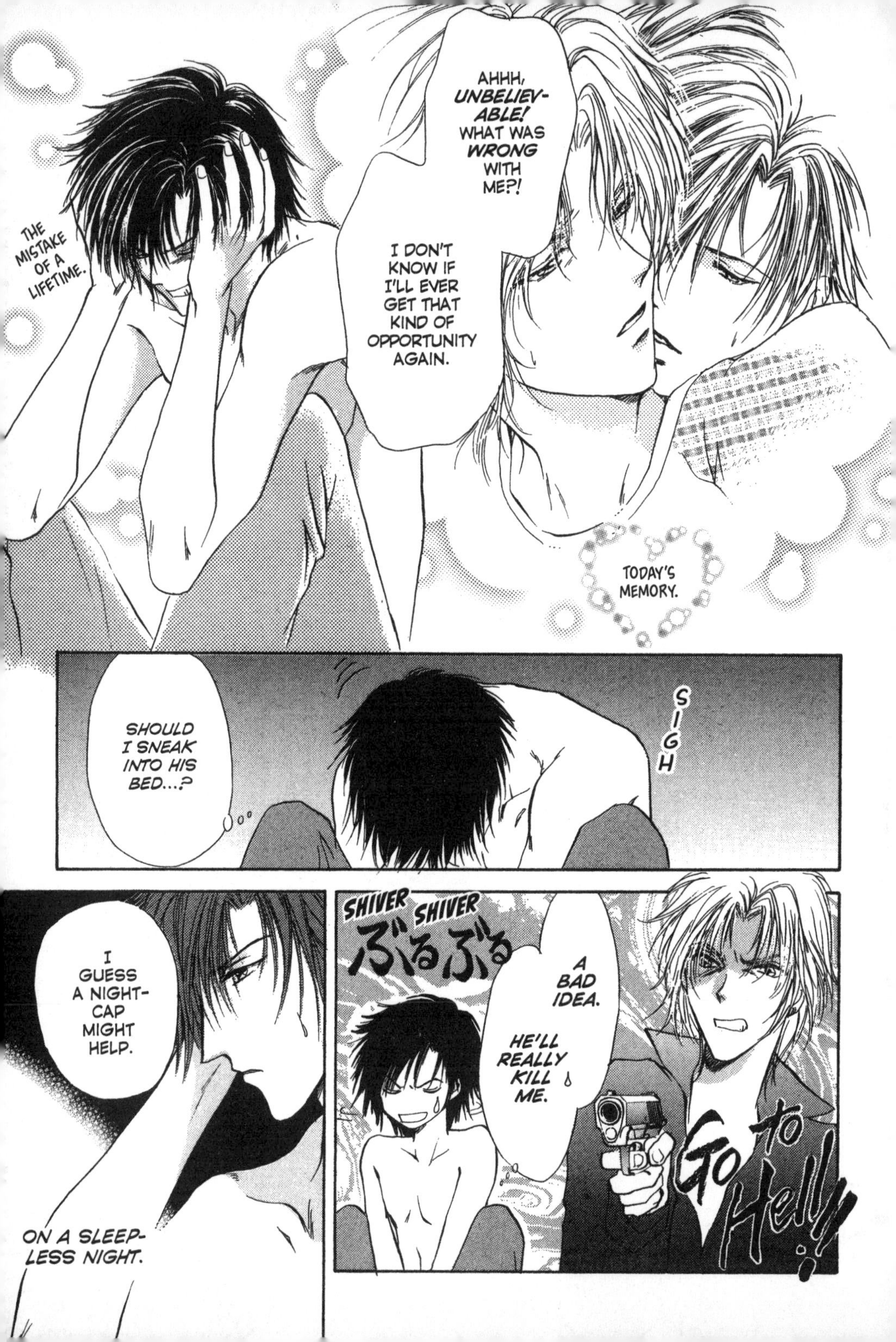
AHHH, UNBELIEVABLE! WHAT WAS WRONG WITH ME?!
I DON'T KNOW IF I'LL EVER GET THAT KIND OF OPPORTUNITY AGAIN.
TODAY'S MEMORY.
THE MISTAKE OF A LIFETIME.
SIGH
SHOULD I SNEAK INTO HIS BED...?
A BAD IDEA.
HE'LL REALLY KILL ME.
SHIVER SHIVER
ぶるぶる
Go to Hell!!
I GUESS A NIGHTCAP MIGHT HELP.
ON A SLEEPLESS NIGHT.

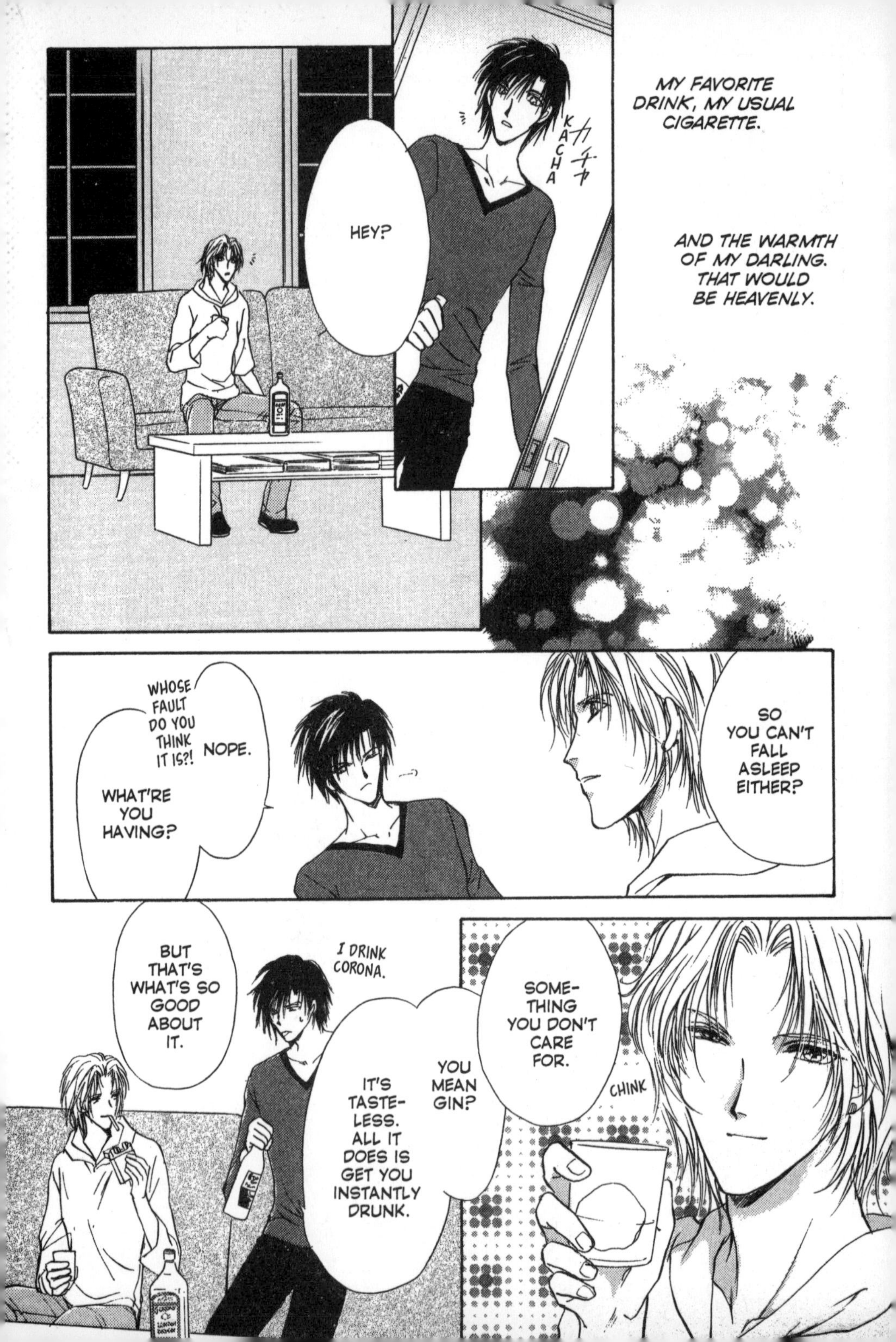
MY FAVORITE DRINK, MY USUAL CIGARETTE.
AND THE WARMTH OF MY DARLING. THAT WOULD BE HEAVENLY.
KACHA カチャ
HEY?
SO YOU CAN'T FALL ASLEEP EITHER?
NOPE.
WHOSE FAULT DO YOU THINK IT IS?!
WHAT'RE YOU HAVING?
SOME-THING YOU DON'T CARE FOR.
CHINK
YOU MEAN GIN?
I DRINK CORONA.
IT'S TASTE-LESS. ALL IT DOES IS GET YOU INSTANTLY DRUNK.
BUT THAT'S WHAT'S SO GOOD ABOUT IT.

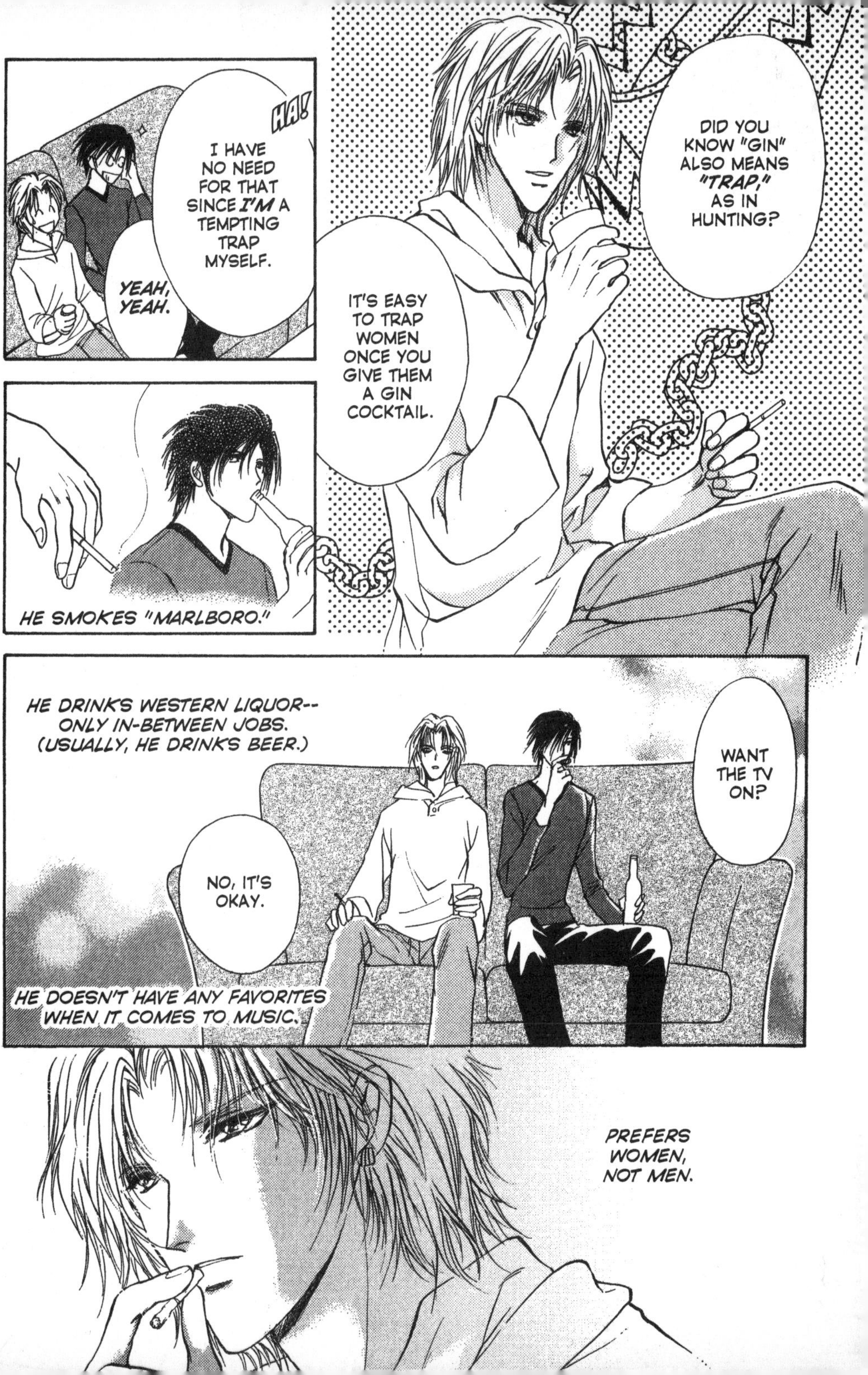
DID YOU KNOW "GIN" ALSO MEANS "TRAP," AS IN HUNTING?
IT'S EASY TO TRAP WOMEN ONCE YOU GIVE THEM A GIN COCKTAIL.
HA!
I HAVE NO NEED FOR THAT SINCE I'M A TEMPTING TRAP MYSELF.
YEAH, YEAH.
HE SMOKES "MARLBORO."
WANT THE TV ON?
HE DRINKS WESTERN LIQUOR-- ONLY IN-BETWEEN JOBS. (USUALLY, HE DRINKS BEER.)
NO, IT'S OKAY.
HE DOESN'T HAVE ANY FAVORITES WHEN IT COMES TO MUSIC.
PREFERS WOMEN, NOT MEN.

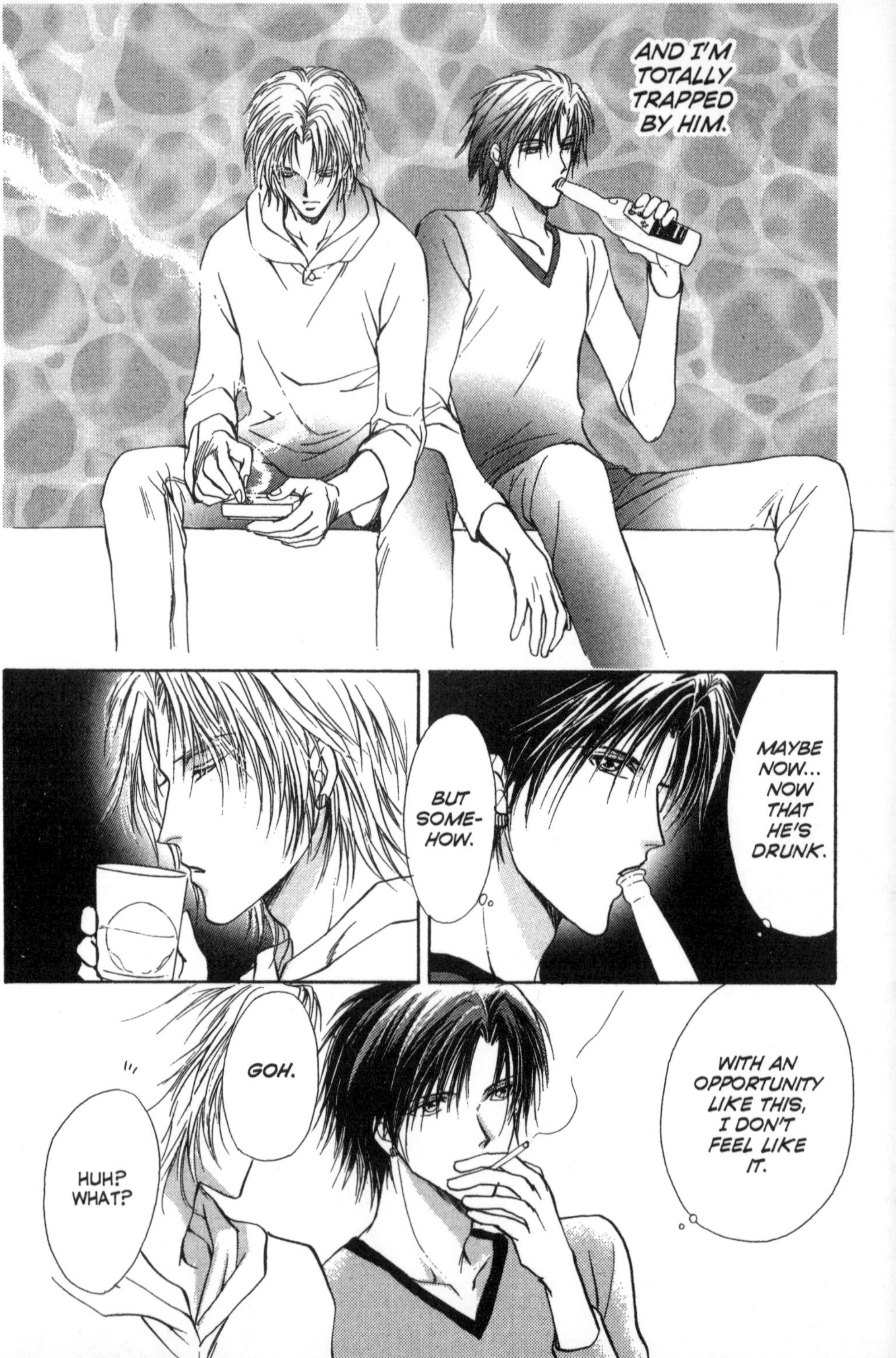
AND I'M TOTALLY TRAPPED BY HIM.
MAYBE NOW... NOW THAT HE'S DRUNK.
BUT SOME-HOW.
WITH AN OPPORTUNITY LIKE THIS, I DON'T FEEL LIKE IT.
GOH.
HUH? WHAT?

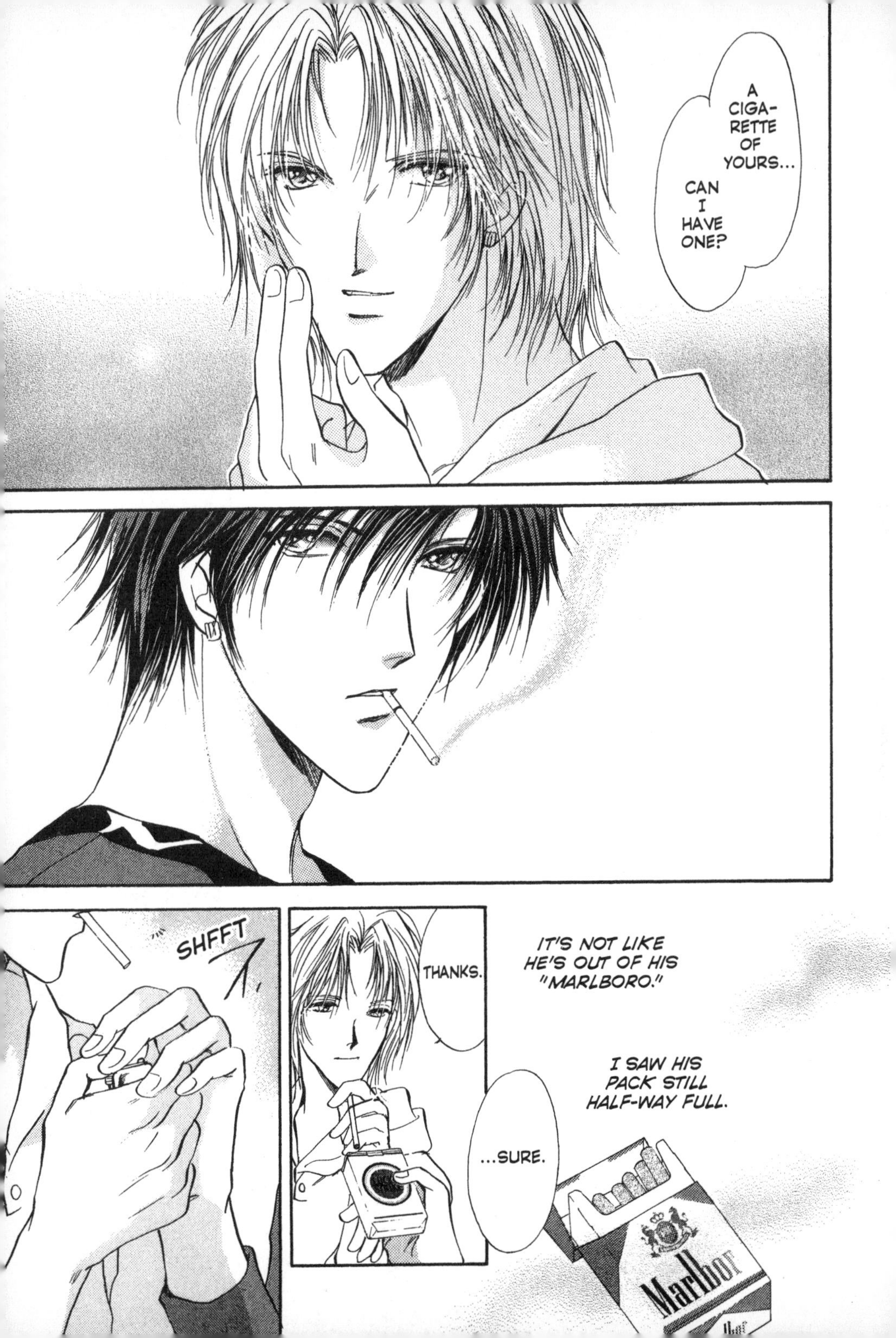
A CIGARETTE OF YOURS...
CAN I HAVE ONE?
IT'S NOT LIKE HE'S OUT OF HIS "MARLBORO."
I SAW HIS PACK STILL HALF-WAY FULL.
Marlbor
THANKS.
...SURE.
SHFFT

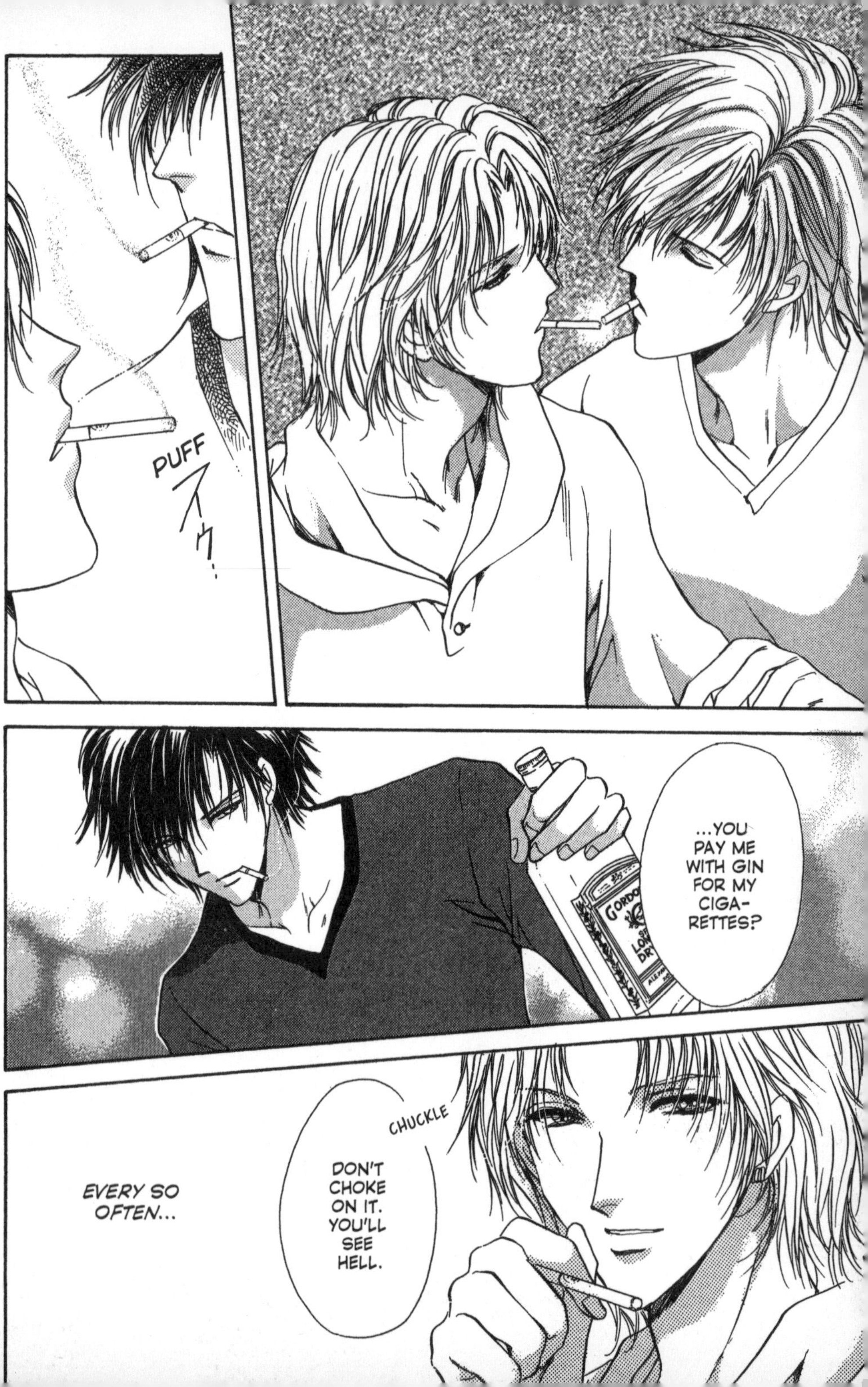
PUFF
...YOU PAY ME WITH GIN FOR MY CIGA-RETTES?
CHUCKLE
DON'T CHOKE ON IT. YOU'LL SEE HELL.
EVERY SO OFTEN...

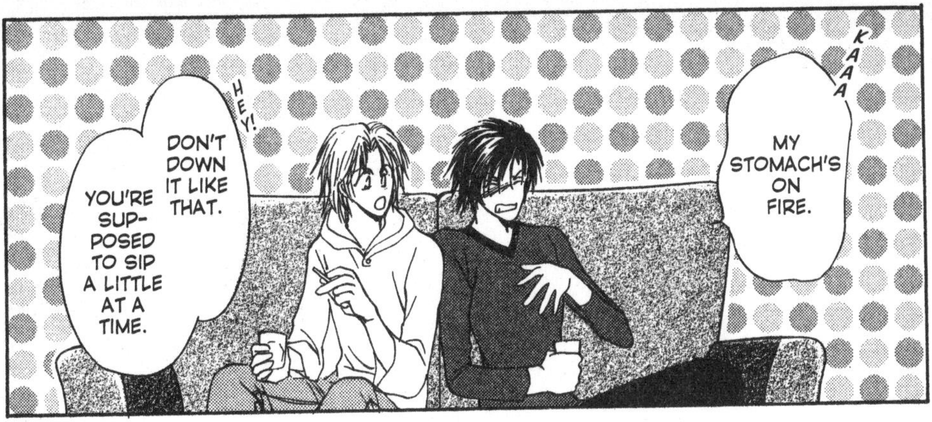
KAAAA
MY STOMACH'S ON FIRE.
HEY!
DON'T DOWN IT LIKE THAT.
YOU'RE SUP-POSED TO SIP A LITTLE AT A TIME.

WE SIT SIDE BY SIDE, AND...

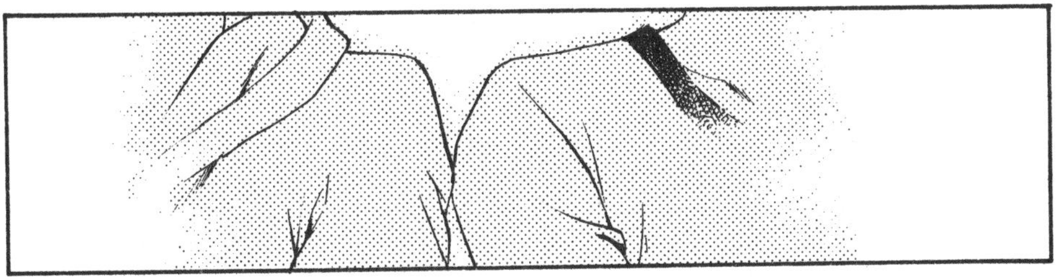

...WE SHARE OUR "SCENT."

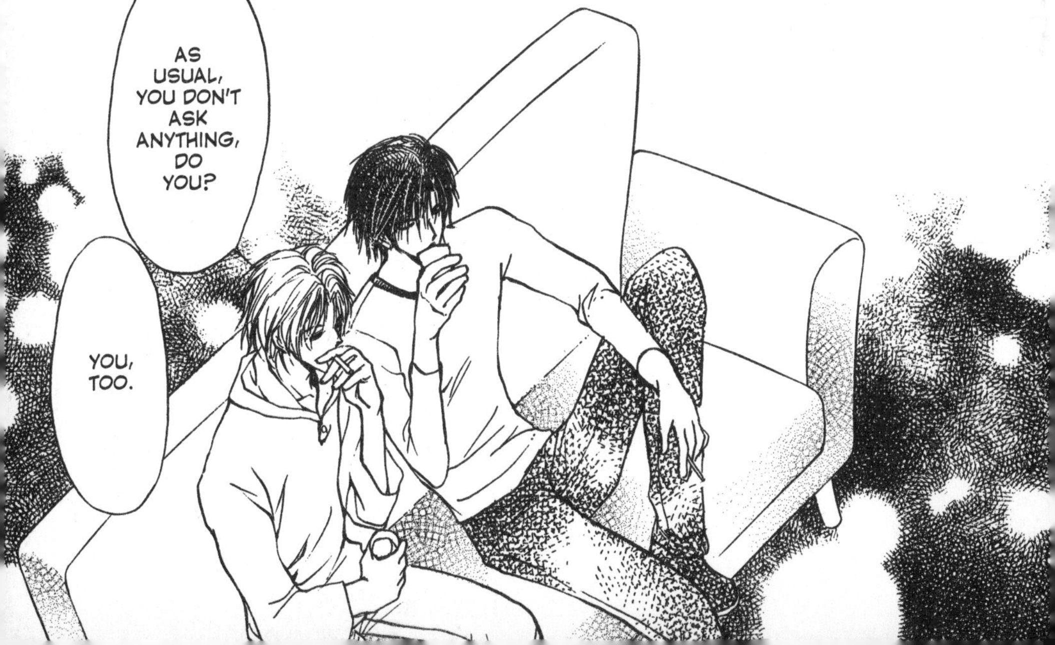
AS USUAL, YOU DON'T ASK ANYTHING, DO YOU?
YOU, TOO.

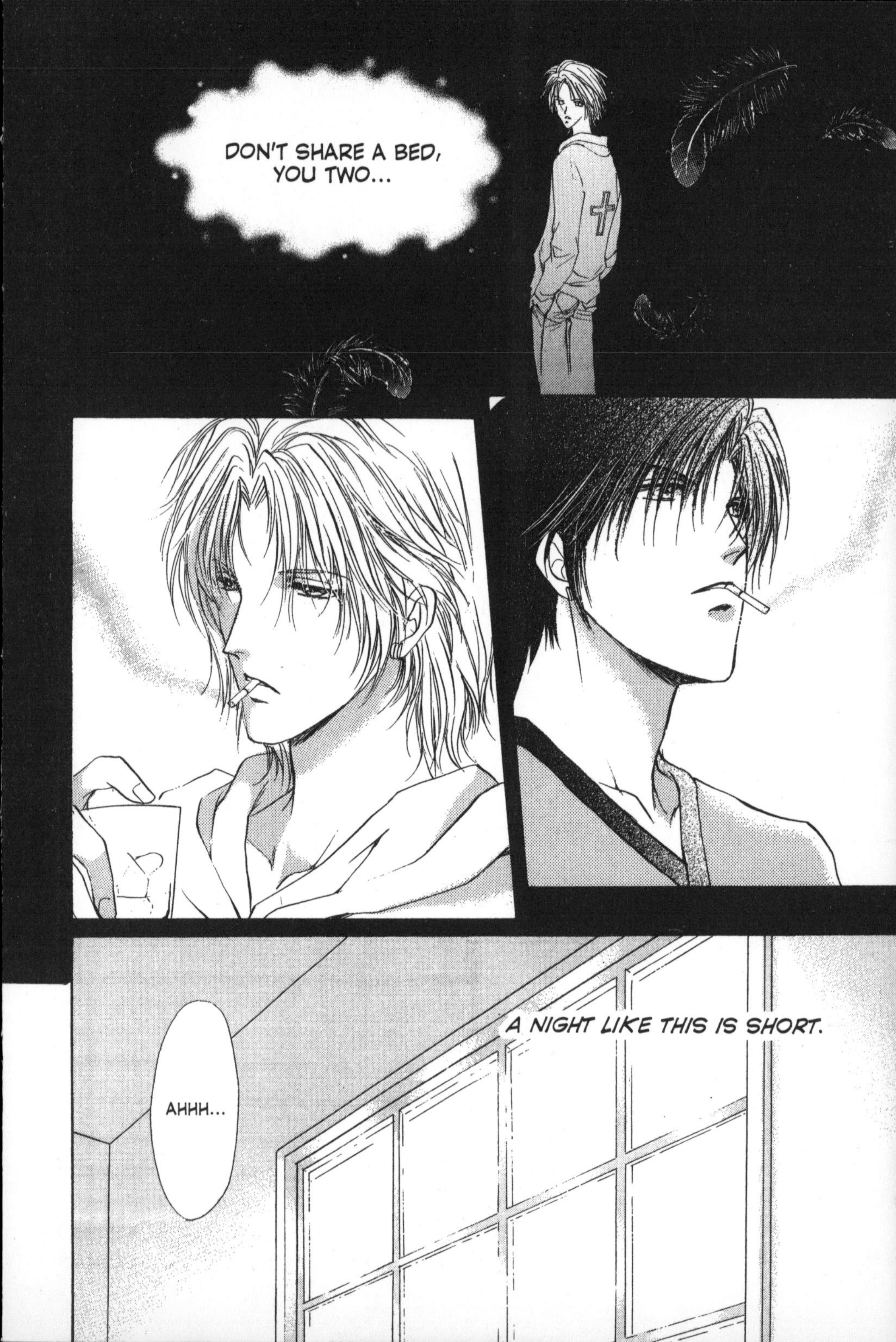
DON'T SHARE A BED, YOU TWO...
A NIGHT LIKE THIS IS SHORT.
AHHH...

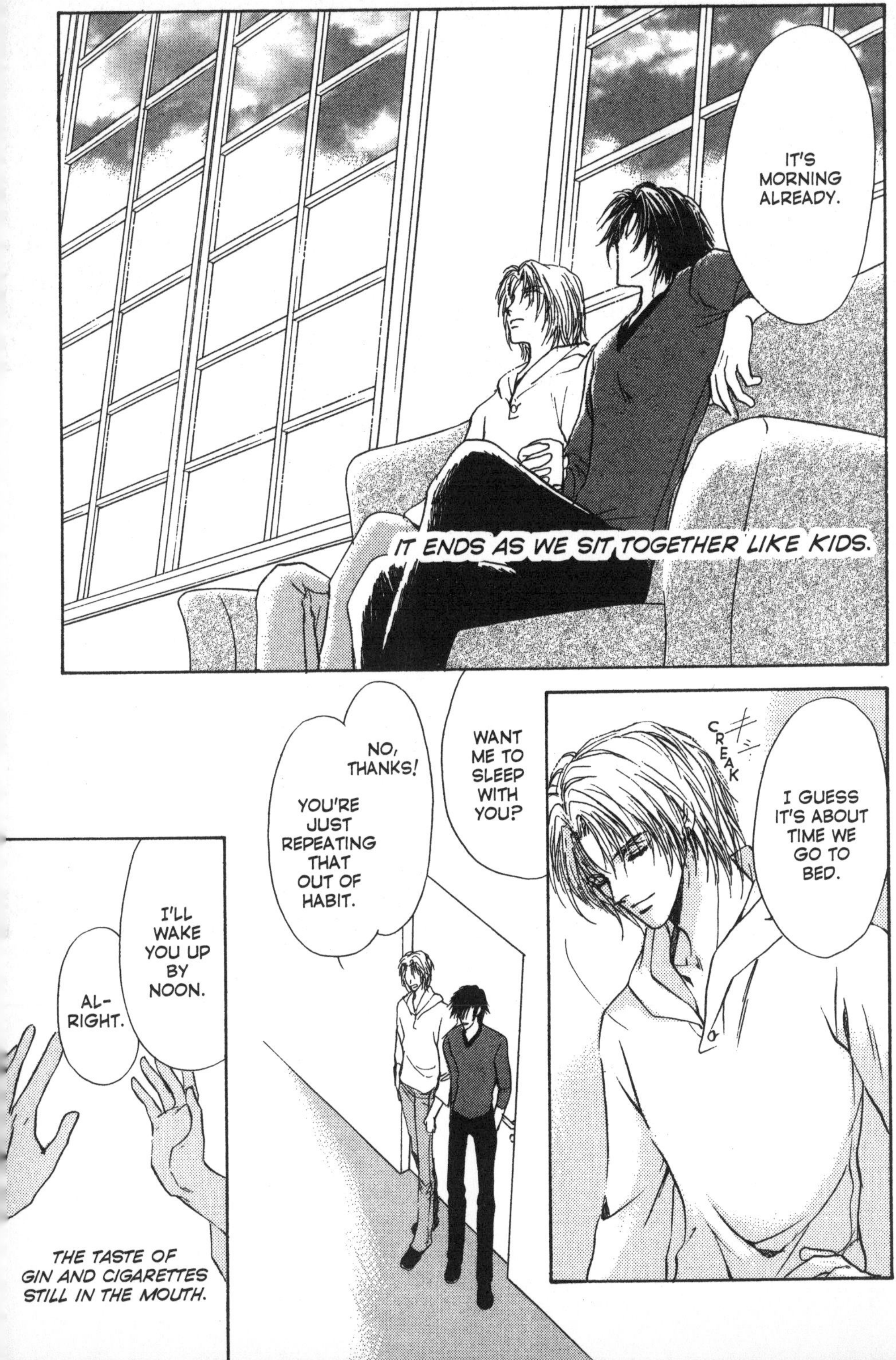
IT'S MORNING ALREADY.
IT ENDS AS WE SIT TOGETHER LIKE KIDS.
CREAK
I GUESS IT'S ABOUT TIME WE GO TO BED.
WANT ME TO SLEEP WITH YOU?
NO, THANKS!
YOU'RE JUST REPEATING THAT OUT OF HABIT.
I'LL WAKE YOU UP BY NOON.
AL-RIGHT.
THE TASTE OF GIN AND CIGARETTES STILL IN THE MOUTH.

IF WE KISSED TONIGHT, THAT'S WHAT I MIGHT HAVE TASTED.

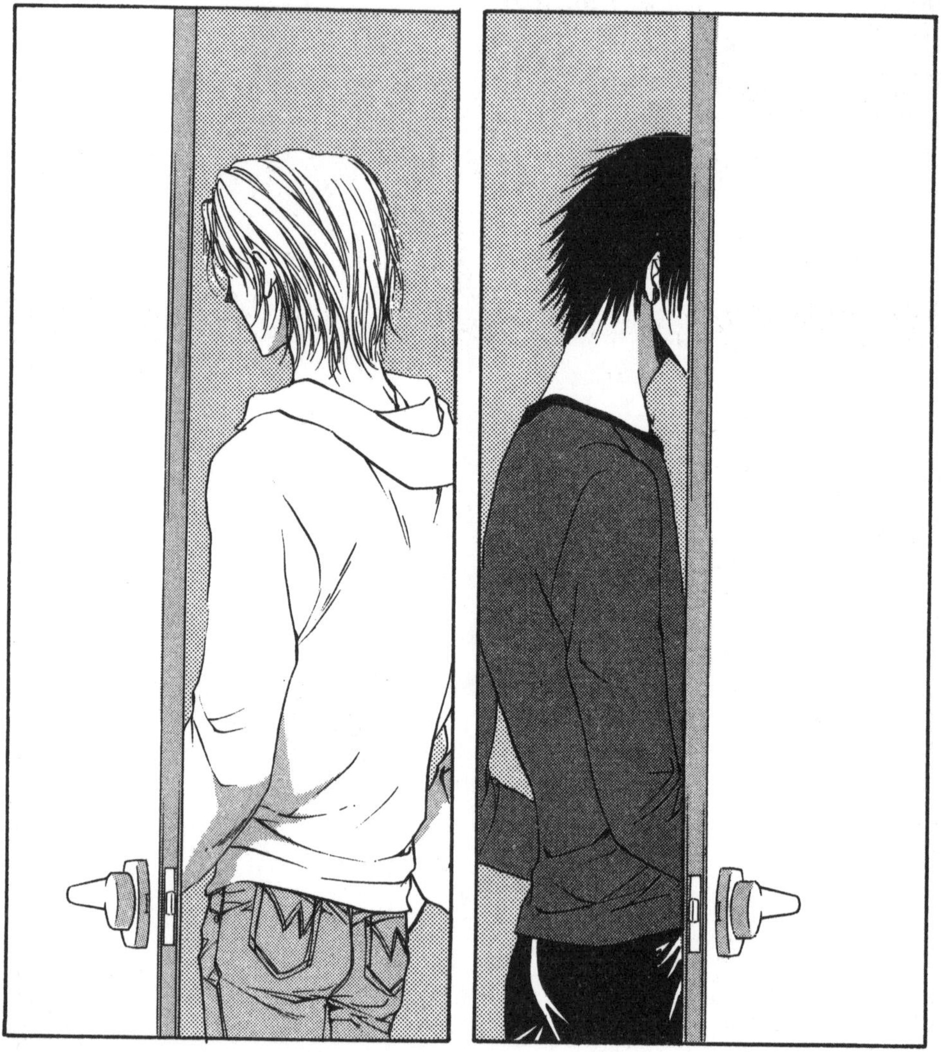

KISS & GIN & CIGARETTE / THE END

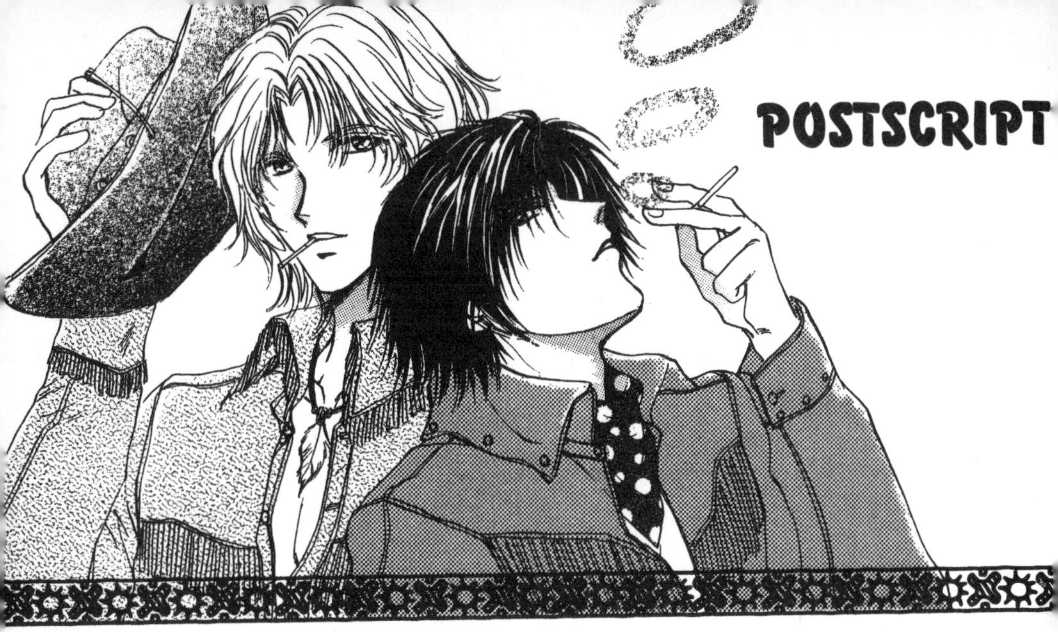
POSTSCRIPT

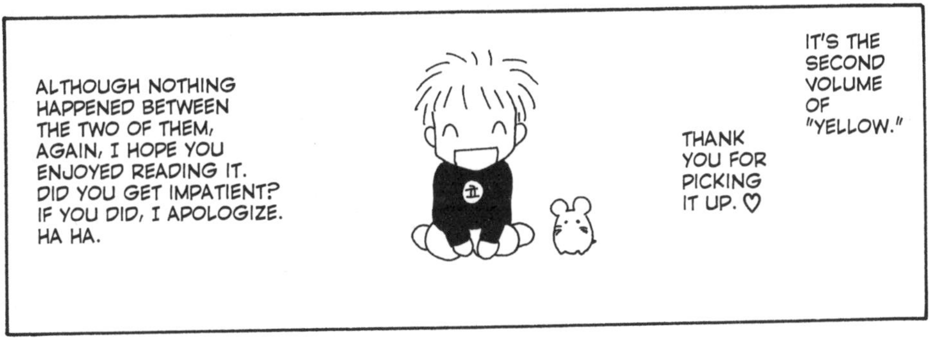
IT'S THE SECOND VOLUME OF "YELLOW."
THANK YOU FOR PICKING IT UP. ♡
ALTHOUGH NOTHING HAPPENED BETWEEN THE TWO OF THEM, AGAIN, I HOPE YOU ENJOYED READING IT. DID YOU GET IMPATIENT? IF YOU DID, I APOLOGIZE. HA HA.

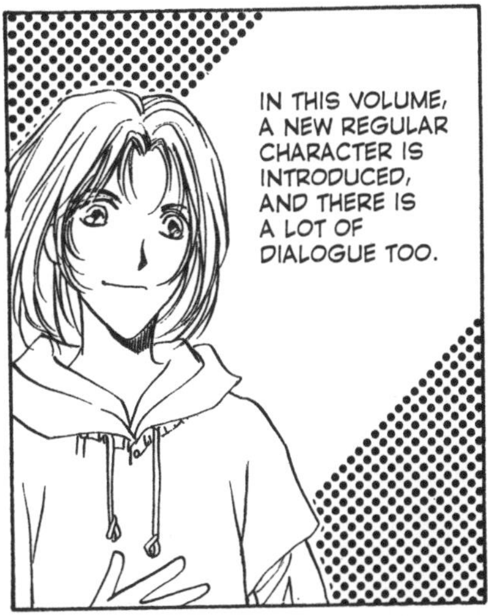
IN THIS VOLUME, A NEW REGULAR CHARACTER IS INTRODUCED, AND THERE IS A LOT OF DIALOGUE TOO.

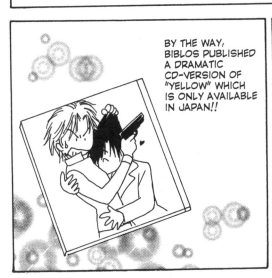

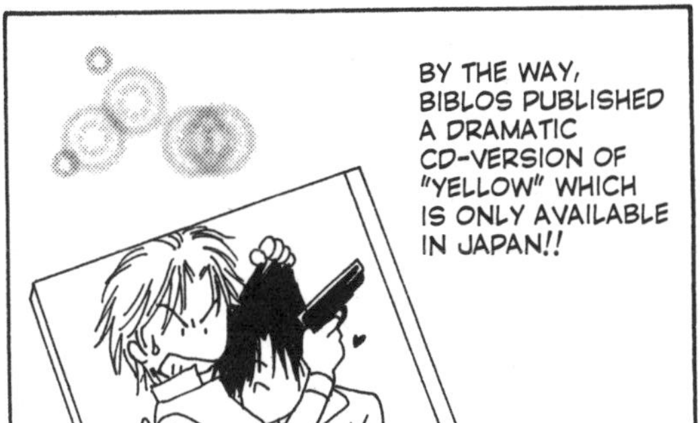
BY THE WAY, BIBLOS PUBLISHED A DRAMATIC CD-VERSION OF "YELLOW" WHICH IS ONLY AVAILABLE IN JAPAN!!

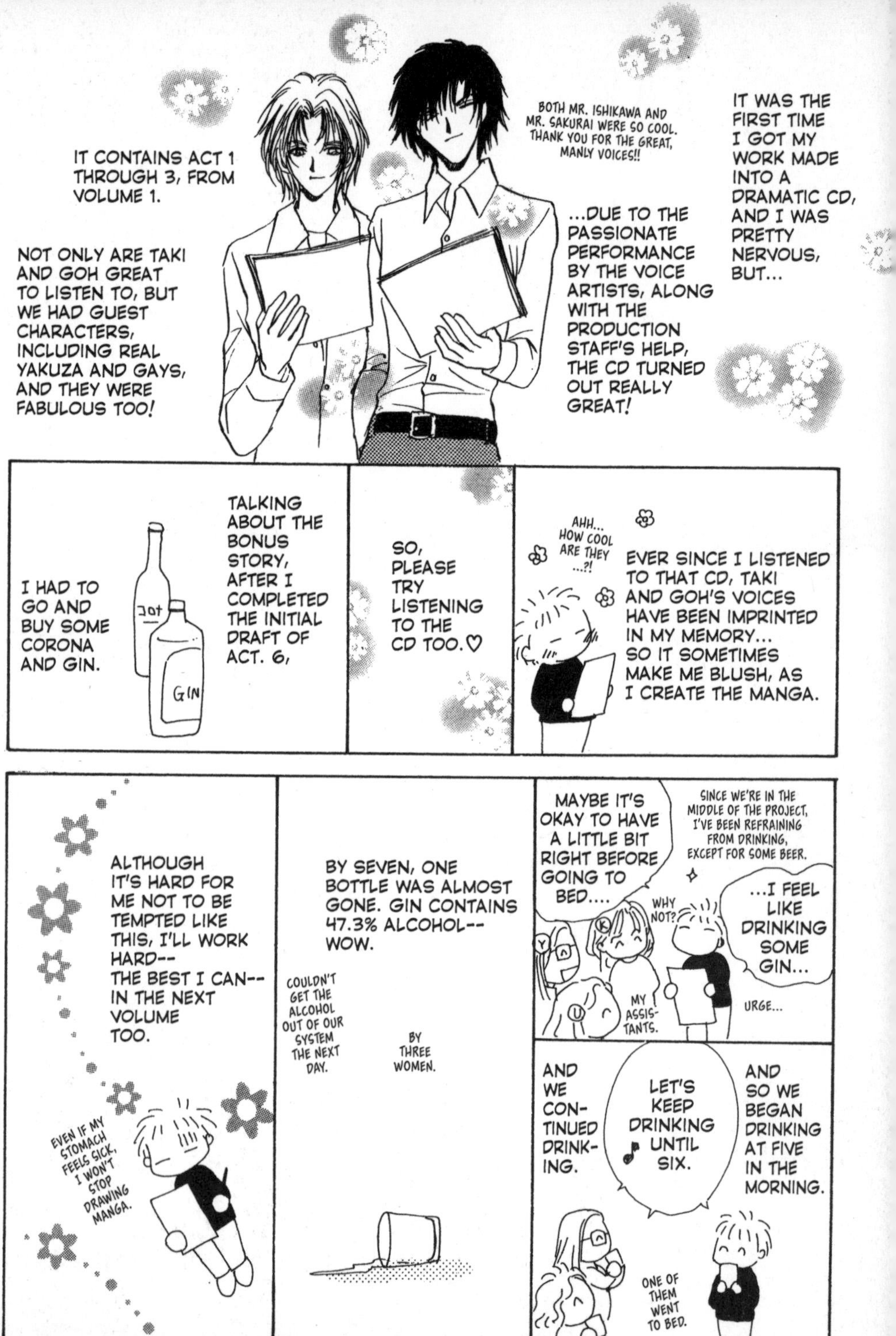
IT WAS THE FIRST TIME I GOT MY WORK MADE INTO A DRAMATIC CD, AND I WAS PRETTY NERVOUS, BUT...
BOTH MR. ISHIKAWA AND MR. SAKURAI WERE SO COOL. THANK YOU FOR THE GREAT, MANLY VOICES!!
...DUE TO THE PASSIONATE PERFORMANCE BY THE VOICE ARTISTS, ALONG WITH THE PRODUCTION STAFF'S HELP, THE CD TURNED OUT REALLY GREAT!
IT CONTAINS ACT 1 THROUGH 3, FROM VOLUME 1.
NOT ONLY ARE TAKI AND GOH GREAT TO LISTEN TO, BUT WE HAD GUEST CHARACTERS, INCLUDING REAL YAKUZA AND GAYS, AND THEY WERE FABULOUS TOO!
EVER SINCE I LISTENED TO THAT CD, TAKI AND GOH'S VOICES HAVE BEEN IMPRINTED IN MY MEMORY... SO IT SOMETIMES MAKE ME BLUSH, AS I CREATE THE MANGA.
AHH... HOW COOL ARE THEY ...?!
SO, PLEASE TRY LISTENING TO THE CD TOO.♡
TALKING ABOUT THE BONUS STORY, AFTER I COMPLETED THE INITIAL DRAFT OF ACT. 6,
I HAD TO GO AND BUY SOME CORONA AND GIN.
GIN
SINCE WE'RE IN THE MIDDLE OF THE PROJECT, I'VE BEEN REFRAINING FROM DRINKING, EXCEPT FOR SOME BEER.
...I FEEL LIKE DRINKING SOME GIN...
URGE...
MAYBE IT'S OKAY TO HAVE A LITTLE BIT RIGHT BEFORE GOING TO BED....
WHY NOT?
MY ASSIS-TANTS.
AND SO WE BEGAN DRINKING AT FIVE IN THE MORNING.
LET'S KEEP DRINKING UNTIL SIX.
AND WE CON-TINUED DRINK-ING.
ONE OF THEM WENT TO BED.
BY SEVEN, ONE BOTTLE WAS ALMOST GONE. GIN CONTAINS 47.3% ALCOHOL--WOW.
BY THREE WOMEN.
COULDN'T GET THE ALCOHOL OUT OF OUR SYSTEM THE NEXT DAY.
ALTHOUGH IT'S HARD FOR ME NOT TO BE TEMPTED LIKE THIS, I'LL WORK HARD-- THE BEST I CAN-- IN THE NEXT VOLUME TOO.
EVEN IF MY STOMACH FEELS SICK, I WON'T STOP DRAWING MANGA.

POSTSCRIPT / THE END

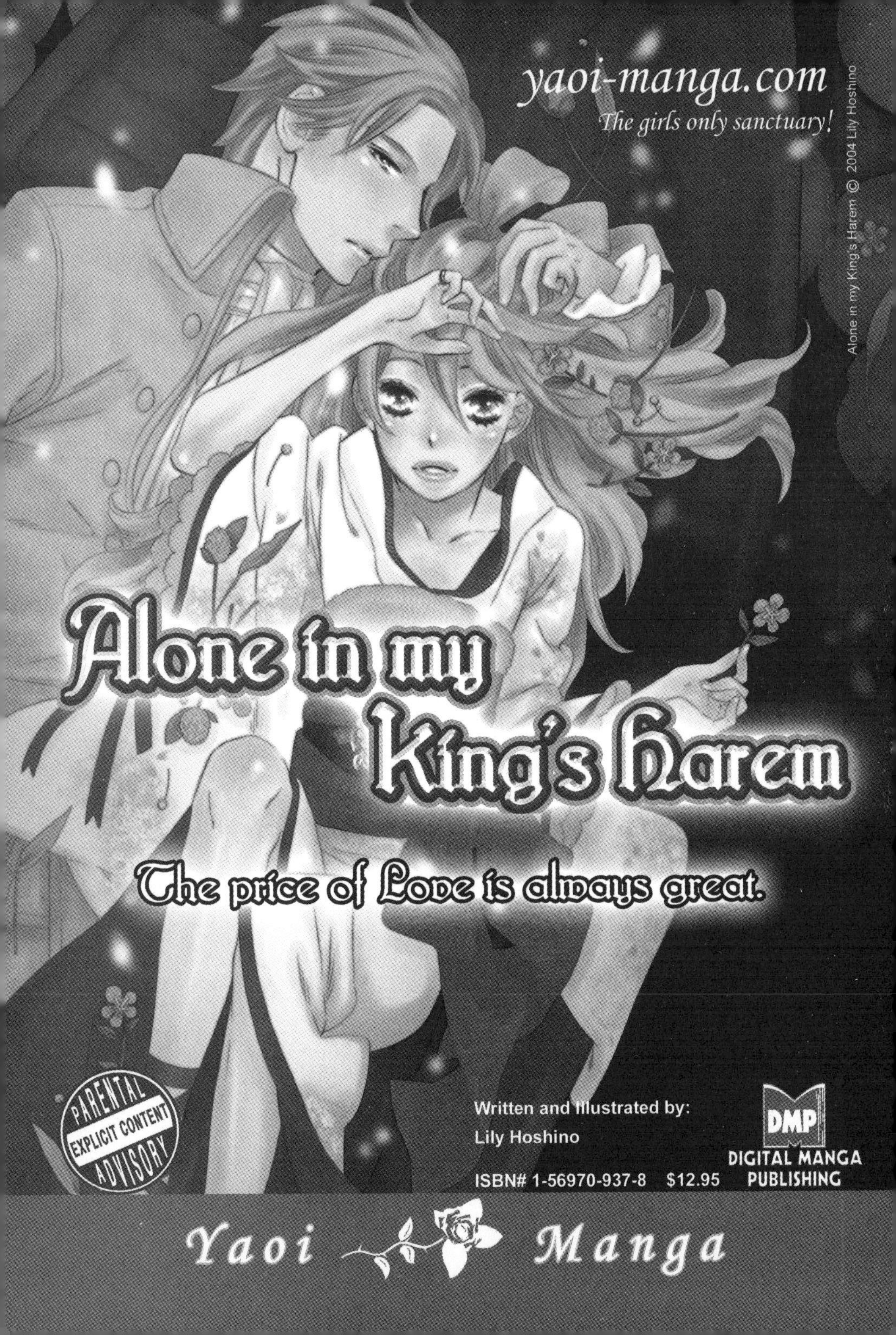

OUR KINGDOM

When the Prince falls for the Pauper...

The family inheritance will be the last
of their concerns.

Written & Illustrated by
Naduki Koujima

ISBN # 1-56970-935-1 $12.95

yaoi-manga.com
The girls only sanctuary!

DMP
DIGITAL MANGA
PUBLISHING

Yaoi Manga

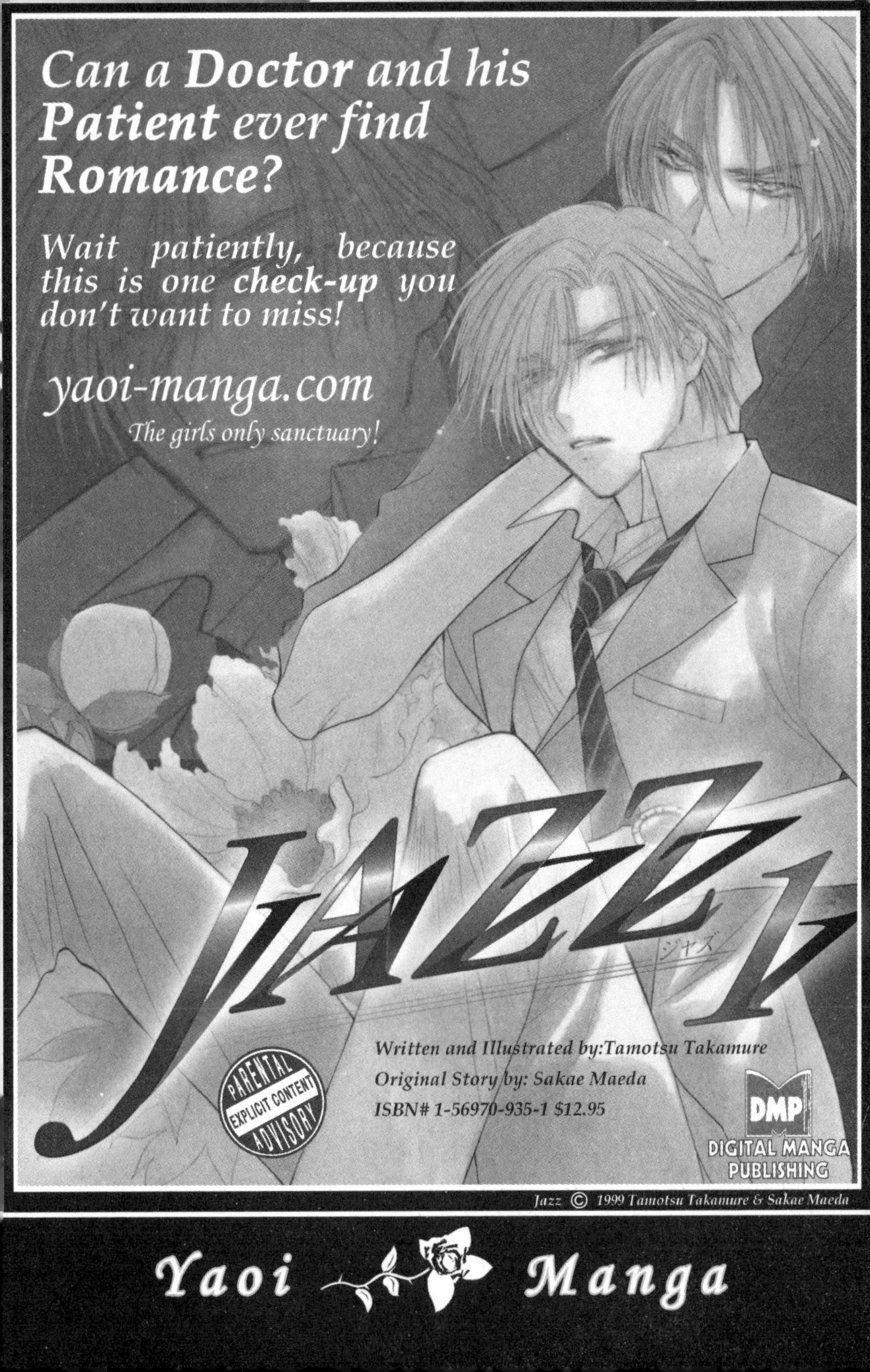
Can a Doctor and his Patient ever find Romance?
Wait patiently, because this is one check-up you don't want to miss!
yaoi-manga.com
The girls only sanctuary!
JAZZ 1
ジャズ
Written and Illustrated by:Tamotsu Takamure
Original Story by: Sakae Maeda
ISBN# 1-56970-935-1 $12.95
PARENTAL EXPLICIT CONTENT ADVISORY
DMP
DIGITAL MANGA PUBLISHING
Jazz © 1999 Tamotsu Takamure & Sakae Maeda
Yaoi Manga

Kimi Shiruya- Dost thou Know?

When Katsuomi and Tsurugi's wooden swords collide, sparks will fly, but as pride gets in the way of love, Tsurugi's brother Saya will profess his love to Katsuomi...

...Will jelousy drive Tsurugi to battle it out with Katsuomi one last time?

ISBN# 1-56970-934-3 $12.95

yaoi-manga.com

The girls only sanctuary

KIMI SHIRUYA "Dost Thou Know" ©SATORU ISHIHARA 2003.
Originally published in Japan in 2003 by SHINSHOKAN CO., LTD.

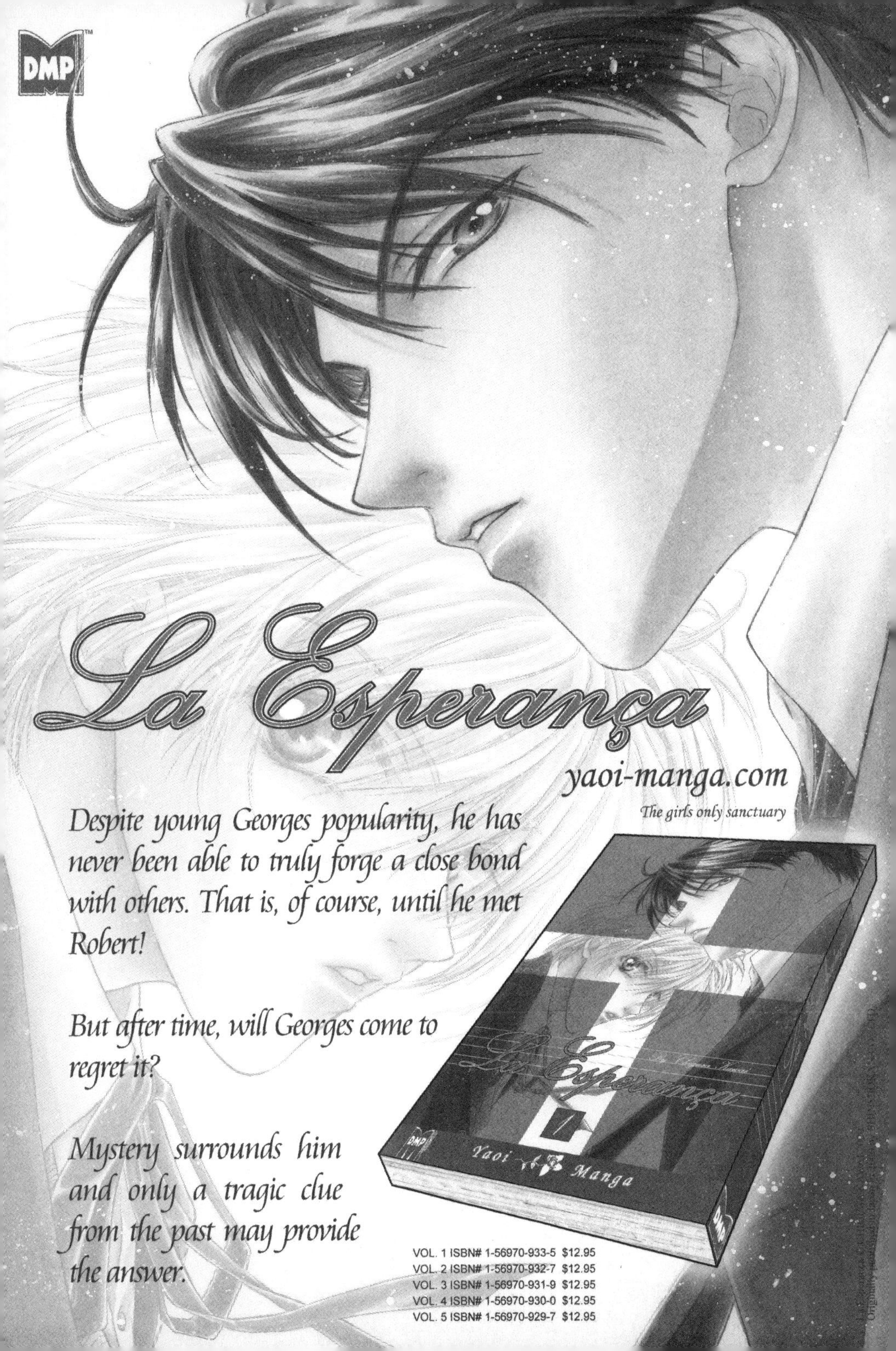

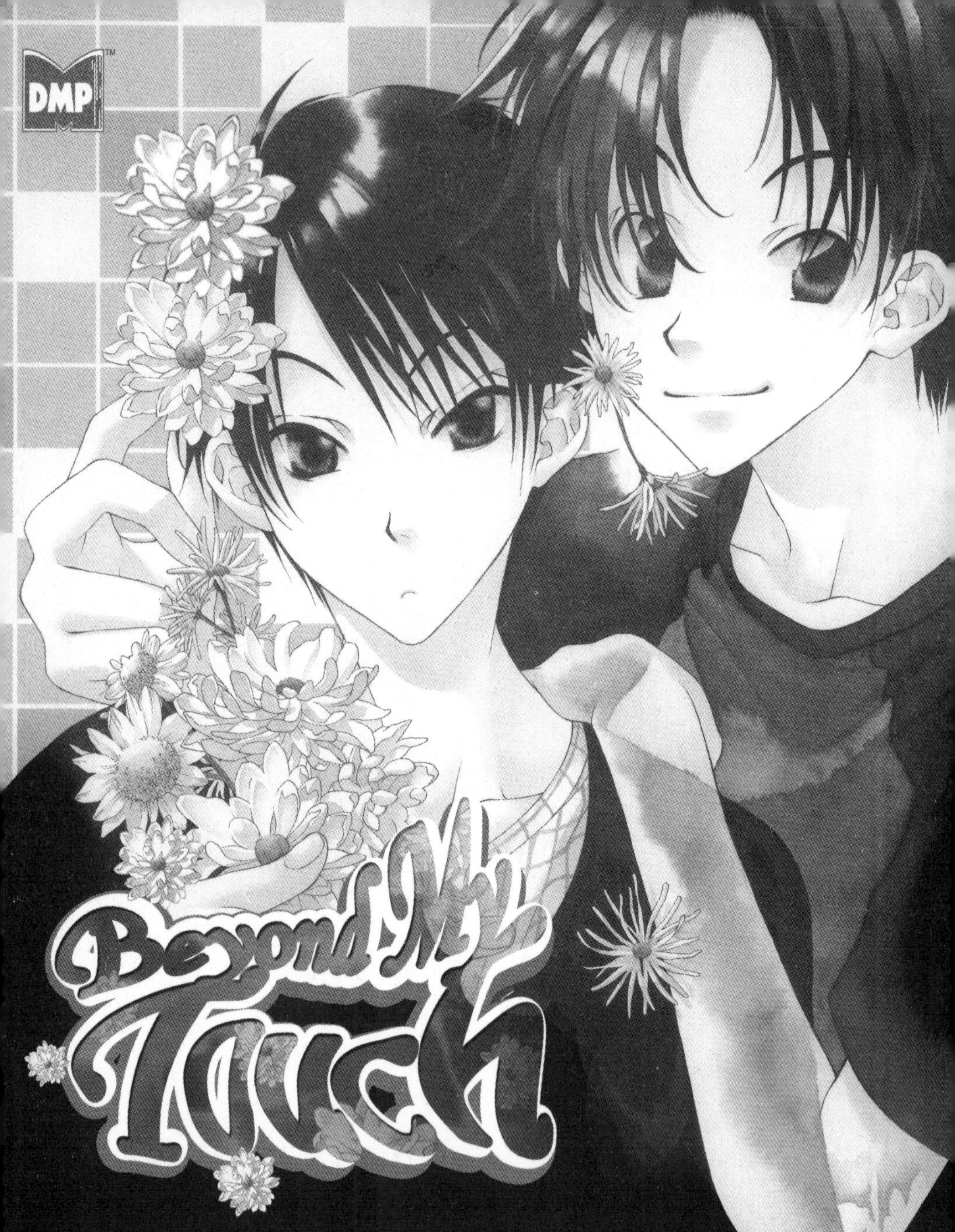
DMP
Beyond My Touch

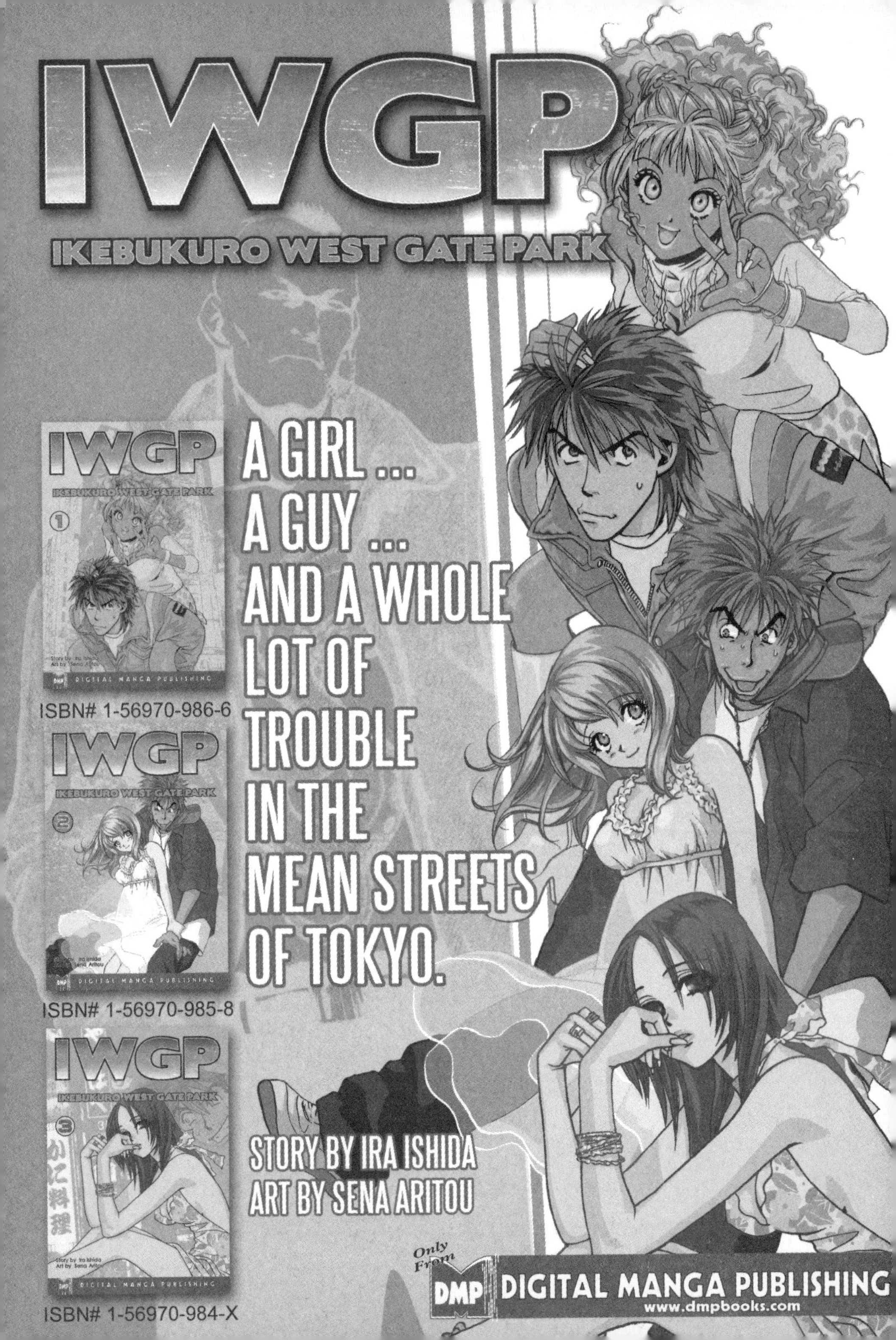
IWGP
IKEBUKURO WEST GATE PARK
IWGP IKEBUKURO WEST GATE PARK 1 DIGITAL MANGA PUBLISHING
ISBN# 1-56970-986-6
IWGP IKEBUKURO WEST GATE PARK 2 DIGITAL MANGA PUBLISHING
ISBN# 1-56970-985-8
IWGP IKEBUKURO WEST GATE PARK 3 Story by Ira Ishida Art by Sena Aritou DIGITAL MANGA PUBLISHING
ISBN# 1-56970-984-X
A GIRL ...
A GUY ...
AND A WHOLE
LOT OF
TROUBLE
IN THE
MEAN STREETS
OF TOKYO.
STORY BY IRA ISHIDA
ART BY SENA ARITOU
Only From
DMP DIGITAL MANGA PUBLISHING
www.dmpbooks.com

This is the back of the book!
Start from the other side.

NATIVE MANGA readers read manga from *right to left*.

If you run into our *Native Manga* logo on any of our books... you'll know that this manga is published in it's true original native Japanese right to left reading format, as it was intended. Turn to the other side of the book and start reading from right to left, top to bottom.

Follow the diagram to see how its done. *Surf's Up!*

NATIVE MANGA
READ RIGHT TO LEFT